# HE
# WENT
# BACK
# FOR HIS
# HAT

# HE WENT BACK FOR HIS HAT

Justice Michael Lee's
judgment on **Bruce Lehrmann**
With a foreword by Chanel Contos

MELBOURNE
UNIVERSITY
PRESS

*Melbourne University Publishing acknowledges the traditional owners of the unceded land on which we work, learn and live: the Wurundjeri Woiwurrung peoples of the Kulin Nation. We pay respect to elders past, present and future, and acknowledge the importance of Indigenous knowledge.*

MELBOURNE UNIVERSITY PRESS
An imprint of Melbourne University Publishing Limited
Level 1, 715 Swanston Street, Carlton, Victoria 3053, Australia
mup-contact@unimelb.edu.au
www.mup.com.au

First published 2024

Cover design by Design by Committee
Typeset by Sonya Murphy, Adala Studio
Printed in Australia by McPherson's Printing Group

NATIONAL LIBRARY OF AUSTRALIA

A catalogue record for this book is available from the National Library of Australia

9780522881127 (paperback)
9780522881134 (ebook)

# CONTENTS

# FOREWORD

## *Chanel Contos*

Justice Michael Lee lays out in detail the intricacies of the law and process around our criminal justice system. A true understanding of these mechanisms tends to be inaccessible to most. Although this is a judgment on the highest profile defamation case of the decade, for many, *Bruce Lehrmann v Network Ten* functioned as a proxy rape trial in disguise.

To accompany his comprehensive judgement, I would like to contextualise the wider problem of pervasive sexual assault and barriers to justice. It is common for defamation to be either threatened or used against women who speak up about men's behavior towards them. This truth made it so that this judgment was not only important to the stakeholders or those in their immediate circles, but one that was significant on both a cultural and a personal level for many.

Justice Lee did a tremendous job of detailing trauma's effect on memory and recollection, as well as how victims often stray from the better understood trauma responses of 'fight' and 'flight'. I would like to add to this a missing piece of discourse about trauma or stress on an individual's behaviour at the time of an act of assault, namely, *fawning*. This is not particularly relevant to the judgment at hand, but drastically important for why our broader criminal system is continuously failing to reach justice for its victims of sex-based violent crimes. Fawning is a response to a stressful situation where the victim tries to get out of danger by taking on a persona that tries to please the perpetrator. This trauma response is triggered when fight or flight are not options to achieve safety. It is common in women in heterosexual situations of assault as, speaking in general terms, a man will be stronger and faster, and trying to physically fight or outrun them would not be an effective attempt at survival.

Accountability doubles as a form of justice for victim-survivors, and a deterrent for potential perpetrators. 'Innocent until proven guilty' and the criminal burden of proof 'beyond reasonable doubt' are both crucial pillars of our legal system, yet simultaneously the largest barriers to accessing justice for victim-survivors of sexual violence. How do we reconcile this? It is an obvious and accepted consequence of a criminal system with a high standard of proof that guilty people will slip through the cracks. In this case, the defence of truth was made easier to accept given that Justice Lee was operating under the civil standard of truth on the 'balance of probabilities' rather than the criminal requirement of 'beyond reasonable doubt'.

When looking at the effectiveness of a disease screening tool, scientists measure sensitivity (the test's ability to correctly identify patients with a disease) and specificity (the test's ability to correctly identify people without the disease). A trade-off between the importance of truly knowing if a person is contaminated, with the importance of truly knowing they are not, is often made based on health risks if the test determines wrongly. If we were to apply this measurement of effectiveness to the criminal system, pretending the disease we are testing for is an act of violence, there has been a priority placed on ensuring there are few false negatives, due to the drastic consequences of false accusations and wrongful convictions. As the adage goes, 'It is better ten guilty persons escape, than one innocent person suffer.' This is one that you will read Justice Lee unpack further in the coming pages.

This priority skew has been enacted to such an extent that we have lost almost all ability to rightly obtain true positive results for crimes of violence against women under the criminal standard of proof. If this were an actual medical test for a disease such as COVID-19 or influenza, it would pose a recognisable public health risk to make decisions based on its high results of false negatives, as many infected people would go freely about their day-to-day lives, impacting others. Consequently, we have a silent epidemic of sexual, domestic and family violence. At a 2024 cabinet meeting in federal parliament that was called to address mass protests by Australian women, state and federal ministers agreed that justice system responses needed to be strengthened, with a focus on high-risk perpetrators and serial offenders to prevent homicides. While the strongest strains of the virus are the ones most likely to test positive and result in death, rather than only focusing on increasing quarantine time for these few, I would like to see the masses of people with weaker strains of the disease be detected.

A new test and a newly imagined form of accountability must be designed and employed, whether that be by state governments, government organisations, banks, schools, universities, private companies, or all of the above – I do not know. We will only know when adequate resources are given to experts to trial and devise one. Other countries have seen high rates of victim satisfaction in restorative justice routes, where empathy, apology and validation are at the heart of the system. This is one I strongly advocate for, particularly for children who are increasingly becoming perpetrators of violence, and who have no place in the court system. This is increasingly necessary given that Australians are in the process of shredding generations of embedded shame about being victims of sexual abuse. The pillars of 'beyond reasonable doubt' and 'innocent until proven guilty' are supported by the metaphorical reinforced beams of stigma and social barriers to prevent reporting. If police stations and courts were faced with reports of real numbers of sex-based crimes occurring in Australia, they would collapse under pressure.

In his judgment, Justice Michael Lee presents an understanding of trauma, and how inconsistencies are often consistent with the behaviours and memories of a traumatised person. You will see the detailed requirements and considerations that were required for a Federal Court judge to take a stand on truth on the balance of probabilities. I hope while reading this methodological judgement – a rarity for victim-survivors – you remember that behind every statistic of sexual violence, there are dynamic, complex and very real humans.

# REASONS FOR JUDGMENT

## A OPENING REMARKS

Mr Bruce Lehrmann sues Network Ten Pty Limited (**Network Ten**) and Ms Lisa Wilkinson (together, the **respondents**) in defamation in relation to an episode of Network Ten's *The Project* programme (**Project programme**). 1

It is a singular case: the underlying controversy has become a cause célèbre. Indeed, given its unexpected detours and the collateral damage it has occasioned, it might be more fitting to describe it as an omnishambles. 2

For some people, any unwelcome findings will be peremptorily dismissed. The reasoning process, including the drawing of fine distinctions based upon the subtleties of the evidence, will be of no interest. This reaction is inevitable given that several observers have a Rorschach test-like response to this controversy and fasten doggedly upon the "truth" as they perceive it. Their response is visceral because the "truth" is revealed and declaimed, rather than proven and explained. Some jump to predetermined conclusions because they are disposed to be sceptical about complaints of sexual assault and hold stereotyped beliefs about the expected behaviour of rape victims, described by social scientists as "rape myths"; others say they "believe all women", surrendering their critical faculties by embracing and acting upon a slogan arising out of the #MeToo movement. Some have predetermined views as to the existence or otherwise of a conspiracy to suppress a rape for political purposes. For more than a few, this dispute has become a proxy for broader cultural and political conflicts. 3

This judgment is not written for people who have made up their mind before any evidence was adduced or are content to rest upon preconceived opinions. It is written to set out my factual findings comprehensively and explain my decision to the parties and to the open and fair-minded. 4

To achieve this end, from the start of this case, I have attempted to ensure as transparent a process as possible, conscious that a trial conducted in 5 public, accessible to the public, and only upon evidence and submissions made fully available to the public, was the best security for confidence of the fair-minded in the impartiality and efficiency of the justice system.

6 An astute observer would have gleaned from the trial that this case is not as straightforward as some commentary might suggest. In part, this is because the primary defence hinges on the truth of an allegation of sexual assault behind closed doors. Only one man and one woman know the truth with certitude.

7 For an impartial outsider seeking to divine the truth (or, more accurately, ascertaining what most likely happened), two connected obstacles emerged.

8 The *first* is, at bottom, this is a credit case involving two people who are both, in different ways, unreliable historians.

9 Countless scholarly articles have been written seeking to explain the frailties of human memory and why it is that different people may remember the same event in different ways. People give unreliable evidence for various reasons and distinguishing between a false memory and a lie can often be difficult. Aspects of so-called "witness demeanour" or physiological signs of deceit are of little use unless the witness is cognitively aware of their deception. Recognising these realities, judges are reluctant to characterise a false representation as a lie unless another explanation is unavailable and it is necessary to do so to resolve a controversy. But as we will see, this is a case where credit findings are central and sometimes an explanation other than mendacity is not rationally available.

10 To remark that Mr Lehrmann was a poor witness is an exercise in understatement. As I will explain, his attachment to the truth was a tenuous one, informed not by faithfulness to his affirmation but by fashioning his responses in what he perceived to be his forensic interests. Ms Brittany Higgins, Mr Lehrmann's accuser, was also an unsatisfactory witness who made some allegations that made her a heroine to one group of partisans, but when examined forensically, have undermined her general credibility to a disinterested fact-finder.

11 The *second* and related obstacle was the assertion that what went on between these two young and relatively immature staffers led to much more. By early 2021, allegations of wrongdoing had burgeoned far beyond sexual assault. It was said a sexual assault victim had been forced by malefactors to choose

between her career and justice. The perceived need to expose misconduct (and the institutional factors that allowed it) meant the rape allegation was not pursued in the orthodox way through the criminal justice system, which provides for complainant anonymity.

As we will also see, when examined properly and without partiality, the cover-up allegation was objectively short on facts, but long on speculation and internal inconsistencies – trying to particularise it during the evidence was like trying to grab a column of smoke. But despite its logical and evidentiary flaws, Ms Higgins' boyfriend selected and contacted two journalists and then Ms Higgins advanced her account to them, and through them, to others. From the first moment, the cover-up component was promoted and recognised as the most important part of the narrative. The various controversies traceable to its publication resulted in the legal challenge of determining what happened late one night in 2019 becoming much more difficult than would otherwise have been the case. 12

I will come to the legal issues, the principles that have guided fact-finding, some observations concerning the credit of various witnesses, and then my findings as to what relevantly went on. But before doing so, I will explain some uncontroversial matters and the issues in the case. 13

# B THE PARTICIPANTS AND SOME BACKGROUND FACTS

14 Most of the important facts are contested. This section records some uncontroversial details as to the principal participants, the publications, and this and related proceedings.

## B.1 The Dramatis Personae

### *I Mr Lehrmann*

15 Mr Lehrmann was born in 1995 in Texas. His father died in Mr Lehrmann's infancy.

16 His mother, who was born in Australia, relocated to northern New South Wales with Mr Lehrmann and his younger sister. The family then moved to Toowoomba in Mr Lehrmann's final years of primary school.

17 From a young age, Mr Lehrmann had a preternatural interest in politics. Upon leaving school, in 2014, he moved to Canberra to undertake study at the Australian National University. His first foray into politics came at the time he started university, as an electorate officer.

18 In March 2016, Mr Lehrmann commenced employment as an office manager with the then Commonwealth Attorney-General, before assuming a role as a health policy advisor to the then Assistant Minister for Health, in August 2017.

19 At the end of 2017, Mr Lehrmann commenced employment as a health policy advisor with the then Minister for Rural Health and Sport, a position he held until October 2018, when he became a policy advisor to the Hon Senator Linda Reynolds CSC, then Assistant Minister for Home Affairs.

### *II Ms Higgins*

20 Ms Higgins was born in Queensland in 1994. She grew up on the Gold Coast, completing her schooling there and later graduated from

Griffith University. In 2017, she was employed as a staffer for Mr Samuel O'Connor MP, a member of the Queensland Parliament.

Ms Higgins moved to Canberra around September 2018 to commence work as an administrative assistant in the Ministerial office of the Hon Steven Ciobo MP. Around this time, she began a relationship with Mr Benjamin Dillaway, the media advisor to Mr Ciobo, which lasted until February or early March 2019. The pair remained close (and at times intimate) friends. 21

In early March 2019, Mr Ciobo announced his pending resignation and, shortly thereafter, Senator Reynolds received a commission to become the Minister for Defence Industry. 22

Ms Higgins was then successful in her application for a role as an administrative officer and junior media advisor in Senator Reynolds' office. 23

### *III Ms Wilkinson*

Ms Wilkinson has been a journalist for over forty years. She has held a wide range of prominent roles. Her beginnings were in print journalism. Her first job was as an editorial assistant and cadet journalist at *Dolly* magazine. She held various roles at *Dolly* and *Cleo* magazines from 1978 to 1995, including rising to become editor-in-chief of both magazines from 1988 to 1995, and was editor-at-large of the *Australian Women's Weekly* from 1999 to 2007. 24

Ms Wilkinson first turned to television in 1996. She rose to lounge-room prominence in the early 2000s, as co-host of *The Morning Shift*. Between 2004 and 2007, she was a news contributor and regular fill-in co-host of the Seven Network's *Sunrise* and *Weekend Sunrise* programmes and, from 2007 to 2017, co-host of *Today* on the Nine Network. 25

In 2017, Ms Wilkinson became co-host of *The Project* and *The Sunday Project*, a role she held at the time of publication. 26

### *IV Mr Angus Llewellyn*

Mr Angus Llewellyn has been a producer for *The Project* since 2019. He is employed by 7PM Company Pty Ltd, which provides Network Ten with production services for *The Project*. 27

Mr Llewellyn is highly experienced and has held various producer roles in radio, including at the ABC, Radio 2UE, and television programmes, including the Seven Network's *Sunday Night*; SBS's *Dateline* and *Insight*; and the ABC's *Lateline*. 28

29 Ms Wilkinson and Mr Llewellyn are both based in Sydney and have frequently worked together since about October 2019. They first met in about 2006 when Mr Llewellyn worked with Ms Wilkinson's husband.

## B.2 Publication of the Impugned Matters

30 On the morning of 15 February 2021, an article entitled "Young staffer Brittany Higgins says she was raped at Parliament House", authored by Ms Samantha Maiden (**Maiden article**), was published on the news.com.au website.

31 Mr Lehrmann became aware of the Maiden article around the time it was published. I have set out the relevant chronology in *Lehrmann v Network Ten Pty Limited (Limitation Extension)* [2023] FCA 385 (**limitation judgment**) and do not propose to repeat it here.

32 It suffices to note that by 2pm that day, Mr Lehrmann had been informed that "government sources" were identifying him as the man accused of sexually assaulting Ms Higgins. His work supervisor, Mr Joshua Fett, informed Mr Lehrmann that Ms Rosie Lewis, a journalist at *The Australian*, had emailed Mr Fett to this effect.

33 That evening, Network Ten broadcast the Project programme, and republished it on the *10 Play* website and *The Project's* YouTube channel shortly thereafter. Mr Lehrmann watched the broadcast live from his then solicitor's office.

34 It is common ground that the television broadcast attracted a national audience of over 725,000 people, from every state and territory. The publication on the *10 Play* website had over 17,000 views, and the publication on YouTube had nearly 190,000 views.

## B.3 The Criminal Proceeding

35 On 17 August 2021, Mr Lehrmann was charged with one count of engaging in sexual intercourse with Ms Higgins without her consent, contrary to s 54(1) of the *Crimes Act 1900* (ACT) (**Crimes Act**). On the same day, Mr Lehrmann was identified by "mainstream" media outlets as the person accused of the offence by Ms Higgins.

36 The trial was originally fixed to commence in the Supreme Court of the Australian Capital Territory on 27 June 2022, but was vacated by McCallum CJ six days earlier for reasons explained in *R v Lehrmann*

*(No 3)* [2022] ACTSC 145; (2022) 299 A Crim R 276. The trial ultimately commenced before McCallum CJ and a jury of sixteen on 4 October 2022. A jury of twelve retired on 19 October 2022 and was discharged eight days later by reason of juror misconduct.

On 2 December 2022, the Director of Public Prosecutions, Mr Shane Drumgold SC, announced that he did not intend to proceed with the prosecution. The reason was said to be the ill-health of the complainant, Ms Higgins. 37

## B.4 Procedural History

Mr Lehrmann brought this proceeding and a (now discontinued) proceeding against News Life Media and Ms Maiden (**News Life proceeding**) out of time, requiring him to seek an extension of the limitation period, which was granted for the reasons given in the limitation judgment. 38

He later commenced a proceeding within time against the ABC (**ABC proceeding**) in relation to the broadcast of an address given by Ms Higgins, alongside Ms Grace Tame, at the National Press Club in February 2022. The ABC proceeding travelled with this proceeding until the first day of the trial, when a settlement was formalised. 39

In December 2023, competing cross-claims were filed in this Court as between Ms Wilkinson and Network Ten in relation to an indemnity for legal costs (**cross-claims**). I directed that the cross-claims be heard separately, and they have been the subject of a judgment (*Lehrmann v Network Ten Pty Limited (Cross-claims)* [2024] FCA 102 (**cross-claims judgment**)). The only present relevance of the cross-claims is that each party agreed that evidence on the cross-claims be evidence in this proceeding. 40

## C THE PUBLICATIONS

41 Mr Lehrmann sues on three matters published on 15 February 2021, being the Project programme:

(1) broadcast on Network Ten;

(2) published on the 10 Play website; and

(3) published on The Project's YouTube channel.

42 The substance of each matter is relevantly identical, and the transcript of the programme, being an aide memoire to Ex 1, is annexed to these reasons as **Annexure A.** I will refer to the impugned matters collectively as the **Project programme**.

43 Mr Lehrmann in the statement of claim (**SOC**) says the Project programme, in its natural and ordinary meaning, was defamatory of him and carried the following imputations:

| SOC Reference | Imputation |
|---|---|
| [4(a)]; [6(a)]; [8(a)] | [Mr Lehrmann] raped Brittany Higgins in Defence Minister Linda Reynolds' office in 2019. |
| [4(b)]; [6(b)]; [8(b)] | [Mr Lehrmann] continued to rape Brittany Higgins after she woke up mid-rape and was crying and telling him to stop at least half a dozen times. |
| [4(c)]; [6(c)]; [8(c)] | [Mr Lehrmann], whilst raping Brittany Higgins, crushed his leg against her leg so forcefully as to cause a large bruise. |
| [4(d)]; [6(d)]; [8(d)] | After [Mr Lehrmann] finished raping Brittany Higgins, he left her on a couch in a state of undress with her dress up around her waist. |

Network Ten and Ms Wilkinson deny the matters concerned Mr Lehrmann but, if they did, they admit the pleaded imputations were conveyed, and are defamatory of Mr Lehrmann: Network Ten's defence (at [4(b)], [6(b)], [8(b)]); Ms Wilkinson's defence (at [4.3], [4.4], [6.3], [6.4], [8.3], [8.4]). 44

Both respondents also say the pleaded imputations do not differ in substance from one another: Network Ten's defence (at [4(c)], [6(c)], [8(c)]); Ms Wilkinson's defence (at [4.5], [6.5], [8.5]). As Ms Wilkinson puts it, the pleaded imputations "contain gratuitous and irrelevant rhetorical flourish that adds nothing to the defamatory sting of rape". 45

What was conveyed by the Project programme was not in issue, and I do not propose to rehearse the uncontroversial principles as to defamatory meaning. In short, the question of what was conveyed and whether it is defamatory depends upon what the ordinary reasonable viewer would understand, and it is common ground that if the Project programme identified Mr Lehrmann, the hypothetical referee would understand it conveyed the pleaded meanings, with the sting being an accusation of rape. 46

# D IDENTIFICATION

## D.1 Introduction

47 Identification is an essential element of defamation and Mr Lehrmann must establish the Project programme is "about" or "of and concerning" him: s 8 of the *Defamation Act 2005* (NSW) (**Defamation Act**). That is, Mr Lehrmann must show that at least one person who viewed the Project programme reasonably understood the allegations concerned him: *David Syme & Co v Canavan* (1918) 25 CLR 234 (at 238 per Isaacs J).

48 Despite the pleadings, the contest in this case is not, however, whether at least one person identified Mr Lehrmann, so as to perfect the cause of action. Instead, what is really in dispute is the *extent* of identification: that is, the persons (or classes of persons) who reasonably identified Mr Lehrmann, which is relevant to damages and the defence of common law qualified privilege.

49 Mr Lehrmann contends he was reasonably identified by three classes of persons, being those:

(1) who either worked in Senator Reynolds' office or had regular dealings with that office and, consequently, knew Mr Lehrmann: (a) was a "senior male advisor" to Senator Reynolds; (b) had previously worked for Senator Reynolds in the Home Affairs portfolio; (c) had attended a drinks event with Ms Higgins and other contacts and colleagues in Defence on the night of the alleged rape; (d) was called into a meeting with Ms Fiona Brown, Chief of Staff to Senator Reynolds, on the following Tuesday, after which he started packing up his belongings; and (e) by February 2021, had obtained a job in Sydney;

(2) who worked in Parliament, being federal politicians, assistants and staffers, journalists, and other persons, including family, friends and acquaintances of Mr Lehrmann; such that Mr Lehrmann's identity must have been known generally to such persons through discussions

and, provided they were not already aware, they would have soon discovered that he was the subject of the Project programme; and

(3) who were invited to speculate as to the identity of the person accused; such that a large, indeterminate number of viewers would have reasonably concluded, having read (or subsequently read) a series of social media posts and/or articles published online, that the programme identified Mr Lehrmann.

In establishing identification, Mr Lehrmann called Ms Kathleen Quinn, 50
Ms Karly Abbott, and Mr David McDonald (**identification witnesses**). Additionally, Mr Lehrmann relies upon other witnesses who gave evidence that they identified Mr Lehrmann (either prior to airing or shortly thereafter).

51I will return to this evidence below, but I will first expand upon the 51
relevant principles.

## D.2 Relevant Principles

The inquiry as to identification has two stages, which reflect the tradi- 52
tional and differing roles of judge and jury in a defamation case.

The *first* concerns whether, as a matter of law, the impugned publica- 53
tion is *capable* of identifying the applicant: that is, whether an ordinary sensible person *could* draw an inference that the publication referred to the applicant, with the Court's function to determine the outer limits of the possible range of meanings: *Corby v Allen & Unwin Pty Ltd* [2014] NSWCA 227 (at [133] per McColl JA, with whom Bathurst CJ and Gleeson JA agreed). Indeed, "great caution" is mandated at this stage because the conclusion which necessarily underpins a finding that the matter is incapable of conveying the pleaded imputations is that no viewer could reasonably understand the publication to bear any meaning outside the range delimited by the judge: *Corby* (at [136] per McColl JA). It is an "exercise in generosity not parsimony": *Berezovsky v Forbes* [2001] EWCA Civ 1251 (at [16] per Sedley LJ).

The *second* stage is for the trier of fact to decide whether the publication actu- 54
ally identified the applicant. As noted above, the fact-finder must determine whether, upon the evidence, persons with special knowledge of the applicant reasonably understood the publication to concern him: *David Syme* (at 238 per Isaacs J). However, identification does not require that readers or

viewers already have the requisite knowledge at the time of the publication: *Fairfax Media Publications Pty Ltd v Pedavoli* [2015] NSWCA 237; (2015) 91 NSWLR 485 (at 503 [81] per Simpson JA, McColl JA agreeing).

55 Identification may be established by direct or indirect evidence. As Mason P observed in *Channel Seven Sydney Pty Ltd v Parras* [2002] NSWCA 202 (at [57]), an indirect way is where the applicant gives evidence of being contacted by people in circumstances showing that such contact was obviously a response to what they read in the publication (it was said of one member of the New South Wales Bar – now deceased – that it was remarkable how often his clients seemed to be importuned by strangers in the street commenting upon defamatory publications).

56 A variant of such evidence is "talk" or "tittle tattle" among readers or viewers indicative of identification. The Court must be satisfied that such evidence is capable of supporting the inference that the responses to the defamatory matter showed that the persons concerned reasonably understood it to refer to the applicant.

57 Whether the identification was correct is relevant to the question of reasonableness. As Bryson JA (with whom Mason P and Tobias JA agreed) observed in *Gardener v Nationwide News Pty Ltd* [2007] NSWCA 10 (at [47]), any purpose for establishing that identification was reasonable is well satisfied if it can be shown the identification was correct: see also *Steele v Mirror Newspapers Ltd* [1974] 2 NSWLR 348 (at 371–374 per Samuels JA).

## D.3 The Witnesses

58 As noted earlier, Mr Lehrmann adduced direct evidence from the identification witnesses, whose evidence I accept.

### *I Ms Abbott*

59 Ms Abbott met Mr Lehrmann around 2016 when he was employed in the Office of the Attorney-General. Since that time, she has "got to know [Mr Lehrmann] reasonably well" and considers him a friend (Abbott (at [6])).

60 Ms Abbott viewed the Project programme when broadcast and identified Mr Lehrmann because she knew he: (a) was an advisor to Senator Reynolds and, although he was not a "senior advisor", he was senior to Ms Higgins; (b) had previously worked for Senator Reynolds in the Home Affairs portfolio; (c) was involved in "an incident involving Brittany" in the office which

resulted in him being "fired" (information received from a conversation in July 2019 with a colleague, Mr Drew Burland); and (d) worked in Sydney.

Ms Abbott was aware of these matters, at least in part, because she had read the Maiden article and connected the allegations to Mr Lehrmann from the conversation with Mr Burland in July 2019 (T48.40–45; T45.20–21). She had a conversation with Mr Dillaway in which he said, concerning the Maiden article, "This is Bruce" (Abbott (at [12])). 61

Ms Abbott explained that following the broadcast, there were conversations and exchanges of text messages among political staffers and other participants in the Canberra rumour mill about identity (Abbott (at [11]); T47.19–48.1; T49.7). In the context of these conversations, Ms Abbott's evidence is that she "[did not] believe that there was any other specific names mentioned to me, but just a 'Do you know who this is?' Or ..." (T47.42–44). 62

### *II Ms Quinn*

Ms Quinn is Ms Abbott's business partner. 63

Ms Quinn met Mr Lehrmann around 2016 and they interacted in work and social settings. She viewed the Project programme and identified Mr Lehrmann because he: (a) was an advisor to Senator Reynolds who was senior to Ms Higgins; (b) had previously worked with Senator Reynolds in the Home Affairs portfolio; and (c) ceased working for Senator Reynolds in about March 2019 and was working in Sydney for British American Tobacco (**BAT**) (Quinn (at [6])). 64

In cross-examination, Ms Quinn explained that prior to airing, she was aware of "a rumour that there had been a security incident in the office, and that was why Bruce had left" (T113.24–42). She discussed the Maiden article, and the fact that it was about Mr Lehrmann, with Ms Abbott prior to the broadcast (T114.34–116.5). 65

In the days following the broadcast, Ms Quinn noted the allegations were a "hot topic" of discussion among staffers (Abbott (at [8])). She recalled conversations with close to a dozen such people over a couple of days and recalled them saying that (T112.13–15): 66

> Bruce was the person that had been identified in The Project broadcast and asking my opinion of his character and whether or not I had ever experienced anything untoward from him.

### *III Mr McDonald*

67 Mr McDonald is a close friend of Mr Lehrmann and his family. He watched the Project programme with his wife when it was aired, to whom he said: "this has to be about Bruce" (McDonald (at [7])).

68 Mr McDonald identified Mr Lehrmann from the programme because: (a) it stated that the former colleague was a male advisor to Senator Reynolds; (b) the person had previously worked for Senator Reynolds in the Home Affairs portfolio; and (c) the person had ceased working for Senator Reynolds in March 2019 and had moved to Sydney (McDonald (at [6]); T56.45–57.20). Mr McDonald promptly discussed the broadcast with his neighbour and said: "it looks like Bruce is in a bit of strife" (McDonald (at [9])).

69 Notwithstanding those identifying facts, in cross-examination, Mr McDonald conceded that he could not exclude the possibility that there were other men working for Senator Reynolds who fell within the description above (T57.40–44).

### *IV Other witnesses*

70 Mr Lehrmann also relies upon other testimony adduced from witnesses of broader significance and to whose evidence I will return, in detail, below. Insofar as they gave evidence relevant to identification, it was as follows.

71 Ms Nicole Hamer explained she watched the broadcast and knew, at that time, that the alleged perpetrator was Mr Lehrmann (T1064.5–1066.4). Prior to publication, she recalled unspecific discussions among people working in Parliament about the upcoming programme, during which Mr Lehrmann was named (T1065.41–45). Ms Hamer did not understand at the time that there was any other person to whom the allegations could relate, but accepted in re-examination that different names were mentioned (T1069.32–41).

72 Mr Austin Wenke gave evidence he read the Maiden article on the morning of the broadcast and watched some (but not all) of the Project programme (T1126.7–8). Following the publication of the Maiden article, Mr Wenke agreed there was "a bit of chatter within Parliament House [about the story]" (T1125.11–22). He concluded the allegations in the Maiden article concerned Mr Lehrmann and he did not recall thinking the allegations could have referred to anyone else (T1125.24–41). He agreed it was fair to characterise the identity of the alleged perpetrator referred to in the Maiden article as an "open secret" within Parliament House (T1126.14–22).

Major Nikita Irvine watched the Project programme. She gave evidence 73 she received questions about it from colleagues in the military but did not want to discuss it (T1207.1–36). Major Irvine identified Mr Lehrmann because (as we will see) Ms Higgins had disclosed details of the incident to her in March 2019 (T1207.35–36) (Irvine (at [60]–[61])).

Mr Dillaway gave evidence he read the Maiden article. He knew the alle- 74 gations concerned Mr Lehrmann because Ms Higgins had told him in March 2019 that Mr Lehrmann had sexually assaulted her (Dillaway (at [42]–[50])). He gave evidence "what was in that story was consistent with what she had told me previously" (T1276.11–25) and that he had a vague recollection of watching the Project programme (T1277.13).

Mr Lehrmann himself gave evidence of the actions of various acquain- 75 tances (with whom he had not remained in contact) following the broadcast (see, for example, Ex 8). In particular, he referred to a screenshot of a Facebook Messenger group chat (which had included Mr Lehrmann) which showed an image of an "EJECT" button, followed by several members leaving the group chat (Ex 11).

## D.4 Identification Established

While there is necessarily some degree of overlap, given it is in issue, it is 76 best not to elide the two stages of the relevant inquiry.

As to the *first*, it is plain as a pikestaff the Project programme 77 was capable of identifying Mr Lehrmann. As noted earlier, there were several tell-tales, being (Ex 1, Annexure A):

(1) he was a "senior male advisor" to Senator Reynolds who had a "special bond" with her (lines 7–8), and was "a bit of a favourite [of the Senator]" (line 9);

(2) he "had been advising her in the home affairs portfolio prior to [working in the Defence Industry portfolio]" (line 10);

(3) he attended drinks with colleagues in Defence on 22 March 2019 (line 11);

(4) the following Tuesday morning, Ms Brown called the alleged perpetrator in for a meeting, following which he "immediately walked out of the office and started packing up his things" (lines 53–55); and

(5) the alleged perpetrator was, as at the date of broadcast, "working in Sydney ... he's got a good job" (line 157).

78 Even accounting for a certain degree of factual inaccuracy (for example, whether Mr Lehrmann was a "senior advisor"), the references above correspond to the particularised knowledge of the applicant possessed by the identification witnesses and other witnesses: see *Plymouth Brethren (Exclusive Brethren) Christian Church v The Age Company Ltd* [2018] NSWCA 95; (2018) 97 NSWLR 739 (at 756 [77] per McColl JA). In the light of that special knowledge, the ordinary reasonable viewer possessing that knowledge *could* understand that Mr Lehrmann was the subject of the allegations.

79 As to the *second* stage, I am amply satisfied that Mr Lehrmann was in fact identified.

80 *First*, Mr Lehrmann was reasonably identified by persons with special knowledge. Each of the identification witnesses identified Mr Lehrmann with knowledge they had acquired by working in Parliament, or by reason of being a friend or family acquaintance. It is immaterial whether they identified Mr Lehrmann from the Maiden article: what matters is the identification witnesses reasonably identified Mr Lehrmann from information contained in the programme. With the exception of Mr McDonald, who could not exclude the possibility he thought the programme may have referred to another person, it is significant for the purposes of assessing reasonableness that Ms Abbott and Ms Quinn were correct in their identification.

81 *Secondly*, it is important that several witnesses gave evidence of gossip and rumour both before and after the Project programme was broadcast. The fact that such "chitter chatter" took place is indicative of the kind of evidence referred to in *Pedavoli* whereby recipients of such information tend to make efforts to discover identity, thereby expanding the circle of people with the requisite knowledge.

82 This is sufficient to establish identification and perfect the cause of action, but given the need to focus on the *extent* of identification, it is necessary to say something more.

83 Reliance by Mr Lehrmann upon the third category, being other persons who may have identified Mr Lehrmann by reason of the Twitter/X "firehose" or "grapevine effect" presents difficulties: see *Kumova v Davison (No 2)* [2023] FCA 1 (at [319]). Unlike other cases where the "Twittersphere" trends with a name following a publication, as Mr Lehrmann conceded in

cross-examination, his solicitors, despite their best efforts, could not locate any Tweets around the time of the broadcast which named Mr Lehrmann as the subject of the Project programme, save for a Tweet published by True Crime Weekly (Ex 7; T484.33–485.33) together with some articles on a website "Kangaroo Court of Australia" (Ex 4, 5 and 6).

All of this, including Mr Lehrmann's evidence as to being contacted on social media following the broadcast, reflects very modest social media dissemination compared to other defamations provoking speculation as to identity. 84

It was less a firehose and more the splutter of an insecurely fastened sprinkler. 85

Before leaving the topic of identification, for completeness, it is worth dealing with a discrete point made by Ms Wilkinson. 86

In her written and oral closing submissions, Ms Wilkinson referred to a number of authorities concerning "small group identification" and, in particular, the decision of Hunt J in *McCormick v John Fairfax & Sons Ltd* (1989) 16 NSWLR 485 as authority for the proposition that in circumstances where there is a small group of persons referred to in an impugned publication, the matter is incapable of conveying an imputation of guilt unless it impugns every member of the class (at 488D–491D). In short, Ms Wilkinson submits this is relevant because Mr Lehrmann has not excluded the possibility that viewers reasonably identified him as one of a small group of persons who could have met the description of the alleged perpetrator, namely Mr Jesse Wotton, who worked for Senator Reynolds in March 2019. 87

I do not accept this submission, for the following reasons. 88

*First*, there were identifying facts which, for those armed with special knowledge, would have ruled Mr Wotton out as the alleged culprit; namely: (1) Mr Wotton did *not* leave Senator Reynolds' office in March 2019; and (2) Mr Wotton was *not* working in Sydney in February 2021. *Secondly*, although not determinative of the question of identification by others, it is telling that when asked whether he was concerned that people might think he was the subject of Ms Higgins' allegations, Mr Wotton gave evidence that he was not concerned because he was "quite confident in the fact that people [knew me well] ... or were in a position to find out should they make their own inquiries" (T1092.32–37). *Thirdly*, prior to 89 broadcast, Network Ten successfully took steps to guard against confusion with any other male who worked in Senator Reynolds' office at the time. As Mr Llewellyn explained (Llewellyn (at [167(a)])):

> We were very conscious that we did not want to inadvertently identify the wrong person as being the alleged perpetrator. We had to give sufficient detail to exclude other males who worked in Linda Reynolds' office at the relevant time.

# E APPROACH TO FACT-FINDING, ONUS, AND THE STANDARD OF PROOF

## E.1 General

It is next appropriate to set out how I have directed myself as to fact-finding, the burden of proof, the standard of proof, and other more particular matters given the nature of the principal allegation. 90

Without introducing complications arising from the differing ways in which the phrase "burden of proof" has been used – and the differences between legal and evidential burdens (as to which see C R Williams, 'Burdens and Standards in Civil Litigation' (2003) 25(2) *Sydney Law Review* 165), I will use the expression burden or onus of proof as simply being the identification of which party has to demonstrate the case or an aspect of the case propounded, whereas the standard of proof is the applicable benchmark that the evidence adduced must meet to discharge that onus. 91

The question of who bears the onus in aspects of this case is straightforward. Mr Lehrmann had (and has successfully discharged) his onus in proving he has been defamed as alleged; the respondents now bear the onus of proof with respect to their defences. If those defences fail and Mr Lehrmann is entitled to damages, he will then be required to prove the compensatory damages he seeks. 92

What this means is that in order to make out the defence of substantial truth, the respondents need to discharge their onus of proving that Mr Lehrmann raped Ms Higgins. The nature of this aspect of the forensic contest brings with it considerations that are necessary to canvass in further detail. 93

I have discussed the relevant principles at length a number of times (see, for example, *Transport Workers' Union of Australia v Qantas Airways Limited* [2021] FCA 873; (2021) 308 IR 244 (at 324–325 [284]–[288])). Notwithstanding this, it is worth referring to Besanko J's recent survey of matters relevant to onus and proof in *Roberts-Smith v Fairfax* 94

*Media Publications Pty Ltd (No. 41)* [2023] FCA 555. In *Roberts-Smith*, his Honour dealt with a number of matters relevant to: (a) the onus of proof in a justification or substantial truth case (at [93]–[94]); and (b) the standard of proof in a case where there is a serious allegation (at [95]–[110]). With respect, his Honour's exposition in relation to these matters is comprehensive. I gratefully adopt the above-mentioned paragraphs.

95 At the risk of supererogation, I will, however, say something in my own words. I will also deal with the agreed facts relevant to Ms Higgins' credit and some miscellaneous matters, which have informed my approach to the evidence.

## E.2 Relevant Observations as to Standard of Proof

96 As to the standard of proof, the starting (and end) point is s 140 of the *Evidence Act 1995* (Cth) (**EA**), which relevantly provides:

> **Civil proceedings: standard of proof**
>
> (1) In a civil proceeding, the court must find the case of a party proved if it is satisfied that the case has been proved on the balance of probabilities.
>
> (2) Without limiting the matters that the court may take into account in deciding whether it is so satisfied, it is to take into account:
>
> (a) the nature of the cause of action or defence; and
>
> (b) the nature of the subject-matter of the proceeding; and
>
> (c) the gravity of the matters alleged.

97 The matters set out in subsection (2)(a), (b) and (c) are mandatory but not exhaustive considerations; other considerations may also be relevant, including the inherent likelihood of the occurrence of the fact alleged and the notion that all evidence is to be weighed according to the proof which it was in the power of one side to have produced, and the other to have contradicted: *Blatch v Archer* (1774) 1 Cowp 63 (at 65 per Lord Mansfield).

98 The concept used in subsection (1), being the "balance of probabilities", is often misunderstood. It does not mean a simple estimate of probabilities; it requires a subjective belief in a state of facts on the part of the tribunal of fact. A party bearing the onus will not succeed unless the whole of the

evidence establishes a "reasonable satisfaction" on the preponderance of probabilities such as to sustain the relevant issue: *Axon v Axon* (1937) 59 CLR 395 (at 403 per Dixon J). The "facts proved must form a reasonable basis for a definite conclusion affirmatively drawn of the truth of which the tribunal of fact may reasonably be satisfied": *Jones v Dunkel* (1959) 101 CLR 298 (at 305 per Dixon CJ). Put another way, as Sir Owen Dixon explained in *Briginshaw v Briginshaw* (1938) 60 CLR 336 (at 361), when the law requires proof of any fact, the tribunal of fact must feel an *actual persuasion* of its occurrence or existence before it can be found.

Justice Hodgson put it differently, but to the same effect, by observing that 99
when deciding facts, a civil tribunal of fact is dealing with two questions: "not just what are the probabilities on the limited material which the court has, but also whether that limited material is an appropriate basis on which to reach a reasonable decision": see D H Hodgson, 'The Scales of Justice: Probability and Proof in Legal Fact-finding' (1995) 69 *Australian Law Journal* 731; *Ho v Powell* [2001] NSWCA 168; (2001) 51 NSWLR 572 (at 576 [14]–[16] per Hodgson JA, Beazley JA agreeing).

Whatever way it is put, a "[m]ere mechanical comparison of probabilities 100
independent of a reasonable satisfaction will not justify a finding of fact": *NOM v DPP* [2012] VSCA 198; (2012) 38 VR 618 (at 655 [124] per Redlich and Harper JJA and Curtain AJA); *Brown v New South Wales Trustee and Guardian* [2012] NSWCA 431; (2012) 10 ASTLR 164 (at 176 [51] per Campbell JA, Bergin CJ in Eq and Sackville AJA agreeing).

Although s 140 EA is now the starting point, the concepts it incorporates 101
are neither new nor novel. Any fact-finding inquiry depends upon context. As Kiefel CJ, Gageler and Jagot JJ recently observed in *GLJ v The Trustees of the Roman Catholic Church for the Diocese of Lismore* [2023] HCA 32; (2023) 97 ALJR 857 (at 874–875 [57]), the statutory provision:

> ... reflects the position of the common law that the gravity of the fact sought to be proved is relevant to "the degree of persuasion of the mind according to the balance of probabilities". By this approach, the common law, in accepting but one standard of proof in civil cases (the balance of probabilities), ensures that "the degree of satisfaction for which the civil standard of proof calls may vary according to the gravity of the fact to be proved".
>
> (Citations omitted)

102 As those acting for Mr Lehrmann correctly state, in *Briginshaw*, Dixon J (at 362) emphasised that reasonable satisfaction is not attained independently of the nature *and* the consequence of the fact to be proved, and his Honour referred to the seriousness of the allegation, the inherent unlikelihood of the alleged occurrence, *or* the gravity of the consequences flowing from the finding in question as matters which could all properly bear upon whether the court is reasonably satisfied or feels actual persuasion. The other members of the Court in *Briginshaw* also referred to the seriousness of the allegation sought to be proved as a matter relevant to whether or not the tribunal of fact could be satisfied of the fact alleged (at 347 per Latham CJ; 350 per Rich J; 353 per Starke J; and 372 per McTiernan J).

103 None of this is inconsistent with what I said in *Kumova v Davison (No 2)* (at [262]), where I noted "the focus on the gravity of the finding is linked to the notion that the Court takes into account the inherent unlikelihood of alleged misconduct". They are linked in that both the inherent unlikelihood of the alleged occurrence and the gravity of the consequences each require consideration.

104 An allegation of rape ranks high in the calendar of criminal conduct, and, at the risk of repetition, the allegation needs to be approached with "much care and caution" and with "weight being given to the presumption of innocence and exactness of proof expected": *Briginshaw* (at 347 per Latham CJ; 363 per Dixon J). Further, a finding of rape would, needless to say, be seriously damaging to Mr Lehrmann's reputation and this consequence properly gives one pause before making it: *Ashby v Slipper* [2014] FCAFC 15; (2014) 219 FCR 322 (at 345–346 [68]–[69] per Mansfield and Gilmour JJ).

## E.3 The Practical Difference Between the Civil and Criminal Standard

105 Although I will explain below why the allegations to be proved in making out the truth defence and the allegations to be made out by the Crown in the criminal proceeding are not identical, this is an example where the same essential wrongdoing is to be assessed by reference to both the criminal and the civil standard. Such cases are not common, and they bring into sharp focus cardinal aspects of our legal system.

106 Most first-year law students are introduced to the possibility of error of wrongful convictions and erroneous acquittals. They are (or at least were) made aware of what is often referred to as "Blackstone's ratio",

being the fourth of five discussions of policy by Sir William Blackstone in his 1765 treatise *Commentaries on the Laws of England*, vol IV, ch 27 (Oxford University Press, 2016) (at 352) that "all presumptive evidence of felony should be admitted cautiously: for the law holds, that it is better that ten guilty persons escape, than that one innocent suffer". I digress to note that this notion is ancient: the idea it is better to allow some guilty to escape rather than punish an innocent has Biblical origins (Genesis, 18:23–32) and later was the subject of discussion by Talmudic scholars (see Maimonides, *The Commandments*, Commandment No 290 (Charles B. Chavel, trans. 1967) (at 270)). Indeed, sixteen years before Blackstone, the concept had been expressed by Voltaire – albeit in a different ratio: "'tis much more prudence to acquit two persons, tho' actually guilty, than to pass Sentence of Condemnation on one that is virtuous and innocent": Voltaire, *Zadig; or, The Book of Fate: An Oriental History* (1749) (at 53).

In any event, this moral choice accommodating the possibility of error 107 has been reflected in fundamental aspects of our criminal justice system, including the presumption of innocence and the logically connected requirement the burden of proof rests with the prosecution. It also finds reflection in the rigour of the criminal law standard of proof.

Hence, although it may be trite, it is worth stressing that in contrast to the 108 present forensic contest, if this allegation of rape was to be determined at a criminal trial, it would not be open for the tribunal of fact to find the case proven unless it is satisfied that it has been proved beyond reasonable doubt: s 141(1) EA.

So even though it is necessary to bear in mind the mandatory s 140(2) EA 109 factors and the cogency of the evidence necessary to establish rape on the balance of probabilities, and that the rape will not be proven unless I feel an actual persuasion of its occurrence, the difference between the criminal and civil standard of proof is substantive and can be decisive in dealing with the same underlying allegation.

Apart from anything else, this difference is evident from the necessity that 110 in a criminal trial, the facts as established must be such as to exclude all reasonable hypotheses consistent with innocence.

By way of useful summary, as was emphasised by the High Court in *Rejfek* 111 *v McElroy* (1965) 112 CLR 517 (at 521 per Barwick CJ, Kitto, Taylor, Menzies and Windeyer JJ):

> [t]he difference between the criminal standard of proof and the civil standard of proof is no mere matter of words: it is a matter of critical substance. No matter how grave the fact which is to be found in a civil case, the mind has only to be reasonably satisfied and has not with respect to any matter in issue in such a proceeding to attain that degree of certainty which is indispensable to the support of a conviction upon a criminal charge.

## E.4 Assessing the Credit of a Complainant of Sexual Assault

112 Another aspect of the context of this fact-finding exercise is that the determination of the justification defence involves, among other things, consideration of the credibility of evidence given by Ms Higgins, a person who alleges she is a victim of a sexual assault.

113 Prior to trial, Network Ten served purported expert evidence seeking to establish that aspects of Ms Higgins' behaviour were not demonstrative of untruthfulness by reference to common or usual patterns of behaviour (as was anticipated would be asserted by Mr Lehrmann in cross-examination). This evidence was not proposed to be adduced by Network Ten in support of a submission that it was probable Ms Higgins was telling the truth, nor that her behaviour following the alleged rape rendered it more or less likely that the assault had occurred as alleged. Rather, the opinion evidence was said to support the proposition that any counterintuitive behaviour relied upon by Mr Lehrmann was of neutral significance.

114 It was a type of evidence discussed by Associate Professor Jacqueline Horan and Professor Jane Goodman-Delahunty in their article 'Expert Evidence to Counteract Jury Misconceptions about Consent in Sexual Assault Cases: Failures and Lessons Learned' (2020) 43(2) *UNSW Law Journal* 707. In that article (dealing with how so-called "rape myths" play a role in jury decision-making), the authors observed (at 710–11):

> Legal authorities in Australia, Canada, New Zealand, the United Kingdom and the United States of America accept that sexual assault myths and misconceptions have a potential to exert an undue influence on triers of fact when deliberating about a sexual assault case. To avoid this undesirable influence, courts rely on traditional processes to educate juries so that they can better assess the

evidence in a sexual assault trial on a sound factual basis. The two primary mechanisms to counteract the undue influence of sexual assault myths are expert evidence and judicial directions.

Over the last decade, counterintuitive expert evidence has been permitted to educate the jury as to how complainants vary in their behaviour both during and following a sexual assault. Legal practitioners and academics have noted that this provision remains underused, despite the widely acknowledged need for this type of educative intervention.

Such opinions as to "counterintuitive evidence" have been admitted under s 108C(1) EA in criminal sexual assault trials in a number of cases, including: *Hoyle v R* [2018] ACTCA 42; (2018) 339 FLR 11 (at 46–48 [223]–[244] per Murrell CJ, Burns and North JJ); *MA v R* [2013] VSCA 20; (2013) 226 A Crim R 575 (at 586–587 [45]–[52] per Osborn JA; at 595 [95] per Redlich and Whelan JJA); *R v Kirkham* [2020] NSWDC 658 (at [41]–[42] per McLennan DCJ); *Aziz (a pseudonym) v R* [2022] NSWCCA 76; (2022) 297 A Crim R 345 (at 355–363 [49]–[92] per Simpson AJA, Lonergan J agreeing). 115

The evidence was objected to by Mr Lehrmann on a number of grounds, which are now unnecessary to detail. Prior to ruling on the objections, I raised with the parties my preliminary view that even if the evidence was admissible, it would be, at best, of marginal utility in circumstances where: (a) this was a judge-alone trial; and (b) that subject to submissions to the contrary, I considered it would be appropriate to direct myself as to the impact of alleged counterintuitive conduct in a manner consistent with some foundational propositions referred to in the proposed evidence which, it seemed to me, simply reflected the accumulated experience of the common law (seen in standard directions) or in ordinary human experience. 116

Sensibly, both parties agreed, and it became unnecessary to deal with admissibility or discretionary exclusion issues, as the following became common ground as agreed facts pursuant to s 191 EA (Agreed Facts dated 18 December 2023 (**agreed facts**)): 117

(1) trauma has a severe impact on memory by splintering and fragmenting memories; such that semantic or meaning elements become separated from emotion; and interfering with the timespan memories require to consolidate and become permanent;

(2) due to the potential for cuing of emotional responses to fragmented memories, memory can change, be subject to reconsolidation effects, and even when these effects are not marked initially, memories may remain labile for some time (thus changes in what the person reports as their memory of an event can be expected);

(3) lack of clarity and confused accounts can be expected until such time as the memory has consolidated;

(4) inconsistencies in reporting following a traumatic event are often observed and explicable through underlying theories of trauma and memory function;

(5) omissions can be understood as alterations in awareness due to high arousal at the time of the event that consolidate over time;

(6) inconsistency is often observed in reliable reports of sexual assault and is not *ipso facto* a measure of deception;

(7) in understanding the account of an alleged "survivor", a person must consider how that account was elicited; this includes the skill and attitudes towards the person by the investigating officers; the time elapsed between the traumatic event and the formal interview; and the psychological/emotional state of the person being interviewed at the time of interview;

(8) the first forensic interview is potentially a trigger for intrusive thoughts that can lead to fragmentation of memory and dissociation; patterns of behaviour such as high confidence and clarity in the account are not helpful in determining whether the account is accurate;

(9) despite the belief that the emergence of inconsistencies across interviews is a sign of lying (people "can't keep their story straight"), the literature on memory, impacts of trauma and the dynamic between interviewee and the interviewer must be considered; and

(10) multiple interviews are typically necessary to construct a clear narrative of events; however, the consequence of these multiple interviews may be patterns of inconsistency or omissions especially early in the interview process (which need to be carefully evaluated but are not in and of themselves necessarily indicative of deception or accuracy).

Consistently with the agreement of the parties, to the extent these propositions are relevant, I will bear them in mind in assessing the impact of any counterintuitive behaviour pointed to by Mr Lehrmann, after the alleged assault, on Ms Higgins' credit. 118

In a similarly helpful and constructive way, the parties also agreed facts as to the impact of acute alcohol intoxication, in that it has: 119

(1) a significant and negative effect on memory as it can impair the memory for behaviour and motivation of all parties involved in a sexual act, including a sexually aggressive act; and

(2) been shown to impair judgment; impact negatively on executive function; and impair attention to environmental cues; it can lead to fragmentary memories that slowly recover and consolidate and from a forensic perspective, this process of fragmentation of memory with at times slow recovery may lead to apparent inconsistency and omissions between interviews.

Although not an agreed fact, there is a further matter worth mentioning about alcohol consumption that is uncontroversial. As was pointed out by Professor Julia Quilter, Professor Luke McNamara and Ms Melissa Porter in their article 'The Nature and Purpose of Complainant Intoxication Evidence in Rape Trials: A Study of Australian Appellate Court Decisions' (2022) 43(2) *Adelaide Law Review* 606, alcohol consumption is "strongly associated with sexual violence crimes, including rape" (at 607). A review of cases, however, suggests that complainant intoxication evidence has historically been more likely to impede, rather than support, the prosecution's ability to prove non-consent, because it can be used to: suggest consent based on a "loss of inhibition" narrative; and/or challenge the credibility of the complainant as a witness and the reliability of their account. 120

But here, of course, the evidence adduced by Mr Lehrmann and the forensic choices he has made means he does not directly advance a "loss of inhibition" narrative and, significantly, any submission made as to the reliability of Ms Higgins as someone affected by alcohol is also relevant (if the evidence otherwise establishes sex took place) to the question of whether she was so affected by alcohol as to be incapable of consenting to sex. 121

## E.5 The Importance of Contemporaneous Representations

122 In a complex commercial case, *Webb v GetSwift Limited (No 5)* [2019] FCA 1533, I noted the following about the process of fact-finding (at [17]–[18]):

> [17] ...what matters most in the determination of the issues in cases such as this is the analysis of such contemporaneous notes and documents as may exist and the probabilities that can be derived from these documents and any other objective facts. ...
>
> [18] As Leggatt J said in *Gestmin SGPS SA v Credit Suisse (UK) Limited* [2013] EWHC 3560 (Comm) at [15]–[23], there are a number of difficulties with oral evidence based on recollection of events given the unreliability of human memory. Moreover, considerable interference with memory is also introduced in civil litigation by the procedure of preparing for trial... [T]he surest guide for deciding the case will be as identified by Leggatt J at [22]:
>
> ... the best approach for a judge to adopt in the trial of a commercial case is, in my view, to place little if any reliance at all on the witnesses' recollections of what was said in meetings and conversations, and to base factual findings on inferences drawn from the documentary evidence and known or probable facts.

123 As the Full Court later observed in *Liberty Mutual Insurance Company Australian Branch trading as Liberty Specialty Markets v Icon Co (NSW) Pty Ltd* [2021] FCAFC 126; (2018) 396 ALR 193 (at 254 [239] per Allsop CJ, Besanko and Middleton JJ), this approach might be best seen as a helpful working hypothesis, rather than something to be enshrined in any rule. Although these observations were made in the context of fact-finding in commercial cases, this does not mean they are anything but apposite to the fact-finding task to be undertaken in this defamation proceeding.

124 Moreover, in this case, in addition to file notes, texts, social media messages and emails, hours of audio, video and closed-circuit television (**CCTV**) footage has been adduced into evidence. I have reviewed this contemporaneous material and, for my manifold sins, have listened or watched all the audio-visual records in evidence. I have trudged unyieldingly through this material because insofar as it casts light on the relevant

issues, these contemporaneous records are a far surer guide as to what happened than *ex post facto* accounts or rationalisations, or unverifiable assertions as to what people "felt".

The helpful working hypothesis of paying close regard to the contemporaneous documents and representations to disinterested third parties is of signal importance, especially where, as I will explain, I have misgivings as to the reliability of aspects of the accounts given by a number of important witnesses. 125

## E.6 The Court is Not Bound to Accept Either of the Parties' Accounts

As I will explain further below, the particularised allegation made by the respondents brings with it the requirement to prove: 126

(1) that, at the time and place alleged (that is, at Parliament House on 23 March 2019), Mr Lehrmann had sexual intercourse with Ms Higgins;

(2) without Ms Higgins' consent; and

(3) knowing Ms Higgins did not consent.

It is notorious that in many rape trials, the forensic battleground is whether the Crown can prove beyond reasonable doubt the second element (**non-consent element**) and the third element (**knowledge element**). In recent times, law reformers have focused attention on whether it is appropriate that consent to sexual activity must be communicated by words or actions, such that there is a responsibility to take steps to find out whether the other person is consenting. This has spurred some recent legislative change: see, for example, the *Crimes Legislation Amendment (Sexual Consent Reforms) Act 2021* (NSW). 127

It is beyond the scope of this judgment to discuss these changes, but as the Victorian Law Reform Commission recently put it in its report *Improving the Justice System Response to Sexual Offences: Report* (September 2021) (at [19.13]), some of the features of the criminal justice system: 128

> make sexual offences more difficult to prove in court. By their nature, sexual offending often happens in private, without other witnesses. The accused does not have to give evidence because they have a right to silence. For rape, the need to prove there was no consent means that many cases will end up focusing on the complainant.

129 What is notable about this civil case, and the criminal case that preceded it, is that by reason of Mr Lehrmann's forensic position to contest the establishment of the first element (that sexual intercourse occurred), he has not engaged directly (through challenging the Crown case at the criminal trial or by way of evidence before me) with the reality and appreciation of consent.

130 Specifically, Mr Lehrmann has advanced an account that he came back to the Ministerial Suite accompanied by Ms Higgins for them to then go their separate ways: not only was there no sex, but no intimacy of any kind.

131 Below I explain why this aspect of Mr Lehrmann's evidence is stuff and nonsense, but for present purposes, this conclusion makes it necessary to point out that in general, disbelief of one witness's account does not establish the contrary, or that a witness giving a contrary account must be believed: *Kuligowski v Metrobus* [2004] HCA 34; (2004) 220 CLR 363 (at 385–386 [60] per Gleeson CJ, McHugh, Gummow, Kirby, Hayne, Callinan and Heydon JJ).

132 Of course, if I am ultimately unable to make a finding one way or another as to what actually happened, it is open to decide the issue on the basis that the party who bears the burden of proof on this issue (that is, the respondents) have failed to discharge their burden: *Rhesa Shipping Co SA v Edmunds* [1985] 1 WLR 948 (at 955–956 per Lord Brandon, Lords Fraser, Diplock, Roskill and Templeman agreeing). Relatedly, and importantly, given my rejection of Mr Lehrmann's account of what went on, it must be borne in mind that a civil onus of proof is not discharged by mere disbelief in opposing evidence (see, for example, in the context of a criminal onus, *Liberato v R* (1985) 159 CLR 507 (at 515 per Brennan J)).

## E.7 Multiple Available Hypotheses and Onus

133 Related to the last point, it is also necessary to consider the existence and cogency of other hypotheses open on the evidence.

134 Recently, in *Palmanova Pty Ltd v Commonwealth of Australia* [2023] FCA 1391, Perram J, in an unusual circumstantial case (and with apologies to those, like me, who thought that algebra would not be involved in this case) observed (at [21]):

> Where there are only two competing hypotheses that between them account for the universe of possibilities open on the evidence, a court's satisfaction that one is more likely than the other will entail

> that the occurrence of the fact supported by the more likely hypothesis is proved on the civil standard. Whilst it is important not to approach the civil standard in an excessively arithmetical way in terms of numeric probabilities it can be useful to do so to illustrate some consequences in a circumstantial case where multiple hypotheses are in competition with each other. For example, where there are only two competing hypotheses and one is more probable than the other then it must follow that the more likely one is more likely than not. (More formally: if $P(A)>P(B)$ then since $P(A)+P(B)=1$ then one may validly infer that $P(A)>1/2$.) But the logic of this breaks down where there are three or more competing hypotheses. If $P(A)>P(B)>P(C)$ then the fact that $P(A)+P(B)+P(C)=1$ does not warrant the conclusion that $P(A)>1/2$ as will be seen if $P(A)=45\%$, $P(B)=30\%$ and $P(C)=25\%$. Thus the court will only be satisfied that a fact is established if the hypothesis supporting it is more likely than *all* of the others considered together (i.e. $P(A)>(P(B)+P(C))$). In particular, the mere fact that one of the hypotheses emerges as more likely than *each* of the others will not suffice, it must be more likely than *all* of them.

Of course, as his Honour recognised, nothing said in *Palmanova* is 135
intended to depart from the realities that: (a) mechanical or arithmetic comparison of probabilities independent of belief will not justify a finding of fact; or (b) each competing hypothesis open on the evidence might range, possibly very significantly, in likelihood of occurrence. The important points made, however, are the need for care when there are a range of possibilities open, and the only way one reaches a state of reasonable satisfaction as to *one* being proven is to conclude its existence is more likely than *all* the other hypotheses available on the evidence.

## E.8 False in One Thing does not mean False in Everything

Moreover, in assessing whether one has reached a state of reasonable satis- 136
faction in making a finding of fact, it is jejune to proceed on the basis that rejecting *part* of an account of a witness of an event must mean one must reject *all* aspects of the account of the witness.

Consistently with ordinary human experience, some witnesses may misre- 137
member or lie about some things but tell the truth about others. Despite my

concerns about the truthfulness of both Mr Lehrmann and Ms Higgins, it would be simplistic to proceed on the basis this means I must reject everything they say. As the Full Court (McKerracher, Robertson and Lee JJ) explained in *CCL Secure Pty Ltd v Berry* [2019] FCAFC 81 (at [94]):

> It has been a long time since the maxim *falsus in uno, falsus in omnibus* (false in one thing, false in everything) was part of the common law, its broad applicability having been rejected long ago (including by no less a judge than Lord Ellenborough CJ in *R v Teal* (1809) 11 East 307; 103 ER 1022). It is trite that the tribunal of fact (be it a judge or jury), having seen and heard the witness, is to decide whether the evidence of the witness is worthy of acceptance and this may involve accepting or rejecting the whole of the evidence, or accepting some of the evidence and rejecting the rest: *Cubillo v Commonwealth* [2000] FCA 1084; (2000) 103 FCR 1 at 45-47 [118]-[123]; *Flint v Lowe* (1995) 22 MVR 1; and *S v M* (1984) 36 SASR 316. It is for this reason a jury is directed that they may accept some parts of a witness's evidence, but not other parts: *Dublin, Wicklow & Wexford Railway Co v Slattery* (1878) 3 App Cas 1155. This reflects the accumulated wisdom and experience of the common law that witnesses may lie about some things and yet tell the truth about others, and the tribunal hearing the evidence is best placed to fix upon the truth. ...

138 Another Full Court (Wigney, Wheelahan and Abraham JJ) in *Kazal v Thunder Studios Inc (California)* [2023] FCAFC 174 recently made the same point (at [272]) as follows:

> ... People sometimes tell lies when giving evidence. What is significant is not the mere fact of the untruthfulness, but its relevance to the issues in dispute. A finding that a witness has lied about a matter need not lead to the rejection of all of the evidence of that witness, but may affect the degree of satisfaction of the existence or otherwise of a fact in issue to which the witness's evidence was directed. ...

## E.9 Implied Admissions and "Consciousness of Guilt"

139 Given, as I will explain, the two principal witnesses in the justification case told lies during their evidence and in the making of out-of-court

representations, the final matter to which I wish to draw attention is how these lies can be used in the fact-finding process.

Ms Higgins is not a party, and although any lies told by her will be central to my assessment of her creditworthiness (and hence reliability), the position of Mr Lehrmann, as a party and as someone who gave evidence contrary to the evidence adduced by the onus-bearing party, needs separate examination. 140

Recently, as part of the Full Court in *Kim v Wang* [2023] FCAFC 115; (2023) 411 ALR 402, I referred (at 428 [150]) to the decision of the High Court in *Kuhl v Zurich Financial Services Australia Ltd* [2011] HCA 11; (2010) 243 CLR 361 (at 384–385 [63]), where Heydon, Crennan and Bell JJ relevantly explained that when a party calls testimony known to be false, this conduct can amount to an implied admission or circumstantial evidence permitting an adverse inference, and I then (at 428–429 [151]) observed as follows: 141

> Recently, in *Roberts-Smith v Fairfax Media Publications Pty Limited (No 41)* [2023] FCA 555, Besanko J addressed the circumstances in which lies can give rise to a finding of a consciousness of guilt or the making of an implied admission and described them as "complex and highly contentious" (at [197]). In summarising the authorities, his Honour observed (at [205]) that a court must "be cautious before treating a lie as an implied admission or evidence of a consciousness of guilt" and, among other things, should bear in mind there may be reasons for the telling of a lie apart from a realisation of guilt: *Edwards v The Queen* (1993) 178 CLR 193 (at 211 per Deane, Dawson and Gaudron JJ).

The concept derives from the criminal law and forms part of the more general principle that the Crown can rely upon an accused's post-offence conduct as evidence of a consciousness of guilt: this could be a lie told in or out-of-court or by other conduct, including suborning witnesses or absconding to avoid arrest: *McKey v R* [2012] NSWCCA 1; (2012) 219 A Crim R 227 (at 233 [26] per Latham J, Hislop J and Whealy JA agreeing). A good example is seen in *Pollard v R* [2011] VSCA 95; (2011) 31 VR 416, where the evidence of the accused hiding a mobile phone was properly admitted as part of the Crown's circumstantial case. 142

When it comes to "*Edwards* lies" as post-offence conduct, as is usefully explained by the Judicial College of Victoria in Pt 4.6 of its *Victorian* 143

*Criminal Charge Book* (which deals with "Incriminating Conduct (Post Offence Lies and Conduct)") (at [25]), at common law, untrue assertions and false denials are only capable of being used as an implied admission if the accused perceives that the truth is inconsistent with innocence and the jury was required to consider the following matters before using such lies as evidence of an implied admission:

(1) the lie was deliberate;

(2) the lie related to a material issue;

(3) the telling of the lie showed knowledge of the offence and was told because the truth would implicate the accused; and

(4) there was no other explanation for the telling of the lie consistent with innocence (see *R v Edwards* (1993) 178 CLR 193; *R v Renzella* [1997] 2 VR 88).

144 But there is a need for adaption of the principles explained in these criminal law authorities in a civil case. In the appeal in Australia's longest running defamation case, Beazley, Giles and Santow JJA in *Amalgamated Television Services Pty Ltd v Marsden* [2002] NSWCA 419 comprehensively dealt with admissions by conduct (at [78]–[88]). In doing so, the Court of Appeal referred to the fourth of the matters noted above and observed the concept that no other rational inference may be drawn is a concept of the criminal law, necessitated by the standard of proof of beyond reasonable doubt. The Court of Appeal went on to explain that in a civil case, it is sufficient for "a lie to be accepted as an admission of guilt, if that is the more probable inference to be drawn" (at [88]). I respectfully agree that such an approach is not only appropriate, but necessary to accommodate the differing standard of proof.

145 How a lie can be used in assessing the reliability of the accounts given by Mr Lehrmann or Ms Higgins is straightforward. What I am presently concerned with is how an identified lie of Mr Lehrmann can and should be used to lend weight to the other evidence said to support the satisfaction of the onus of proof by the respondents. I will return below in Section H.2 to implied admissions and simply note for present purposes that the identification and use of "*Edwards* lies" should be approached with caution, including in the light of the warning in *Briginshaw* (reflected in s 140 EA) that reasonable satisfaction should not be produced by, among other things, indirect inferences.

# F OBSERVATIONS AS TO THE CENTRAL WITNESSES

This section sets out my general assessment of the creditworthiness of the evidence given by a dozen (of a total of 33) witnesses who gave oral evidence. I will then turn to make specific factual findings. In the course of doing so, I will address the evidence of these and other witnesses in greater specificity where relevant. 146

In another defamation case (*Russell v Australian Broadcasting Corporation (No 3)* [2023] FCA 1223), I said (at [438]) that many experienced judges have expressed the caution that any criticisms of a witness, which go beyond the legitimate necessities of the occasion, should be avoided. Unnecessary credit findings should be eschewed. Part of this reticence reflects a body of research casting doubt on the ability of judges to make accurate credibility findings based on demeanour: see *Fox v Percy* [2003] HCA 22; (2003) 214 CLR 118 (at 129 [31] per Gleeson CJ, Gummow and Kirby JJ). 147

But like *Russell*, this is a case where several of the deficiencies were both patent and telling. Moreover, this is a case where credit, given the way it impacts upon the resolution of the determinative issues in the case, requires close and especially nuanced examination. 148

## F.1 Mr Lehrmann

### *I General Remarks*

I will deal below in Section G.4 with the account given by Mr Lehrmann as to why he went back to the Ministerial Suite on the fateful night. I can make general observations as to his creditworthiness by reference to other aspects of his evidence. 149

Network Ten described Mr Lehrmann as "a fundamentally dishonest man, prepared to say or do anything he perceived to advance his interests" (T2215.5). Senior counsel for Ms Wilkinson described him as "an active 150 and deliberate liar" and wondered aloud whether "Mr Lehrmann is just a compulsive liar" (T2316.43).

151 Hyperbolic submissions made about the lack of credit of a party witness are not uncommon. In a recent speech ("Seven Random Points About Judging", *National Judicial Orientation Program*, 17 March 2024), Justice Beech-Jones made a similar point to that made in my introductory remarks: that is, a judge should be reticent about accepting such submissions "unless you really have to".

152 But even taking this wisdom into account, this is one of those cases where expressing criticism is warranted. But one must not be simplistic. A falsehood told by a witness will be especially serious if the maker is under a legal obligation to tell the truth. But irrespective of legal obligation, there are gradations of the seriousness of untruths: an untruthful person may just be all mouth and trousers; or be recklessly indifferent to the truth or, by way of compulsion, finds it difficult to discern between what is true and untrue; or finally, and most culpably, may be someone who tells calculated, deliberate lies.

153 I do not think Mr Lehrmann is a compulsive liar, and some of the untruths he told during his evidence may sometimes have been due to carelessness and confusion, but I am satisfied that in important respects he told deliberate lies. I would not accept anything he said except where it amounted to an admission, accorded with the inherent probabilities, or was corroborated by a contemporaneous document or a witness whose evidence I accept.

## *II Miscellaneous Examples of False Statements during the Hearing*

154 Instances of Mr Lehrmann's false out-of-court statements or unsatisfactory evidence are legion, but the following important examples illustrate the point sufficiently.

155 *First*, there was the evidence denying that he found Ms Higgins alluring as at March 2019. As I will explain, from the start, Mr Lehrmann thought that Ms Higgins was attractive. This attraction informed a number of his later actions. Moreover, his denial of this fact was unwary as it contradicted what he had said on the *Spotlight* programme. When confronted by this inconsistency, his attempt to explain it away by suggesting the attraction he felt for Ms Higgins was "just like [the attraction] I can find

[in] anybody else in this [court]room, irrespective of gender" (T351.8–11) was as disconcerting as it was unconvincing.

*Secondly*, and relatedly, Mr Lehrmann initially gave evidence that he had not met Ms Higgins prior to attending the Kingston Hotel on 2 March 2019 and downplayed his awareness of her (T175.9–11). This was supplemented by saying Ms Hamer initiated Ms Higgins being invited to the Kingston Hotel, a contention I reject below. All of this was directed to avoiding admitting that he thought Ms Higgins was comely and wanted to get to know her (as was his evidence denying he entreated her to stay after she wished to move on from the hotel that day (T1049)). 156

*Thirdly*, there was false evidence about what occurred at The Dock on 22 March 2019. Mr Lehrmann, in chief and initially in cross-examination, gave evidence to the effect: (a) he purchased one drink for Mr Wenke and one for himself, and that Mr Wenke then returned the shout (T244.14–19); (b) he did not purchase drinks for anyone else (T95.1–2); (c) the only money he spent was $16 (Ex 15; T244.40–41); and (d) he had minimal contact with Ms Higgins (T94.38). Going back to the hierarchy of untruths referred to at the beginning of this subsection, this was an aspect of Mr Lehrmann's evidence where I am unsure whether he was being recklessly indifferent to the truth; or was finding it difficult to remember what was true; or was confused (or a combination of these things). 157

Mr Lehrmann must have known that the relevant CCTV footage (Ex R42 / Ex 17A) would be examined by some with the intensity that others analyse the Zapruder film. Hence, even if one was willing to give false evidence, it was odd to dissemble as to these matters. There was an inevitability the CCTV footage would demonstrate that: (a) he had purchased drinks for Ms Higgins and had seen her consume significant quantities of alcohol; (b) his prior explanation for how he had paid for the drinks would not pass muster; and (c) he spent most of the evening with Ms Higgins. Even if one puts the best complexion on what occurred, it confirms that Mr Lehrmann's evidence is unreliable. 158

*Fourthly*, there was the evidence as to what occurred at the Canberra bar, 88mph. Mr Lehrmann emphatically denied any intimacy with Ms Higgins at 88mph (T298.19–20). This evidence was not only false (as I will later explain) but was in tension with representations to the Australian Federal Police (**AFP**) (Ex 31) that he could not recall any intimacy but accepted that he and Ms Higgins "were close" (T298.36; T299.29–43). In trying 159 to reconcile these positions, Mr Lehrmann was then forced to draw a distinction between intimacy and flirtatious behaviour, which resulted in the following nonsensical exchange (T300.5–7):

> DR COLLINS: Well, explain what you mean by you engaged in minimal flirtatious behaviour with Ms Higgins. What did you do? ---Well, nothing – nothing – nothing beyond that would indicate an attraction or anything more than, you know.

160 Mr Lehrmann later said he had been truthful in posing and answering a rhetorical question to AFP officers in these terms (T301.28–36):

> DR COLLINS: You were asked the question:
>
> > *Is it possible* [you engaged in intimate behaviour with Ms Higgins at 88mph]*?*
>
> Your answer is:
>
> > *Yeah, yeah, it's possible, but um, would I have – would I have acted beyond anything that was a bit flirtatious? Absolutely not, because I was in a relationship, so.*
>
> ?---Yes.
>
> Remember giving that answer?---Yes, I remember that answer.

161 As I will come to, Ms Lauren Gain's account that she observed Mr Lehrmann and Ms Higgins "being quite touchy with one another" and her memory of both engaging in a "passionate kiss" and of Ms Higgins "taking selfies of the two of them" (T1106.19) was compelling. It also reveals the hollowness of Mr Lehrmann's suggestion that his relationship with a girlfriend morally inhibited him from engaging in intimacy with Ms Higgins. This was an example of Mr Lehrmann being mendacious about a centrally important part of the case.

162 *Fifthly*, as detailed below, Mr Lehrmann gave false evidence about a litany of other matters, such as: being reprimanded by Senator Reynolds; the classified document security breach; as to securing entry into Parliament House; the circumstances in which he came to be accompanied by Ms Higgins when securing entry; about whisky; and about his representations made to Ms Brown. All these falsehoods, together with his Walter Mitty-like imaginings in skiting to Ms Gain about the Australian Secret Intelligence Service (**ASIS**), demonstrate that Mr Lehrmann had no compunction about departing from the truth if he thought it expedient.

*Finally*, was his assertion (which received intense attention from Network Ten) that Ms Gain colluded with Ms Higgins to invent an account of what happened. Mr Lehrmann alleged that Ms Gain presented a false account under oath in his criminal trial to attempt to pervert the course of justice. Mr Lehrmann's counsel in written submissions accepted he gave "strident evidence" about Ms Gain but then explained that this was prompted by the fact that "Ms Gain had been contacted by Ms Higgins in a deceptive and calculated manner ahead of the Project broadcast in a manner suggestive of an attempt to pollute Ms Gain's evidence and 'recruit' her". As I will explain when I discuss Ex 47, I am satisfied that Ms Higgins did seek to prompt Ms Gain's recollection in a calculated fashion – but it does not follow that Ms Gain was prepared to do anything but recount her truthful recollection when she was called upon to give evidence. Although I understand Mr Lehrmann's concern over Ms Higgins' conduct reflected in the creation and deletion of Ex 47, it was wrong for Mr Lehrmann to make a serious allegation against Ms Gain to dissimulate the true nature of his then attraction to Ms Higgins. 163

### *III The Spotlight Detour*

The conclusions expressed in the preceding section had been drafted prior to Easter Sunday when, less than four days prior to the notified date of delivery of this judgment, my Associate was contacted by the solicitors for Network Ten concerning an application to reopen, which I then listed and resolved as soon as practicable, after hours, the next business day. 164

Although the application was an unusual one and there is a need for caution in allowing a re-opening of the evidence after reservation except on well-founded grounds, I gave leave because: doing so was consistent with the authorities in relation to fresh evidence; the material was said to have some relevance to matters that went beyond the question of Mr Lehrmann's credit; and, moreover, its receipt would assist in ensuring this controversy was quelled, and be *seen* to have been quelled, on the basis of *all* admissible evidence the parties wished to adduce. Further, doing so would not cause any real delay (and hence be inimical to resolving justly this dispute quickly and efficiently). 165

Following the reopening, Mr Taylor Auerbach, a former Senior Producer on the *Spotlight* programme, was called to establish the propositions that: 166

(1) the extent of what might be described as collateral rewards given to Mr Lehrmann for his co-operation with the Seven Network was more extensive than had been previously stated; and

(2) contrary to: (a) assurances given by the solicitors for Mr Lehrmann to the solicitors for Network Ten; (b) assurances given to the Court by senior counsel for Mr Lehrmann acting on instructions; and (c) Mr Lehrmann's evidence before me, Mr Lehrmann provided materials to the makers of the *Spotlight* programme contrary to his subsisting legal obligations.

167 I deal with each topic below, but it is worth initially making two points.

168 *First*, Mr Auerbach accepted in cross-examination that he "hated" his former colleague and friend, *Spotlight* producer Mr Steve Jackson (blaming him, "in part", for the fact his contract at the Seven Network was not renewed) (T2786.35; T2788.45). Given his cast of mind, and his more general resentment as to how he was treated over the *Spotlight* programme, it is unsurprising he has an animus towards the Seven Network, and this was manifest in his evidence and in his manner of giving it. His resentment was palpable upon viewing the wanton and vaguely disturbing destruction of what appeared to be a perfectly serviceable set of golf clubs. It is unnecessary to make factual findings in relation to many aspects of his evidence, but one would generally be cautious in making findings based upon incomplete evidence and resting solely upon the word of a man motivated by such rancour.

169 *Secondly*, and connected to my first point, the evidence of Mr Auerbach travelled beyond seeking to impeach the credit of Mr Lehrmann. He laid the allegations on thick against a variety of persons – somewhat like the paint in an early work of his namesake, Frank. One of these allegations was that he was instructed (apparently implicitly) by a solicitor, Mr Richard Keegan, to "delete any materials that could be damaging for Seven" (Auerbach 30 March 2024 (at [20])). I reject this assertion – it is unbelievable on its face. As to his allegations of improper conduct against his erstwhile work colleagues, they are irrelevant to the facts in issue, except in one limited respect.

*Collateral Rewards*

170 I can deal with Mr Auerbach's evidence of profligate behaviour very briefly. He gave evidence, consistent with contemporaneous documents and uncontradicted by any evidence in reply by Mr Lehrmann, that he

became Mr Lehrmann's "babysitter" or "minder" as the Seven Network worked to secure an exclusive interview with Mr Lehrmann (T2776.15–20). At some stage, it appears Mr Auerbach was discomforted in being placed in this role (Ex R899), but he nonetheless performed it, sometimes, it appears, ardently. I assume that Mr Lehrmann thought any joint activities with Mr Auerbach would be kept private.

The specifics are unedifying, and it is unnecessary to make granular findings. In the end, it is fair to conclude that Mr Lehrmann was less than candid in his account of the extent of the benefits he received prior to, and exchange for, his bargain to participate in giving exclusive interviews to the Seven Network. It is fair to remark that the evidence reveals that some of the pre-compact inducements and consideration flowing in the direction of one contractual counterparty was of an unorthodox and undocumented kind. But given the other matters going to credit in this case, it is an inconsequential point. 171

*Hearne v Street*

The second point has more significance. 172

As is well known, and as was explained by the High Court in *Hearne v Street* [2008] HCA 36; (2008) 235 CLR 125, where one party to litigation is compelled, either by reason of a rule of court, or by reason of a specific order of the court, or otherwise, to disclose documents or information, the party obtaining the disclosure cannot, without the leave of the court, use it for any purpose than that for which it was given unless it is received into evidence. The obligation extends to anyone who receives the documents or information knowing the documents or information have been disclosed by compulsion. The circumstances in which this substantive legal obligation, which I will call the *Hearne v Street* obligation, no longer subsist are broader than receipt into evidence, but this detail need not detain us: see *Treasury Wine Estates Limited v Maurice Blackburn Pty Ltd* [2020] FCAFC 226; (2020) 282 FCR 95. 173

After the first *Spotlight* programme, the broadcast of material apparently subject to the *Hearne v Street* obligation caused much perturbation on the part of the respondents. Following demands for an explanation, upon instructions, Mr Lehrmann's solicitors repeatedly denied he breached the *Hearne v Street* obligation (on 5, 8 and 9 June 2023 (Ex R895; R898; and R896); and 10 August 2023 (Ex R897)). His senior counsel, again no 174 doubt acting on express instructions, did the same before me on 9 June 2023. Consistently with the instructions provided to his lawyers, Mr Lehrmann gave evidence during the trial to the effect that he did not give documents to the Seven Network, he just gave an interview (T523.32–7).

175 As I explained at the trial, I am not some sort of roving law enforcement official, and if any issue concerning an alleged breach of the *Hearne v Street* obligation is to be pursued in relation to anyone, it will not be by me, and it will not be by this Court. My role is more limited: it is to ascertain whether Mr Lehrmann made (or caused to be made) false representations as to this topic. I am comfortably satisfied he did.

176 Three documents or categories of documents were relied upon by Network Ten, namely those the parties agree were either contained in the "AFP eBrief" served on Mr Lehrmann in the criminal proceeding (or make reference to such material), being: (a) 2,312 pages of text messages between Ms Higgins and Mr Dillaway, of which only 17 pages were tendered at the criminal trial (**Dillaway Messages**); (b) a "Master Chronology" (obviously prepared by Mr Lehrmann's counsel for the purpose of the trial) which contains references to material and documents contained in the eBrief (this is defined elsewhere in these reasons as "MC", being an annexure to the affidavit of Mr Auerbach sworn 2 April 2024); and (c) PDF files of messages passing between Ms Higgins and Mr Peter FitzSimons (Ms Wilkinson's husband), which were not adduced into evidence (**FitzSimons Messages**).

177 As to (a), although the file names for the versions of the Dillaway Messages from the eBrief and those produced by Mr Auerbach match and bear the same date (Ex R892; R889; and R890), and Mr Auerbach says he located them in his iCloud storage, there is no independent proof as to them being provided electronically by Mr Lehrmann to Mr Auerbach during their joint golfing trip to Tasmania as he alleges. As to (b), although the MC does contain some material sourced from materials subject to the *Hearne v Street* obligation, it was a document prepared by counsel and the evidence is somewhat opaque as to how it came to be in the hands of the Seven Network. Although it is fair to remark the evidence tends to support the contentions as to misuse made by Network Ten, and it is also true Mr Lehrmann elected not to lead evidence to refute Mr Auerbach's evidence despite having the opportunity to do so, I do not consider it necessary to reach any conclusion as to the Dillaway Messages or the MC,

given the state of satisfaction I have reached as to the matter to which I will now turn.

It is sufficient for present purposes to find: 178

(1) photographs of a computer screen displaying the FitzSimons Messages were taken, being the photographs annexed to Auerbach 30 March 2024 (**Relevant Photographs**);

(2) the Relevant Photographs also show that on the computer screen, tabs were open which record web pages which are not inconsistent with the computer being one operated by Mr Lehrmann (one of the tabs is for "Current students" and another is for the "University of N …": Mr Lehrmann has deposed that, in 2023, he was a law student (Lehrmann (at [38]));

(3) the Relevant Photographs were taken at a house on Barker St, Randwick on Saturday, 4 March 2023;

(4) the Randwick house was then being licensed by the Seven Network for Mr Lehrmann;

(5) at 8:13am on Monday, 6 March 2023, there is a text message between Mr Jackson and Mr Auerbach by which Mr Jackson informs Mr Auerbach he has "mail" being that "Mark went to Bruce's on Saturday" (and forwarding a screenshot of an exchange of messages between Mr Jackson and Mr Mark Llewellyn, the Executive Producer of the *Spotlight* programme, who had, it appears, been at the Royal Randwick that Saturday (at, I would think, around the time of commencement of the Autumn Carnival) as he is asked by Mr Jackson "Did you pick a winner at Randwick on Saturday?" (Ex R905 (at 89)); those messages are consistent with Mr Lehrmann meeting Mr Llewellyn at the Randwick house on the day the Relevant Photographs were taken; and

(6) some of the Relevant Photographs show the reflection of a man identified as Mr Llewellyn who, from the location indicated by the images, must have taken the Relevant Photographs.

In the absence of any other explanation, the inescapable conclusion is 179
that Mr Lehrmann provided access to Mr Llewellyn to take the Relevant Photographs, and thus wrongly provided him with access to the information contained in the FitzSimons Messages. His representations and

evidence to the contrary were false to his knowledge on a serious matter, and this conclusion fortifies my assessment as to his general credit.

## F.2 Ms Higgins

### *I General Remarks*

180 It is necessary to assess the credit of Ms Higgins circumspectly. She is someone who has the intense, uncritical support of some but has also been the subject of widespread social media abuse. As with Mr Lehrmann, I am conscious that giving evidence would have been a daunting and stressful experience.

181 I am in the unusual position of receiving submissions from a witness as to her credit directly. This came about because I was anxious to ensure procedural fairness was provided concerning submissions made as to the falsity of certain out-of-court representations (in circumstances I explain in detail below).

182 Ms Higgins' submissions extended beyond these out-of-court representations. Notwithstanding this, I have considered them, although they largely repeat points made by the respondents. But Ms Higgins does make the bespoke and valid point that it is the parties who identify and frame the issues (including issues concerning credit) and the evidence adduced as to those issues. It ought not to be assumed that if Ms Higgins had been a party she would not have adduced further and different evidence, both from herself and others. Consequently, she may have been able to place the credit attacks made upon her in a different light and, in making credit findings, it is necessary to be cognisant of potentially missing context.

183 The other general point emphasised, although also made by the respondents, is that to the extent that so-called "peripheral details" of her reconstructed memory were wrong, they do not reflect dishonesty even though they may raise an issue as to reliability. As to reliability, one must not only take account of the well-known general features of human memory, but also the mental state of Ms Higgins and the well-known specific effect of trauma, and in particular sexual assault, on her memory.

184 This submission has merit up to a point, and it has informed my consideration of important, indeed critical, aspects of Ms Higgins' evidence, but, as I will explain, I am comfortably satisfied that a number of credit issues arising from a fair assessment of the evidence of Ms Higgins cannot be minimised in this way.

## *II Contrast with Mr Lehrmann*

Those studying political science in the late twentieth century were inevitably introduced to the work of Hannah Arendt who discussed the importance of public truth while coining and explaining the notion of "organised lying". 185

There is a significant difference between the distortions of Mr Lehrmann and Ms Higgins. In the case of Mr Lehrmann, the untruths were all over the shop (being a form of what might be called "disorganised lying"); whereas the untruths of Ms Higgins: (a) can be placed in two temporal categories; (b) were, in the latter category, quite organised; and (c) within both categories, generally had a common thread. In 2019, this was to paint aspects of her conduct in a better light at a time when she did not wish to pursue a complaint; but by 2021 and afterwards, most were part of a broader narrative or theme she and her boyfriend wished others to believe (and, it appears, others wanted to believe). 186

Unsurprisingly, counsel for Mr Lehrmann made several detailed attacks on the credit of Ms Higgins in final submissions. But no distinction was recognised between the two periods and the different contexts I have described. 187

Ms Higgins was described "as a fundamentally dishonest witness such that the Court could not act on anything she says without independent corroborative evidence". The submission was developed by asserting that her evidence "has been so discredited, and she has been shown to be so manipulative that the Court cannot safely rely on anything she has said". It was further said that whenever Ms Higgins was challenged in cross-examination, she felt she had a safe harbour in repeatedly giving "unresponsive and self-serving speeches" and exhibiting frustration at the process of being challenged (Network Ten itself described some of these incidents as "emotional outbursts"). 188

Like with Mr Lehrmann, I will not evaluate her evidence as to what occurred in the Ministerial Suite in this section, but it is convenient to specify ten points going to credit made by Mr Lehrmann and then evaluate the merits of them and other matters. 189

## *III The Points Made by Mr Lehrmann in Submissions*

*First*, reliance was placed on allegedly dishonest conduct or false statements shortly after the incident being: (a) asking Ms Brown for a day 190 off to go to a doctor's appointment on 28 March 2019 when, in reality, she was apparently spending time with Mr Dillaway who was staying in Canberra (Ex R4; T782–3); and (b) telling the AFP on 1 April 2019 that she had gone to Phillip Medical Centre and had tests done, and was awaiting results (Ex R77 (at 6); T1406).

191 *Secondly*, Mr Lehrmann pointed to a series of representations made to Mr Dillaway before and shortly after the alleged rape that are inconsistent, or at least apparently inconsistent, with Ms Higgins' later account, for example:

(1) despite giving evidence that Mr Lehrmann was treating her poorly when she commenced work in Senator Reynolds' office, on 6 March 2019, Ms Higgins asserted to Mr Dillaway (in response to a question as to how her day had been) that it was "actually, pretty good. I really like the Reynolds team. They are super relaxed. The remaining defence industry people are being such a pain though" (indicating that people were becoming annoying and territorial), but that she was "super happy just to go hang with Bruce on the Senate side and work" (T935.35) – before leaving this message, Ms Higgins' evidence to me that she was "not really" being truthful in making this entirely benign representation to Mr Dillaway (T936.24) is a good example of her willingness to rewrite history in aspects of her evidence when she later thought it was in her interests;

(2) asserting that she had already spoken to her father about the incident and her father was flying down – when Ms Higgins had not, in truth, discussed any incident with her father and there was a pre-existing arrangement for her father to come to Canberra (T979.25–34);

(3) telling Mr Dillaway that she went to the doctor and had a sexually transmitted infection test, when she did not – said to be a far from benign lie in the circumstances (T782.13–24); and

(4) despite giving evidence she was suicidal and lonely in Western Australia (T682.26–33) sending text messages that are inconsistent with such claims (see Ex R99 (at 1077, 1086, 1089, 1109, 1145, 1146, 1171, 1185, 1198, 1216)).

192 *Thirdly*, Mr Lehrmann relies upon false statements in Ms Higgins' 2021 records of interview with the AFP, such as: (a) while trying to gain entry to Parliament House she was "falling all over the place, I fell over at Parliament,

I couldn't sign my own name" (Ex R884, Q33–4) when the CCTV footage does not support these assertions (Ex 17); and (b) telling the AFP she did not receive any emails from Mr Lehrmann before work on the Monday after the weekend of the incident, when she clearly had (Ex R885).

*Fourthly*, reliance was placed on her conduct in telling the AFP in 2021 (T813.17–21) and the criminal trial in 2022 (Ex 71 (at T130)) that she did not wear the dress she wore on the night of the alleged rape again for months, notwithstanding she was photographed wearing it only weeks later. 193

*Fifthly*, Mr Lehrmann relied upon what is said to be the suspicious evidence as to the "bruise photograph" and, more generally, the selective deletion of data from her phone other than data that might be perceived as being either supportive (or at least non-contradictory) to her allegations. 194

*Sixthly*, there was the belated accusation during her second interview with the AFP in May 2021 that Mr Lehrmann attempted to kiss her on the evening of Friday, 15 March (T607.33–38) notwithstanding Ms Higgins' failure to mention this striking incident at an earlier time, including to Mr Dillaway (T1277.33–34) and in response to direct questions as to whether Mr Lehrmann had given any inkling of his attraction towards her, prior to the fateful night. 195

*Seventhly*, her inconsistent and contradictory evidence at trial about having a panic attack and missing the start of Mr Ciobo's valedictory speech (T676.16–28; T715.28–32; T717.1–4; T723.43–25.7). 196

*Eighthly*, her evidence the Commonwealth "came to an agreement that a failure of a duty of care was made" (T1025.28–29) when the Commonwealth made no such admission of liability (Ex 59). 197

*Ninthly*, Mr Lehrmann submitted that Ms Higgins' draft manuscript (Ex 49), "was full of inaccuracies and inconsistencies with her evidence" and her unsatisfactory excuse that "the book is crap" (T743.44), notwithstanding she was under a contractual obligation to tell the truth in the manuscript (T735.29–34). 198

*Tenthly*, Mr Lehrmann relies upon what he describes as Ms Higgins' "misleading and dishonest claims about lack of forensic analysis of Mr Lehrmann's phone in her speech to the media after the mistrial", when she well knew Mr Lehrmann's phone had been analysed by the AFP. 199

200 Before moving on, it is convenient to deal with the last two points shortly. They are not of real significance. As to the book, as the saying goes, an autobiography usually reveals nothing bad about its writer except his memory. I propose to focus on representations made on more solemn occasions than those appearing in a draft of what, by its very nature, is a self-serving account. As to the final point, senior counsel for Mr Lehrmann suggested (not unfairly) that these factually inaccurate comments reflect a broader aim of Ms Higgins to engage in commentary to shape the public relations narrative from 2021 to draw attention to what she and her supporters consider to be the unfairness of her account being scrutinised or questioned in any way, but the speech was given at a highly emotional time, and it does not seem to me to have much present relevance.

***IV 2019 Conduct Issues***

201 Consistently with what I have identified as temporal differences, I will initially deal with these matters raised by Mr Lehrmann to the extent they involve Ms Higgins' conduct immediately after the incident in 2019.

202 The notion Ms Higgins' evidence has been so discredited by post-incident representations to Mr Dillaway or the AFP (or Ms Brown as discussed below), such that the Court cannot safely rely on *anything* she has said, not only puts the point much too highly but is simplistic.

203 There are inconsistencies and untruths in 2019, but, as the respondents and Ms Higgins point out, they must be contextualised. Additionally, there is the lack of nuance and superficiality of dismissing a witness as *always* untruthful or unreliable just because aspects, even important aspects of their evidence, fall into that description.

204 Moreover, given the potential agreed effects of trauma, I do not consider any of this 2019 conduct (or any other of the alleged counterintuitive conduct I examine below, such as her email contact with Mr Lehrmann) is necessarily inconsistent with a victim of sexual assault seeking to process what had occurred; working her way through feelings of confusion; questioning her conduct; considering what she should do; and reflecting upon how people would perceive her if she made a complaint.

205 In making these comments, I am not discounting the important untruths Ms Higgins told the AFP in her 2019 interactions with them. These require some extended consideration but, in the end, I consider they are examples of Ms Higgins, then under stress but decidedly uninterested

in pursuing a formal complaint, trying to develop an account she could rationalise and perceived made her look better in the eyes of others. For convenience, I will deal with them in Section I.2 below.

### *V Subsequen't Conduct Issues*

Numerous aspects of the conduct of Ms Higgins in the years following 2019 were far more troubling. 206

#### *The Development of the Cover-up Narrative*

The most important aspect of this later conduct, commencing in early 2021, was the way in which Ms Higgins crafted a narrative accusing others of putting up roadblocks and forcing her two years earlier of having to choose between her career and seeking justice by making and pursuing a complaint. 207

As I have already noted, this cover-up or victimisation allegation was perceived by the Project team as being the most important aspect of the Project programme and its deployment meant her account achieved much notoriety and public interest. 208

As we will see, the articulation of the core aspects of this claim commenced shortly before Ms Higgins' boyfriend, Mr David Sharaz, made the necessary arrangements for Ms Higgins to tell her account. She then did so to Ms Maiden (Ex 50), leading to the Maiden article and to Ms Wilkinson (and then to Mr Llewellyn and, through them, to those that worked on the Project programme (**Project team**)). 209

As I will explain below, what is notable about this aspect of the account of Ms Higgins is not only its inconsistency with the contemporaneous records and its falsities, particularly as to Ms Higgins' dealings with Ms Brown, but also its imprecisions and its reliance upon speculation and conjecture. Eschewing specifics, and primarily concentrating upon her alleged feelings rather than the actions or words of others, the initial account given to the Project team on 27 January 2021 had Ms Higgins use the highly ambiguous word "weird" (or variations, such as people were "acting weirdly") no less than *82 times* (Ex 36). The same nebulous word, in some grammatical form, was also used *34 times* during the much shorter interview with Ms Maiden (Ex 50). 210

Although there are differences, what Ms Higgins said to Ms Maiden is broadly the same as that conveyed to the Project team and save for the odd exchanges (at [300] and [751] below), the credit point is sufficient 211 to be made by reference to the latter representations. Although, of course, I am conscious that the underlying truth of what was conveyed to the Project team is not directly relevant to the statutory qualified privilege defence (for reasons I will explain), these representations are conveniently dealt with in Section I.2 below.

*The Victimisation Allegation and the Commonwealth Deed*

212 In the febrile atmosphere of 2021, many instinctively believed what Ms Higgins asserted about the rape and the subsequent cover-up of the crime. In advance of any trial where the rape allegation would be examined, the broader allegations of Ms Higgins resulted in her being feted by many; becoming a celebrated speaker at a mass demonstration, being nominated for awards, receiving invitations to make a nationally televised speech at the National Press Club and a book deal with Penguin Random House (apparently worth $325,000 (T735.1–5)).

213 Further, the allegations were relied upon (together with other things), in support of several claims for compensation asserted to be "variously available against the Commonwealth of Australia as Ms Higgins' employer and in addition ... other employees of the Commonwealth, the Hon Senator Reynolds, the Hon Senator Cash, the Commonwealth and the Liberal Party". More particularly, these claims involved the allegation that following her reporting a sexual assault she suffered "victimisation, including ostracism and being pressured not to discuss the assault or the [Commonwealth's, the then Prime Minister's and Senators Cash and Reynolds'] handling of it" and "workplace bullying and harassment" (Ex 59, Draft Statement of Particulars (cl 1.3)).

214 Ms Higgins' claims were compromised, after the criminal trial, on the terms set out in a Deed of Settlement and Release between her and the Commonwealth of Australia (as represented by the Department of Finance) dated 13 December 2022 (**Commonwealth Deed**) (Ex 59)).

215 Despite the submissions of Mr Lehrmann, I do not consider I should place any significant weight on the fact that Ms Higgins asserted in evidence before me (and before the Commonwealth Deed was produced) that the Commonwealth came "to an agreement that a failure of a duty of care was made" (T1025.28–29). Given the quantum paid by the Commonwealth, as a layperson, she might have come to believe that the Commonwealth must have accepted the underlying merit of her factual

and legal claims. Similarly, although Ms Higgins understated the amount the Commonwealth paid to her benefit, this is again perhaps understandable, as like many litigants she was no doubt focused on the net sum she was able to pocket following the payment of disbursements.

What is of more importance is that the Commonwealth Deed provided: 216
(a) an express warranty was given by Ms Higgins (cl 7.1(a)) that the matters referred to in the Commonwealth Deed "are true and correct" (including the particulars provided by her to the Commonwealth in support of her claims: see Recital H); (b) that the warranty as to truthfulness was given "with the intention of inducing the Commonwealth" to enter into the Commonwealth Deed (cl 7.1(i)); (c) for an acknowledgment that the Commonwealth was relying upon this and other warranties given by Ms Higgins (cl 7.1(j)); and (d) the Commonwealth was to pay to Ms Higgins (or for her benefit) the total sum of $2,445,000 as "compensation in respect of" claims "potentially available to Ms Higgins" under the *Australian Human Rights Commission Act 1986* (Cth), the *Sex Discrimination Act 1984* (Cth) and the *Disability Discrimination Act 1992* (Cth) (cl 2.1.1, cl 1.1).

That is, in broad terms, the payment was made for any potential claim 217
under defined "Statutory Causes of Action" and was given in exchange for releases (cl 4) – except that those releases did not extend to releasing Senator Reynolds and Senator Cash from any actions that "do not relate to the performance or non-performance of their ministerial duties; or fines or penalties" (cl 4.2).

I stress that Ms Higgins is not a party: no findings in this proceeding bind 218
her and, of course, no relief is sought in this proceeding in relation to the Commonwealth Deed. It is not my role to comment upon the merits or otherwise of the Statutory Causes of Action made against the Commonwealth or others; the nature or quantum of the compensation sought; the process by which the settlement occurred; nor the quantum of the resolution sum or the scope of releases. My focus is solely upon Ms Higgins' present creditworthiness.

As **Annexure E** reveals, submissions were made on this 219
topic of credit as it related to the Commonwealth Deed consistently with the express agreement between the parties. I initially thought that in its written submissions, Network Ten was backsliding and flirting with a contention it would be procedurally unfair to

make findings as to the falsity of representations made by Ms Higgins in the Commonwealth Deed, but I was disabused of my misapprehension in supplementary submissions and Network Ten further acknowledged that any false representations made in the Commonwealth Deed could be relevant to the credit of Ms Higgins.

220 One would have thought this was an obvious and proper concession given the nature of the occasion upon which the representations were made, but it is now necessary to deal also with separate submissions made by Ms Higgins.

221 Ms Higgins makes points which can be dealt with in two broad categories:

(1) there are *procedural* difficulties in that it would be "grossly unfair" for any allegations concerning the Commonwealth Deed to be used against Ms Higgins given the lack of cross-examination by Mr Lehrmann's counsel on the topic;

(2) there are *evidentiary* difficulties in that: (a) the circumstances in which the Commonwealth Deed came to be prepared, agreed and executed have not been explored; (b) Ms Higgins should not be presumed to comprehend or be familiar with a complex formal document in the same way as a lawyer; and (c) the mediation occurred shortly after she was hospitalised, and there is "an enormous lacuna" in the evidence as to Ms Higgins' subjective state of mind upon which any finding of dishonesty could be made in relation to the contents of the Commonwealth Deed.

*Suggested Procedural Difficulties*

222 There is no unfairness in Mr Lehrmann making this aspect of his submissions as to credit. Regrettably, to explain why takes some time and requires close examination of the record.

223 The issue as to the Commonwealth Deed arose initially from an exchange on 5 December 2023, at the end of a lengthy period of Ms Higgins giving evidence. To provide context, by this stage, the cross-examination had been going on since 30 November 2023 (T706.16). I had taken frequent breaks when I considered it appropriate and had counselled Ms Higgins to request breaks if she thought she needed them to give a proper account of her evidence. Senior counsel for Network Ten, had also referred to his concerns as to the welfare of the witness and later made a submission

about the cross-examination becoming "oppressive" (T899.14). In the end, without imposing time limits, I did ask senior counsel of Mr Lehrmann to attempt to conclude the cross-examination on 5 December 2023 (T906.39). This request was informed by my close observation of the witness and my assessment of the stress the length of the cross-examination was occasioning.

In any event, the issue of the Commonwealth Deed arose right at the end of the cross-examination after Ms Higgins had, shortly before, given evidence as to the Commonwealth coming to "an agreement that a failure of a duty of care was made, and they did pay me" and that she thought the settlement "was around [$]2.3[m]" (T1026.2). The relevant exchange was as follows (T1028–9): 224

> MR WHYBROW: And as you sit there today, there has never been any finding as to whether or not your allegations are true or not? ---The Commonwealth admitted that they breached their duty of care and that they didn't go through proper processes, so that's actually why they settled with me.
>
> HIS HONOUR: Did the Commonwealth make an admission of liability, did they?---I believe so, but you might have to double-check with them.
>
> MR WHYBROW: Was Mr Zwier your solicitor in relation to those proceedings or was he involved in them?---He was present, but it – it wasn't his. It was – I had Noor Blumer. Blumers were my lawyers for the – the civil case. For the civil – the potential civil case, and we also almost filed a civil case against Bruce, but they didn't want me to do a double action or something for some reason.
>
> I call for production of the deed – was there a deed or was it just a settlement?---I – I – I don't know.
>
> Okay?---I'm not sure.
>
> I make that call.
>
> ***
>
> HIS HONOUR: Who are you making the call to?
>
> MR WHYBROW: Mr Zwier. I understand he's in court.

HIS HONOUR: That's not a call [to a party]. So you're seeking an order - - -

MR WHYBROW: Sorry.

HIS HONOUR: - - - under section 36 - - -

MR WHYBROW: I apologise. Yes.

HIS HONOUR: Section 36 of the Evidence Act - - -

MR WHYBROW: Yes.

HIS HONOUR: - - - directed to someone who's within the confines of the court, being Mr Zwier, for production of the deed.

MR WHYBROW: Yes, your Honour.

MS CHRYSANTHOU: I object to that order being made, your Honour, on the basis of relevance.

HIS HONOUR: Well, it's apparently relevant. I mean, the witness has given evidence about what the settlement was and what it involved, including an admission of liability by the Commonwealth, and there may or may not be permissible questions based on it, but it's a much lower standard, being apparent relevance.

MS CHRYSANTHOU: Yes, your Honour.

HIS HONOUR: Yes. Mr Zwier, is there anything to produce?

MR L. ZWIER: Your Honour, I can't say I was really prepared for this moment.

HIS HONOUR: Well, here you are. You're in the spotlight.

MR ZWIER: I know. I know. I can't see that it's relevant, but I've heard your Honour's observations about that. I'm not sure, even if your Honour is inclined to make an order to require to me to produce, that – I should have it, but I would have to check.

HIS HONOUR: All right. Thank you. Yes.

MR WHYBROW: Thank you. Just excuse me one moment, your Honour. Your Honour, Ms Higgins, they're my questions in cross-examination.

225 Ms Higgins proceeded to complete her re-examination and was excused (T1033.15). I recall turning my mind at the time as to whether I should excuse the witness notwithstanding an outstanding order for production directed to her solicitor, but given my (admittedly impressionistic)

perception of Ms Higgins' condition following the long cross-examination and in the absence of knowing what was in the Commonwealth Deed (and hence knowing there would be any allegation of a prior inconsistent statement), and the absence of any application, I considered it prudent to excuse her, so to relieve any concerns she may have that any further cross-examination was likely to take place.

It sometimes seems in this case that no good deed goes unpunished. 226

When the Commonwealth Deed had still not been produced pursuant 227
to the order by the following morning (6 December 2023), the following occurred:

> HIS HONOUR: … Can I deal with, then, a few matters before we deal with the witnesses that are outstanding. The first is the order that I made yesterday afternoon, page 1029 of the transcript, being the oral subpoena directed to Mr Zwier. Is there production pursuant to that oral subpoena?
>
> DR COLLINS: He doesn't appear to be in court. Your Honour, we will make some inquiries.
>
> HIS HONOUR: Well, the order that I made has the same effect as the subpoena to produce documents, so that document the subject of the order under section 36 should be produced.
>
> DR COLLINS: Yes.
>
> HIS HONOUR: Can I direct your solicitors to get in contact - - -
>
> DR COLLINS: Yes, of course.
>
> HIS HONOUR: - - - with Mr Zwier and find out when production is going to occur of the document, please.
>
> DR COLLINS: Yes. We will attend to that.
>
> HIS HONOUR: It should have already occurred.

Later that morning, the following exchange occurred (T1078): 228

> HIS HONOUR: I see Mr Zwier is here. Mr Zwier, have you got a document to produce?
>
> MR ZWIER: I do, your Honour.
>
> HIS HONOUR: Yes.

MR ZWIER: I have a deed of settlement.

HIS HONOUR: Thank you.

MR ZWIER: And I will produce it. I just want to apologise. I hadn't appreciated that it was the making of a direction.

HIS HONOUR: No, that's all right, Mr Zwier. Thank you very much for your attendance.

MR ZWIER: Your Honour, can I just make a couple of observations about it.

HIS HONOUR: Of course.

MR ZWIER: First, it contains obligations of confidence within the terms of the document, and it arises following a mediation which is governed by a mediation agreement, the details of which I am not presently across, and therefore there might be other parties with an interest in relation to it. Can I also say this. To the extent that a party might seek to tender the document, my client may wish to be heard in relation to that application, because it has, for example, certain particulars about her that ...

HIS HONOUR: I certainly give – I would be disposed, now that it has been produced, to give access to the parties, but I certainly, Mr Zwier, would give your client the opportunity of being heard in relation to any matter she wishes to be heard to before it would be tendered.

MR ZWIER: Thank you, your Honour.

HIS HONOUR: And also seek whatever confidentiality orders that it might be thought appropriate to seek, even if it was tendered. So, thank you very much.

229 An application was made for access and granted. The next day, the following relevantly took place (T1158):

HIS HONOUR: At page 1078 to 79 of the transcript, the document was produced by the solicitor for Ms Higgins. No objection was made to access to the legal practitioners. Although, an objection was made to access to other persons, and you will recall that I said, well, I'm not going to make it an access order simply to legal practitioners, so, therefore, access [was] exercised by each of the parties. I did, however, indicate that I would give Ms Higgins the opportunity to be heard in relation to any confidentiality order, so I think the appropriate course is for me, if you're proposing to tender it, to tender it, mark it, but I will make – I won't make an interim confidentiality order, but what I will say is I will not allow access to any non-party to the document at present until, say, 4 pm today. So if there's an application that can be made, it can be made - -

MR WHYBROW: Your Honour, I can indicate that - - -

HIS HONOUR: - - - at the conclusion of the day.

MR WHYBROW: - - - yesterday evening, we advised Mr Zwier that, in accordance with what he said in the transcript of our intention to tender the deed of settlement, and in open correspondence, he replied and added:

*Strictly and private confidential –*

to the header, so I'm not sure if - - -

HIS HONOUR: Well, do you want to show it to me? I don't want to – first, and then – if you think it's consistent with me seeing, I just - - -

MR WHYBROW: Yes, I do, your Honour. It's consistent with what is expressed - - -

HIS HONOUR: Is everyone happy at the bar table for me to see this letter?

DR COLLINS: Yes, your Honour.

HIS HONOUR: Yes. Well, I'm sorry, but if someone wants to make application in respect of confidentiality of a document of which unopposed access has been given to the parties, then they should do it today.

MR WHYBROW: Yes.

HIS HONOUR: And I will allow them to do it today, and is your – do you propose to make an application to further re-examination [*sic*] Ms Higgins in relation to the document or not?

MR WHYBROW: Yes, your Honour. We engaged in some preliminary discussions as to whether or not it might be able to be tendered and then simply made submissions on some of the matters, including some new matters without a Browne v Dunn point being taken.

HIS HONOUR: Yes.

MR WHYBROW: But some of those matters are so significant that it's our - - -

HIS HONOUR: Well, one of the – well, I think I will have to hear argument about that because one of the things I did – and you may recall this – I did offer, I think on more than one occasion, the applicant to seek third party discovery, and I was told that, notwithstanding I was open – and that would have meant that this document would have been discovered by the third party, and secondly, also what would have been discovered is matters relating in Part 2 of that list when certain things were deleted. Now, I was told expressly you did not want that order. So this – you would have had a list of documents well in advance.

You would have been able to inspect this deed well in advance of the hearing, but a forensic decision was made by the applicant, notwithstanding, I said I was prepared to make such an order not to seek it. So in a sense, you're the author of your own misfortune in relation to that, it coming up during the hearing, so that's one thing I would want assistance about when it came to any application to bring a witness back to cross-examination, but I'm not going to determine that application now or hear you further in relation to it, because, no doubt, not only will – there may be some evidence about that. There may be all sorts of argument about it, but I just raise that because that, in my mind, is quite relevant a consideration. In any event, there's no reason why the document can't be tendered, so a document – unless there's any objection?

MS CHRYSANTHOU: Your Honour, so long as it doesn't prejudice our ability to oppose any application under section 46, it's tendered without objection, because we do oppose any application under section 46 to recall the witness, and we don't want it to be said that not objecting to the document in any way prejudices our ability to oppose that application, if it's persisted in.

HIS HONOUR: Well, I've provided you judicial advice, so - - -

MS CHRYSANTHOU: Well, I object if the tender of the document is in aid of recalling the witness under section 46.

HIS HONOUR: Well, no, it's admissible and I'm going to receive it.

MS CHRYSANTHOU: Yes, your Honour.

DR COLLINS: We understood it to be implicit in the exchange between your Honour and Mr Whybrow that the argument about whether Ms Higgins ought be recalled, was an argument for an other day ... I didn't mean literally another day.

HIS HONOUR: And the confidentiality issue will certainly be dealt with today. So that will become – the deed of settlement and release between the Commonwealth of Australia v Brittany Higgins will now become exhibit 59.

**EXHIBIT #59 DEED OF SETTLEMENT AND RELEASE BETWEEN THE COMMONWEALTH OF AUSTRALIA AND BRITTANY HIGGINS**

Later that day, I interrupted a witness to accommodate senior counsel for Ms 230
Higgins appearing (T1248) and determined a confidentiality application, which was only pressed in limited respects, and then delivered *ex tempore* reasons: *Lehrmann v Network Ten Pty Limited (Confidentiality) (No 2)* [2023] FCA 1561. Immediately after the delivery of reasons on Ms Higgins' application, the following then took place (T1252–3):

HIS HONOUR: And is there agreement between the parties that they say that they won't take the point about procedural fairness? Are you not putting the prior inconsistent statements to the – to Ms Higgins, that is, concerning a true amount payable pursuant to the deed and the fact that, contrary to the evidence given to me, there was no admission of liability - - -

MR WHYBROW: As I understand it, it's - - -

HIS HONOUR: - - - and other matters?

MR WHYBROW: Yes, it's accepting those. There are some matters where they are strictly completely new. I have spoken to Ms Chrysanthou on those. I haven't had a chance to speak to Dr Collins, but - - -

> HIS HONOUR: All right.
>
> MR WHYBROW: - - - in the circumstances where, effectively, the gist of all of those matters were put - - -
>
> HIS HONOUR: Yes.
>
> MR WHYBROW: - - - to Ms Higgins, we don't - - -
>
> HIS HONOUR: Well, I must say my preliminary view was that it wouldn't have been appropriate to have Ms Higgins recalled if there was some sort of sensible resolution.
>
> MR WHYBROW: Yes.
>
> HIS HONOUR: So I congratulate the parties on sensible approach to that because I did wish to spare her the necessity to come back.
>
> MR WHYBROW: Yes. Indeed.
>
> **HIS HONOUR: But it doesn't inhibit you in making whatever submissions you wish to make between the inconsistencies about what's contained in the deed and the evidence given by Ms Higgins.**
>
> **MR WHYBROW: Yes, your Honour.**
>
> **HIS HONOUR: All right. Thank you.**

231 Following review of the evidence and the receipt of submissions, it became evident to me the possible importance of the representations made in the Commonwealth Deed by Ms Higgins, and Annexure E details the steps I have taken to guard against any residual issue as to procedural fairness including, in the circumstances set out above, allowing for Ms Higgins to make any submission she wished to make about the submissions advanced by Mr Lehrmann. Given what occurred at trial, there is no basis to contend *inter partes* that there is any fetter upon Mr Lehrmann making the submissions he now advances (and none is suggested to arise). But even so, to make doubly sure, as Annexure E indicates, given Ms Higgins herself has now raised a point about procedural unfairness, notwithstanding: (a) the background set out above; (b) the other matters in Annexure E; and (c) the appearance of her representatives on 7 December 2023 when the agreement between the parties was announced, I allowed Ms Higgins the opportunity of making an application to seek to defer judgment to allow her to be recalled to give evidence if she so wished. Such an application to address the supposed procedural

unfairness to a witness, by a witness, would not, obviously enough, have been an application under s 46 EA, but there would have been ample power to make an order facilitating that course if I was convinced it was necessary to assure fairness: see s 11 EA. She did not do so.

*Suggested Evidentiary Difficulties*

To the extent Ms Higgins suggests the Court would not make an adverse finding as to the evidence she gave regarding her understanding of the Commonwealth Deed when she was cross-examined on its effect prior to production, as is evident from [215] above, that issue can be put to one side. 232

Although how the Commonwealth Deed came to be agreed and executed has not been the subject of detailed evidence, Ms Higgins accepts she was represented by "Blumers Lawyers, personal injury lawyers, to act for her in relation to her civil claims against the Commonwealth, which were settled following a mediation on 13 December 2022" (Ex 59). Moreover, if one has regard to Ms Higgins' evidence (see [224] above), and the execution page of the Commonwealth Deed, she signed, sealed, and delivered the document on that day in front of her current solicitor, Mr Zwier. 233

There is no evidence before me as to the extent of Mr Zwier's retainer at the mediation, and I am well aware the act of attestation of a deed only indicates the witness was present and witnessed the execution, and the obligation owed by an attesting witness is to perform this function properly (*Ellison v Vukicevic* (1986) 7 NSWLR 104 (at 112 per Young J); *Graham v Hall* [2006] NSWCA 208; (2006) 67 NSWLR 135). But even leaving aside the precise content of any duty of either of her two solicitors present, as a matter of commonsense, it is difficult to accept that I ought not infer it is more likely than not that a senior and highly experienced solicitor would only witness the execution of a document of such importance if satisfied the person executing under seal was mentally competent to do so and understood, at least in general terms, the nature of what was happening (*a fortiori* if that person, in one form or another, was a client). 234

However, for reasons I will now come to, by reason of the limited relevance of the Commonwealth Deed for present purposes, it is unnecessary to make any findings as to the mental state of Ms Higgins or her subjective understanding of particular contractual provisions when the representations were made. 235

*Conclusion on the Commonwealth Deed and Credit*

236 Having dealt with these unnecessary complications raised at the heel of the hunt, I now go back to the real point.

237 To repeat, I do not consider it necessary nor appropriate that I attempt to characterise or reach any legal conclusion as to Ms Higgins' conduct in giving the warranties contained in the Commonwealth Deed. I am only dealing with issues as to credit.

238 It is sufficient to find that through her personal injury solicitors, and more likely than not on instructions, Ms Higgins was in 2022 advancing a claim for compensation based on allegations materially the same as those she had articulated to Ms Maiden and to the Project team, the core aspects of which she had consistently maintained since at least January 2021. More specifically, representations, materially identical to central representations made in the Commonwealth Deed, had been made for almost two years and were now being used to ground the Statutory Causes of Action articulated by her solicitors. The Commonwealth Deed is useful in going some way in collecting, formalising, and providing some belated degree of coherent particularisation to what might broadly be described as the coverup allegation.

239 In this regard, and contrary to the submissions of Network Ten, the relevant issue is not whether Ms Higgins made representations (repeated in the Commonwealth Deed) in a manner consistent with *her evidence*, but rather whether Ms Higgins made representations contrary to *the facts*.

240 It is evident several things being alleged were untrue. As my findings below will establish, and without seeking to be exhaustive, it is convenient to identify sufficient examples by reference to the Particulars of Liability (**PL**) and Attachment 2, "Event Complained About" (**A2**) as follows:

(1) that on 26 May 2019: (a) Ms Higgins told Ms Brown that Mr Lehrmann had "sexually assaulted" her (PL cl 3.4; A2 cl 4.4); and (b) Ms Brown confirmed to Ms Higgins that CCTV footage demonstrated that Ms Higgins was "visibly drunk when coming through the entrance to the Ministerial wing of Parliament House and that Mr Lehrmann had said that he had not been drinking that evening" (PL cl 3.5);

(2) that during the week following the sexual assault, Mr Yaron Finklestein, Principal Secretary to the Prime Minister, was a "regular presence" in Senator Reynolds' office advising Ms Brown on "how to

deal with [Ms Higgins] in light of the sexual assault by Mr Lehrmann" (PL cl 3.9);

(3) that Ms Brown "rebuffed [Ms Higgins'] request" to view the CCTV footage from 22/23 March 2019 (PL cl 3.12; A2 4.12);

(4) that on 27 March 2019, members of the AFP Parliament House unit informed Ms Higgins that "they had been told to investigate a sexual assault" (PL cl 3.13);

(5) at or around 11 April 2019, Ms Higgins raised with Ms Brown the issue of sick leave for her mental health and also needing time off work to assist the AFP in its investigation but "Ms Brown demonstrated an unwillingness to discuss the issue and made it clear to [Ms Higgins] that it was her problem to deal with" (PL cl 3.22; A2 cl 4.22);

(6) that "Ms Brown informed Ms Higgins that she had two options. She could return home to the Gold Coast on paid leave for the duration of the election campaign, but this would negatively impact her prospects of having a job to reapply for after the election. Alternatively, [Ms Higgins] could "stay onboard" Senator Reynolds' team and work on the election campaign in Western Australia" (PL cl 3.23);

(7) that "Ms Brown made it clear by her words and demeanour that the events of 22/23 March 2019 must be put to one side; that [Ms Higgins] ought remain silent about the sexual assault, in order to keep her job/career" (PL cl 3.24; A2 cl 4.24);

(8) that it was in the context of electing to go to Western Australia to assist with Senator Reynolds' election campaign that Ms Higgins "felt she had no choice but to abandon pursuit of the complaint of sexual assault with the AFP" (PL cl 3.25);

(9) that "Minister Reynolds did not engage with [Ms Higgins] at all during the election campaign. She avoided [Ms Higgins] and made clear that she did not want the claimant attending events with her" (PL cl 3.28).

I have not included in these examples matters where the (at least underly- 241
ing) falsifying proposition was not put to Ms Higgins. Nor have I placed any significant weight on incorrect but relatively minor inaccuracies, such as the assertion Mr Lehrmann: (a) without invitation or agreement with Ms Higgins: (i) got into the taxi and directed it to stop at Parliament House (PL cll 2.4, 2.5; A2 cl 3.4, 3.5); (ii) paid the taxi fare and then directed Ms Higgins to get out of the taxi and go with him to Parliament House (PL

cl 2.6; A2 cl 3.6); (b) "led [Ms Higgins] to the Ministerial Suite" (A2 cl 3.9); or (c) had his staff pass which allowed him to enter the building and that Ms Higgins had to be signed in via a "guest sign in book" and she had "difficulty remaining upright and signing her name" (PL cl 2.8).

*The Bruise Photograph*

242 A *third* aspect of the post-2019 conduct causing concern relates to Ms Higgins' so-called bruise photograph. The bruise photograph was said by Ms Higgins in her statutory declaration and on oath as being a record of an injury suffered during the rape – and hence being contemporaneous documentary evidence supporting her accusation (Ex R532 (at [7])). Indeed, as we will see, at the beginning of her first meeting with the Project team, this photograph is raised specifically by Mr Sharaz and Ms Higgins as being the only evidence that elevated Ms Higgins' account from simply being one person's word against another. Its forensic importance is manifest and while she was under an obligation to tell the truth, it was put forward by her as corroborative material.

243 Despite this, Ms Higgins distanced herself from embracing it as evidence of the rape in evidence-in-chief before me (T672.11) and, indeed, she ended up saying in cross-examination (T712.12–19) that:

> At the time, I believed it was caused by the assault, but with hindsight and with, you know, like, yourself [Mr Whybrow SC] in the criminal trial, put to me, it was possible that it came from another source, so I've now had to accept that it may not have necessarily come from the assault itself. It may have come from falling up the stairs, but I accepted that during the criminal trial, but at the time, I was 100 per cent sold on the – sold – that I – I thought it was because I was in pain when he was raping me, but because of the criminal trial, I've had to accept that I don't 100 per cent know it was from the assault. It could have been falling up the stairs, so that's where I'm at.

244 In the witness box at this trial, she seemed irritated that the cross-examiner would challenge her on the photograph. But the evidence as to her inconsistencies on this topic are both important and vexing.

245 We know the original photograph, despite its obvious importance, was not mentioned or provided to the AFP in 2019. This is despite Ms Higgins meeting, a few days after the bruise photograph was supposedly

taken, with highly experienced AFP sexual assault investigators sensitively asking her for any relevant information over a lengthy period in the presence of a sexual assault counsellor providing her with support (see [680] below). Further, the metadata of the original photograph has never been produced. The earliest record of a bruise or the photograph is in 2021 and, when this reproduction is examined, it shows a bruise on Ms Higgins' right leg, in circumstances where she gave evidence that Mr Lehrmann had "crushed" her left leg during the alleged rape (Ex 71 (at T128–129)).

What is equally odd are the singular circumstances by which Ms Higgins' 246
phone was "completely wiped" and her photos had disappeared from her iCloud records (Ex 36 (at 0:05:56; 0:07:53–0:08:00)), and yet the bruise photograph and some other limited material survived, allowing it to be deployed by Ms Higgins and Mr Sharaz to lend verisimilitude to the account she gave to Network Ten.

I will go into further detail as to this topic below, but it suffices for pres- 247
ent purposes to note that despite her evidence before me, I consider it unlikely there could be genuine confusion in Ms Higgins' recollection as to how she got the bruise recorded in the bruise photograph given the way she and Mr Sharaz deployed it in 2021 and their subjective understanding of its importance.

*Selective Retention and Curation of Data*

Nextly, and relatedly, was the missing messages, including one on the 248
morning she left the Ministerial Suite with a security guard, Mr Alex Woods (with whom Ms Higgins had earlier matched on Bumble (T910.45)), and with Ms Hamer, Major Irvine, and Ms Gain – including, tellingly, Ex 47, being the deleted text message automatically saved separately in the "notes" section of the phone whereby Ms Higgins, on 27 January 2021 (and just after the five-hour conversation with Ms Wilkinson and Mr Llewellyn) sought to prompt Ms Gain as to the detail of Ms Higgins' narrative of what occurred in 2019 (T910–11; T925–6). Also missing was the important and truthful message to Mr Dillaway on 9 April 2019 in which Ms Higgins tells Mr Dillaway that she was "not interested in pursuing [a police complaint]" (Ex 45).

Moreover, the missing data went beyond text messages, but included 249
photos taken on the night in question, which may have shown interactions

between Ms Higgins and Mr Lehrmann. This is in circumstances where: (a) the evidence establishes that Ms Higgins had been asked by Detective Senior Constable Sarah Harman of the AFP on 8 April 2019 not to delete photos taken on the evening, including photos Ms Higgins had said she had taken of her and Mr Lehrmann on 22 March 2019 (T1294.17–30; T1324.37–39); (b) it is evident from the CCTV video from The Dock (Ex R42 / Ex 17A) that Ms Higgins had taken photographs at The Dock (T2353.45); (c) Ms Gain gave evidence of Ms Higgins having taken "selfies" at 88mph at around the time Ms Higgins and Mr Lehrmann were being intimate (T1106.19–21); and (d) the AFP did belatedly access Ms Higgins' phone on 26 May 2021, approximately 8,000 photographs were downloaded, but they did not include any photographs taken by her on the fateful night (T2354.2–4; Ex 67 (at T662.25–33)).

250 When confronted with this issue, the evidence of Ms Higgins was (T908.39–909.41):

> MR WHYBROW: ... in May of 2021, after you had made public allegations and spoken to the police, you handed your phone to the police, so that they could do [an] extraction of any data on it?---Yes. I – I don't remember the exact date but I handed over my phones, the ones that I had at the time.
>
> Sure. And you recall that that – you had been asked since about February if the police could access your phone to try and get the data off it?---Yes, I was worried about leaks I was seeking legal advice at the time.
>
> ... do you agree that it was about three or four times you were asked by the police and it was not for a period of three months from when The Project went to air until approximately 23 May 2021, that you finally consented to the contents of your phone being downloaded?---Yes, they asked during the first DIC and I said seek legal advice and then during the second DIC I provided my phone.
>
> Before you handed over your phone to police, you would [delete] some things off it?---Yes, I deleted one particular photo that I was worried about.
>
> What was that?---It was at a party and someone put a make America great hat on my head and I was ashamed that it was in existence, so

I deleted it. I knew it wasn't – it wasn't relevant or anything, but I was just worried that it would leak, and it was something I was really ashamed off, so I deleted it.

Well, I want to suggest to you, you deleted a lot more than just one photograph off your phone before you gave it to the police?---That was the only one of note that I deleted.

Leaving aside "of note" you're aware, aren't you, that on 21 May there was a text recovered by the police where you had been sending various audio and photographs to Mr Sharaz and he asked you, "What's this", and you said:

*I am cleaning out my phone ahead of the police.*

?---But it didn't actually take place, as I sought legal advice and they said that would be dumb and I handed over all the audio recordings which are the ones I was worried about, which was the Cash one and the Try one and I gave it to them upfront.

My question is do you recall that you sent a text to Mr Sharaz on 21 May saying:

*I am cleaning out my phone ahead of the police*?

?---I did send that text message.

Yes. And you were deleting things off your phone ahead go giving it to the police, were you not?---I deleted a photo of me that I was ashamed of; yes.

Well, can I suggest that you deleted any messages you had with a significant number of people who may have been in a position to contradict your narrative of events?---No, that's not true.

The reference in this extract to the representation made to Mr Sharaz 251
via WhatsApp on 21 May 2021 requires some context. At this time, Ms Higgins was sending Mr Sharaz "old audio", and Ms Higgins said, "I'm cleaning out my phone ahead of the police" (T909.30). It is plain she was sending media to Mr Sharaz; what is also clear is that she retained material not apparently inconsistent with the allegation of rape (T709.30). From Mr Sharaz's response, it appears the specific audio sent to him on 21 May was a covertly recorded conversation, and he reassured her and there was some discussion as to whether she could trust the police.

252 But what matters is the existence of the various contradictory explanations given (or suggestions floated) by Ms Higgins as to why some material was preserved and some was missing. Some data might conceivably have gone missing when changing phones, but it was never made clear to me why such an event (or events) would cause her iCloud data to disappear like a will-o'-the-wisp? Or, more strangely, to disappear from her backups selectively? Or, even stranger still, why, as detailed below, would she toy with a conspiracy theory that her data was wiped remotely? Moreover, why would she not be careful to save the data concerning the original version and metadata of a photograph she (and Mr Sharaz) later considered in 2021 the most important corroborative material supporting her account of what occurred?

253 I do not think it is a co-incidence that the material she did not provide to the AFP when her phone was belatedly handed over (but has since been obtained from other sources) often sits uncomfortably with aspects of her 2021 cover-up narrative.

254 Although some unspecified material may have been lost through a faulty transfer between devices, the weight of the evidence requires the conclusion that it is more likely than not that she curated data because she thought deleting some material assisted in her maintaining the cogency of her 2021 account. This went well beyond any concern about being seen in a photograph taken after someone had apparently placed a "MAGA hat" on her head.

*2021 False Accusations*

255 Finally, there is an example of an untruth about what, in the overall scheme of things, might be thought inconsequential, but which is revealing.

256 Ms Higgins asserted that Nick, her Bumble date, left The Dock because he "was bullied mercilessly by everyone at the event, um, they were all poking fun at him and laughing at him. And he pretty quickly was sort of driven out of the event" (T940.15–19). But what the CCTV footage irrefragably proves is that no-one did anything that could be remotely described as bullying Nick. Ms Higgins abandoned her date as she preferred to go and sit at the same table as Mr Lehrmann (Ex R42 / Ex 17A (at 20:51:38)). Ms Higgins, after being taken to the video, had to accept (albeit in what, at the time, struck me as a curiously light-hearted tone) that "I did ignore my date, and I was really rude" (T944.3).

Although on one level minor in itself, this untrue representation is one example of a willingness to make an accusation cut out of whole cloth because it suited Ms Higgins to make it. I will come to other examples below, including a substantively more important one relating to Mr Payne recounted to Ms Maiden. 257

### *VI Conclusion on General Credit*

When closely analysed, Ms Higgins' out-of-court representations in 2019 are of a different character than those out-of-court representations from 2021 and in court thereafter. Any inconsistent or untrue representations in 2019 are not inconsistent with the conduct of a genuine victim of sexual assault struggling to process what happened, seeking to cope, and working through her options. But whatever the truth of the evidence she gave as to what occurred in the Ministerial Suite one night in 2019, the cogency of her evidence as to this central aspect of the case must be evaluated and closely scrutinised in the light of the fact that my findings establish that has since 2021, Ms Higgins: 258

(1) made false representations as to what had occurred following the incident to Ms Maiden and the Project team and thereafter more generally;

(2) asserted definitively that she retained contemporaneous evidence of the rape that she knew bolstered her credibility and rely upon it when (on the most generous view of it) it ought to have been apparent to her – as she recognised at this trial – there was an infirm basis for doing so;

(3) selectively curated material on her phone prior to giving it to the AFP; and

(4) sometimes told untruths when it suited her.

In summary, and after having had the opportunity of observing Ms Higgins' demeanour closely over approximately four and a half days and comparing her testimony to other documentary and oral evidence I accept as being cogent, it would be fair to describe her as a complex and, in several respects, unsatisfactory witness. Nuance is required in evaluating her evidence and any contentious or uncorroborated aspect needs to be scrutinised warily. 259

## F.3 Ms Brown

260 Both Mr Lehrmann and Network Ten subpoenaed Ms Brown to give evidence and foreshadowed calling her in their case. I have not, of course, seen any outline of anticipated evidence served, but assume Network Ten wished to lead evidence relevant to the termination of Mr Lehrmann and about the falsity of what he said about his reasons for going to Parliament House and what he did while he was there.

261 Prior to trial, my Associate received a communication from the solicitors from all parties asking me, in effect, to give them an advance ruling on the tender of various documents and, if I allowed them to be adduced, foreshadowed that the parties "would not call upon their subpoenas".

262 As I explained through my Associate, this was misconceived on at least four bases. *First*, no application had been made for an advance ruling in accordance with s 192A EA and, in the circumstances, I was not disposed to give notice until a document of the type indicated was tendered; *secondly*, as I had already explained, I wanted all relevant matters to be dealt with in open court; *thirdly*, a *subpoena ad testificandum* is an order, in terms, requiring a third party to appear before the Court at a specified time and place, and the order remains in force until set aside by the Court; and *fourthly*, if an application to set aside the subpoena was to be made, it should be made on proper evidence, in an orthodox way and determined in Court.

263 An application was then made by Ms Brown to be relieved from compliance with the subpoenas. I set aside the Network Ten subpoena (as I was informed that Network Ten did not now propose to call Ms Brown in their case). Despite initially pressing the application to set aside the subpoena issued on the application of Mr Lehrmann, after I indicated I would make some accommodations to meet the problems identified in medical evidence put before the Court on behalf of Ms Brown, the application was not pressed.

264 The respondents contend it is important not to overstate the significance of Ms Brown's evidence because her management of the allegations in March 2019 is "simply not in issue, save to the extent that it has a bearing on the assessment of Ms Higgins' credit in relation to the allegation of rape". They do, however, embrace Ms Brown's evidence insofar as:

(1) she gave evidence as to her interactions with Mr Lehrmann from 26 March to 5 April 2019, which evidence "proves that he lied about various significant matters at the time and to this court";

(2) she documented that Mr Lehrmann said: (a) when asked about what else he did in the office, that he "didn't wish to get into that" (T2052.4–5); he "chatted" with Ms Higgins and they went into the "outer office" or the "general area" – being the support staff area (T2051.31–38); and (c) that Ms Higgins was "fine" when he left (T2054.21–29); and

(3) that there was never any risk to Ms Higgins' job (T2157.17–20).

The submission is also made that whether Ms Higgins told Ms Brown that she remembered Mr Lehrmann being "on top of me" (T2096.30–31) at their first (as Ms Higgins asserts) or second meeting (as Ms Brown asserts) is "immaterial", because Ms Brown's account favours Network Ten as "Mr Lehrmann's case theory that Ms Higgins said she had been sexually assaulted at the first meeting to save her job, falls apart". 265

Despite all this, Network Ten says the evidence of Ms Brown "has to be treated with some caution" because: (a) she made "selective" and not literally contemporaneous notes; (b) Ms Brown professed recollection of matters not recorded in her notes (T2031.6–10); (c) she had a "general tendency to understate the obvious significance of what she had learned about the incident" and it is "difficult to accept her evidence" that sexual intercourse or a sexual assault had been committed and it was something that could "not be ruled in, and could not be ruled out", notwithstanding she was worried that something terrible had happened (T2041.4–5) and it had entered her mind that there had been non-consensual sex (T2055.5–47; T2058.42–44). 266

Ms Wilkinson makes the submission it is open to the Court to form the view that Ms Brown is not being dishonest about her insight as to what she had learned about the incident, but "rather she completely lacks ordinary human insight into such matters" perhaps because she lacked training and what was peculiarly called "general human experience". 267

I had the opportunity of closely observing Ms Brown giving evidence over two days for approximately five hours. Without any intended disrespect or (I hope) stereotyping, Ms Brown struck me as an archetype of 268 a successful professional administrator of a certain age and disposition. She had a conservative outlook and conducted herself in a careful and (generally) risk adverse way. Despite having her health seriously affected by allegations of shameful conduct and (like the other principal actors) experiencing a torrent of social media abuse, she gave evidence in a calm way, and was responsive to questions.

269 One aspect of her evidence was particularly striking. Despite Ms Brown facing sustained pressure from her Minister and one of the Minister's colleagues to report the incident to the AFP – even though she was unsure an allegation was then being made of rape and irrespective of the wishes of Ms Higgins – she pushed back.

270 She explained her reasoning in this exchange where I sought to summarise and clarify the evidence given on this topic (T2129.1–27):

> HIS HONOUR: I'm just trying to get this in my mind. I'm sorry if I'm being obtuse.
>
> You had your third meeting with Ms Higgins. You knew the information that had previously been conveyed to you: young people, intoxicated, come back by themselves to an office, drinking whisky, someone wakes up naked. You also know by the end of the third meeting that, as I understand your evidence, that Ms Higgins had said to you, "I remember him being on top of me." Just pausing there. At that stage, did you have a view one way or the other as to whether or not it's likely - let's leave aside the question of rape for the moment, at that stage, putting all those things together, did you believe that they had been engaged in some sort of sexual activity?---It was a possibility. Consensual, non-consensual, you couldn't rule it in, couldn't rule it out.
>
> No. I'm not talking about consent. I'm just talking about whether or not - - -?---It was possible.
>
> ...I presume it's a very serious thing in your mind to push back against two Ministers about whether or not something be reported to the police?---Yes.
>
> And, as I understand your evidence, your motivation in doing that is because you thought it would be disempowering of the person

> whose interests are most acutely affected; that is, the person who may have something to report?---Yes.
>
> It's really for her to make a decision about whether she wants to start a process about going to the police and that was the reason you were pushing back?---Yes.

We are not all the same. I have no doubt that if apprised of the information identified above, many in her place would have concluded that sex had taken place with a question mark hovering over consent. For all I know, the Senator (who was not called), may have done so by this time and I suspect that is the conclusion I would have drawn. But I accept Ms Brown's evidence of her circumspection was given genuinely, and this reflected what the contemporaneous record demonstrates was her guarded personality and careful, even pedantic, approach. 271

She was not someone to speculate or jump to conclusions and I reject any suggestion Ms Higgins expressly said to Ms Brown at either their first or second meeting that she had been raped or sexually assaulted. As Ms Higgins later said to Ms Maiden (Ex 50 (at 12)): 272

> I don't know, I think for like the longest time I was really weird about actually saying it was rape, I couldn't ... I don't know why but I was really delicate around that whole subject. So maybe I didn't say to her directly that he was raping me ... he was on top of me and I just ... And from our exchange, I think she understood the inference of what was being made.

She did not draw a definitive conclusion in the light of the ambiguous words used by Ms Higgins – she adopted the more cautious view that sex and something untoward *may* have happened. 273

But what does not reflect caution was standing up to her Minister and the Chief of Staff of another Minister when Ms Brown thought they were intent on protecting their own interests at the expense of allowing a young woman to make her own decision as to whether she would involve the police – even at some risk to her professional career. This showed integrity in resisting pressure she subjectively considered inappropriate and evinced a concern for the autonomy and welfare of Ms Higgins. In these circumstances, to be later vilified as an unfeeling apparatchik willing to throw up 274 roadblocks in covering up criminal conduct at the behest of one's political overlords must be worse than galling.

275 The attempts in cross-examination to impeach the integrity of Ms Brown's contemporaneous note taking went nowhere. The contemporaneous record supports the notes being prepared when and how Ms Brown said they were prepared. They do not purport to record everything, but only what was regarded then to be the key points. They are, like in so many cases where there is an honest and careful note taker, the best record of the dealings they document, rather than later recollections. They are of such importance that I reproduce them as **Annexure B** to these reasons, and I find that to the extent they record the dealings of Ms Brown, they are accurate and reliable. Further, to the extent there is a conflict between those notes and the evidence of Ms Brown with that of Mr Lehrmann, I unhesitatingly prefer the evidence of Ms Brown; the same goes for any conflict between the evidence of Ms Brown or the notes with that of Ms Higgins.

276 Indeed, in assessing the critical evidence of Mr Lehrmann, as I will later explain, aspects of Ms Brown's contemporaneous notes, which did not receive particularly close attention at trial, are of signal importance, in that they record Mr Lehrmann's initial responses to queries made of his actions by Ms Brown. Importantly, as to activities in the Ministerial Suite on the fateful night he represented: (a) he did not access any documents (26 March); (b) he came back to drink whisky and ended up drinking two glasses (26 March); (c) he "chatted" with Ms Higgins but "didn't wish to get into" anything else they did (26 March); (d) "they [that is, Ms Higgins and Mr Lehrmann] had a whisky" (5 April); and (e) Ms Higgins was "happy" when he left and he "said he had to go home and she said bye see you next week and he said ye [*sic*]. He said he had to get home" (5 April).

277 Returning to Ms Brown, she may not have been schooled by health and psychological professionals in dealing with sexual assaults, and may have not, by reason of her personality and age, been as empathetic as some others or have the acute sensitivity of many millennials. She no doubt could have done some things differently, for example, even though Ms Higgins did not raise it at the time, the unprompted failure to recognise the inappropriateness of holding the initial meeting with Senator Reynolds in the Minister's office was maladroit. But whatever

shortcomings can be identified (including with the benefit of hindsight), she ensured she took considered advice from those in whom she reposed confidence, recorded, and acted upon that advice and, subject to the above, showed commonsense and compassion by her own lights (demonstrated by all her contemporaneous records, including text messages).

Despite the express and implied criticisms of her, Ms Brown also went 278
out of her way to reassure Ms Higgins and supported and assisted her in contacting the police. It is worth noting that the AFP officers Ms Brown assisted Ms Higgins in seeing promptly are (even now) described by Ms Higgins as having been "wonderful and were really lovely to me", "amazing" and "great" (T821).

As Ms Brown herself put it, she did her "professional best with what was 279
given" to her (T2060.4; T2066.46). If one wants to get a real reflection of the contemporaneous 2019 views of Ms Higgins, well before the attitude of Ms Higgins towards Ms Brown evolved in 2021 consistently with the development of the broader narrative of a cover-up, they are reflected in her text message of 7 June 2019 (Ex R810):

> I wanted to say this in person but– I cannot overstate how much I've valued your support and advice throughout this period. You've been absolutely incredible and I'm so appreciative.

## F.4 Ms Gain

Ms Gain was a significant witness. 280

As at March 2019, Ms Gain was employed as a communications advisor 281
in the Department of Defence, having previously worked as an advisor in the office of Mr Ciobo. She came to know Ms Higgins in this role and to have a good working relationship with her, involving socialising at work events and discussing their shared interests and experiences in media and communications (Gain (at [4]–[11])). The pair did not, however, consider each other to be friends. To her recollection, Ms Gain had not met Mr Lehrmann prior to 22 March 2019, but had heard his name in staffing circles (Gain (at [27])).

Ms Gain was impressive and credible. Unlike a number of other important 282
witnesses, she was refreshingly responsive to questions asked of her and made appropriate concessions and she did not pretend a highly detailed

recollection of everything that occurred on the critical night when she was drinking. Moreover, her evidence was consistent with contemporaneous material including, importantly, Ex R59, being a Telegram message in which Ms Gain gossiped to her friend, Major Irvine, that "Brittany hooked up with Bruce" the night before.

283 The submission made on behalf of Mr Lehrmann that Ms Gain should not be believed because she could not recall other, less significant details is one I reject. Rather, this is a pointer to the fact that she was being frank in the variability of her recollection, which is generally how memory works.

284 I should make specific reference to Ex 47 when it comes to the credit of Ms Gain. After Ms Higgins had decided to appear on the Project programme, it will be recalled she sent and then deleted a text message to Ms Gain after almost two years of no contact (T926.4). It is a message that does Ms Higgins no credit, worsened by her fortunately unsuccessful attempt to delete any record she had of it. The message was said by Ms Higgins to be a "cathartic thing for me to get off my chest" and "random" (T923.30–924.21) – but it was no such thing. I am comfortably satisfied it amounted to an attempt to prompt Ms Gain of the details of the night in question and impress upon her the allegation of Ms Higgins that she had been sexually assaulted (and the effect of that assault) before anyone spoke to Ms Gain to get her independent account of what may have been said to her. Despite this, Ms Gain forcefully pushed back on assertions that her genuine independent recollection may have been polluted.

285 Ms Gain gave considered answers to all questions asked of her, was forthcoming as to the quality of her recollection, and was unflappable when tested under cross-examination. I have no reason to disbelieve any of her evidence and I accept it.

## F.5 Major Irvine

286 Major Irvine was also an important and impressive witness who generally gave responsive, careful, and considered evidence.

287 I reject the suggestion made on behalf of Mr Lehrmann in submissions that Major Irvine's evidence should be approached with caution because of a lack of contemporaneous notes and the possibility of subconscious

infection of her recollection "from other information". Although the suggestion was put that she might have difficulty delineating between recollection and reconstruction, she gave evidence, which seems to me to make intuitive sense, that she deliberately decided not to make any records so as to be protective of Ms Higgins' information and disagreed that this meant her independent recollection of events (which, in her mind, were significant) were distorted by subsequent publicity.

Unlike Ms Gain, it is fair to say that she was, at times, a combative wit- 288
ness, but having observed her closely, I think this was more the result of her personality than seeking to be an advocate against Mr Lehrmann's interests.

There were two aspects of Major Irvine's evidence which initially gave me 289
some pause, being: *first*, her assertion, when tested about her ability to recall what happened at The Dock, that she had an independent recollection of "who was sitting where or who drank what ... because someone told me she was raped three days later" (T1190.19–24). This seemed a somewhat forced and non-responsive riposte (although on one level understandable). I was reassured, however, when Major Irvine later fairly agreed with the proposition that her recollection of "general details as to whether you had bought drinks for people and they were all gin and tonics, or vodka, lime and soda or whether you asked for rounds, or things like that" was potentially affected by the alcohol that she had consumed on the night and the passage of time (T1193.15–24).

*Secondly*, when asked in chief about declining Ms Gain's invitation to 290
kick on to 88mph, she responded by saying not only did she not want to mix work and pleasure by going to a club with people with whom she worked (which is entirely understandable), but also that she did not want to socialise or spend time with Mr Lehrmann because he had "bad vibes", which she put down to "women's intuition" (T1178.43–1179.3; T1196.4–15).

At first blush, this speculation might be thought to be a tell-tale of some- 291
one seeking to poison the well against a party whose interests they were seeking to damage, or be reflective of some hostility. But what is evident upon close examination of the contemporaneous documentary material is that her general wariness of Mr Lehrmann is supported by her Telegram exchange with Ms Gain the following day (at 2:07pm) in which she

explained, albeit Delphically: "Bruce is in a bit of trouble in our office [at the moment] so I tried to keep distance" (Ex R59).

292 Moreover, there was one aspect of her evidence that was of importance, and which struck me as being a truthful recounting by Major Irvine of a genuine recollection. After noting Ms Higgins was "very down" on the Wednesday or Thursday after the incident, Major Irvine walked with Ms Higgins and had the following conversation with her (T1180.41–46):

> I said, "Are you okay". She said no. I – she said, "No, have you heard what has happened"? I said no. She said, "**On the weekend, ... Bruce, Austin, Lauren and I went to 88. Bruce and I were in a[n] Uber to go home and he wanted to come back to Parliament House. He had some whisky to show me or something. When we came back to Parliament House, I fell asleep on the couch and I woke up and he was on top of me**".

293 Ms Higgins did not use the word rape or assault expressly, but Major Irvine went on (T1180.46–1181.22):

> **And I said, okay, was it – and I paused. And she said, "Yes, definitely"**. And I took that to mean it was an assault. I asked if she had spoken to the Minister or Fiona Brown about it yet. At that stage, she had spoken to Fiona but had not yet spoken to the Minister. I am confident that police were mentioned in that interview – in that meeting – sorry, that conversation with her. I'm confident that she had either booked to see into the police or was going to book in to see the police.
>
> ...
>
> I also told her that, you know, this is big news, and she said, "Yes, with the election so close".
>
> ...
>
> She did talk about CCTV footage. I'm unsure if – it was definitely in the topic of conversation, either it would show how drunk she was or she wanted to see it or someone had seen it and told her how drunk she was ...
>
> (Emphasis added)

Senior counsel for Network Ten then asked her to do the best she could as to which of the reasons she gave for asking for mentioning the CCTV footage and the following exchange occurred (T1181.24–32): 294

> **I'm sorry. It was a long time ago. Yes?---It would show how drunk she was. She said the word "CCTV" in that conversation.**
>
> Thank you. And how did that conversation end?---I said, "I'm really sorry," and, you know, "I really want you to press this. It's really bad what's happened," and I gave her reassurances that I was here if she needed to talk to me.

Although Major Irvine rightly conceded the conversation was a long time ago, I accept these exchanges occurred as recounted. 295

## F.6 Mr Payne

Mr Christopher Payne was a departmental liaison officer. The impression I gleaned was that he was not at all fond of Mr Lehrmann. He gave extensive evidence, which I generally accept, about a security breach, but was quite fuzzy about the timing of some other events. At trial, Mr Payne augmented some details of a conversation with Ms Brown absent from earlier accounts which, together with his manner of giving this evidence, leads me to treat his account of his communications with Ms Brown with some hesitation. 296

However, one aspect of his evidence that was given clearly and firmly was in relation to a contemporaneous representation by Ms Higgins, which I consider to be of real importance. 297

It occurred during a conversation between Ms Higgins and Mr Payne, probably on 28 March 2019, which Mr Payne had initiated after Mr Payne had observed Ms Higgins was teary and upset. Parts of his evidence are worth setting out at length to see the context of the emphasised representation (T1422–3): 298

> DR COLLINS: ... can you take his Honour through, again, doing the best you can, what words did she use and what words did you use?---Certainly. So once Brittany was in the room, the door was closed, we were the only two in the room at the time. I asked her words to the effect of, "what's wrong?" Brittany responded by

outlining the events of Saturday after they had arrived back at Parliament House, or on the approach to Parliament House.

So just doing the best you can, what words did she use to you?---She said that she and Bruce had arrived in an Uber at Parliament House. And they had come through security and come back to the Minister's suite. She told me that she had been sitting on a window-sill and didn't remember anything after that until she woke up on the couch in the Minister's office.

All right. And did she say what was happening when she woke up on the couch in the Minister's office?---She did. She said to me that at that time, Mr Lehrmann was having sex with her on the couch.

All right. Did she say anything else?---She was very upset at that point. So I paused to let her collect herself. And I then asked her, "may I ask you a very direct question?" And she said "Sure. Go for it". **And I remember, those were the exact words, were "Sure. Go for it." And I said, "did he rape you?" And her response was, "I could not have consented. It would have been like f***ing a log."**

And you're very clear in those words, Mr Payne. Why is that?---They were quite confronting words, as you can imagine. I mean, I don't know how to – a twenty- something year old female in tears saying those words to you is extremely confronting. So they stuck with me.

And did you say anything in response to that?---I let her collect herself because she was very upset. And I said to her, "if you want my advice, you must go and see a doctor and you should go to the police. And I can help you do those things. If you want to go now, I will take you". And her response was that – she thanked me for my concern and said she didn't want to proceed with that at that time.

299 I accept Mr Payne's evidence that these confronting words were said by Ms Higgins and that they resonated with Mr Payne.

300 In making this finding, I am conscious Ms Higgins had the following enigmatic exchange with Ms Maiden (Ex 50 (at 24–25)), characteristic of so many of her allegations in 2021:

*Ms Higgins*:

Everyone was weirded out that [Mr Lehrmann] had suddenly left, no good-bye, he packed up a box and he was gone, and it was like weird because he was one of Linda Reynolds kind of more senior advisers in that space. Everyone was like, that's weird. They knew obviously it was connected because Fiona called both of us in together. **One of the advisers asked me one day, like oh, like something weird's going on, like are you okay. And I was like, oh, not really and I was like, do you want to know what's wrong? And he was like, no, no, I don't need to know that. And I said, okay, this is fun.**

*Ms Maiden*:

How old was he?

*Ms Higgins*:

Forty-something. He's another Defence guy.

*Ms Maiden*:

Yeah.

*Ms Higgins*:

Yeah.

*Ms Maiden*:

**So he's like anything weird going on but don't tell me.**

*Ms Higgins*:

**Yeah.**

The parties accept these were comments about Mr Payne. It says something about Ms Higgins' desire by 2021 to paint others as having behaved inappropriately (and also her suggestibility to leading propositions) that she represented these things about one of her former colleagues, who after seeing her in distress in shortly after the incident, was concerned to enquire about her wellbeing. 301

## F.7 Mr Dillaway

I do not need to deal with Mr Dillaway at any length. He tried to assist the 302
Court with his genuine recollection, but it is fair to say that unless aided

by contemporaneous documents, his recollection was poor. I am not being critical of him, but save for one matter in respect of which I think he had a good recollection (contacting, with Ms Higgins' permission, a friend to assist Ms Higgins) by far the surest guide as to any interactions of Ms Higgins or others with him in 2019 comes not from his affidavit or unprompted recollection, but from the text messages that have been placed into evidence.

303 As I will explain, one of these messages is of some significance. That is the exchange on 26 March 2019, where Mr Dillaway asked: "Was it just you and Bruce who went back there or a group of people? Did you hook up in there or did someone take advantage of you?" (Ex R99 (at 695)) to which Ms Higgins replied:

> Yeah, it was just Bruce and I from what I recall. I was barely lucid. **I really don't feel like it was consensual at all".**
>
> (Emphasis added)

## F.8 Ms Wilkinson

304 Ms Wilkinson's evidence did not lack self-assuredness. As one would expect from someone with her professional background, Ms Wilkinson was a polished and articulate witness. Regrettably, however, these not inconsiderable skills were often deployed by her in the witness box to advocate for her views.

305 Her counsel made the point, not unfairly, that Ms Wilkinson has "spent decades in a professional environment which involved conversational style interviews and debates" and in those circumstances it is unsurprising "she had difficulty within the structure of giving evidence for the first time in a Court". This submission may have some merit because when she gave evidence for a second time at the trial, she was a candid and far more responsive witness. Be that as it may, and notwithstanding allowances for her background as a presenter, some aspects of her initial spell in the witness box caused me concern: for present purposes, it is worth mentioning four.

306 *First*, was her refusal to make the obvious concession in response to her cross-examiner's questions that her speech at the 62nd Annual TV Week Logie Awards on 19 June 2022 conveyed the message that Ms Higgins was credible and to be believed, and therefore, by necessary implication, that her allegation of rape was true.

This was a speech given by a proposed Crown witness – eight days before the criminal trial was due to begin – during a televised programme, broadcast in the ACT. In a judgment given two days later, the Chief Justice of the Australian Capital Territory in *R v Lehrmann (No 3)* (at 279–280 [22]–[25]; 280 [29]–[30]) said this: 307

> [22] ... upon receiving the award, Ms Wilkinson gave a speech in which she openly referred to and praised the complainant in the present trial. Unsurprisingly, the award and the content of the speech have been the subject of extensive further commentary.
>
> [23] The recent commentary includes remarks made on the popular morning radio program, "Jonesy and Amanda". The relevant segment from that program in evidence on the present application opened as follows:
>
> > Amanda: But there were some really lovely moments last night. One of which was the award that Lisa Wilkinson and The Project picked up for the story they did on Brittany Higgins. They just – it was a phone call that came to Lisa. She answered Brittany Higgins' phone call. Brittany had – the back story here, I'm sure you remember, was raped in Parliament House.
>
> [24] The transcript attributes to "Jonesy" his assent to that recollection. He later refers to the fact that, "...the whole story was dreadful. Absolutely dreadful", adding, "[j]ust the very fact that she had to have a meeting in the very room that she was raped with her superiors and then her career was virtually finished." And so on.
>
> [25] In case it is not clear, my purpose in quoting those remarks is the fact that each of the radio presenters assumed the guilt of the accused. The evidence before me on the present application also includes other social commentary including a copy of the complainant's own post effectively repeating remarks made by Ms Wilkinson in her speech. **In other words, as was put in argument before me this morning, the combination of the speech and the posts amounted to Ms Wilkinson endorsing the credibility of the complainant who, in turn,**

**celebrated Ms Wilkinson's endorsement of the complainant's credibility.**

***

[29] What can be known is that, somewhere in this debate, the distinction between an untested allegation and the fact of guilt has been lost. The Crown accepted that the Logie awards acceptance speech was unfortunate for that reason. He also accepted that Ms Wilkinson's status as a respected journalist is such as to lend credence to the representation of the complainant as a woman of courage whose story must be believed.

[30] **The prejudice of such representations so widely reported so close to the date of empanelment of the jury cannot be overstated. The trial of the allegation against the accused has occurred, not in the constitutionally established forum in which it must, as a matter of law, but in the media.** The law of contempt, which has as its object the protection of the integrity of the court but which, incidentally, operates to protect freedom of speech and freedom of the press, has proved ineffective in this case. The public at large has been given to believe that guilt is established. The importance of the rule of law has been set at nil.

(Emphasis added)

308 Despite, with respect, these measured but pointed criticisms, when the topic of this speech was canvassed in cross-examination, Ms Wilkinson took comfort in: (a) the fact that she did not say in express terms that Mr Lehrmann was a rapist and that she was only "celebrating her courage" (T1730.8); (b) the Chief Justice had acted on the basis of an incorrect representation that Ms Wilkinson had received a warning about the possible consequences of the proposed speech by the Director of Public Prosecutions; and (c) she had taken legal advice from Ms Tasha Smithies, the Senior Litigation Counsel for Network Ten, and the speech was made with the encouragement of Network Ten.

309 As to (a), as Ms Wilkinson eventually and inevitably conceded, by necessary implication she was celebrating Ms Higgins' courage in making a true

allegation of rape; and as to (b) it was common ground before me that no warning was given by Mr Drumgold (and this is consistent with the evidence of Ms Wilkinson and also Ms Smithies).

As to (c), it emerged belatedly during the hearing that Ms Wilkinson was correct in saying Network Ten, through Ms Smithies, did provide express advice as to the giving and the content of the speech (T2550.6) and Ms Cat Donovan, the Network Ten Head of PR (who had seen an advance copy) had led Ms Wilkinson to believe that "Network Ten had given full approval" (Wilkinson 5 December 2023 (at [27])). Consistently with this encouragement, that evening at 11:07pm, Ms Beverly McGarvey, the Chief Executive Officer of Network Ten, acclaimed Ms Wilkinson for having given what Ms McGarvey described as a "Beautiful speech" (Wilkinson 5 December 2023 (at [29])). It will be necessary to return to aspects of this conduct that can be attributed to Network Ten below. 310

What became apparent by the end of the evidence was the action in giving the speech was not, as many suggested at the time, a case of Ms Wilkinson going off on a frolic and irresponsibly saying something off the top of her head. She was sufficiently prudent to seek advice. She only came to give the speech as a result of being badly let down by those to whom she turned for advice and counsel. One can well understand Ms Wilkinson's frustration at the true picture being obscured by Network Ten maintaining its joint claim for privilege until the eleventh hour. 311

But although the reality of this advice and encouragement provides important context, Ms Wilkinson was a fourth estate éminence grise with 40 years' experience – she gave evidence she was appointed a Member of the Order of Australia in 2016 for, among other things, services to broadcast and print journalism. If she had of thought matters through as an experienced journalist, and less as a champion for Ms Higgins, she ought to have known the speech was fraught with danger and recognised that lauding a complainant on the eve of a rape trial in the terms she did would be apt to undermine the due administration of justice. 312

She was keen to give the speech not because of pressure from her employer (as seems to be suggested by her final submissions) but because, in the words of Ms Smithies, Ms Wilkinson had become "inextricably intertwined with Ms Higgins" and had provided her with "clear and unequivocal" support 313 for the preceding 18 months (T2616.18–25). The speech was part of a continuum of conduct of Ms Wilkinson celebrating and lending credence to Ms Higgins as a woman of courage whose story *must* be believed.

314 I accept Ms Wilkinson did not fully appreciate the extent of the problem, given the advice and encouragement of Network Ten and perhaps because of the approbation the speech received by way of applause from her professional peers on the night (notwithstanding some of them, surely, must have been aware of the pending jury trial).

315 But in the end, what matters for present purposes is less any lack of judgment in giving the speech, but rather her lack of candour in the witness box by refusing initially to admit it conveyed the representation that Ms Higgins' rape allegation was credible and to be believed. I disagree with the submissions made on behalf of Ms Wilkinson that the questions of the cross-examiner were imprecise. This evidence illustrated a tendency of Ms Wilkinson to try to avoid making concessions, even an obvious one.

316 *Secondly*, some of her evidence about the content of the Project programme displayed an allied tendency to make assertions that she thought supported her case but lacked a factual foundation. One notable example was the evidence that an aspect of the Project programme conveyed the notion that Ms Brown was caring; or that aspects could be construed as complimentary about Ms Brown and Senator Reynolds.

317 Counsel for Ms Wilkinson defended specific answers relating to Ms Brown at some length in written submissions, but the notion that the Project programme was not very critical of Ms Brown, as well as Senator Reynolds, is utterly unsustainable. Her evidence also embraced the concept that the Project programme conveyed to viewers that Ms Higgins was putting pressure on herself not to go to the AFP, rather than alleging she was experiencing such pressure from Ms Brown and Senator Reynolds. Self-created roadblocks were put up, the argument apparently goes. Not only is that wrong on any objective review of the broadcast, but is disingenuous – as the contemporaneous observations of the participants demonstrate (and as I will explain below).

318 A further example of making such assertions was her evidence-in-chief that every new piece of information which came to her attention prior to broadcast corroborated Ms Higgins' version of events (as relayed to her on 27 January and 2 February 2021) (Wilkinson 28 July 2023 (at

[110])). She stood by this evidence in cross-examination (T1724.14–25), notwithstanding the fact she admitted she had read, prior to broadcast, a communication from what she described as "some nameless person from the Prime Minister's Office" (T1868.9) stating (contrary to Ms Higgins representations) that (Ex R716; T1866.35–41):

> The Minister reiterated to the staff member that whatever the staff member chose to do, they would be supported. The Minister stated to the staff member that her only concern was for the staff member's welfare and stated there would be no impact on their career. The Minister encouraged the staff member to speak with police in order to assess the options available to them. At this meeting, the staff member indicated they would like to speak to the AFP, which the Minister supported and the office facilitated.

She dismissed this material as a "very official response to a very difficult 319
political situation that the government was in" (T1866.45–6). In a similar way, according to Ms Wilkinson, she had been told by Mr Llewellyn at some point that the reason for the loss of data from Ms Higgins' mobile phone related to transfers from multiple mobiles. There is no contemporaneous record of this communication (and given its obvious importance, the lack of record is intuitively surprising) but assuming it was said, this information was inconsistent with what Ms Higgins had earlier said about the cause of her alleged loss of data – how this corroborated Ms Higgins' version of events (rather than undermined her credibility on a topic considered at the time by Ms Wilkinson to be important) was unexplained.

*Thirdly*, was her willingness on affirmation to double down on an allega- 320
tion that Ms Brown and Senator Reynolds were active participants in a systemic cover-up of alleged criminal conduct when, upon any fair review of the available material, the basis for such a grave allegation is infirm (even taking the evidence of Ms Higgins as to what she "felt" or what was "weird", and the assertion senior staffers from the Prime Minister's Office (**PMO**) had met with Senator Reynolds in her office, at their highest). The willingness to maintain that such conduct occurred in the absence of any solid, verifiable material in her possession, demonstrates her willingness to engage in speculation (or, to use her words, to "read ... between the lines" (T1781.38)). Indeed, the maintenance of this allegation seems odder in circumstances where, by the end of the trial, Ms Wilkinson was

emphasising her reliance on the investigative work of others. In any event, for the purposes of assessing her evidence, this willingness to speculate causes me to approach her testimony with some caution.

321 *Fourthly*, and picking up on the last point, there is the evidence upon which rests Ms Wilkinson's final submissions that her job in relation to the publication was to "to read the pre-prepared script" and that "she acted not only reasonably in reading that pre-prepared script but perfectly, in that she read it word for word". As I will develop below when dealing with the reasonableness of her conduct in relation to publication, this picture is hard to reconcile with Ms Wilkinson getting up on the night of the Logies; accepting a prestigious award on behalf of *The Project*; and declaiming "this interview and this story is by far the most important work *I* have ever done". Moreover, the evidence given as to any degree of professional scepticism or rigour in analysing the allegations must be seen in the light of her assertion immediately thereafter: "I knew it [that is, it would be the most important work I would ever do] from that very first phone call I had early last year with a young woman, whose name, she told me, was Brittany Higgins" (Ex 12).

322 Balanced against this is that I accept Ms Wilkinson was sincere and genuine in parts of her evidence and, most particularly, consistently with what she said at the Logies, she never questioned the underlying truth of any of Ms Higgins' allegations from the first moment they were articulated. I also accept she held genuine concerns about the procedures and assistance available to Ms Higgins, and as to what she alleged she experienced. In particular, I accept she fully believed what Ms Higgins told her on 2 February 2021 about the state of Senator Reynolds' knowledge as at the time of the 1 April meeting.

323 I also accept Ms Wilkinson reposed confidence in the producers and executive producers at Network Ten who were responsible for different aspects of the production, editing, and approval of the Project programme.

## F.9 Mr Llewellyn

324 I can be briefer with the other statutory qualified privilege witnesses, including Mr Llewellyn, whose evidence I address in considerable depth below. He was cross-examined at length.

Mr Lehrmann submitted that Mr Llewellyn was an unimpressive witness who made non-responsive speeches and struggled to give answers to questions, and that his evidence ought not be accepted "unless it is corroborated by documents or other witnesses, not including Ms Wilkinson". 325

To the extent this submission suggests my focus should be on contemporaneous materials and what inferences should be drawn from what is revealed in recordings and other candid communications, rather than *ex post facto* assertions in an affidavit, it is well made. I further accept that Mr Llewellyn was often non-responsive, and several aspects of his evidence were less than satisfactory, such as: 326

(1) his testimony as to the lack of a political motivation of Mr Sharaz (T1630), a conclusion which cannot be reconciled with the contemporaneous material including, as just one of a number of examples, Mr Sharaz saying to him on 27 January 2021 that (Ex 36 (at 1:14:09–1:14:17)):

> ... the reason we've chosen the timeline we've had is because it's a sitting week when we want the story to come out. A break and then–
>
> ... the Senate goes in March, and that's when I'm going to talk to - I've got a friend in Labor, Katy Gallagher on the Labor side, who will probe and continue it going. So sitting week, story comes out. They have to answer questions at Question Time. It's a mess for them. March, Senate estimates. Hopefully we can try and get the footage, that sort of stuff, for Britt's clarity and then he's going to call an election whenever he calls it.

(2) relatedly, his initial refusal to accept that he knew that Mr Sharaz intended to assist the then Opposition to pursue the issues being discussed in Parliament (T1629–30); and

(3) his refusal to accept the reality that the Project programme conveyed the impression that Ms Higgins would not be supported if she went to police (T1574.1–46).

327 Mr Llewellyn did provide generally credible testimony in cross-examination as to aspects of what he did. Whether those steps were all he should have reasonably done is discussed below.

## F.10 Mr Meakin

328 Mr Peter Meakin is an editorial consultant with over 60 years' experience as a journalist with a high reputation built by being in a number of senior roles in commercial television.

329 I will deal with some of his evidence below when dealing with the s 30 defence. If suffices to note for present purposes that he was an impressive witness who gave thoughtful, responsive answers and, refreshingly, was willing to make concessions adverse to the case of Network Ten when he thought it was appropriate.

## F.11 Dr Robertson

330 During the course of final submissions, I described Dr Robertson, a toxicologist called by Network Ten, as a "very impressive expert [witness]" (T2328). I adhere to that view. It is unnecessary to say more than he was a disinterested and cautious witness who understood the role of an expert is to assist the Court. In the end, however, his evidence is only relevant to the extent I can accept as reliable the assumptions upon which he based his opinions.

## F.12 Mr Reedy

331 In two interlocutory judgments delivered *ex tempore* during the trial, I detailed the background of Mr Tim Reedy (the forensic lipreading expert) and the nature of his evidence: *Lehrmann v Network Ten Pty Limited (Expert Evidence)* [2023] FCA 1577 and *Lehrmann v Network Ten Pty Limited (Expert Evidence) (No 2)* [2023] FCA 1647.

332 In the latter judgment, in allowing the tender of Mr Reedy's evidence (initially given on the *voir dire*) in the trial, I said (at [17]) that the arguments raised by counsel for Mr Lehrmann in the context of seeking discretionary exclusion of the evidence of the lipreader "are matters which will need to be considered carefully when I assess the *weight* of the evidence, including my personal observations and assessments of the interactions captured by the relevant CCTV footage" (original emphasis).

Mr Reedy was an impressive and accomplished man who did his best to assist the Court but, in the end, there is no need for me to form definitive views about his evidence. This is because I do not intend to place weight upon it. 333

This is no reflection upon Mr Reedy. After the hearing, I have had the opportunity of considering the interactions captured by the relevant CCTV footage closely and repeatedly. I have formed my own views from my observations as to the nature of the interactions and communications between Mr Lehrmann and Ms Higgins, which emerge tolerably clearly from many reviews of the recording. 334

In not placing weight on Mr Reedy's evidence, I am additionally conscious of the limitations on the process of lipreading from video (readily acknowledged by Mr Reedy) and, more importantly, that the opinion lipreading evidence may, at least to some extent, have been affected by the fact that when Mr Reedy viewed the video, he "saw that the man was encouraging her, enticing her to drink everything that was on the table" (T2181.5). I am grateful for Mr Reedy's assistance, but I am in as good a position as him to assess whether this is a fair characterisation of what occurred. 335

# G FACTUAL FINDINGS OF RELEVANCE TO THE SECTION 25 DEFENCE

336 Before going further, I should make four preliminary points.

337 *First*, although I have considered all the evidence adduced, in this section I will make findings about what relevantly occurred without necessarily setting out conflicting accounts. I have already explained my general approach to the evidence of various witnesses, and it would expand an already burdensome judgment to proceed otherwise, particularly when the important facts leading up to and following the incident emerge fairly clearly; *secondly*, the evidence ranged far and wide and a number of incidents recounted have no bearing on the resolution of the case, hence I will try to avoid making findings on immaterial matters; *thirdly*, from time to time I make reference to the transcript – these references are not necessarily meant to be exhaustive references but are often illustrative, and point to an example of where the relevant evidence can be usefully found; and *fourthly*, and most significantly, at Section I below, I make findings as to the relevant post-incident conduct, which was the subject of much and disputed evidence; although these findings are located chronologically, and after I have expressed my conclusions on the substantial truth defence, I have taken them into account in forming views as to credit and in reaching my ultimate conclusion on the substantial truth defence.

## G.1 Pre-Incident Events

### *I The Reynolds' Office*

338 In the Reynolds' office, there was a clear pecking order. Although Ms Higgins overstated the seniority of Mr Lehrmann in her 2021 accounts to Ms Maiden and the Project team, Mr Lehrmann was more senior than Ms Higgins in his role as policy advisor, while Ms Higgins was an administrative officer and junior media advisor. I am not satisfied the issue of

Mr Lehrmann "bullying" Ms Higgins had been escalated within the office as Ms Higgins asserted in 2021, but accept Mr Lehrmann would give her tasks, such as organising a new phone list so that Mr Lehrmann was listed at a particular spot and moving a fridge, which Ms Higgins recalled as being "particularly annoying" tasks (T602.16–603.9). Whether she actually did feel like Mr Lehrmann's secretary (T934.20) is unnecessary to resolve, but what matters is that she did feel he was in a position of power in the office and in his dealings with her.

The office was in a state of flux, owing to the Senator's recent change in 339
portfolio, and the spectre of the May 2019 federal election, which most observers confidently expected the Coalition Government would lose. Many of the Ministerial staff were in what is known as a "deferral period", when a person is temporarily employed by a Minister pending the final selection of Ministerial staff (T87–88). Mr Lehrmann was in a deferral period of approximately one month following Senator Reynolds' swearing-in to the portfolio of Minister for Defence Industry on 2 March, and all staff, including Ms Higgins, would enter a deferral period in the weeks prior to the election. There was no security in any of these jobs and, as contemporaneous messages discussed below confirm, Ms Higgins understood this to be the case.

Work hours were long and, like in many demanding professional offices, it 340
was common for staff members to socialise outside work hours, including by having dinner and drinks.

The floorplan of the Minister's Suite is of some significance 341
– although it is not a matter of disputation. In evidence are two marked-up versions of the floorplan, the *first* being a copy annotated by Mr Lehrmann (Ex 19); and the *second* being a copy marked-up by Ms Higgins (Ex R1), the latter of which I have reproduced as **Annexure C.**

As can be seen, upon entering the Minister's Suite, one passes through 342
a reception waiting area, at the end of which there is a perpendicular corridor, which leads to the support staff area (where the desks of Mr Lehrmann and Ms Higgins were located) to the left, and to the Minister's office to the right. In the support staff area, there are large window ledges, upon which one can sit, overlooking what is known as the Prime Minister's Courtyard.

### *II Mr Lehrmann's Knowledge of Ms Higgins*

343 Mr Lehrmann told the Court he did not know Ms Higgins or her aspirations in working for Senator Reynolds until their interaction at the Kingston Hotel (colloquially, the "Kingo") on 2 March 2019, discussed below (T175.9–26). He later admitted the pair had interacted in passing, when Mr Lehrmann went to visit Ms Abbott in Mr Ciobo's office, where Ms Higgins worked at the front desk (T175.36–42).

344 Despite his denials (see, for example, T176.14–37; T350.43–44), as noted above (at [156]), I am satisfied Mr Lehrmann was taken with Ms Higgins from the outset. He told Ms Hamer as much in early March 2019 (T1047.1–19), and agreed he found her attractive when interviewed for the *Spotlight* programme in June 2023 (T351.1–12).

### *III 2-3 March 2019: Drinks at the Kingston Hotel and Related Events*

345 At the Kingo on 2 March, a telling incident occurred, and the event and its reverberations are consistent with: (a) Mr Lehrmann's attraction to Ms Higgins; (b) Mr Lehrmann's immaturity and lack of self-awareness; and (c) Senator Reynolds being given information that may have caused her to question whether Mr Lehrmann was someone in whom she could repose confidence.

346 Mr Lehrmann attended Senator Reynolds' swearing-in ceremony and then attended a celebratory lunch at the Kingo together with some colleagues, being Ms Hamer, Mr Wotton and Ms Michelle Lewis, the office manager of Senator Reynolds' Perth office.

347 At some point, Messrs Lehrmann and Wotton were playing pool and drinking. Ms Hamer and Ms Lewis were near the snooker table. Mr Lehrmann told Mr Wotton, in substance, that he wanted to invite Ms Higgins for a drink because he knew her; that she worked for Mr Ciobo; and that she was looking for another job. Ms Lewis left at some point.

348 Ms Hamer and Messrs Lehrmann and Wotton discussed who might move across to work in Senator Reynolds' office. Mr Lehrmann asked Ms Hamer whether she knew Ms Higgins. Ms Hamer had not met Ms Higgins but had obtained her contact details through Instagram. Upon being apprised of this fact, Mr Lehrmann asked Ms Hamer to contact the "good looking" Ms Higgins on Instagram and invite her to the pub (T1047.3–5).

Ms Hamer then messaged Ms Higgins on Instagram, asking her to come to the Kingo for a drink if she was free. Ms Higgins responded saying she would drop in before attending to other plans. 349

Ms Higgins understood, or at least suspected, this would amount to an informal job interview. Ms Higgins arrived and after some time passed, she and Ms Hamer split off from Messrs Lehrmann and Wotton to have a private conversation in the courtyard, which lasted somewhere between thirty minutes and an hour. Ms Hamer and Ms Higgins apparently clicked and discussed their journeys into politics, and Ms Hamer asked Ms Higgins her plans in the light of Mr Ciobo's resignation (T1048). 350

When Ms Hamer and Ms Higgins rejoined the others, Ms Hamer informed everyone she was impressed by Ms Higgins and discussed a plan whereby Ms Higgins would have carriage of the Minister's Canberra-based media matters, while Ms Hamer would be responsible for those that were Perth-based. Ms Hamer indicated she would inform the Minister that Messrs Lehrmann and Wotton had met Ms Higgins and supported her joining the team (T1082.39–44). 351

Following this happy news, Ms Higgins informed everyone she would be heading off and took out her phone and began to order an Uber (T1048.47–8). 352

Mr Lehrmann and Mr Wotton both asked Ms Higgins not to depart and to stay for a drink. Ms Higgins demurred, and Mr Lehrmann took Ms Higgins' phone from her so that she could not complete the Uber booking and again entreated her to tarry with them awhile. Ms Higgins responded by repeating she had to go and said she was already running late (T1049.10). 353

Ms Hamer then intervened and protested, telling Mr Lehrmann something to the effect of "she told us she could only stay for a little while. She has to go" (T1049.12–14). Mr Lehrmann then returned Ms Higgins' phone, which Ms Higgins accepted while laughing the incident off (which might be seen as a non-confrontational approach to an awkward situation, which was understandable given the power dynamic and Ms Higgins' hopes to secure the job). 354

After Ms Higgins left, Ms Hamer was sensitive to what had happened and told Messrs Lehrmann and Wotton to "shut the f**k up" (T1083.32). She considered both men had behaved boorishly and in such a way as to make 355

Ms Higgins feel she would not get a job because she had not fallen in with their plans to stay for a drink.

356 Mr Wotton was displeased at her reaction and responded, "quite passionately" (T1083.37). Mr Lehrmann chimed in and told Ms Hamer she had overreacted in defending Ms Higgins and that he had only been joking. Ms Hamer disagreed and left shortly thereafter.

357 Ms Hamer was distressed by the incident. Once she left, she spoke to a relative and resolved to then send an email to Senator Reynolds at 4:47pm, resigning from her position as media advisor (Ex 56). The email did not elaborate upon her reasons for resigning. Ms Hamer had been unhappy at work, was missing her home in Perth, and felt "ganged up" on by Mr Lehrmann. In her mind, this was the final straw and she wanted to move on.

358 In the meantime, Mr Wotton returned to his hotel. On his way back, he contacted Ms Lewis and later met with her at the restaurant of the hotel, where Ms Lewis was also staying, to report the incident, being the "heated discussion" with Ms Hamer (T1085.34). During their meeting, Ms Lewis informed Mr Wotton that Ms Hamer had resigned (T1085.41–42).

359 Ms Hamer and Messrs Lehrmann and Wotton attended Parliament House the following day, Sunday, 3 March. Each was only made aware of the presence of the others upon their arrival.

360 When Mr Wotton arrived, he overheard what appeared to him to be a "jovial" meeting between Senator Reynolds and Ms Hamer. What evidently was happening was that Senator Reynolds had asked Ms Hamer why she had resigned, and, in response, Ms Hamer had recounted the incident the previous night and had told the Minister "when the phone was taken away from Brittany, I, kind of, stepped in to defend her. Bruce then, kind of, got defensive, made a comment about me always feeling the need to stand up for women. I got defensive and then I just, kind of, just from there, said that I was – it was enough. I didn't want to be here anymore" (T1068.10–23). The Minister talked her out of resigning.

361 In any event, when Ms Hamer emerged from the room, Mr Lehrmann was then called in (despite his peculiar evidence, he does not recall being reprimanded by Senator Reynolds and yet recollects attending Parliament House and overhearing Mr Wotton being told off (T225)).

When Mr Lehrmann emerged from the meeting room after his reprimand, Mr Wotton took from the abashed look on Mr Lehrmann's face that he was next, and that he would not be in for a pleasant time (T1084–5). 362

Senator Reynolds called Mr Wotton into her office and asked for his version of events. He gave an account, but she was not mollified and ticked him off. She explained that Messrs Lehrmann and Wotton were senior males in the office, in positions of power, and that they should have understood how their conduct may have made Ms Hamer and Ms Higgins feel (T1086.1–11). Senator Reynolds told him that the events of the previous day had "put her in a very difficult position in terms of whether or not Ms Higgins ultimately ended up with a job in her office" (T1086.2–4). 363

Messrs Lehrmann and Wotton later discussed the matter and consoled each other by both expressing they were unhappy with the way Senator Reynolds had dealt with the issue (T1086.31–35). 364

### *IV 15 March 2019: "Team Reynolds" Dinner*

On 15 March, Senator Reynolds held a dinner at the Kingo for her newly integrated staff, apparently attended by Mr Lehrmann, Ms Higgins, Ms Hamer, Mr Wotton, and Ms Lewis. 365

Mr Lehrmann said he did not recall the dinner occurring (T205.16–40). But I accept it happened. 366

Ms Higgins said she left the Kingo at about the same time as Mr Lehrmann (approximately 9 or 9:30pm), and the pair waited outside the venue for their respective rideshares. Around the time Mr Lehrmann's vehicle arrived, Ms Higgins alleges Mr Lehrmann tried to kiss her, an advance she rebuffed. Mr Lehrmann does not recall waiting outside the Kingo with Ms Higgins and denies trying to kiss her or ever making an advance towards her (T206.7–14). 367

This advance might have happened, but I am not satisfied it did. I am chary in accepting this version of events for two reasons: *first*, this far from unremarkable incident was not raised in 2019 and is not even mentioned in the five-hour interview between Ms Higgins, Ms Wilkinson and Messrs Llewellyn and Sharaz (Ex 36); nor is it raised in the uncut, two-hour interview between Ms Wilkinson and Ms Higgins (Ex 37) – even when Ms Wilkinson (and for that matter, Ms Maiden) asked Ms Higgins if she had an inkling that Mr Lehrmann may have been interested in her; *secondly*, it 368 is raised for the first time when Ms Higgins was already being disingenuous about a number of things and I cannot discount the possibility this might amount to an attempt to buttress her allegations by pointing to a prior incident of inappropriate conduct that cannot be definitively disproved by any contemporaneous document or independent witness. Notably, this alleged occurrence paints Ms Higgins in a good light by showing her rebuffing Mr Lehrmann's unwelcome attempts at intimacy (which cogent evidence establishes she did not do a week or so later at 88mph).

369 The effect of giving this evidence is reflected in the submission now made by Network Ten as painting Ms Higgins as experiencing a well-known phenomenon: "Ms Higgins' first reaction was depressingly familiar to many women – she blamed herself for doing something that had unintentionally led Mr Lehrmann on or encouraged him to kiss her".

370 In any event, nothing really turns on this incident. What matters, to the extent it does matter, is that Mr Lehrmann was attracted to Ms Higgins at this time and later in March (irrespective as to whether he made a clumsy and unwelcome attempt at osculation outside the Kingo).

### *V 20 March 2019: Mr Lehrmann's First Security Breach*

371 On Wednesday, 20 March, an incident took place involving Mr Lehrmann and a secure document. In the witness box, and on the *Spotlight* programme, Mr Lehrmann described it as a "very brief minor incident" (see, for example, T89.8–11) for which he was briefly scolded by a subordinate, Mr Payne. But, as he eventually conceded (T219.9–12; T219.35–36), it was much more than that.

372 In an incident report (Ex R79 (at 2)), Mr Payne explained Mr Lehrmann left a "Top Secret - Codeword classified document uncovered and uncontrolled on a desk". When this was brought to Mr Payne's attention, Mr Payne informed Mr Lehrmann documents at that classification level could not be handled in such a manner and offered to provide him with appropriate document handling procedures. Mr Lehrmann declined and thought Mr Payne was straying outside his lane. He requested Mr Payne give him the document in order for him to return it to the originating agency, claiming he had a secure means by which to transport it. He was then observed leaving the Minister's Suite with the document in an opaque plastic folder (which, hardly surprisingly, was not consistent with appropriate procedure).

Ms Brown promptly became aware a security incident had taken place (T1415.46–47). She understandably took the incident seriously and subsequently initiated an office-wide audit in response (T1419.10–23). Ms Brown gave evidence, which I accept, that the Home Affairs DLO stated Mr Lehrmann's actions would be a sackable offence (Brown (at [25])). She discussed the issue with Mr Lehrmann in what she described as a "low key way" (T2039.28–30). 373

All in all, this was far more than a minor lapse and the matter was unsurprisingly referred to, and relied upon, by Senator Reynolds in a letter sent to Mr Lehrmann on 4 April, in which the Minister indicated she was considering terminating his employment "on the basis of serious misconduct" (Ex 23) (**show cause letter**). In an email in response to the show cause letter, Mr Lehrmann stated he felt "embarrassed, ashamed and deeply remorseful" (Ex 24). 374

### *VI 22 March 2019: Before the Dock*

On 22 March, Mr Ben Couch, an aide-de-camp, messaged a group of friends within the Department of Defence and adjacent offices, including a number of aides-de-camp from the Royal Australian Navy, arranging a plan for drinks at The Dock at around 7pm. 375

Ms Higgins was invited along separately by Ms Gain, whom she had known for a couple of months (T610.15–19). She viewed the event as a networking opportunity, and a chance to demonstrate to her professional peers she "wasn't just a receptionist" and she had "contacts" (T610.31–35). Ms Higgins extended the invitation to a number of others, including Mr Wenke (who worked for the Minister for Home Affairs and occasionally socialised with Mr Lehrmann), Mr Lehrmann and a man she was in contact with on the dating application Bumble, who also worked in politics (T610.37–40; T611.1–9). Ms Higgins' hapless date was referred to initially as "Bumble guy", but as noted above (at [256]), later was given the dignity of being described by his Christian name, "Nick". 376

Ms Higgins went home after work to ready herself for the night ahead. She had worn her favourite white pencil dress to work that day with a cardigan "to make it ... more office appropriate" (T611.36–40). She swapped her cardigan, work bag and work items (including her Parliamentary pass) for a smaller handbag and had a glass of wine before catching a taxi or Uber to The Dock (T611.35–45). 377

378 Quite separately, Mr Lehrmann and Mr Wenke made plans to have "a couple of beers and a bite" at the Kingo after work (T240.37–41). Unconvincingly, Mr Lehrmann told the Court he "recall[ed] Austin and I working on something" and could not "recall if it was necessary to go home after the Kingston or return ... to Parliament" (T240.41–47), while Mr Wenke was clear, and I accept, he had finished his work for the week by the time he set off for the Kingo (T1121.37–38). There is no record of Mr Lehrmann telling his girlfriend of his plans. At some point over the course of their repast or afterwards, Mr Lehrmann and Mr Wenke decided to accept the invitation to "kick on" to The Dock.

## *VII The Dock*

379 Fortunately, we can identify with some precision what went on at The Dock given the existence of what Mr Reedy correctly described as high quality and clear CCTV footage (Ex R42 / Ex 17A). Over an extended period, it shows a group seated together around a long table, variously chatting, mingling, drinking, tucking away pizza and chips, going to the bar and moving to and fro.

380 Ms Higgins arrived at about 7:19pm and greeted the group of about eight, including Ms Gain and Major Irvine who had each arrived slightly earlier at around 7pm or so.

381 Mr Wenke's evidence was that he and Mr Lehrmann arrived at The Dock around 8pm or 8:30pm (T1121.40–41) but the CCTV records the group at the large courtyard table with Mr Lehrmann and Mr Wenke approaching at 8:39pm (Ex R42 / Ex 17A (at 20:39:31)), at which time Ms Higgins was in conversation with Nick. Mr Lehrmann agreed that the image recorded him and Mr Wenke arriving at The Dock (T252.24). After being introduced and exchanging pleasantries with those at the large table, Mr Lehrmann and Mr Wenke then went inside to the bar to order their first round, and then went to the courtyard and sat at a smaller table at around 8:44pm (Ex R19) (T264). Ms Gain was seated with them (T1105.21–25).

382 Ms Gain had not previously met Mr Lehrmann (T1113.7), and she asked him where he worked. Mr Lehrmann told her that he was in Senator Reynolds' office (T1103.1–16) and, at some point in the conversation, Mr Lehrmann spun the tall tale he was waiting on a clearance to come through so that he could go and work at ASIS. Ms Gain, politely, kept her well-founded incredulity to herself.

Not much time passed when Ms Higgins entered the courtyard at 8:51pm with a drink in her hand and then joined a conversation about the previous federal election and then imminent poll with Mr Lehrmann, Mr Wenke and Ms Gain (T616.7–11). Nick, alas, was left chatting to a man in a blue shirt (Ex R42 / Ex 17A (at 20:51:38)). After being forsaken like a shag on a rock for an extended period and despite then making successful attempts to interact with some of the group on the larger table, Nick understandably left The Dock, no doubt ruing swiping right. 383

With the exception of Mr Lehrmann, no-one who gave evidence as to their time at The Dock could recall discussing Australia's submarine contracts with France at either table. The lack of recollection of any discussion of this topic is intuitively unsurprising. Declaiming on the topics of who was building submarines and where they were being built was not quite the repartee one would usually expect to hear over a convivial drink on a Friday night between twenty-year-olds out for a good time – even if (with respect) one would not expect the badinage of the Algonquin Round Table (and that some attending were political "junkies" or had an interest in defence matters). 384

The lack of detailed conversation on this topic is also consistent with Mr Lehrmann's evidence that he was aware he could not discuss sensitive matters in public, and so kept the conversation at The Dock friendly and social (T258.30–38; T259.1–2). Moreover, I accept the evidence of Ms Gain and Ms Irvine who told the Court that even if the submarine contracts had been discussed at the pub on a busy Friday night, the discussion would have been generalised, unclassified and based on what was already in the media (T1119.3–15). The suggestions made in Mr Lehrmann's written submissions that I should draw adverse inferences because the respondents did not call various unnamed Naval officers to give evidence, or adduce evidence-in-chief as to the mention of submarines from the lipreader Mr Reedy, are wholly unrealistic (as the Naval officers were in neither side's camp and any inference from the absence of evidence would not affect the combined weight of the evidence actually given by those present and commonsense conclusions drawn from the nature of the occasion). 385

Having explained the timing and nature of the social occasion, it is worthwhile organising the further and important factual findings relating to events that took place at The Dock into three topics: *first*, Mr Lehrmann's 386 payments; *secondly*, the drinks consumed by Ms Higgins; and *thirdly*, a summary of the interactions between Mr Lehrmann and Ms Higgins.

*Mr Lehrmann's Payments*

387 As I have already noted, Mr Lehrmann had initially said in his evidence, when asked how much he had to drink at The Dock, that he had "only a couple of rounds with Austin. We – we were in – so I think it would have been one round for me, one round for him" (T94.43–45), that is, each shouted the other once (T244.14–39). This, of course, was consistent with his evidence he did not have any cash with him on the night (T249.8); his adamant insistence he only had two sources of funds that he could access (an EFTPOS debit card and a credit card (T249.17–47)); that he only used one of these cards (T250.9–19); and his relevant account statements provided by him to the AFP and which were adduced into evidence.

388 As I will come to shortly, the CCTV establishes beyond argument what happened and inevitably Mr Lehrmann was required to accept the answers he had given about not having bought drinks for anyone other than Mr Wenke had been false (T260.18; T288.30–40).

389 Mr Wenke does not recall lending his credit card to Mr Lehrmann (T1126.28–29) and it would not have been consistent with his usual practice to have done so (T1126.31–32). By the end of Mr Lehrmann's evidence, no rational explanation had been forthcoming.

390 How then did he purchase them?

391 The answer can be seen in a portion of the CCTV footage which demonstrates that at about 9:35pm, Mr Lehrmann handed over a card in payment of a $42.50 charge for a round of drinks "one of which is for Ms Higgins" (Ex R42 / Ex 17A (at 21:34:56); T2359). Despite his persistent representations to both the AFP and this Court that he only had access to the cards in respect of which he provided statements, it is evident this was untrue.

392 This issue is essentially ignored in Mr Lehrmann's written submissions, with the comment being made that Mr Lehrmann's evidence "about the number of drinks purchased" at The Dock was "less problematic than it was made out to be" because it was not just him "who was clearly wrong about various details" and he "had no reason to retain minute details of this night and it is unrealistic to expect anyone to do so, almost [two] years later". But it is much more than that.

This is far from a picayune point. I do not accept that having access to another source of funds to allow payment by way of card at The Dock (and possibly later at 88mph) is a "minute detail" or is something that would have been forgotten. Moreover, Mr Lehrmann did not say he may have had access to other funds but could not now recall – he repeatedly denied it. The purchase of drinks on behalf of Ms Higgins by Mr Lehrmann was, and must have been known by Mr Lehrmann to be, an important aspect of their interactions leading up to the incident later that night. 393

*Drinks Consumed by Ms Higgins*

There was no agreement and hence no comprehensive table provided by the parties in their final submissions about what the evidence reveals as to all the drinks consumed by Ms Higgins on the evening of 22 March and early hours of 23 March 2019. 394

I have prepared such a table and reproduce it at this point of my reasons [see following pages 108–9] as a guide to what the evidence reveals, even though it anticipates my findings as to what occurred after Ms Higgins left The Dock and I consider may well underestimate alcohol consumption, for reasons I will explain when it comes to making findings as to why Ms Higgins and Mr Lehrmann went to the Ministerial Suite and what occurred there. 395

A review of the CCTV footage does not always show empty glasses. It is difficult to be certain as to whether Ms Higgins drained the dregs, but I am satisfied it is more likely than not that she would have, given she was not challenged on her evidence she consumed the drinks (which accords with commonsense, given the prices that were being paid for them). 396

The evidence also establishes that Mr Lehrmann was aware of the following consumption by Ms Higgins (using the drink numbers from the table) while at the Dock: 397

(1) at around 8:51pm, shortly after Mr Lehrmann's arrival, Ms Higgins, with a spirit-based drink in hand (**Drink 6**), joins the smaller courtyard table with Mr Lehrmann, Mr Wenke, and Ms Gain (Ex R42 / Ex 17A (at 20:51:38));

(2) at around 9:34pm, Mr Lehrmann buys a spirit-based drink for Ms Higgins (**Drink** 7) and three beers for the small table (Ex R42 / Ex 17A (at 21:34:58));

| Drink | Where | What | Bought by | When | Reference |
|---|---|---|---|---|---|
| 1 | Home | Glass of wine | - | Unknown (after work but before 7pm) | T611.42 (Ms Higgins) |
| Ms Higgins arrives at The Dock | | | | 7:19pm | Ex R42 / Ex 17A (at 19:19:02) |
| 2 | The Dock | Spirit-based drink | Ms Higgins | 7:25pm | Ex R42 / Ex 17A (at 19:25:21) |
| 3 | The Dock | Spirit-based drink | "Blue polo shirt guy" | 7:50pm | Ex R42 / Ex 17A (at 19:50:22) |
| 4 | The Dock | Spirit-based drink | Nick | 8:05pm | Ex R42 / Ex 17A (at 20:05:02) |
| 5 | The Dock | Spirit-based drink | Nick | 8:34pm | Ex R42 / Ex 17A (at 20:34:04) |
| Mr Lehrmann and Mr Wenke arrive at The Dock | | | | 8:39pm | Ex R42 / Ex 17A (at 20:39:31) |
| 6 | The Dock | Spirit-based drink | Unknown | 8:51pm | Ex R42 / Ex 17A (at 20:51:38) |
| 7 | The Dock | Spirit-based drink | Mr Lehrmann | 9:34pm | Ex R42 / Ex 17A (at 21:34:58) |
| 8 | The Dock | Spirit-based drink | Ms Higgins | 10:09pm | Ex R42 / Ex 17A (at 22:09:31) |
| 9 | The Dock | Spirit-based drink | Unknown (Mr Lehrmann passes drink to Ms Higgins) | 10:42pm | Ex R42 / Ex 17A (at 22:42:21) |

| Drink | Where | What | Bought by | When | Reference |
|---|---|---|---|---|---|
| **10** | The Dock | Spirit-based drink | Mr Lehrmann | 11:10pm | Ex R42 / Ex 17A (at 23:10:21) |
| **11** | The Dock | Spirit-based drink | "Dark jacket guy" (Mr Lehrmann gestures Ms Higgins to finish drink) | 11:50pm | Ex R42 / Ex 17A (at 23:50:55) |
| **Mr Lehrmann, Ms Higgins, Ms Gain and Mr Wenke leave The Dock for 88mph** | | | | **11:51pm** | **Ex R42 / Ex 17A (at 23:51:35)** |
| **12–14** | 88mph | Between one to three 30ml shots or nips (as I will explain below, my finding is that Ms Higgins had at least two, but possibly more, spirit-based drinks at 88mph) | Unknown | 12:00am–1:30am | T295.33–4 (Mr Lehrmann); T619.17–20 (Ms Higgins); Wenke (at [13]); Gain (at [41], [47]) |

(3) slightly over half an hour later, at around 10:09pm, Ms Higgins buys herself another drink (**Drink 8**) and returns to the small courtyard table (Ex R42 / Ex 17A (at 22:09:31); T270.11–23) – incidentally, in the absence of Mr Lehrmann, the CCTV captures Ms Higgins showing apparent signs of impairment, swaying back and forth and struggling to maintain balance while standing at the bar before returning to the small table (Ex R42 / Ex 17A (at 22:08:28));

(4) about twenty minutes later, Mr Lehrmann, Ms Higgins and Ms Gain had returned to the large table; and about ten minutes after that (at 10:34pm), it is evident Mr Lehrmann collects three spirit-based drinks on the table and pushes them towards the corner of the large table close to where Ms Higgins was standing (Ex R42 / Ex 17A (at 22:34:20–28); T272.14–16); my close review of the video has not allowed me to conclude that in doing so he said "All hers, all hers" to Ms Gain (indicating that the three drinks were for Ms Higgins) or exactly what words passed between Ms Higgins and Mr Lehrmann, but whatever was said, I am amply satisfied from viewings of the video that Mr Lehrmann was, by his actions, encouraging Ms Higgins not to let the collected drinks go to waste and encouraging further consumption by her (with Ms Higgins playfully resisting the suggestion she drink them by patting Mr Lehrmann on the shoulder) (Ex R42 / Ex 17A (at 22:34:31));

(5) at around 10:42pm, Mr Lehrmann handed Ms Higgins a spirit-based drink (**Drink 9**) (Ex R42 / Ex 17A (at 22:42:21); T275.6–8) after she came back to the large table – being, it appears, the fourth such drink he had observed Ms Higgins consume since he had arrived (T275.10–11) (cf MFI 64 (at 22:34:02)); it is not entirely clear that Ms Higgins, in response, said "come on"; and although something was said by her, I cannot be certain of the precise words;

(6) at around 11:08pm, Ms Higgins finished Drink 9 in one hit, looks a tad unsteady on her feet (Ex R42 / Ex 17A (at 23:08:03–14)), and then joins Mr Lehrmann (who then quickly finished his drink) in walking towards the bar area (Ex R42 / Ex 17A (at 23:08:28); T278.46–279.5); Ms Higgins seems by this stage to be ebullient, putting her hands in the air and is evidently in high spirits; although it is easy to be distracted at this point in the video by two happy middle-aged ladies re-enacting what might be a scene out of *Mamma Mia* in the background, Mr Lehrmann can be seen talking with Ms Higgins

and purchasing drinks, including a further spirit-based drink for Ms Higgins (**Drink 10**) (Ex R42 / Ex 17A (at 23:09:51); T280.27), which she subsequently consumed;

(7) thereafter, as time moves towards 11:20pm, Ms Higgins looks again less than entirely steady on her feet; and, by half-past eleven, things seem to be winding down: Ms Higgins can be seen focused on her phone; and, after speaking on her phone to Mr Dillaway at 11:36pm, at around 11:37pm, Ms Higgins got up while holding Drink 10 and engaged with Mr Lehrmann, Ms Gain and Mr Wenke (Ex R42 / Ex 17A (at 23:37:28); T282.25–33);

(8) at around 11:50pm, Ms Higgins picked up and skolled another drink (**Drink 11**) (Ex R42 / Ex 17A (at 23:51:03); T284.40–43) – notably the sixth spirit-based drink which Mr Lehrmann had observed Ms Higgins consume since his arrival – from a close review of the video, it is clear that Mr Lehrmann had again actively encouraged her to consume the drink.

I have no doubt that from his own observation, Mr Lehrmann must have 398
been aware that a woman of Ms Higgins' stature consuming this much alcohol was likely to have become significantly inebriated.

Attached as **Annexure D** to these reasons are screenshots 399
taken by Network Ten's legal representatives from the CCTV video (Ex R17–R30 inclusive), which record ten drinks consumed by Ms Higgins at The Dock (including the six drinks Mr Lehrmann observed Ms Higgins consume already mentioned above (at [397])).

The oral evidence of Ms Higgins was that by the time she left The 400
Dock, she had consumed 11 vodka, lime and sodas or vodka diet cokes (T614.20–33; T617.37–40) (together with **Drink 1**, being a glass of wine consumed at home, being 12 drinks in total). She said that night she was "drinking for a purpose. I was drinking to get drunk" (T946.33–38). The consumption of her first drink at home was unchallenged, and as would already be evident from my findings, I accept it occurred. Although her behaviour as revealed in the CCTV footage is consistent with someone proposing to get drunk (and succeeding in that effort), my reservations as to Ms Higgins' reliability cause me some hesitation in accepting her uncorroborated testimony as to how much she drank by the time she left The Dock. A far surer guide is the CCTV recording (Ex R42 / Ex 17A).

401 The written submissions made on behalf of Mr Lehrmann assert that the foundation for the assumption Ms Higgins consumed ten drinks at The Dock (and three others elsewhere) "is tenuous". More specifically, he asserts that a close review of MFI 64 (being a 20-minute selection relied upon by Mr Lehrmann taken from the whole of the CCTV footage in evidence and from the cameras operating that night) "suggests Ms Higgins consumed not more than [nine] drinks at [The] Dock" and "no more than [ten] drinks all night".

402 In the end, doing my best from viewing the CCTV footage and the other evidence, I find Ms Higgins had the drinks I have identified, and I do not accept Mr Lehrmann's submissions. But if for some reason I am wrong, and only nine were consumed, I do not think it really matters because it is not possible to be precise as to the full extent of her further consumption, and she continued to "kick on".

*Interactions between Mr Lehrmann and Ms Higgins*

403 In final submissions, Mr Whybrow contended that if one has regard to the whole of the CCTV footage (Ex R42), rather than selected extracts, it is: "not accurate to say that [Mr] Lehrmann is spending all his time with [Ms] Higgins, keeping an eye on her, plying her with drinks, all of those things that are put as significant credit issues against him" (T2363.25–37; T2361.35). In amplification of this submission, as noted above, the 20-minute selection relied upon by Mr Lehrmann (said fairly not to amount to "a subjective and selective view") (being MFI 64) was played in Court (T2352–3).

404 It is true that Mr Lehrmann was not constantly with Ms Higgins and was not encouraging her to drink earlier in the evening, but it is equally true that his evidence-in-chief that his interactions with Ms Higgins at The Dock "were professional and cordial" and that "I recall them being minimal, to an extent" (T94.38–39) was a serious distortion of their dealings. Those interactions cannot be properly characterised, as Mr Lehrmann attempted to do, as "some brief social interactions" or "incidental conversations" and "nothing of substance" (T246.19–26). Contrary to his evidence, he did spend most of the evening with Ms Higgins and, as the night wore on, was aware of her drinking and, towards the end of the evening, was encouraging her to drink well beyond the bounds of sobriety.

He was also keen to continue the evening and his interactions with her. As events at The Dock were winding up, a plan was made for a group to then go to an "80s themed" bar, known as "88mph", and located in the Canberra Civic. Although it does not matter, no evidence was adduced as to why the bar had this name, but one might speculate the owner was an aficionado of the popular 1985 film *Back to the Future* where Marty McFly (Michael J Fox) travels in a DeLorean time machine from the 1950s back to the 1980s at that speed. 405

## *VIII 88mph*

As it happened, only Mr Lehrmann, Ms Higgins, Mr Wenke and Ms Gain continued on to 88mph. Perhaps unsurprisingly, given the hour of the visit and the amount of alcohol that had been consumed, the evidence as to aspects of what occurred at 88mph was somewhat hazy. 406

Mr Lehrmann submits there is "no consistent or reliable evidence as to how many drinks Ms Higgins consumed at 88mph", other than what can be inferred from the fact Mr Lehrmann spent $40 at 88mph (or, more accurately, $40 shown on what we now know are incomplete card statements) (Ex 15). But Ms Higgins did give evidence Mr Lehrmann and Mr Wenke bought her and Ms Gain drinks and that they were shots (T619.11–12). Although she could not recall how many shots she had, her recollection was that there were *rounds* of drinks, plural (T619.19). Ms Gain said she could "remember having at least one drink; I don't recall what that drink was" (T1106.15–16) and Mr Wenke explained he recalled "talking and drinking" but did not recall the specifics (T1123.9). 407

It is not entirely clear, but I think it is highly likely that Ms Higgins had at least two and possibly more shots at 88mph given the context of the earlier drinking (particularly towards the end of the festivities at The Dock), Mr Lehrmann's encouragement of the drinking, and the solecism of taking the benefit of shouting and not reciprocating. This is consistent with Ms Higgins' evidence and suggests that she had a least two shots (which, with the benefit of s 144 EA, I assume would have been 30ml nips). I am fortified in this view given that the group stayed in 88mph for a period in excess of an hour and a half. 408

But whatever else may be less than pellucid, one thing did emerge with clarity from the evidence of Ms Gain: that at 88mph "Brittany hooked up with Bruce" (Ex R59). 409

410 I am amply satisfied that I ought to reject the evidence of Mr Lehrmann and Ms Higgins which is inconsistent with this account of Ms Gain. In particular, I reject Mr Lehrmann's denial of "pash[ing]" Ms Higgins (T297.5–11) and "any intimate behaviour" with Ms Higgins at 88mph (T301.16–17).

411 As to Ms Higgins, she asserted that Mr Lehrmann was "all over her space" (T620.17–24) and gave evidence that (T620.7–10):

> I remember him having his arm around my shoulder. I remember him touching me and I remember having, like, a thought process of – of discomfort, but not wanting to vocalise a discomfort, so I remember that. I – I called it handsy. I felt him being handsy with me.

412 Ms Higgins' evidence that she was passive and discomforted is an example, on one level understandably, of Ms Higgins moulding her recollection. Despite her evidence, and as much as Ms Higgins might regret it, as Ms Gain recalled, they were "quite touchy with one another" (T1106.20) and "his hands [were] on her thighs and her hands [were] on his thighs" (T1107.1–2) and they engaged in a mutually passionate kiss. This was "a real kiss"; more than "a peck, it was very much a kiss kiss", a "passionate kiss" and a "pash" (T1107.4–21). The submission made by Network Ten that Ms Gain's account is "entirely consistent with Ms Higgins' account" is, with respect, silly. One does not "pash" passively.

413 Mr Lehrmann was acting upon his attraction to Ms Higgins, and the less than sober Ms Higgins was sufficiently uninhibited to be a not unwilling participant in the level of intimacy Ms Gain described. Any discomfort was not evident to Ms Gain, who viewed what was happening as mutually intimate conduct by two young people "hooking up" in a nightclub.

414 I also accept the evidence of Ms Gain that Ms Higgins fell over and was required to be helped back up (T1106.18). This happened close to the booth, and Mr Lehrmann was the one to help her to her feet and back into the booth (T1106.35–46). She could not recall if Ms Higgins injured herself in the fall (T1116.30–35). Although, based upon Ms Gain's evidence, this incident occurred and there may have been other stumbling, including on the stairs, I am not satisfied that there was any "falling up the stairs" so as to sustain the bruise recorded in the bruise photograph as Ms Higgins belatedly suggested (and given how a body would likely "fall up" to strike ascending stairs, it is not immediately obvious to me how

the bruise photograph depicts such an injury – assuming the photograph existed in 2019).

Ms Gain also told the Court she formed a view, based on her previous observations of alcohol on Ms Higgins, that Ms Higgins was intoxicated. She knew the difference between when Ms Higgins was and was not drunk, and she characterised Ms Higgins as drunk at 88mph (T1106.25–33; T1116.37–43). I accept that this was her genuine view informed by observing her over an extended period that night, that this view accorded with the reality of Ms Higgins' condition. 415

### *IX Leaving 88mph and the Journey to Parliament House*

By about 1:30am, the group resolved it was time to go. 416

Ms Gain and Mr Wenke agreed to share an Uber or taxi as they lived in the same direction (T1123.23–31). Ms Gain could not recollect leaving 88mph (T1107.27–31). 417

Ms Higgins' present recollection was that someone told her that she and Mr Lehrmann lived in the same direction and by that stage, she was "so compliant" that she agreed and got into a cab or Uber with him (T621.23–41). 418

Mr Lehrmann's evidence was that everyone left 88mph at the same time and that he indicated to the group that he had to go back to Parliament House to get his keys (T121.1–2). He further asserted that Ms Higgins indicated that she needed to go to Parliament House and, consequently, he suggested that they should share an Uber (T121.9–12). 419

I reject both these accounts. 420

Mr Lehrmann's account is risible. Ms Higgins was the most junior and recent member of Senator Reynolds' office. What possible reason was there for this heavily intoxicated young woman, who had earlier seen no need to carry her parliamentary pass, go back to work after a night on the tiles? It is not as if one can readily envisage what work was necessary to be done by a junior media advisor at a ridiculous hour on a Saturday morning. Further, if the reason Mr Lehrmann needed to return to Parliament House was to collect his keys, he could have texted his girlfriend to have her meet him at the door or called her (T306.13–14). 421

Mr Lehrmann asks me to accept the proposition that it was "a process to get in" to his shared flat (T306.10) and that to avoid this complication, he 422 preferred to: (a) go out of his way to go back to work in the early hours; (b) lie to Parliament House security; (c) sign the necessary register; (d) be issued with a pass; (e) go through a metal detector; (f) be escorted by a security guard to his office; (g) obtain his keys from his office; (h) book another Uber; (i) go back through a Parliamentary exit; (j) meet the rideshare car; and then (k) ride home. Even if he was in the doghouse because he had stayed out late, I think it is safe to conclude that the process of getting into a flat he shared with his girlfriend would have been a significantly less elaborate exercise.

423 Moreover, the incoherence of this evidence is also shown by the fact that if he really needed to collect his keys from Parliament House, he could have just said so, and the sensible security guards who gave evidence before me would, no doubt, have assisted him to get them.

424 Ms Higgins' evidence was that she thought she was going home. She said that at some point during the ride, Mr Lehrmann said something to the effect: "I have to just pick something up from work" (T621.46). This account has a kernel of truth in that it explains why she agreed to leave with Mr Lehrmann (or even explains why she got into the Uber with Mr Lehrmann), but otherwise does not withstand analysis.

425 Like with so much fact-finding in litigation, the key to unlocking what most likely happened is found in examining the most contemporaneous accounts; in this case, what they both initially and spontaneously said as to why they ended up in an Uber and going back to Parliament House. As we will see, as for Mr Lehrmann, this comes from his conversation with Ms Brown in their second meeting on 26 March 2019 where he told her that he "came back to drink some whisky or something like that" (T153.45–47). Notably, and as I have already explained, at this meeting, after Mr Lehrmann said he "chatted" with Ms Higgins, when pressed by Ms Brown's question "what else did you do whilst in the office?", Mr Lehrmann revealingly said he "didn't wish to get into that" (T2052.4–5).

426 As for Ms Higgins, as I have referred to in dealing with the credit of Major Irvine, on the Wednesday or Thursday after the incident, Ms Higgins said to her (T1180.41–45): "Bruce and I were in a[n] Uber to go home and he wanted to come back to Parliament House. *He had some whisky to show me or something*" (see also Irvine (at [60])). This is also consistent with her representation to Mr Dillaway on the day after the incident (despite

at the time being "cagey"), that "we brought the party back to Parliament House" (T1216.29–30).

I am satisfied that regardless of whether there was ever any settled initial plan to share an Uber home, at some stage, and with the acquiescence of the inebriated Ms Higgins, the plan became for the Uber to go to Parliament House following what Mr Lehrmann had said about whisky. Needless to say, based on this finding (and even on the evidence she gave at the trial), the representations made by Ms Higgins in the PL that it was without "agreement" between Mr Lehrmann and Ms Higgins that Mr Lehrmann got into the taxi and directed it to stop at Parliament House (cf PL cll 2.4, 2.5) are incorrect. 427

## G.2 A Snapshot in Time: Things We Know as to the Position as at 1:40am

I previously commenced a defamation judgment (*Oliver v Nine Network Australia Pty Ltd* [2019] FCA 583 (at [1]–[2])) by referring to the saw that "nothing good happens after two o'clock in the morning" and observing it reflected the wisdom that "drink and the wee hours often occasions trouble". 428

Here too there was a combination of drink and the wee hours, and it led, on any view of it, to trouble: but before we examine what that trouble entailed, it is worth pausing to consider what was likely in the minds of one man and one woman who found themselves being conveyed by an unknown Uber driver to Parliament House shortly before twenty to two in the morning. 429

Dealing *first* with Mr Lehrmann, he had been attracted to Ms Higgins for a while and, for the first time, had just been able to kiss the object of his attraction passionately, placed his hand intimately on her leg and thigh, and had his physical displays of affection requited. 430

*Secondly*, as is reflected by what had just taken place, he was a man who had already acted unfaithfully towards his girlfriend by the standards of right-thinking people and had no scruples about doing so again that evening. 431

*Thirdly*, he likely wanted to continue to be intimate with Ms Higgins. Put bluntly, he was a 23-year-old male cheating on his girlfriend, having just "hooked up" with a woman he found sexually attractive. Human 432 experience suggests what he then wanted to happen is not exactly shrouded in mystery.

433 *Fourthly*, Mr Lehrmann had been drinking, and he knew Ms Higgins was inebriated – indeed, as I have explained, he had encouraged Ms Higgins' consumption of alcohol; and although he may not have understood precisely how alcohol affects the cerebral cortex of the brain and works to impair cognitive and psychomotor functions, like most young men, he must have known that excessive alcohol consumption leads to impaired judgment, and lowered inhibitions.

434 *Fifthly*, he could not go to his place (for obvious reasons), and if he wanted to continue to be intimate with Ms Higgins, he knew this was best done at a place he could access and where they could be alone; of course, he knew such a place, being the Minister's office at Parliament House.

435 *Sixthly*, he would have been buoyed by getting Ms Higgins into an Uber and securing her agreement to come back to the Ministerial Suite by telling her something along the lines of: "that he had some whisky to show [her] or something" (T1180.41–45).

436 *Seventhly*, he would have thought the presence of whisky in the Ministerial Suite made it a perfect location and a better option than suggesting going back to Ms Higgins' shared accommodation (as Parliament House afforded the opportunity of continuing to drink whisky, which would only assist his aim of continued or enhanced intimacy). Incidentally, this probably means his comment about seeing his whisky had a broader significance than just being Mr Lehrmann's functional equivalent of a clichéd pick-up line used by men of ill intention to lure women to a private place.

437 *Eighthly*, in the light of the above, commonsense suggests that it is obvious there was one dominant thought running through the mind of Mr Lehrmann as he was approaching Parliament House, and it was nothing to do with French submarine contracts.

438 Then we have Ms Higgins.

439 She was in a very different and potentially difficult position. She was working in a professional office where she correctly perceived Mr Lehrmann as having greater power and, in fact, he had been dealing with her as a subordinate. Earlier in the evening she felt Mr Lehrmann was "nice to me for the first time and I was pleased with how it was going" (T617.22–26)

and felt "like an equal", like they were "peers almost" (T617.25–31). She wanted to get on with him and, moreover, was keen to interact – even at the expense of abandoning her date. She was drunk and had been drunk for some time and, for whatever combination of reasons, she had not only not rebuffed the advances of Mr Lehrmann, but had reciprocated in the manner described by Ms Gain.

Given the state of the evidence, apart from the uncertainties of trying to draw conclusions from what one can gauge impressionistically from the Parliamentary CCTV, how keen Ms Higgins was to go back to Parliament House is difficult to tell. But even if she found the prospect a tad unwelcome, going back was understandable, as like many professionals the subject of an advance by a work colleague with more power, Ms Higgins did not want to alienate someone she perceived could be of real importance to her career. If she agreed to go back somewhat reluctantly, it would have been for a reason not dissimilar as to why she made light of the incident three weeks earlier, when Mr Lehrmann had taken her mobile phone when she was trying to leave the Kingo. In this regard, there is no evidence Ms Higgins was aware that Mr Lehrmann had already decided to move on from working with the Minister. 440

In any event, she agreed to go to Parliament House after Mr Lehrmann had said he "had some whisky to show [her] or something"; but the extent of her genuine enthusiasm and whether in her affected state she thought she was just going back for a drink, or whether she thought the reference to whisky was simply a pretext for more intimacy, is difficult to tell (and, in the end, does not really matter). Notably, Ms Wilkinson submits that it may be (having regard to Ms Higgins' interactions with Mr Lehrmann at 88mph) that "it was [Ms Higgins] intention to have sexual intercourse with [Mr Lehrmann] at that time and that she no longer recalls that given her level of intoxication" and that this "would be one explanation why she exited with [Mr Lehrmann] at [Parliament House] rather than staying in the Uber and going home by herself". 441

It is also worth noting, before we go on, a number of the above matters bring into sharp focus the central importance of my findings based on the acceptance of the independent evidence of both Ms Gain (as to what occurred earlier that night) and Major Irvine (being the recipient of a recounting by Ms Higgins of what occurred around four days later) and, 442 as I will explain, are consistent with other representations made by both Mr Lehrmann and Ms Higgins in the immediate wake of the incident.

## G.3 Security and Entry to the Ministerial Suite

443 Upon arrival at the gate to the entry into Parliament House, Mr Lehrmann pressed the intercom and said: "Oh, hi mate. Bruce Lehrmann here with Minister Linda Reynolds. *We've* been requested to pick up some documents. I've forgotten my pass" (Ex 16; T306.40–42). I emphasise the word "we've" because during the trial it was often said "[I've] been requested ..." (T123.36), but it is clear upon listening closely to Ex 16 that Mr Lehrmann uses the word "we've".

444 The reason for this lie, according to Mr Lehrmann, was that if he had suggested his reason for returning to Parliament House was to collect his keys, security would "have thought that was a minor thing" and told him to "bugger off and come back next week" (T351.14–34). I do not accept this speculative evidence and notably this suggestion was never put to the security guards for their comment.

445 A further flaw in Mr Lehrmann's account is that although he says he thought Ms Higgins had some unarticulated reason to access Parliament House, he never ascertained whether she had a security pass or a better reason to enter, which would have obviated his reason to lie (T310.1–19).

446 Ms Higgins recalled getting out of the car and walking to the "Point 8" entrance to the back of Parliament House. She says she could not recall why she had got out of the car; she gave the evidence that she just thought that because Mr Lehrmann had got out, she should too (T622.17–22). But I do not accept this evidence – as I have explained, she knew she was going to the Ministerial Suite and had acquiesced in doing so.

447 At around 1:41am on 23 March 2019, Mr Lehrmann and Ms Higgins came into Point 8 (Fairweather (at [9]); Anderson (at [11]); Ex 17 (at 01:41:43)). Ms Higgins could not remember much conversation between her and the security guards (T623.17–18).

448 The evidence of one of the security guards, Ms Nikola Anderson, was that she paid particular attention to Ms Higgins because she thought she looked nice, and she noticed that she had what appeared to be grass stains down one side of her dress (Anderson (at [12])). She also recorded in her

later incident report that she was advised "that [Mr Lehrmann and Ms Higgins] had urgent business that needed tending to" (Ex R67).

The evidence of the other security officer, Mr Mark Fairweather, was that he had previously seen Mr Lehrmann and Ms Higgins at Parliament House, but he did not know their names; and that Mr Lehrmann told him: "We're here to do some work" and that [Mr Lehrmann and Ms Higgins] had to go to Senator Reynolds Suite" (Fairweather (at [12], [14]–[15]); T307.39–47). Mr Fairweather was able to confirm relevant details as to Mr Lehrmann and Ms Higgins from computer records (Fairweather (at [16]–[21]); Anderson (at [17]–[19])). But they were required to fill out the visitor pass register, and Mr Fairweather's evidence (corroborated by the CCTV footage) was that Mr Lehrmann completed the register for himself and for Ms Higgins (Fairweather (at [22]–[27], [61]); T1172.42–45). 449

Bizarrely, Mr Lehrmann denied signing the register on behalf of Ms Higgins, but accepted that at no point is Ms Higgins recorded as bending down to write anything on the visitor pass register (as seemed to be initially suggested by Ms Anderson). One does not need the assistance of an expert to be confident the handwriting in the register is the same for both relevant entries (Ex R2). 450

Mr Fairweather recalled a general smell of alcohol but did not think that the visitors were overly affected (by which he meant slurring, falling over, vomiting level drunk) so as to be refused entry (Fairweather (at [29]–[32], [62])). He considered the scale of intoxication to be "very moderate" and not "heavily intoxicated" because otherwise he would have refused entry (T1172.4–27). Mr Fairweather, although an experienced security guard, was not a breathalyser in human form. He said at the time they were "half pissed" (Ex R69). I have no doubt his evidence was given genuinely, but without prolonged examination and complete information as to what had occurred earlier in the evening (and although Mr Lehrmann may only have been "half pissed"), he mistakenly but honestly underestimated the extent of the intoxication of Ms Higgins. Similarly, Ms Anderson realised Ms Higgins was intoxicated after she observed her struggling to get her shoes back on coming through the metal detector (Anderson (at [27]–[28])) and later recorded this observation in her incident report (Ex R67). 451

452 I pause to note that the trenchant criticism of Ms Anderson and Mr Fairweather in the submissions of Network Ten is both unfair and over the top. Those submissions censoriously assert that "Mr Lehrmann and Ms Higgins ought to have been denied entry to Parliament House having regard to their state upon arrival, or they ought to have been supervised when going to the Ministerial Suite and then immediately escorted out" and the security guards "are open to criticism" and letting them in "was a very serious misjudgement on their part".

453 These prim criticisms were never put to them for their comment, and as anyone with the life experience of being in pubs frequently would readily understand, drunk people are often able to compose themselves for a fleeting or short interaction and it is often difficult to form an immediate and accurate view as to the extent of intoxication of a person with whom one has not had any extended contact. I have little doubt that what happened with staff obtaining entry this night was no different than what would happen if staff presented themselves in the same way at entry points of countless professional offices throughout the country. On the information the security guards had available to them, they had no concerns that something untoward was going to happen. After having had the benefit of hearing them in the witness box, I have no doubt the security guards were conscientiously trying to do their jobs and the submissions critical of them, which smack of both hindsight distortion and Grundyism, ought not to be accepted.

454 In any event, Mr Lehrmann and Ms Higgins then proceeded to put personal items into trays that went through a security scanner. Mr Lehrmann walked through a metal detector and Ms Higgins followed him. The metal detector was activated twice by Ms Higgins (Ex 17 (at 01:45:02–12)) and Ms Anderson realised the culprit was Ms Higgins' shoes. Ms Higgins then returned through the metal detector and removed her shoes. She put her shoes in a white tray and pushed the tray through the scanning machine. She came through the metal detector without wearing her shoes, and it was not activated (Ex 17 (at 01:45:50)).

455 The CCTV then records Ms Higgins making unsuccessful attempts to put on her shoes. Ms Anderson then said: "Don't worry about it, just carry your shoes. It's okay but put them on when you get up there" (Anderson (at [29])); Ms Higgins then collected her items from the tray and hurried through a set of double doors towards the lift (Ex 17 (at 01:46:57)). I have

no doubt that Ms Higgins' inability to put on her shoes was caused by her state of inebriation. This is consistent with her walking barefoot through Parliament House, and then tossing her head back and looking towards the ceiling while she waited to be let into the Ministerial Suite (Ex 17 (at 01:47:56)).

It is worth pausing at this point in the narrative to make a miscellaneous point relevant to Mr Lehrmann's credit. Mr Lehrmann said he had two phones and a wallet with him for the whole evening (T92.5–6; T249.12; T316.6–9). In cross-examination, he denied having just one phone when he entered Parliament House and says that he took out both devices when he came through the security door (T250.21–251.4; T314.3–16). I am satisfied that a close review of the CCTV footage (Ex 17 (at 01:45:13–25)) establishes that Mr Lehrmann removed but one phone from the security tray. 456

Ms Anderson then escorted Mr Lehrmann and Ms Higgins to the Ministerial Suite, which she then opened with a key (Ex 17 (at 01:48:10); Anderson (at [35])). 457

## G.4 Whisky, and the Accounts of What Happened Inside the Ministerial Suite

I will set out each account and comment upon them before detailing my findings and coming to my conclusions below. Prior to doing so, however, it is worth making findings about whisky. 458

### *I The Whisky at the Office*

I am satisfied that being conscious of the importance of the whisky, Mr Lehrmann has made several false statements about this topic. 459

There is no doubt that Mr Lehrmann had at least three bottles of whisky and other alcoholic beverages in the old Senate office, which he moved to the Ministerial Suite (T196.33–38; Ex 29 and 30; T191.18–193.33). If it was ever in doubt, which it is not, Ms Hamer and Mr Wotton confirmed this was the case (T1061.7–9; Hamer (at [6]); Wotton 28 September 2023 (at [38])). Hence the terms of the invitation given to Ms Higgins to accompany him to the Ministerial Suite. 460

I am also satisfied that Mr Lehrmann gave deliberately false answers to the AFP during his 19 April 2021 interview when he said: "yeah, I didn't 461 have any alcohol in my office" (Ex 31, Q762) and that to his knowledge, there was no alcohol in the Ministerial Suite (Ex 31, Q754; T196.28–38). Importantly, when the AFP put to him that Ms Brown had told the AFP that: "he just came in to have a drink – to drink his whisky", Mr Lehrmann doubled down and asserted: "... there's no alcohol, I didn't have any alcohol, so, to access" (Ex 31, Q764).

462 Demonstrating his forensic difficulty with his representations concerning the Scottish libation, his evidence on this topic at trial was all over the shop. Despite saying in his evidence-in-chief that he had told Ms Brown that he "came back to drink some whisky or something like that" (T153.45–47), in cross-examination, Mr Lehrmann said that what in fact he had said to Ms Brown was that he "came back to have a drink" (T228.19–24). But he should have known this excuse would not fly as he had accepted that he told Ms Brown in their second meeting on 26 March 2019 that he went back to drink whisky (T228.26–32) and, as recently as June 2023, he had told the *Spotlight* programme (T228.42–229.48; Ex R16) that he had given Ms Brown the whisky excuse on 26 March 2019 (T230.1–20).

463 This is not just another unsatisfactory aspect of Mr Lehrmann's evidence. This is an important lie. It was his way of distancing himself from the rationale he had originally given for going to the Ministerial Suite, being the same reason conveyed to Ms Brown, immediately and spontaneously, when first confronted with having to account for his actions in the days after the incident. Moreover, it was a lie that had serious consequences, because with knowledge of the truth, he allowed his denial of having alcohol in his office to go uncorrected throughout his criminal trial, and allowed submissions to be advanced to the jury that the account he had given to police was truthful and accurate (T202.1–3). I hasten to add that I have no doubt his senior counsel acted in accordance with appropriate ethical constraints at the criminal trial, and so it must follow he did not apprise his own trial lawyers as to the true position.

### *II Mr Lehrmann's Account*

464 Turning to Mr Lehrmann's current account, as we know, he says he came back from a nightclub in the early hours of a Saturday morning to get his keys, but then decided to work on Question Time briefs prompted by information that he had received at The Dock. Despite its length, it is worth setting out his account given in chief (T142–145.30):

MR WHYBROW: Mr Lehrmann, you have already given evidence that you're in – you had come back to Parliament House to get your keys?---Yes.

What did you do when you reached the end of the line, or the route that you have drawn on that map?---I placed my phones down on my desk and I observed the Question Time folders opposite me.

Okay. Can you describe what that means?---So against the wall, I had carriage of about five or six Question Time briefing folders about the size of the court books here.

And are they documents that needed to be kept in a secure cabinet, or anything of that nature?---No, they're not.

What's the nature of a Question Time folder?---Primarily political in nature, to prepare a minister for Question Time and senate estimates that are also utilised for as well. As well as some media and other external things, if a minister was travelling to an event, we had a brief ready.

In relation to Senator Reynolds, did that encompass a single portfolio or a single subject area?---It did not.

And why was that?---In the Senate, senators who are ministers have representing arrangements as well, and Senator Reynolds still had carriage of some of the Home Affairs portfolio as well, as she was still sworn, I believe, as the emergency management minister as well.

Okay. Now, you said that you saw these folders there on your desk?---Yes.

What happened?---Based on the conversations that I had at the dock, I took it upon myself to make some notes while it was fresh in my mind against various briefs in those folders.

What sort of briefs?---From my recollection, it was heavily focused on the submarine issue, given the political sensitivity at the time.

To your recollection, were there documents in any of those briefs relating to that subject?---Many, yes.

And what did you do?---I would have, to the best of my recollection, I would have firstly, identified the brief, read the briefs - - -

Sorry. I just want to ask, were you standing, sitting, or what did you do?---Sitting, yes.

Okay. And you said you put your phone down, or phones?---Yes.

***

MR WHYBROW: What happened?---I loaded up the Question Time folders, read the briefs, identified the relevant ones that were on my mind to make those notes.

My recollection was I didn't turn around – my computers were behind me at that point, because my desk was a U-shape.

What form did these notes take?---Either handwritten on the – on the brief itself or via Post It notes. The Question Time briefs had a pink overlay cover sheet that would go over the top of the departmental produced Question Time brief, so if I can explain. The Question Time brief would come up from the department in a raw form and a – policy advisors would then annotate and make notes and for certain politically sensitive issues, would put a pink slip over the top of that Question Time brief with political talking points, if you will.

Okay. And do you recall how long you spent doing this task?---My recollection was 30 to 40 minutes.

Okay. And did you finish that task?---Yes.

And what did you do when you finished it?---I turned around to my phones and saw that I had missed calls and got my keys and went out the back door.

Did you hear – sorry, I wanted to ask you this – were your phones, or was there any practice as to whether your phones were on loud, soft or anything?---They're always on silent.

***

When you were sitting at your desk, were you able to see what work Ms Higgins was doing?---No.

Okay. How far away was her workstation from yours, based on your recollection?---Centimetres, if you – you know, but behind – between a divider.

> Okay. During the time that you were at your desk, did you have any further interaction with Ms Higgins?---I did not, no.
>
> Did you hear her?---No.
>
> ***
>
> When you had finished annotating the Question Time briefs and you said you picked up your phone, what happened?---I - - -
>
> HIS HONOUR: Sorry, did you say phone?
>
> MR WHYBROW: Phones.
>
> HIS HONOUR: Yes.
>
> MR WHYBROW: Sorry, you said something about a phone after you had finished?---Yes, I had my work phone and my personal phone.
>
> Okay. Going back to having annotated the briefs, what happened then?---I ordered an Uber on one of my phones. I can't recall which one, whatever one had the Uber app.
>
> Okay, and what did you do then?---I exited the back door, right beside my desk and left.
>
> Did you make any inquiries as to the whereabouts of Ms Higgins? ---I did not.
>
> Why not?---I wasn't – I wasn't even sure that she was still there and I had indicated, as I entered as well, that I would get what I – what I need and head off. I thought that was sufficient.

### *III Consideration of the Account of Mr Lehrmann*

I have already said enough to indicate that I consider Mr Lehrmann's 465
account to be an elaborate fancy.

*First*, there are my findings as to what happened at 88mph, and the ratio- 466
nale given by Mr Lehrmann to have Ms Higgins come back to a private place at Parliament House. As I have already noted, put in stark terms, it is fanciful a somewhat lubricated male staffer accompanied by a woman he found attractive, who he had just been "pashing" in a nightclub despite having a girlfriend, would then be interested, after coming to a private place very late, to just say "cheerio", and then soberly proceed to note up briefs for a Question Time that was not to occur for one and a half weeks,

*a fortiori* when the staffer had already resigned; had no outstanding tasks; was not ordinarily involved in work concerning the Defence portfolio (T1424.39–42); and hitherto had demonstrated no outward signs of being a workaholic.

467 *Secondly*, even if we leave to one side my findings as to what was on Mr Lehrmann's mind, the account itself lacks coherence. Mr Lehrmann was unable to identify any information he obtained at The Dock (or 88mph) relevant to the work he was supposedly doing for the Minister on the Question Time folders (T387.30–33). He said that the only information that he could recall was about "the French submarine contract" (T387.36) but he was unable to specify who had provided him with information about the contract (T387.39; T388.1). I have already rejected his evidence that he was having detailed discussions about politically sensitive matters at The Dock with, among others, aides-de-camp (T388.32; T389.35).

468 *Thirdly*, and although less significant, Mr Lehrmann did not mention being so conscientious that he decided to work on Question Time folders early on a Saturday morning when asked what he was doing by Ms Brown or when he was later asked to show cause why he should not be terminated for serious misconduct by the Minister. Mr Lehrmann did not explain why he had not raised his supposed diligence other than he thought Ms Brown would be more concerned about someone coming back to the office doing work. Although I appreciate that Ms Brown would have escalated the security breach in the event Mr Lehrmann had accessed sensitive work information, if Mr Lehrmann had, in truth, been working manually in recording important information, one assumes there would have been ways of painting this information more favourably than coming back to the office for no reason other than to luxuriate while imbibing strong liquor.

469 *Fourthly*, it is not lost on me that doing manual marking up on paper with a pen, moving documents around or sticking tabs on paper is perhaps the only work that would not require Mr Lehrmann to log into a computer and leave some form of retrievable electronic record. I do not believe I am being unduly cynical to remark that this strikes me as being convenient.

470 *Fifthly*, it may be a minor point in the scheme of things, but if we are to assume that Mr Lehrmann had shared an Uber with Ms Higgins and understood she was attending to some unexplained work task early on

Saturday morning, why would Mr Lehrmann just bolt from the office after attending to his tasks without attempting to extend the courtesy of checking whether she was there or saying he was going? One would expect a man with any manners faced with the possibility he was leaving a young woman late at night and unaccompanied, who he knew had been drinking, would check whether she had gone and, if not, how she was getting home safely; but it suffices for present purposes to say that Mr Lehrmann's account, as to this aspect alone, is intuitively odd.

*Sixthly*, and importantly, there is the contradiction between this account and what he first told Ms Brown before there was any allegation of sexual assault. As noted at [276] above, he first represented to Ms Brown he did not access any documents, he came back to drink whisky, and had a whisky with Ms Higgins. 471

All in all, I accept the submission made by Network Ten that Mr Lehrmann's evidence about writing on Question Time folders was a "transparent lie, and yet it remains the only explanation Mr Lehrmann has offered to this Court for his presence in the Ministerial Suite for 40 minutes on 23 March 2019". It also is unsurprising that Mr Lehrmann made his spontaneous and telling comment noted earlier to Ms Brown a couple of days later when asked "what else [did you do] while in the office?", Mr Lehrmann replied "I don't wish to get into that" (T2052.4–5). 472

### *IV Ms Higgins' Account*

Ms Higgins has no recollection of being escorted to the Ministerial Suite and did not even know there had been a security guard accompanying her and Mr Lehrmann. Her first memory within the Suite was sitting on a ledge, being the ledge by the windows overlooking the Prime Minister's Courtyard (T626.19–22). 473

She initially said she sat on the ledge for a "long period of time" (T626.38–41). The evidence Ms Higgins would just sit there for a "long" period alone when, according to her account, Mr Lehrmann had said to her (and she understood) that he was just picking something up immediately struck me as strange, and I asked her to clarify it as follows (T627.17): 474

> HIS HONOUR: ... you said you have a recollection of being there I think you mentioned for a long period?---It could have been five minutes.

475 Very soon thereafter, the evidence-in-chief changed as Dr Collins KC went back to the topic, and the following exchange took place:

> DR COLLINS: Okay. And I think you said to his Honour you don't have a recollection of how long you were there?---No, I'm not sure. It could have been a minute, but it – for me, it – I thought we were going in and out quickly, so it probably wasn't a very long period of time.

476 Later, in cross-examination, Mr Whybrow also explored this issue and the following exchange occurred (T954–5):

> MR WHYBROW: You have a recollection of waiting for some period of time for Mr Lehrmann?---Yes, but when I say "a long time", I feel like it was – it was, like, minutes, like, but in my mind, it felt like a long time.
>
> Right. You don't like the words "long time" now, do you? And you want to make it minutes, do you?---No, it's just – I've used the word "a long time", a lot, and people have issue with it, because they don't understand the context in which I'm trying to convey, so I have to be more specific, especially now in this field. So it felt like a long time to drunk me, but realistically, it was, like, minutes.

477 Later, Mr Whybrow put to Ms Higgins that she had previously said to Ms Wilkinson that (T961.21):

> I remember he was, sort of, taking a really long time with something. I don't know, it felt like he was taking a really long time. And I was sitting on the ledge of the office, sort of, windows that overlook the Prime Minister's courtyard, and was feeling – I was feeling very out of it and so I got to the point where – I don't know if he guided me there or if I went by myself – went the myself – but I ended up lying down and passing out on the Minister's couch.
>
> ?---Yes. And I'm saying that on the basis that I woke up on the couch with your client raping me - - -
>
> Yes, you've said - - -?--- - - - so I was on the couch.

478 In any event, for reasons that were unclear in her inebriated state, she was apparently alone for some period (being variously a really long time, or a long time, or five minutes and it just "felt" long, or it was a minute) and

she did not understand where Mr Lehrmann had gone and why she was still at Parliament and wanted to go home.

She also said she was looking for Mr Lehrmann and was not able to see him (T628.1–5) and because he was not within eyeshot (and therefore not at his desk), she speculated he was either in the kitchen or the DLO area (T627.5–9; T954.18–45). She denied that she sat at the ledge in the Minister's office (T956.4–5). 479

In her account in chief before me, her memory is then blank. She had said to Ms Wilkinson (T961.21) that she "was feeling very out of it and so I got to the point where … I ended up lying down and passing out on the Minister's couch". She had also said to Ms Maiden (Ex 50 (at 6–7)) that she was sitting on one of "these little window ledges that face into the Prime Minister's Courtyard" and then had the following exchange (Ex 50 (at 7)): 480

*Ms Maiden*:

And what was he doing?

*Ms Higgins*:

I don't know, a really …

*Ms Maiden*:

Yeah, you don't remember, no.

*Ms Higgins*:

> **No, but I just remember I was laying down on the Minister's couch. So I was really, really drunk and the world felt like it was spinning and I thought I was going to die …**

Ms Higgins at trial denied she remembered (that is, had a real memory) of laying down on the Minister's couch in the private office, although the above extract has a degree of tension with this evidence. Before me, after being on the ledge, the next thing Ms Higgins said she remembers (or, as she put it, the next "touchpoint") is only when she awakes on the Minister's couch. 481

Despite its length and graphic nature, it is appropriate to set out her next memories in some detail. She explained (T628.23–28): 482

> So the first thing I remember when I woke up was a pain in my leg; that was the thing that kind of stirred me up. Bruce was on top of me. I was – so my head was in the back corner of the couch. He was on top of me, his arms were over the top of the couch. He was having sex with me at that point in time. And that was what I first woke up to at that point in time and is, like, the next touchpoint that I have. It's the next thing.

483 She was asked to describe where her head was located on the couch. She said (T628.36–40):

> I was lodged in between the armrest and the back of the couch. My head was jammed in the corner and he was on top of me, over – he wasn't looking at me, he was lurched over the top of me. I was spread open and exposed. I had one leg open, on the side of the couch, and then one open, which is where his knee was, in my leg.

484 After being asked to further describe what she recollected, Ms Higgins went on (T629.29–45):

> I told him "No", on a loop. I don't know how many times I said it. I told him to stop. I couldn't – I couldn't scream for some reason. I don't know, it was just, like, trapped in my throat; I couldn't do it. I know I felt really, like, waterlogged and heavy and I couldn't – I couldn't move. I was under the impression it had been going on for, like a little bit of time. I used the expression, like, "I was – I was late to the party". Yes, I felt like it had been going on for a little while and I was only, kind of, coming to right at the end.
>
> I just – it seemed like he was going quite fast and he kind of seemed a bit sweaty, or I don't know, maybe I was the one who was sweaty. But it, like, it wasn't – there was no, like – there was no, like – it – he was very much in the throes of it. It was very much rough and happening, and it didn't matter that I was talking or awake or whatever, it just felt like he was doing it and – like, it didn't matter, like I was an afterthought, like, he was – it felt like he was going to climax soon, or, like it had been going on for a while and that he was – I don't know. I don't know if "speeding up" is the right word, I don't know. Yes, that's – that was my impression at the time. Yes.

Pausing the narrative in chief for a moment, it is useful to refer to some evidence given in cross-examination, where Ms Higgins said (T962.29–963.6): 485

> MR WHYBROW: You've given evidence to his Honour that when you were, on your evidence, being sexually assaulted by Mr Lehrmann, your head was towards the door?---Yes.
>
> And you previously gave evidence in the trial that his knee was on your leg - - -?---Yes.
>
> - - - whilst he was penetrating you?---Yes.
>
> And you asserted that the bruise photograph was caused by that conduct?---It hurt. I had a bruise and made an assumption, but I – I – I have to accept that it may not have been from that.
>
> Okay. And do you recall that when you gave your evidence before the jury and you were describing these events, you were describing that this knee on your thigh was on your left thigh?---I didn't remember the left or right, but my head was in the corner. One was up against the couch and one was spread open, and so that would have been the left side, yes.
>
> And the photograph that you have provided was a photograph of your right thigh?---Yes.
>
> Okay. And I take it you have no recollection of turning around?---Not in the middle of the night, but I know – not in the middle of the night. I don't recall moving in my sleep when I was passed out after the rape.

Going back to her account in chief, Dr Collins adduced the following evidence (T630.1–31): 486

> DR COLLINS: You said you couldn't scream; did you try?---I don't know, I just – I couldn't – like, you think of a scream and you, like, want to – it didn't come out. I was saying "No" and I was telling him to stop, and there was an urgency to it, but I couldn't – I couldn't, like, scream like you see in, like, the horror movies, like, I couldn't – I don't know. I don't know why I couldn't.
>
> To your recollection, did Mr Lehrmann respond to you asking him to stop?---No, he didn't even acknowledge it.

> You said you had the impression he was close to a climax. Do you have a recollection of how the incident ended?---I don't know, but I – I believe he finished and I believe he finished inside of me.
>
> Why do you have that belief?---I don't know. I just – it stopped suddenly and I don't remember him – I don't remember it being anywhere else, or him – I just remember when he stopped, it stopped and he got off me.
>
> And sorry to press it, but can you describe where your legs where at the time of the - - -?---Yes.
>
> - - - the sex?---So I was laying down. My head was obviously in the back, and my legs were pinned open. So he was on top of me. One leg was kind of pinned against the side of the couch and the other one was pinned open. And all of a sudden, once he finished, he stopped and he got off me. So I don't believe he came anywhere else but inside of me.
>
> And when he stopped, do you have a recollection of what he did? ---I remember him getting up. And I didn't say anything at that point. And he looked at me and then he left.
>
> Did any – was there any words spoken?---No, we didn't say anything.

487 Ms Higgins then recalled Mr Lehrmann leaving (either through the back exit or the back slip door) and after Mr Lehrmann had left that she: "couldn't get up off the couch. I don't know if it was, like, shock, or if I was just so drunk that I physically couldn't get up, but I couldn't pick up my body off the couch. And then I passed out" (T630.38–40; T631.31–32). She did not want to be there, but she could not get up and did not know why (T630.42–44).

488 Ms Higgins said that her breasts and bottom half were exposed. She was not sure where her dress was, but it was conceivable that it was around her waist, or it may have been taken off (T631.18-20; T631.27–29).

### *V Consideration of the Account of Ms Higgins*

489 The first thing to be said about Ms Higgins' account is that it involves a grave allegation by a witness with general credibility problems and whose contentious evidence, in accordance with the fact-finding principles explained above in Section E, must be approached with great care. But by

reference to my findings as to the circumstances in which Mr Lehrmann and Ms Higgins found themselves, taken as a whole, it does not strike me as inherently implausible (unlike the account of Mr Lehrmann).

Before drawing conclusions as to the extent to which this account should be accepted, three matters merit particular focus. This is despite these matters not being the subject of detailed submissions from Mr Lehrmann (because of the case theory of no contact adopted by him). 490

*First*, as my findings establish, Ms Higgins' account commences with a false characterisation of how it is she came back to the Ministerial Suite in the first place. As Ms Gain made plain, she had "hooked up" with Mr Lehrmann, and what occurred thereafter must be viewed in the light of the fact that Ms Higgins had been in a nightclub being intimate with Mr Lehrmann and had then agreed to accompany him. 491

*Secondly*, and relatedly, is the pretext of coming back, being what Mr Lehrmann had said to her about whisky – she did not accompany Mr Lehrmann to the Suite just to sit passively on a ledge for a very long period (or a short period, or something in between) for no apparent reason waiting for a person who had wandered off (unless, of course, it was to grab the whisky and some glasses, a task which would have taken no time at all). 492

*Thirdly*, and in a quite different category, is a subtle tension between Ms Higgins' various accounts of the assault. As I said at the commencement of these reasons, the surest guide to what went on are the probabilities arising from the logic of events, the testimony of independent and honest witnesses, and contemporaneous and apparently candid representations. Falling within the last two of these categories, is the evidence of two assertions made by Ms Higgins, being a representation: 493

(1) made only three days after the incident, and immediately after Mr Payne had asked "Did he rape you?", being her immediate and spontaneous response: "I could not have consented. **It would have been like f**king a log**" (T1422.39–43);

(2) with her ex-boyfriend (noted in above Section F.7), again just days after the incident, where in response to his direct question "Did you hook up in there or did someone take advantage of you?", Ms Higgins replied: "Yeah, **it was just Bruce and I from what I recall. I was barely lucid. I really don't feel like it was consensual at all**" (Ex R99 (at 695)).

494 These representations, which suggest she was passive and hence incapable of consenting, reflect an interaction somewhat different from one where Ms Higgins had repeatedly, and unequivocally, said "no on a loop". This must be qualified by noting that consistently with the notion of passivity, there was alleged immobility, in that she also said at trial (as I have reproduced in context above), that she: "couldn't scream for some reason ... it was just, like, trapped in my throat; I couldn't do it. I know I felt really, like, waterlogged and heavy and I couldn't – I couldn't move"; and later: "I couldn't, like, scream like you see in, like, the horror movies, like, I couldn't – I don't know. I don't know why I couldn't" (T629).

495 In pointing this out, I am conscious that shortly after the incident, on 1 April 2019, Ms Higgins also told AFP officers that "Bruce had said something about finishing – I said something about "no don't" or "no don't" (Ex R77 (at 4)). As I will explain, however, this was said by Ms Higgins while she was conveying a number of untruths to AFP officers which seemed to paint her actions in what she, at the time, perceived to be a better light and at a time she was not intending to proceed with a criminal complaint.

496 What is one to make of this?

497 It might have been said to be a possible pointer to a lack of reliability of this aspect of her evidence given at trial, but the point was not relied upon by those acting for Mr Lehrmann, presumably because what commonsense and the agreed facts go some way in explaining is that a tension or inconsistency of this type must not be dealt with superficially and there may be an entirely benign explanation for its existence.

498 If Ms Higgins had been the victim of the assault she recounted, this could simply reflect the lability and frailty of memory following such an event and how someone can come to process trauma and later recount a consolidated memory of a highly distressing incident which has come to dominate her life in recent times. Whatever the truth of what happened, I have little doubt Ms Higgins' current account at trial reflects how I expect she would have wanted to act in such a situation, that is, to demonstrate active and repeated resistance to her assaulter.

499 I will come back to this issue, but before leaving it, it is worth recalling her almost ebullient reaction when told the news by Ms Maiden that Mr Lehrmann denied that any sex took place and, as she said in chief (T703.22):

> DR COLLINS: And just explain what was going through your mind as you heard for the first time that Mr Lehrmann's position was that he had not had any sexual contact with you?---I was really relieved. **I thought that, like, we were going to have this very nuanced debate about consent and alcohol and all this kind of stuff,** and I was really shocked and kind of happy at the time that he was saying that nothing had happened, because to my mind it was so preposterous ...

There is, of course, no nuanced debate about consent if a woman repeatedly says no and a man proceeds on regardless. Or, going back to the words Ms Higgins used to Mr Dillaway, there is no need in such circumstances to only "feel like" what happened was not consensual. There is, however, the real possibility of some form of nuanced debate if a woman is barely lucid, she later processes what occurred, and she realises she has been assaulted while initially lacking proper awareness of what was going on. 500

## G.5 Findings as to What Occurred in the Ministerial Suite

Having made a series of factual findings leading up to the entry of Mr Lehrmann and Ms Higgins into the Ministerial Suite, identified what had motivated them to come back to the Suite, and as to aspects of their accounts of what then occurred, in this section I will: *first*, identify and consider five incontrovertible facts; *secondly*, summarise my findings as to the condition of Ms Higgins in the Suite; *thirdly*, identify post-incident events not already dealt with that might rationally bear upon what happened in the Suite; and *fourthly*, state my conclusions. 501

### *I Five Incontrovertible Facts*

It is worth commencing this aspect of my reasons by identifying some matters relevant to what happened that are indubitably true, and then draw some logical and direct inferences from those facts. 502

*First*, is that Mr Lehrmann and Ms Higgins were alone in the Ministerial Suite for about 40 minutes between 1:48 and 2:30am. 503

*Secondly*, during this time, Mr Lehrmann did not answer six telephone calls from his girlfriend between 2:16 and 2:18am (T320.16; Ex R85A). 504

*Thirdly*, at about 2:33am, Mr Lehrmann departed alone through the security gate and was collected by an Uber (Ex 17 (at 02:33:18); Fairweather (at [42])). 505

506 *Fourthly*, immediately after, or shortly after Mr Lehrmann left, Ms Higgins, having been affected by alcohol, fell into a very deep sleep on the couch in the Suite in a state of undress. Indeed, in this regard, as Mr Lehrmann accepts in his final submissions, Ms Higgins, at some time, "passed out ... in the Minister's suite".

507 *Fifthly*, given no-one had seen Ms Higgins leave, it was decided between Mr Fairweather, Ms Anderson and Mr Kevin Callan, their supervisor, that Ms Anderson should go up to the Minister's office to do a "welfare check" (Anderson (at [39]–[43]); Fairweather (at [51]–[54])); which she then did, and at about 4:20am, Ms Anderson:

(1) entered the Suite shouting "Security, hello security" (Anderson (at [45]));

(2) went to the door of the Minister's office and said "Security. Hello? Security" and there was no answer (Anderson (at [45]));

(3) opened the door to the Minister's office and then saw Ms Higgins lying on her back on the couch in a state of undress such that she saw Ms Higgins' vagina and Ms Higgins' knees were up and slightly apart (Anderson (at [46]–[49]); T1166.15–20);

(4) Ms Higgins opened her eyes and looked at Ms Anderson but then proceeded to roll into the foetal position (Anderson (at [50]–[55])).

508 I have deliberately used the term "state of undress" because there is some question as to whether Ms Higgins was fully naked, which I will resolve below, but with that qualification, all the matters specified above are not in contest.

509 What one can directly infer from these incontrovertible facts is that: (a) there was sufficient time for Mr Lehrmann and Ms Higgins to continue to drink whisky together and/or to have coitus; (b) Mr Lehrmann was either engaged in sexual intercourse, conduct preparatory to this act, or some other activity between 2:16 and 2:18am and did not appreciate his girlfriend was calling him, or was aware of the calls but ignored them; (c) by the end of the 40 minutes, Ms Higgins was sufficiently affected by alcohol not to leave the Suite to go home but in her state had come to be lying naked or semi-naked on the couch; and (d) one hour and fifty minutes

later, Ms Higgins was, although not in obvious distress, sufficiently discombobulated that when seen by a uniformed stranger, did not interact verbally and did not move immediately to recover her modesty by putting on her dress or covering herself.

I now turn to making findings as to Ms Higgins' condition at the critical time, which, for reasons I will explain, I regard as being towards the end of the 40-minute period and shortly before Mr Lehrmann left, that is, around 2:20am or thereabouts (or about two hours prior to being found by Ms Anderson). 510

### *II The Condition of Ms Higgins in the Suite*

Dr Robertson's video observations of Ms Higgins half an hour earlier (at around 1:50am) were that she exhibited no "obvious" signs of intoxication in the sense of being able to walk through the check point unassisted, although he observed that: (a) she was required to support herself by holding on to the table when seeking to put her shoes back on (T1997.8–13) (Ex R877 (at [3.4])); and (b) at this stage, it was likely that Ms Higgins had developed some acute tolerance to alcohol and, as such, was likely to appear less intoxicated, particularly if her Blood Alcohol Content (**BAC**) (being a measure of alcohol in the blood as a percentage calculated in grams per 100 millilitre of blood) was falling at this time (Ex R877 (at [3.4])). 511

Dr Robertson was asked to opine on the likelihood of Ms Higgins falling asleep having regard to her level of intoxication between 1:50am and 2:15am. Dr Robertson's evidence (on the highly contestable and conservative assumptions as to the extent of drinking at 88mph and that drinking ended at or shortly prior to 1:30am), was that it is likely that at 1:50am and 2:15am, Ms Higgins' BAC would have peaked and was likely falling. Assuming a BAC of approximately 0.25% and a falling BAC, the effects of alcohol would likely have included sedation and increased tiredness, and would have increased the likelihood of falling asleep (Ex 877 (at [3.6]–[3.7])). 512

Despite the efforts of both parties to lend a patina of precision to what in truth is an inherently imprecise exercise based wholly upon assumptions, it is impossible to be certain as to Ms Higgins' BAC as at about 2:20am. What is far more important than any pinpoint BAC (which we will never know with certainty), is her general condition, that is, how her level of 513 drunkenness affected her early that morning, and how I find it would have appeared to Mr Lehrmann.

514 I have already made findings that as early as four hours before, Ms Higgins was sufficiently affected such that the CCTV shows her losing her balance and stepping backwards to maintain balance (and there are later but less obvious indications recorded on the CCTV of her being less than entirely steady on her feet). CCTV suggests Mr Lehrmann must have been aware of at least one incident at The Dock demonstrating a lack of balance, and things then progressed (see above at [397]). He knew she was drinking excessively. It was evident to Ms Gain that Ms Higgins was drunk, and I am satisfied that the same observation would have been made by any sentient person observing her over an *extended* period.

515 Further, and importantly, there is the evidence I accept of Ms Gain, that Ms Higgins fell over, and Mr Lehrmann helped her to her feet and back into the seating booth. It must have been obvious to anyone that had seen (and been a party to) this incident that alcohol consumption had decreased Ms Higgins' motor co-ordination, and whatever may have been her precise BAC, she was seriously inebriated.

516 One then comes to the question of what happened in the Ministerial Suite. Intuitively, given what had been happening, one would think it likely the drinking continued given what we know about Mr Lehrmann encouraging Ms Higgins to imbibe and the rationale given by him for them both to come back to the Suite. After all, Mr Lehrmann said he was going to show Ms Higgins *whisky* – not Qing Dynasty ceramics. Moreover, very shortly after the incident, and before any allegation of sexual assault was made, Mr Lehrmann represented to Ms Brown (Annexure B) that he came back to drink whisky and ended up drinking two glasses; "chatted" with Ms Higgins but "didn't wish to get into" anything else they did; and said "they [that is, Ms Higgins and Mr Lehrmann] had a whisky".

517 Despite these contemporaneous representations, additional drinking with Ms Higgins in the Ministerial Suite was not put to Mr Lehrmann in cross-examination because Dr Collins embraced the account given by Ms Higgins as to why she came back to Parliament House, which I have rejected. Mr Whybrow did not put additional drinking to Ms Higgins because it was the antithesis of his case theory. This is a good illustration

of the difficulties with fact-finding when the only two witnesses to an event do not tell the whole truth. If I had my druthers, I would have liked to have seen Mr Lehrmann tested on his previous representations as to drinking with Ms Higgins and to hear Ms Higgins' response, but I understand forensically why that was not the case. Although I strongly suspect that additional joint drinking did take place in the Ministerial Suite, it is unnecessary for me to make a positive finding.

There is, of course, other evidence as to intoxication. There are the various assertions of Ms Higgins that her intoxication was "worse than even the worst night at schoolies" and "10 out of 10 drunk" (T927.38–45) and those of Mr Lehrmann downplaying her level of intoxication. Given my concerns as to the self-serving nature of this testimony, it is unsafe to place any significant weight upon this evidence, save to the extent that I accept Ms Higgins' inherently probable evidence that she felt very drunk. 518

There is also the important CCTV footage of Ms Higgins entering Parliament House at about 1:45am (Ex 17) and walking through security. Mr Lehrmann submits this demonstrates Ms Higgins: (a) walked in a straight line through the metal detectors wearing high heels twice; (b) bent over multiple times without falling over or stumbling, including once bending from the hip and standing on one foot without any support; (c) skipped along the corridor to catch up to Mr Lehrmann; (d) smiled and acknowledged someone out of shot and acknowledged a security guard; and (e) did not fall over or need to be carried through security. 519

This is all substantially true, but drunk people sometimes walk in a roughly straight line, and it also shows Ms Higgins trying to put her shoes back on (which, I presume would not be a complex task), struggling for a considerable period and steadying herself against the security desk. Her difficulty was so obvious that Ms Anderson called out to her: "Don't worry about it, just carry your shoes. It's okay but put them on when you get up there" (Anderson (at [29])). Ms Higgins then gave up trying to put her shoes back on, collected her items from the tray and then Ms Higgins engaged in the unrestrained behaviour of skipping after Ms Anderson and Mr Lehrmann *sans* shoes (Ex 17 (at 01:46:57)). 520

During her entry, the CCTV footage demonstrates she was not paralytically drunk and was, at this time, able to function to a certain level. Consistently with this, the experienced Mr Fairweather let her in. But 521 understandably given the nature of his limited observations, he was not able to appreciate how far her cognition had been affected and, in particular, how her inhibitions and decision-making capacity had been impaired.

522 Unlike the security guards, but like Ms Gain on the night, we have an excellent idea of the extent of Ms Higgins' drinking and, taking all the evidence together, by 2:20am or so, I am comfortably satisfied that Ms Higgins was a very drunk 24-year-old woman, and her cognitive abilities were significantly impacted. Given this state and the late hour, it is highly likely she was prone to drowsiness. This is strongly supported by the fact, as Mr Lehrmann put it in his final submissions, that she "*passed out* naked in the Minister's suite" (emphasis added) and my finding she was still very significantly affected two hours after she was left alone.

523 Further, in the light of my findings as to Mr Lehrmann's conduct, I am also satisfied he was aware of her condition.

524 For completeness, I should mention that in Section I.2 below, I refer to a contemporaneous note of Assistant Commissioner Close of a meeting on 4 April, which contains a reference to "info that alleged victim may have been drugged". This representation is in evidence before me because no objection was made by Mr Lehrmann as to its admissibility, no application was made for its discretionary exclusion, nor was any application made for a limitation on its use under s 136 EA. Despite this, it is of such a speculative nature to have no probative value. No other suggestion of this type has been made in the evidence and no party has made submissions about this topic. In these circumstances, I ought to give it no weight and put it (and a related representation made in the same document as to any other incident) out of my mind.

### *III Post-incident Conduct*

525 It is next worth pausing to check the suggested counterintuitive behaviour pointed to by Mr Lehrmann that might rationally bear upon what happened in the Minister's office and any other relevant post-incident conduct. In this regard, it is, of course, necessary to again have regard to the agreed facts as to the effect of trauma and alcohol on recollection.

526 The events upon which most emphasis was placed were some exchanges between Mr Lehrmann and Ms Higgins immediately in the days following the incident, which commenced by Mr Lehrmann emailing Ms

Higgins eight hours after leaving Parliament House by forwarding a news summary with the following message (Ex 20):

> Might see about getting you on this list! :)

Ms Higgins did not read this message until Monday, 25 March (T638), 527
and also on that day, at 7:34am, Mr Lehrmann forwarded Ms Higgins another news summary with the following message (Ex 21):

> Not letting me send to private email! Will email David and get your gmail on the mail list!
>
> BL

Ms Higgins responded at 1:15pm in the following terms (Ex 21): 528

> So weird!
>
> Honestly, that would be the best if you could.

That morning, Mr Lehrmann purchased Ms Higgins an unsolicited cup 529
of coffee, left it on her desk, said it was for her and then kept walking (T325.30–43); notably Mr Lehrmann did not seek to repeat the suggestion he "went out" for a coffee with Ms Higgins (as he had told the *Spotlight* programme (T327.12–13)).

The next day, at 10:28am, Ms Higgins sent the "phoning a friend" email to 530
Mr Lehrmann asking for some help with a task in preparing some "portfolio stats" to "generate some [talking points]" to put into a campaign "prep pack" (Ex 22).

With regard to how she felt around this time, Ms Higgins gave evidence 531
that she was worried that Mr Lehrmann may have "gone around and told [people] we had had consensual sex", but that his normalising the situation (for example, by sending the emails) made her feel "weirdly relieved" because "it's my word against him, trying to verify that it was rape and that there was no consent" and she was not in a position to deal with having a fight about whether or not it had been consensual right at that moment (T639.28–44).

At best, I agree with the respondents that this evidence is essentially 532
neutral. The evidence is consistent with a rape not having occurred, but *on the assumption Ms Higgins was a victim*, this reaction does not offend commonsense. I have already explained why it was unnecessary for me to accept opinion evidence explaining the danger of making assumptions as

to the reliability of sexual assault complaints by reason of some *a priori* view as to how victims of sexual assault are expected to behave. Reasoning based upon so-called "typical" behaviour of genuine victims, such as shunning or exhibiting hostile behaviours towards the perpetrator or avoiding contact is superficial and distorts the process of fact-finding.

533 In considering the validity of Ms Higgins' allegation, I do not consider Ms Higgins' actions in accepting a cup of coffee or responding to emails about news alerts or requesting Mr Lehrmann's professional help as important. They are consistent with there not being any issue between them but again, *on the assumption she was a victim*, they can be readily characterised as the actions of a woman who had not yet come to terms with what had happened to her but needed to confront the reality that she had to work out a way of being in the same professional office as a male colleague who had assaulted her. No doubt the struggle to work out how to respond would resonate with many women working in any type of workplace who have had to find some way of coping with such a predicament.

534 I have little doubt that if she had been raped, that by the time of these interactions, it is quite conceivable that Ms Higgins would be driven by conflicting emotions: self-doubt, concern that she would be humiliated by word leaking out to her colleagues and questioning the prudence of her own behaviour.

535 Moreover, these incidents cannot be assessed in a vacuum. It is also necessary to have regard to the fact that other contemporaneous actions of Ms Higgins are consistent with her being a victim of sexual assault. I have already considered her important contemporaneous representations to Mr Payne, Mr Dillaway, and Major Irvine. Below, in Section I, I make detailed findings as to relevant post-incident conduct, but it is worth mentioning some aspects of this behaviour in this part of my reasons, as they provide important context to the alleged counterintuitive behaviour.

536 *First*, was what was said to Mr Dillaway during their first discussion after the incident, while Ms Higgins is still in the Ministerial Suite. Because of what was said during that discussion, Mr Dillaway recounted his impression as follows in the Master Chronology (as recorded in Annexure H to the affidavit of Mr Auerbach sworn 2 April 2024 (**MC**) (at 15)):

> I'd got the impression that she'd done - something had happened that she didn't want to tell me about. Um, but I wasn't sure what

> it was at that time, I probably assumed that maybe she just – she'd hooked up with another guy or something like that. Um, you know, had been out partying. Um, and then, you know, I was trying to- it didn't - it didn't - I remember thinking it didn't make any sense at all what she was telling me because she said, "They were out, then they went back to a minister's office to have drinks." And having worked in that building for a long time, like I know you just - you can't just go have a party in a minister's office. Like when Parliament's sitting, yeah, you can get people into an office pretty easy. But when Parliament's not sitting, you can't just go from a nightclub, zoom by Parliament and bring everyone from the bar and have a party in the minister's office. And kind of when she said that to me initially, I remember thinking like -you know, WTF, I'm like that doesn't make any sense. "What do you mean youse [*sic*] went back to the minister's office and had drinks and partied there?" I'm like, "That doesn't make any sense." And I think as I stated to probe those questions, um, she tried to kind of shut it down. And, you know, she said, "Look, I don't want to talk about it."

This is not inconsistent with a victim of sexual assault still trying to pro- 537
cess what happened, and being initially reticent in discussing the details with someone with whom they were close.

*Secondly*, and importantly, are the representations made by Ms 538
Higgins in meetings with Ms Brown recorded in Annexure B. Those communications show a woman working through a traumatic event and providing further information notwithstanding she did not, at that time, feel able to say to Ms Brown in express words that she had been "raped" (which was a graphic word she initially had some – but not uniform – difficulty in applying to her experience). Hence, even when she first articulated to Ms Brown at the end of her third meeting on Thursday, 28 March, that she recalled Mr Lehrmann "being on top of me" (and which caused Ms Brown to be shocked) (T2129.1–27), she did not expressly say she had been raped. As noted above (at [272]), as she said to Ms Maiden (Ex 50 (at 12)) "I think for like the longest time I was really weird about actually saying it was rape". Given the agreed facts as to the effects of trauma, this is hardly surprising.

*Thirdly*, are the prompt communication of allegations with the AFP and 539
the Sexual Assault and Child Abuse Team (**SACAT**) in 2019 and the

subsequent counselling, which will be examined in further detail below, and which are consistent with a sexual assault having taken place (even though it would be unsafe to rely on a lack of complaint and counselling as counterintuitive behaviour, for reasons I have explained).

540 *Fourthly*, was Ms Higgins' message to Mr O'Connor (the Queensland MP and friend of Ms Higgins) on 29 March 2019, where she represented that a "super f****ed up thing happened little while ago" (T1920.44–1921.4) and a subsequent telephone conversation during which Mr O'Connor (T1921.37–40):

> absolutely remember[ed] the word "rape" [being used]. That's not something that you forget, and she absolutely did say that he had taken her back to Parliament House.

541 *Fifthly*, there was some relatively insignificant evidence of a change of demeanour in the wake of the incident given by Ms Kellie Jago (Ms Higgins' mother), Ms Hamer, Ms Alex Humphries (Ms Higgins' housemate) or, more significantly, of distress by Ms Cripps, the crisis counsellor.

542 *Sixthly*, is the conduct on 3 April 2019 responding to Mr Dillaway's offer to "reach out to the PMO" (Ex R99 (at 814)) which was accepted by Ms Higgins, and which led to a conversation with Mr Julian Leembruggen which was the subject of a contemporaneous record by Mr Dillaway:

> Spoke to PMO. He was mortified to hear about it and how things have been handled. He's going to discuss with COS [Dr John Kunkel] – no one else. I flagged need for councillor [*sic*] and desire to be closer to home during election.

543 To which Ms Higgins replied (Ex R99 (at 814)) – incidentally, in terms in stark contrast to her later narrative:

> Thank you for doing that. Honestly, I really appreciate it. The help is beyond welcomed.
>
> I wouldn't say it's been handled poorly, just a difficult situation to manage. Seriously, Fiona is great. I just think there has been a lot of competing things going on.

544 Again, for present purposes this does not prove a rape occurred, but a person in the position of Ms Higgins agreeing for a friend to "reach out to the PMO" in relation to matters relevant to the incident is not behaviour counterintuitive to a sexual assault having occurred.

*Finally*, was a representation made to her father which falls into a somewhat different category because it occurred much later. Mr Higgins gave raw and palpably believable evidence that after the trip to Canberra at the end of March 2019, he did not hear from his daughter and felt something was wrong (T1469.41–47). He then explained on 2 February 2020, his daughter sent him a message that said: "When you are free this week, we probably need to have a chat. So much has gone on in the past year, and I haven't fully kept you in the loop. You have to keep your cool, though, and back me up" (Ex R882; T1470.15–19). Mr Higgins and his daughter subsequently had a call (T1476.32–33) during which Ms Higgins told him that "the inappropriate [thing] that had happened at Parliament House was that she had been raped ..." (T1470.35–36). Again, this sort of statement must be put in its proper context, but one wonders why a daughter would say such a thing to a clearly loving father absent a genuine belief a sexual assault had taken place. For completeness, it is worth stressing these apparently candid communications with her father might be thought to have cogency because they occurred before the person later charged with the responsibility of "pitching" the project of the cover-up, Mr Sharaz, came into her life on 29 May 2020 (MC (at 63)), the important *Four Corners* programme, and the subsequent development of the cover-up narrative. 545

A further aspect of Ms Higgins' post-incident behaviour said by Mr Lehrmann to be "powerful evidence that Ms Higgins knew no sexual activity had taken place" was her failure to have a sexually transmitted infection check performed, despite telling Mr Dillaway she was doing so and her evidence she believed Mr Lehrmann "'finished' inside [of her]" (T630.10–12). I reject this submission. It suggests a pattern of typical or "normal" behaviour of rape victims that takes insufficient account of the agreed facts as to the possible effects of trauma and the variability of reaction sexual trauma can cause. There may be many reasons *on the assumption Ms Higgins was a victim of rape* for her not wanting to subject herself to such a process, particularly when the surrounding contemporaneous material suggests she had no intention of pursuing a complaint with the police at this time. 546

In summary, despite other concerns as to her creditworthiness, any alleged post-incident counterintuitive behaviour of Ms Higgins does not materially affect my assessment of the underlying cogency of her allegation 547 she was assaulted. Further, considering all the post-incident conduct to which I have referred as a whole, it is not inconsistent with the conduct of a genuine victim of sexual assault struggling to process what happened, seeking to cope, and working through her options.

### *IV Complaint Evidence or Prior Consistent Statements*

548 Before leaving the topic of the contemporaneous representations made by Ms Higgins which provide context to her other post-incident conduct, it is convenient here to make a further point.

549 This is a civil proceeding and so s 66(2) EA, applicable to complaint evidence, is not relevant. In this civil case, no objection was made as to the admissibility of any evidence of complaint or alleged prior consistent statements made by Ms Higgins, and I was not asked to exercise my discretion to limit the use of any such evidence under s 136 EA.

550 Hence the evidence of her contemporaneous representations to Ms Brown, Mr Payne, Mr Dillaway, Major Irvine, Mr O'Connor and, as we will see, the AFP on 1 April, can go beyond merely putting other post-incident conduct in proper context but can also be used to show consistency of conduct by Ms Higgins, some proof of the fact of what was asserted in the representations; in this way, the previous representations are relevant to the reliability of Ms Higgins in this aspect of her evidence.

### *V What Happened?*

551 As can be seen from the above, I have: (a) directed myself as to the principled approach to fact-finding; (b) identified why, on the basis of my credibility assessments and other reliable contemporaneous evidence: (i) I reject the entirety of Mr Lehrmann's account as to what occurred in the Ministerial Suite; and (ii) have identified aspects of the account of Ms Higgins that are inaccurately based or exhibit an apparent inconsistency; (c) made findings as to: (i) the condition of Ms Higgins; and (ii) the preceding proximate interactions between Mr Lehrmann and Ms Higgins and their states of mind when they arrived at Parliament House; (d) identified incontrovertible facts and drawn some conclusions from the existence of those facts; and (e) considered any alleged counterintuitive behaviour and relevant post-incident representations in evidence.

552 Against this background, and in the context of my other conclusions as to what occurred, I now come to identifying what happened within the

Ministerial Suite. In doing so, I will distinguish between something that *might* have happened (but where I am unable to reach a sufficient level of satisfaction to allow a finding of fact to be made), and something that on the balance of probabilities *did* happen (where I have reached the requisite level of satisfaction to make a finding of fact).

As to the former, it is possible, for example, that Mr Lehrmann left Ms Higgins on the office ledge for a period as she asserts, but only while he obtained his whisky and glasses and was ready to usher her into the Minister's office – but I cannot be satisfied that this was the case. Although I suspect Ms Higgins was telling the truth about being on the ledge for some short period, it is also possible that they both entered the Minister's office and immediately started drinking, but again I have not reached the requisite level of satisfaction. 553

Whatever be the true position as to additional drinking, I am convinced, however, that sexual intercourse did take place and that it took place with Mr Lehrmann on top of Ms Higgins on the couch in the Minister's office. I will come back below to whether I accept Ms Higgins' evidence she was not aware of what was happening when Mr Lehrmann commenced the sexual act. 554

I am also amply satisfied, in accordance with the inherent probabilities, that coitus (and any other physical contact) concluded quickly upon Mr Lehrmann ejaculating, and that he thereafter promptly left the Minister's office and the Ministerial Suite. It follows that it is far more likely than not that sexual intercourse occurred towards the end of the period when both Mr Lehrmann and Ms Higgins were in the Minister's office and at around, or shortly after, the time Mr Lehrmann's girlfriend was trying to telephone him. 555

Given the evidence I have already discussed and the weight I place on contemporaneous representations, I have not reached a level of satisfaction that during the sexual act Ms Higgins said, "no on a loop" and I think it is more likely than not that she did not, or was not, able to articulate anything. On balance, I find it is more likely than not that she was passive (as she later said, "like a log") during the entirety of the sexual act. 556

I am further satisfied she felt unable to get up from the couch immediately following Mr Lehrmann leaving and she then passed out into a deep 557 sleep. The fact she "passed out", at some time, is common ground in final submissions.

558 When it comes to the dress, I accept the evidence of Ms Anderson, who encountered her about two hours later. It is unclear to me whether the dress had been completely removed prior to the sexual act, or during it, or had just been scrunched around the waist of Ms Higgins (thus exposing her breasts and genitalia). If it was the latter, then I think it is likely the dress was taken off by Ms Higgins at some time prior to the arrival of Ms Anderson, despite her not being fully aware of her surroundings, presumably to allow her to be unencumbered by it while sleeping.

559 As to the bruise, I fall well short of being satisfied that Mr Lehrmann placed his leg against either of Ms Higgins' legs so forcefully as to cause a large bruise (particularly given my considerable doubts about the authenticity of the bruise photograph).

560 I will make some further findings as to what occurred when I consider the elements of rape in Section H.2 below.

# H THE SECTION 25 DEFENCE

## H.1 Introduction

As mentioned above (at [93]), to establish a defence under s 25 of the Defamation Act, the respondents are required to prove the substantial truth of each imputation, meaning it is true in substance or not materially different from the truth. Further, and again as noted above, it is sufficient if the "sting" or gravamen of an imputation is substantially true. Recognising the sting of each imputation pleaded in this case, all parties agreed in a statement of agreed issues that the only question on truth is question 4: "Whether [Mr Lehrmann] raped Brittany Higgins in Parliament House in 2019?". 561

## H.2 Substantial Truth: Was there a Rape?

### *I What Needs to be Proven*

The submissions of all parties were less than helpful in relation to this aspect of the case. This is not a criticism of the barristers but reflects the reality that the respondents say sexual intercourse happened in such a way as to mean it follows axiomatically that there must have been a rape; whereas Mr Lehrmann's case is that no sexual intercourse took place at all. 562

More particularly, Network Ten contends that because Mr Lehrmann denied any sexual contact, this: 563

> ... obviate[ed] the need for any enquiry as to whether the intercourse described by Ms Higgins could have been consensual or as to whether his conduct was other than wilful or reckless (*Crimes Act 1900* (ACT), s 54). If intercourse occurred as described by Ms Higgins, it was obviously rape.

But it is not as easy as that for at least two reasons: *first*, as I have explained, although I have found intercourse took place, I am not reasonably satisfied as to an aspect of the account of Ms Higgins as to what occurred, that 564 is, she repeatedly and expressly said to Mr Lehrmann that he should stop; and *secondly*, the relevant inquiry on the substantial truth defence is not governed by whether Mr Lehrmann breached a particular statutory norm, being s 54(1) of the Crimes Act.

565 This second point requires some elaboration.

566 It is agreed the respondents must prove Mr Lehrmann raped Ms Higgins, but what does one mean by "rape" in this context? Does it mean something different from what can be described as the penetrative sexual offence that existed in the ACT at the time of the alleged assault or at the time of publication? Put another way, does it mean something different from the charge Mr Lehrmann faced in the criminal proceeding?

567 Historically, rape was defined at common law as carnal knowledge by a man of a woman (who is not the man's wife) against her will. Consistently with this definition, the crime of rape required proof of physical force and resistance: Cyril J Smith, 'History of Rape and Rape Laws' (1974) 60(4) *Women Lawyers Journal* 188 (at 189–91). Further, the crime was subject to a narrow definition of sexual intercourse and, as the years have passed, statutory extensions and modifications to the common law crime of rape have been made in all jurisdictions to varying degrees. For example, there is no longer any principle in Australian common law respecting the single legal personality of spouses (hence rape can occur within marriage), and the penetrative sexual offence is no longer gender-specific and, despite some inconsistencies, generally includes penetration of the genitalia by a penis, object, or part of a body or mouth. There has now been removal of express references to force and the introduction of a consent standard based upon voluntary agreement. Further, the penetrative sexual offence is still described as "rape" in some jurisdictions (Victoria, Queensland, South Australia and Tasmania); but by 2010 was described as "sexual assault" in New South Wales, "sexual intercourse without consent" in the ACT and the Northern Territory; and "sexual penetration without consent" in Western Australia: see Australian Law Reform Commission, *Family Violence – A National Legal Response* (Report 114, October 2010) (at [25.8]–[25.13]).

568 It may be stating the obvious, but given some submissions made by the parties, it is important to stress that I am not dealing with whether, by reference to the civil standard of proof, Mr Lehrmann has breached a specific criminal

provision under a law of the Australian Capital Territory. My inquiry is different and is relevantly focused upon the *natural and ordinary meaning* of the word "rape". Moreover, it must be borne in mind that language is not static; it evolves, and a word's denotation or connotation is not immune from development and change. Our focus is on what rape means in contemporary Australia – not by reference to what it may have meant historically or may mean in the future (if, for example, legislative change eventually causes the ordinary perception of what constitutes consent to also change).

Although the elements of the penetrative sexual offence can differ 569
somewhat between jurisdictions and by reference to the time when the offending is alleged to have taken place, the natural and ordinary meaning of rape is tolerably plain. As noted above, given the contemporary ordinary understanding of rape and how it has been particularised in this case, the respondents are required to prove:

(1) that, at the time and place alleged, that is, at Parliament House on 23 March 2019, Mr Lehrmann had sexual intercourse with Ms Higgins;

(2) without Ms Higgins' consent;

(3) knowing Ms Higgins did not consent.

I have already explained how I consider the respondents have made out 570
the first element.

Network Ten deals with the non-consent element and the knowledge ele- 571
ment briefly and simply relies on the fact that Mr Lehrmann said he did not at any stage seek to procure consent to have any sexual intercourse with Ms Higgins (T319.6–20). It then says that because "Mr Lehrmann knew that Ms Higgins had had at least six spirit-based drinks at The Dock and then several further drinks at 88mph" that "his conduct in respect of consent to intercourse was at least reckless".

Ms Wilkinson oddly submits with regard to the non-consent element 572
that "Ms Higgins gave evidence that she did not consent to sex with Mr Lehrmann" and this should be accepted because "she was not challenged on that evidence". More logically, she also submits that "[b]y reason of the toxicology evidence, the Court should find that Ms Higgins was incapable of consent due to her level of intoxication". Ms Wilkinson then tends to elide the last two elements by submitting that even if I was to reject the evidence given as to Ms Higgins' protestations:

(1) if the sexual intercourse had been consensual, then it is likely that Ms Higgins and Mr Lehrmann would have left together but Mr Lehrmann leaving her there, semi-lucid "is indicative of his knowledge that Ms Higgins did not consent to what he had just done"; and

(2) Mr Lehrmann had knowledge of Ms Higgins' lack of consent "by the fact that he observed her drinking heavily throughout the night, saw her fall over and observed her going through security and being unable to put on her shoes".

573 Before setting out my reasons in relation to each element, which ought be considered separately, it is convenient to first consider (and then reject) the notion that if consensual sex took place, then it is likely that Ms Higgins and Mr Lehrmann would have left together. I do not consider this logic to be at all compelling. This is because, *on the assumption the sex was consensual*, Mr Lehrmann was still behaving dishonourably by having sexual intercourse with Ms Higgins while in a relationship, and his girlfriend was trying to contact him – presumably trying to work out where he was and why he was there at 2:15am. Given he had satisfied himself, and that he knew his girlfriend was awake and was attempting to contact him, calling an Uber and getting out of the Ministerial private office with celerity (and leaving Ms Higgins undressed) is the action of a cad, but is nonetheless explicable.

574 That argument put to one side; I now turn to the issues of more substance and proceed to deal with the question of whether the respondents have discharged their burden on the balance of probabilities of proving the second element (non-consent element) and then separately deal with the third element (knowledge element).

### *II Non-Consent Element*

575 Unlike the first element, this second element, obviously enough concerns Ms Higgins' state of mind.

576 Although I am not satisfied there was a clear verbal protest being made by Ms Higgins, and find it is more likely that Ms Higgins was "passive" during the sexual act, any suggestion that some form of "active resistance" is determinative of the question of consent would be misguided.

577 Ordinary human experience suggests that sexual assault victims vary in their behaviour, including during a sexual assault – the notion a woman is expected to attempt either "fight or flight" to then be accepted as having

been a victim of sexual assault is not only not reasonably open but wrong-headed. It is redolent of historical conceptions of rape, which relied upon notions of force and resistance, rather than the contemporary focus on voluntary consent.

This is not to suggest that in order to conclude there was a want of consent 578
it is appropriate I have regard to, let alone form a considered view about, the extensive empirical studies of persons alleging sexual assault and the voluminous academic literature (not referred to by any party) as to how humans exposed to extreme threats may react with disassociation or a state of involuntary, temporary motor inhibition known as "tonic immobility" and the suggested widespread phenomenon of the occurrence of tonic immobility during sexual assaults: see, for example, T Fusé et al, 'Factor structure of the Tonic Immobility Scale in female sexual assault survivors: An exploratory and Confirmatory Factor Analysis' (2007) 21(3) *Journal of Anxiety Disorders* 265; A W Coxell and M B King, 'Adult male rape and sexual assault: Prevalence, re-victimisation and the tonic immobility response' (2010) 25(4) *Sexual and relationship Therapy* 372; M A Hagenaars, 'Tonic immobility and PTSD in a large community sample' (2016) 7(2) *Journal of Experimental Psychopathology* 246; and M L Covers et al, 'The Tonic Immobility Scale in adolescent and young adult rape victims: Support for three-factor model' (2022) 14(5) *Psychological Trauma: Theory, Research, Practice, and Policy* 780.

I am not to rely on matters not in evidence. 579

What I am required to do, in applying the fact-finding principles I have 580
explained, the facts found and agreed, and commonsense, is to assess the reliability of Ms Higgins' evidence as to her state of mind. That is, she did not consent because she was so drunk on the couch that at some point, she was not aware of her surroundings but then suddenly became aware of Mr Lehrmann being on top of her, at which time he was performing the sexual act, which he then continued to a conclusion.

In evaluating the cogency of this aspect of her evidence, I am required to 581
have regard to all of the evidence, including contemporaneous representations made by Ms Higgins shortly after the incident, and a number of other matters, including:

(1) the s 140(2)(a), (b) and (c) EA mandatory considerations, reflecting the necessity to approach the allegation with much care and caution

and with weight being given to the presumption of innocence and exactness of proof expected;

(2) the other fact-finding principles I have explained in Section E above, including but not limited to: (a) the need for me to reach a state of a reasonable satisfaction on the preponderance of probabilities; (b) the care required when there are a range of possibilities open and the only way one reaches a state of reasonable satisfaction as to *one* being proven is to conclude its existence is more likely than *all* the other hypotheses available on the evidence; and (c) that witnesses may be untruthful about some things and yet be truthful about others;

(3) Ms Higgins' *general* lack of creditworthiness and the heightened caution therefore necessary in assessing any aspect of her evidence; and more *particularly*, the fact I have not accepted she expressly and repeatedly voiced her lack of consent.

582 But in the end, it comes down to my assessment of whether Ms Higgins was telling the truth in the witness box when she gave this evidence as to her state of mind, having paid close attention to not only what she said, but her manner of saying it.

583 Notwithstanding the cautions to which I have referred, the full range of other possibilities combined, and taking all my reservations as to the credibility and reliability of Ms Higgins into account, her evidence that she was not fully aware of her surroundings but then suddenly became aware of Mr Lehrmann on top of her, at which time he was performing the sexual act, when given orally before me, struck me forcefully as being credible and as having the ring of truth. I use the term "fully aware" advisedly, as consciousness is best understood as not being a binary concept but rather as being on a continuum, and the evidence defies a finding as to her *precise* state of consciousness at a specific time.

584 In accepting this specific aspect of Ms Higgins' evidence, I have directed myself to bear in mind that like in any case where criminal conduct is sought to be proven based largely or exclusively on a single witness, it is important I am satisfied to the appropriate standard that the witness is both honest and accurate in the account given.

585 I have also been conscious of the dangers of too readily drawing conclusions about truthfulness and reliability based upon the appearance or demeanour of a witness while giving evidence. It is for this reason I have

tried, as best I can, to limit my reliance on the appearances of witnesses and have attempted to reason my conclusions, as far as possible, based on contemporary materials, objectively established facts, and the apparent logic of events. But there is nothing about this finding that conflicts with objectively established facts or logic (and indeed when one has regard to the other events of the night and Ms Higgins' immediate post-incident conduct taken as a whole, including the consistency of her core allegation of sexual assault, the opposite is true).

At the risk of repetition, I am conscious of the fact that I must eschew 586 inexact proofs, indefinite testimony, or indirect inferences and, in doing so, I am acutely aware that working out when a compromised witness such as Ms Higgins is telling the truth in one aspect of her evidence presents real challenges. But bearing all these matters in mind, I have reached a state of actual persuasion on the balance of probabilities that Ms Higgins: (a) was not fully aware of her surroundings when sexual intercourse commenced; and (b) did not consent to intercourse when she became aware Mr Lehrmann was "on top of her".

The non-consent element is made out. 587

## *III Knowledge Element*

This third element also involves consideration of state of mind, but this 588 time of Mr Lehrmann.

If one accepts sexual intercourse happened, and also accepts that Ms 589 Higgins did not consent to intercourse as I have found, the issue arises as to whether one can draw the inference that Mr Lehrmann must have known that Ms Higgins was not consenting.

If I was to accept that Ms Higgins was obviously unconscious when sexual 590 intercourse commenced, then proof of the knowledge element would follow readily. That may well have been the case, but it is equally probable this may not have been obvious, thus requiring focus on the issue as to whether Mr Lehrmann understood that Ms Higgins, in her inebriated state, was not fully aware of what was happening to her.

Given what I have found about it being likely Ms Higgins did not expressly 591 voice her resistance, and the other findings I have made of their interactions (that Ms Higgins was "like a log"), I do not consider I can be positively satisfied on the balance of probabilities that Mr Lehrmann turned his mind to consent and had, at the relevant time, a state of mind of actual cognitive awareness that Ms Higgins did not consent to having sex.

592 But this is not the end of the matter.

593 It is not in dispute that the knowledge element can be established by recklessness and Mr Lehrmann in his closing submissions, when in dealing with differences between imputations, accepts that "the bare fact of rape ... might be committed simply by being recklessly indifferent to whether or not there was consent".

594 Much ink has been spilled and significant attention of law reformers and legislators has been directed in recent years to the issue of what constitutes recklessness as it relates to the fault element in sexual offences (although this topic, for reasons I have explained, was wholly unexplored in the submissions and the parties have not engaged with the question as to what recklessness means having regard to the ordinary, contemporary conception of rape).

595 Recklessness can, of course, mean different things, such as an awareness the complainant might not be consenting (possibility recklessness), indifference as to whether the complainant is consenting (indifference recklessness) and failure to give any thought as to whether the complainant is consenting (inadvertence recklessness) – although possibility recklessness might be best seen as a variant of indifference recklessness: see D A Smith, "Reckless Rape in Victoria" (2008) 32(3) *Melbourne University Law Review* 1007.

596 This sort of taxonomy can distract, and, in any event, it is sufficient for our purposes to consider what has been usefully called in the cases "non-advertent recklessness". In *R v Stevens (No 2)* [2017] ACTSC 296, Mossop J was requested to indicate in advance of closing submissions what direction his Honour would give the jury in relation to non-advertent recklessness. In doing so, his Honour, with respect, usefully summarised and explained the position as follows (at [1]–[11]):

> [1] ... The New South Wales Bench Book incorporates the elements of the description of nonadvertent recklessness described in the headnote to the decision in *R v Tolmie* (1995) 37 NSWLR 660. This is the formulation articulated by Kirby P. It differs somewhat from the formulation of Newman J, who adopted the earlier decision of *R v Kitchener* (1993) 29 NSWLR 696 at 697, where Kirby P said:

> This can be shown not only where the accused adverts to the possibility of consent but ignores it, but also where the accused is so bent on gratification and indifferent to the rights of the victim as to ignore completely the requirement for consent.

[2] Barr AJ agreed with both the reasons of Kirby P and the reasons of Newman J and hence there is no clear majority formulation of the appropriate test. The headnote, however, picked up the formulation of Kirby P.

[3] In *Gillard v The Queen* [2014] HCA 16; 88 ALJR 606, the High Court, while approving various formulations in the House of Lords in *Director of Public Prosecutions v Morgan* [1976] AC 182, expressly said that it was not necessary to consider whether recklessness extends to the state of mind of inadvertence to consent in the way described in *Tolm ie* (see *Gillard* at [26].) The Court said:

> It is sufficient in order to address the issues raised by the appeal, to observe that recklessness is a mental state captured by the concept of indifference to the complainant's consent, as explained in the joint reasons in [*Banditt v The Queen* [2005] HCA 80; 224 CLR 262].

[4] The authorities in this jurisdiction since 2008 have not explored the possible different formulations of non-advertent consent. Those decisions involve approval of the decision of Besanko J in *Sims v Drewson* [2008] ACTSC 91; 2 ACTLR 307, as is made clear by his Honour's judgment at [32]. The issue that his Honour was called upon to decide was whether or not non-advertent recklessness was within the concept of recklessness in s 60 of the *Crimes Act 1900* (ACT). His Honour formulated the concept of non-advertent recklessness as follows:

> Non-advertent recklessness is where the accused person is so indifferent to the rights of the alleged victim as to ignore completely the requirement of consent.

[5] It is worth noting that this picks up the language of Lord Cross in *Morgan*. Besanko J also made reference to

the decision of the New South Wales Court of Appeal in *Kitchener* and the Court of Appeal decision in *Fitzgerald v Kennard* (1995) 38 NSWLR 184, which followed the decision in *Kitchener*. Finally he referred to the decision in *Banditt v The Queen* [2005] HCA 80; 224 CLR 262, which was consistent with the acceptance of nonadvertent recklessness being within the scope of the concept of recklessness. His Honour's discussion of *Tolmie* was limited and he did not discuss the correctness of the particular formulation captured by the headnote in *Tolmie*. The correctness of Besanko J's reasoning in *Sims* was confirmed by the Court of Appeal in *Director of Public Prosecutions v Walker* [2011] ACTCA 1 at [53].

[6] The Court of Appeal in *Gillard v The Queen* [2013] ACTCA 17 at [105] approves the test for recklessness articulated in *Sims* and describes *Sims* as "[a]pplying the test for recklessness found in *R v Tolmie*". Having regard to the decision in *Sims*, the express reference to *Tolmie* must be to the acceptance of the concept of non-advertent recklessness rather than to the specific approval of the formulation as set out in the headnote. I note also that the pinpoint reference to [25] in *Sims* must be incorrect. It is probably intended to be a reference to [23].

[7] As I have indicated above, the High Court in *Gillard*, while dealing with a slightly different point, expressly left open the question of whether or not the formulation reflected in the headnote in *Tolmie* was correct. In my view, the ACT authorities confirm the applicability of the concept of non-advertent recklessness but do not mandate any particular formulation of it.

[8] Having regard to the manner in which the decision in *Tolmie* was dealt with in *Sims*, I do not consider that it involved a specific approval of Kirby P's formulation of the concept. In the circumstances, it would be consistent with the decision of the High Court in *Banditt* and *Gillard* if the direction that I gave in relation to non-advertent recklessness was to the effect of that given by the trial judge in *Banditt*, with additional references to the verbal formulae expressed in *Morgan*, which were approved in *Gillard*, namely:

> Recklessness does not have to be the product of conscious thought. If the accused does not even consider whether the complainant is going to consent or not then that is reckless. This can be described in various ways: namely, that the accused's state of mind is at least indifferent to the complainant's consent, if he just goes ahead willy-nilly not even caring whether she consented or not, or that he has gone ahead without caring whether she was a consenting party. If the accused was reckless in that sense then the law says that he is reckless.

[9] That direction appears to me to be consistent with the formulation of Besanko J at [23] in *Sims*; namely:

> Non-advertent recklessness is where the accused person is so indifferent to the rights of the alleged victim as to ignore completely the requirement of consent.

[10] It also appears to be consistent with the decisions of the New South Wales courts relied upon by Besanko J in *Sims*; namely, *Kitchener* and the decision of Newman J in *Tolmie*. Although the references to proceeding willy-nilly or having a state of mind of indifference tend to suggest a higher test than a mere failure to consider the issue of consent, because they might suggest a positive state of mind rather than an absence of consideration, I do not consider that there is a difference of substance if the circumstances are such that there is a possible absence of consent.

[11] I consider that the formulation based on Kirby P's reasons in *Tolmie*, reflected in the headnote, is a test which appropriately captures the essence of non-advertent recklessness: failing to consider something that in the circumstances one should. The President's formulation has the benefit of avoiding the uncertain implications from the varying form of expression in *Morgan*. However, any potential difference between that formulation and those expressly approved by the High Court in *Gillard* have not been explored in the High Court or the Court of Appeal and it is therefore appropriate in this case to attempt to adopt a formulation that has been so approved.

597 These were observations made, of course, in the context of a direction being sought as to what was required to be established by the Crown in a prosecution of the ACT penetrative sexual offence. But in my view, they apply equally to an element embedded in the natural and ordinary meaning of rape in contemporary Australia. I have no doubt that the ordinary person on the Belconnen omnibus, who went home to watch the Project programme, would think a man would have raped a woman if he was so bent on his gratification and indifferent to the rights of the woman that he ignored or was indifferent to the requirement for her consent.

598 I consider that the knowledge element can be established if the respondents prove, to the civil standard, that at the time sexual intercourse took place, Mr Lehrmann's state of mind was such that he was indifferent to Ms Higgins' consent, and he just went ahead willy-nilly. Put another way, the knowledge element is established if Mr Lehrmann was so indifferent to the rights of Ms Higgins as to ignore the requirement of consent.

599 I will not repeat what I have set out in the preceding section. Needless to say, like with my findings as to the other two elements, I have again reminded myself of the principles explained above in Section E, including the need to feel an actual persuasion of the existence of a fact before it can be found; the seriousness of the allegation of knowledge of non-consent; the extent of its unlikelihood; and separately, the gravity of the consequences flowing from the finding.

600 Notwithstanding the need for pause, I am satisfied that it is more likely than not that Mr Lehrmann's state of mind was such that he was so intent upon gratification to be indifferent to Ms Higgins' consent, and hence went ahead with sexual intercourse without caring whether she consented. This conclusion is not mandated by, but is consistent with, my finding that intercourse commenced when Ms Higgins was not fully cognitively aware of what was happening.

601 In summary, I consider it more likely than not that in those early hours, after a long night of conviviality and drinking, and having successfully brought Ms Higgins back to a secluded place, Mr Lehrmann was hell-bent on having sex with a woman he: (a) found sexually attractive; (b) had been mutually passionately kissing and touching; (c) had encouraged to drink; and (d) knew had reduced inhibitions because she was very drunk. In his pursuit of gratification, he did not care one way or another whether Ms Higgins understood or agreed to what was going on.

Because of what I find to be Mr Lehrmann's state of mind of non-advertent recklessness, the knowledge element has been made out. 602

## *IV Further Observations as to Mr Lehrmann's "Critical" Submission*

For completeness, I note that in reaching this conclusion, I have fully considered all the submissions made by Mr Lehrmann, including one his counsel described as "critical". It is worth making three short points as to aspects of Mr Lehrmann's submissions, to the extent I have not otherwise sufficiently dealt with them. 603

*First*, the important corroborative evidence of Ms Anderson is minimised by asserting her observations as to the state of Ms Higgins' make-up create a difficulty for the respondents and that although "Ms Higgins was found asleep on the couch naked", this could be because "it simply made her feel more comfortable" or "she decided to remove her dress before she lay down on the couch as she may have wanted or tried to avoid vomiting on her dress, and then passed out asleep". I do not regard these submissions as being in the least persuasive. Ms Anderson's fleeting observations upon being confronted by the surprising sight of Ms Higgins looking up at her, not in obvious distress but sufficiently unaware of her surroundings to just stir herself to turn over into the foetal position like a naked newborn babe, are hardly likely to have precision as to such a minor matter. In any event, without getting into the vulgarities, commonsense suggests the sort of sexual activity I find took place would not necessarily result in a woman's make-up being smeared all over her face (as the submission implicitly suggests). As to the point about the dress, ingenuity may be able to conjure up a number of possibilities (short of her frock just falling off) but we are here dealing with questions of likelihood, which leads to the next, more general, and so-called "critical" point. 604

*Secondly*, Mr Lehrmann submits that there are: 605

> a number of plausible explanations for why Ms Higgins, being affected by alcohol, took off her dress and lay down naked on the Minister's couch. The existence of these plausible alternative explanations, coupled with a lack of independent reliable evidence to support the [r]espondents' submissions, makes any positive finding to the requisite standard that sexual activity took place, consensual or otherwise, unable to be supported by the evidence. Mr

Lehrmann submits that the facts and circumstances of this case are archetypal of a '*Palmanova*' situation – where no one hypothesis emerges as more likely to be correct than all of the other possibilities considered together.

606 Between the two poles advanced by Mr Lehrmann and Ms Higgins as to what happened are a range of possibilities, including "various permutations of consensual sexual activity (including anything from kissing or touching to sexual intercourse), or intercourse which was at law not consensual, but which Mr Lehrmann believed was consensual". Mr Lehrmann also submits it is necessary to consider scenarios where no sexual contact occurred despite a prior intention to engage in such activity on the part of either or both of them and, although such hypotheses were not explored in evidence, as a matter of ordinary human experience they naturally arise as possibilities and must therefore be considered.

607 These submissions are unquestionably correct so far as they go. No doubt inadvertently, however, some of the submissions, when articulated, came close to suggesting that to find the respondents' onus had been discharged, it was necessary I exclude all reasonable hypotheses consistent with the rape not having occurred (as if I was determining the case beyond reasonable doubt).

608 All these scenarios have been considered and some rank higher on the likelihood range than others. For example, scenarios that consensual sex occurred, or Mr Lehrmann was not reckless while having non-consensual sex, are more likely than scenarios they just "pashed" and drank whisky and Ms Higgins later just decided to take off her clothes for a lark or because she was feeling close or had a fit of the vapours, or that Ms Higgins "prepared herself" to have sex by lying down naked but fell asleep and Mr Lehrmann departed because of scruples as to not taking advantage of the otherwise willing Ms Higgins. Whether they are fanciful or just unpersuasive, they are all individually far less likely eventualities than what I have found took place. Further, and critically, upon a review of the whole of my findings on the evidence, even taking all these other possibilities of what might have occurred together, the sum of the likelihood they occurred is outweighed by the likelihood Ms Higgins was raped as she asserted in the critical part of her oral testimony.

609 *Thirdly*, there is the issue of Ms Higgins' motive to lie. During the hearing, those acting for Mr Lehrmann suggested that fabricating the rape

allegation was conduct directed to saving Ms Higgins' job. More particularly, it was said that having been found passed out in the Minister's office would be highly damaging to her reputation and career prospects as an aspiring staffer or Member of Parliament and, as a consequence, she needed to construct a different narrative to rehabilitate her reputation. Ms Higgins did express some fear for the early termination of her job when the incident first became known. She had, after all, explained to the Project team in the initial interview (Ex 36 (at 0:46:59)) that: (a) she "immediately thought [she] was going to be sacked"; (b) that it "felt like [Ms Brown] was going to fire me" (Ex 36 (at 0:49:31)); and (c) agreed that she "thought I'm about to be fired" (Ex 36 (at 1:00:12–24)). To similar effect, at the criminal trial, she gave the following evidence (Ex 71 (at T269.19–25)) as to her state of mind when she was first called in to see Ms Brown:

> MR WHYBROW: You had seen Mr Lehrmann effectively to your mind be sacked? – Yes
>
> ...
>
> And you were called in to what you anticipated would be a meeting where you might also be terminated? – Yes.

Network Ten's response to the suggestion Ms Higgins had a motivation to lie is, among other things, to say: (a) this would mean her conduct, more than two years later, in quitting her job, publicising her false rape allegation, and reinstating a police investigation "would be utterly irrational"; and (b) Ms Brown acknowledged that Ms Higgins' job was never at risk (T2157.17–35). 610

As to (a), this seems to assume her motivations could not have changed in those two years and the correctness of the related proposition advanced by Network Ten (in the teeth of the 2021 representations of Ms Higgins to Ms Maiden and the Project team and her exchanges with Mr Sharaz) that Ms Higgins in 2021 still "loved the Liberal Party" (Ex 71 (at T192.5)). As to (b), that might have been Ms Brown's view and is no doubt correct, but what mattered was the *perception* of Ms Higgins. 611

The lack of merit in the suggested motive, to my mind, is somewhat different. *First*, although she would not want to be peremptorily terminated, as her contemporaneous messages reproduced below make clear, she well understood she was to be unemployed very soon and had no long-term 612 job security. *Secondly*, even if one can point to it being somehow in Ms Higgins' interests to suggest her work colleague behaved inappropriately towards her, to invent a rape allegation in such circumstances would not only be malevolent, but one would expect it be done by being definitive and clear about the allegation, and not responding to the incident in the traumatic, halting way evident in Ms Higgins' 2019 actions (consistent with the actions of a sexual assault victim dealing with trauma); nor *thirdly*, would it explain her evolving and evidently candid contemporaneous exchanges with those in whom she decided to confide in the process of confirming her initial instinct not to press her complaint.

### *V The Role of Implied Admissions and Consciousness of Guilt*

613 I have referred to many lies of Mr Lehrmann but the lies that presently matter are those lies that relate to an issue material to the question as whether sexual intercourse without consent took place as alleged. Only three seem to me to matter and they do not include such things as his various lies told to Ms Brown and in his response to the show cause letter, which are also consistent with him trying to downplay any security breach aspect of the incident, which could lead to his dismissal.

614 As to the *first*, until he got into the witness box in this civil case there was no need for Mr Lehrmann to recount what happened. As I observed in the limitation judgment, notwithstanding Mr Lehrmann had the privilege to refuse to answer any question on the ground of self-incrimination, after retaining legal advice, he gave his account of no sex taking place to the AFP and subsequently, his then legal representative, Mr John Korn, made a statement that Mr Lehrmann "absolutely and unequivocally denies that any form of sexual activity took place at all" (Ex R98).

615 I am conscious that counsel for Mr Lehrmann submitted that it was the "gamble of [Mr Lehrmann's] life to assert there had been no sex" if he "had no idea whether any forensic evidence existed". But this assumes a sophistication and rationality in Mr Lehrmann's approach notably absent from his evidence, such as his silly lies about whisky, French submarines or as to what happened at The Dock when the CCTV records establish what happened. Moreover, in truth it was a gamble either way once Mr Lehrmann decided to give an account and, if there had been corroborative medical records, then Mr Lehrmann would, I expect, have thought it likely some use would have been made of them in the broadcast – particularly given

the way the Project team had used, as "contemporaneous" corroborative material bolstering Ms Higgins' credit, the bruise photograph. In any event, I am comfortably satisfied on the balance of probabilities that the instructions he gave his trial lawyers about no contact and a lack of sex were given because he knew the admission of sex with a drunk woman would mean the possibility of her lack of consent was brought squarely into issue and he feared the truth.

As to the *second*, as is already clear, I am satisfied Mr Lehrmann knew his account given to the AFP and to his legal representatives at the trial as to why he came back to Parliament House and what he did there was false. It is passing strange the account to the AFP was given in the absence of his then retained legal representative, but there is no need to speculate as to why this was the case. 616

As to the *third*, I am also satisfied the lies about there being no alcohol in the Ministerial Suite were deliberate and were said to divert the AFP from the truth and were advanced by him because he well realised that an admission he had sex with Ms Higgins, after she had been drinking heavily, could put him in some peril as implicating him in non-consensual sex. It is notable that his account to the AFP came after the broadcast of the last of three relevant *Four Corners* programmes (discussed below), which featured Ms Anderson saying Ms Higgins was inebriated when entering Parliament House and her subsequent discovery of Ms Higgins less than alert and naked on the couch. 617

But as Besanko J observed in *Roberts-Smith*, the circumstances in which lies can give rise to a finding of a consciousness of guilt or the making of an implied admission are complex and highly contentious, and one must be cautious before treating a lie as an implied admission. 618

An implied admission is, in the end, a piece of circumstantial evidence, which proves a fact from which another fact may be inferred. I have reached a level of satisfaction to the requisite standard as to what occurred in this case without the necessity to have regard to any reasoning based upon an implied admission or a consciousness of guilt on the part of Mr Lehrmann. Having said that, the fact that Mr Lehrmann has told the deliberate and material lies identified when he knew the truth, would, if that fact had been considered by me, only have served to fortify the conclusion I have reached independently of taking into account any implied admission. 619

## *VI Conclusion on Rape*

620 Mr Lehrmann raped Ms Higgins.

621 I hasten to stress; this is a finding on the balance of probabilities. This finding should not be misconstrued or mischaracterised as a finding that I can exclude all reasonable hypotheses consistent with innocence. As I have explained, there is a substantive difference between the criminal standard of proof and the civil standard of proof and, as the tribunal of fact, I have only to be reasonably satisfied that Mr Lehrmann has acted as I have found, and I am not obliged to reach that degree of certainty necessary to support conviction upon a criminal charge.

## *VII Differences between Imputations*

622 Given the agreement between the parties as reflected in the agreed issues for determination document, one would have thought that this necessarily means that the substantial truth defence is made out. But in final written submissions, Mr Lehrmann has raised a further issue the scope of which was, at least initially, unclear.

623 To understand it, for ease of reference, it is worth again setting out the imputations which are admitted were conveyed:

(1) [Mr Lehrmann] raped [Ms] Higgins in Defence Minister Linda Reynolds' office in 2019 (**Imputation A**).

(2) [Mr Lehrmann] continued to rape [Ms] Higgins after she woke up mid-rape and was crying and telling him to stop at least half a dozen times (**Imputation B**).

(3) [Mr Lehrmann], whilst raping [Ms] Higgins, crushed his leg against her leg so forcefully as to cause a large bruise (**Imputation C**).

(4) after [Mr Lehrmann] finished raping [Ms] Higgins, he left her on a couch in a state of undress with her dress up around her waist (**Imputation D**).

624 Mr Lehrmann contends that there are differences between the imputations in that the ordinary reasonable person might think that for Mr Lehrmann to continue raping Ms Higgins after she had pleaded multiple times for him to stop (Imputation B) was especially heinous, "and more so than the bare fact of rape (Imputation A), which might be committed simply by being recklessly indifferent to whether or not there was

consent". The ordinary reasonable person might also think that "for him to leave her half-naked on the couch afterwards (Imputation D) was callous, in a way which aggravates the sting of the imputation somewhat".

Why this might be thought to be significant is that as can be seen from my findings, although I am satisfied a rape took place, I do not accept it has been established that: 625

(1) Ms Higgins woke up mid-rape and was crying and telling Mr Lehrmann to stop at least half a dozen times (cf Imputation B); or

(2) Mr Lehrmann crushed "his leg against her leg so forcefully as to cause a large bruise" (cf Imputation C); or

(3) Mr Lehrmann left Ms Higgins "with her dress up around her waist" (cf Imputation D).

It is not enough simply to make out a defence to one imputation. It is now beyond doubt that a defence of justification requires a respondent to prove that *each* of the defamatory imputations conveyed by the matter was substantially true at the time of the publication: *Herron v HarperCollins Publishers Australia Pty Ltd (No 2)* [2022] FCAFC 119; (2022) 292 FCR 490 (at 342–345 [7]–[17] per Rares J, with whom Wigney and Lee JJ agreed). 626

But it does not matter here. For the purposes of the truth defence, as I have previously noted, I consider the four imputations pleaded by Mr Lehrmann do not differ in their essential substance, and the defamatory sting of each is that Mr Lehrmann raped Ms Higgins in Parliament House. 627

This proposition has been proven and thus the defence is made out. 628

It follows it is unnecessary for me to proceed to deal with the other pleaded defences and damages, as the respondents are entitled to judgment. It is tempting to take such a course, but I have been urged by the parties to find the facts necessary to deal with the statutory qualified privilege defence and determine that defence against the prospect my conclusions as to the substantial truth defence may miscarry. I will proceed to do so, but first I will turn to some aspects of what next happened, being the immediate post-incident conduct. 629

# I FINDINGS AS TO RELEVANT POST-INCIDENT CONDUCT

## I.1 Introduction

630 It is important to stress the relevance of any immediate post-incident conduct. As I have indicated in Section G.5, alleged counterintuitive behaviour after the incident cannot be assessed in a vacuum and, to get a complete picture, it is appropriate to have regard to all relevant contemporaneous actions of Ms Higgins, that is, not just alleged counterintuitive conduct but also conduct not inconsistent with her being a victim of sexual assault.

631 Moreover, given the central importance of the creditworthiness of Ms Higgins and the care necessary in dealing with her evidence, as I have explained, it is relevant to ascertain whether Ms Higgins has made false representations (both in and out-of-court), including as to matters other than just leading up to her being in the Minister's office. All these matters need to be considered in evaluating her credit and factored into my assessment as to whether the respondents discharged their onus (as I have done). As I have already noted, the findings in this section, although considered by me in assessing the credit of Ms Higgins for the purposes of the determination of the substantial truth defence, only appear in this part of my reasons to keep my findings in roughly chronological order as an aid to comprehension.

## I.2 The Immediate Aftermath: Miscellaneous Matters Referred to in Submissions

632 I have already touched upon some aspects of the immediate post-incident conduct. What also relevantly happened in 2019 is set out below. These facts, like those above, are found primarily by reference to the contemporaneous records, objectively established facts, and the apparent logic of events.

The contemporaneous records reveal that the security incident was escalated quickly and further demonstrate the lack of substance in the notion (implicit and sometimes explicit in the respondents' submissions) that Ms Higgins was treated poorly by members of the Department of Parliamentary Security (**DPS**). These records, usefully collected in MC, demonstrate that: 633

(1) At approximately 6:10am, Ms Anderson rang her team leader to let him know that Ms Higgins had not left; she was told to apprise her day shift relief and to keep it as discreet as possible "given the compromising position the female had been in" and her "potential loss of dignity"; she was also told the relieving day shift team leader would attempt to find a day shift female security officer to do another welfare check later in the morning (at 12).

(2) At 7:15am, the team leader was instructed to perform another welfare check (at 12).

(3) While Ms Higgins remained in the Ministerial Suite and was texting Mr Dillaway about a missed call from the evening before (saying "Hahah all good. I truly have zero recall on what I was calling about") (Ex R99 (at 667)) and having a telephone calls, including with Mr Dillaway, the Chief of Staff of the DPS had been informed about the incident "involving ministerial staff members" and that "a female, who was believed to have been intoxicated, had been found naked in an unlocked ministerial suite"; the Chief of Staff immediately called Ms Cate Saunders, the Deputy Secretary of DPS to advise her of the situation and they agreed to both go to Parliament House (at 13).

(4) At 9:14am, while Ms Higgins was alone in the Ministerial Suite and in a position to text and make telephone calls, there was discussion as to whether "there is a need to call an ambulance based on welfare of the female remaining in the suite and the need to maintain discretion to avoid gossip and unnecessary humiliation"; a minute or so later, a female DPS officer entered and had a conversation with Ms Higgins through a closed door, when Ms Higgins indicated that "everything was OK"; the Chief of Staff was apprised of this fact and immediately advised Ms Saunders by text that Ms Higgins "was conscious and she did not believe an ambulance was required" (at 13).

(5) At 10:01am, Ms Higgins approached the security desk and handed an item to security, before waving goodbye and departing (at 14).

634 Although DPS were, obviously enough, aware of the serious security lapse, as at 11am on Tuesday, 26 March, Ms Brown did not know of either the existence of the security incident or that involved Mr Lehrmann. Nonetheless, she had a meeting at that time with Mr Lehrmann to finalise the end of his contract. The meeting did not last long.

635 Shortly after that meeting, at 11:45am, Ms Brown received a call from Ms Lauren Barons Assistant Secretary, Advice and Support Branch of the Ministerial and Parliamentary Services (**M&PS**) division of the Department of Finance and Administration. M&PS administered the employment framework for staff of Parliamentarians and provided several human resources and support services, including advice on general employment matters and work health and safety. M&PS also provided an independent counselling service provided by an external service provider with a network of associated registered psychologists and social workers across Australia.

636 Ms Brown was told by Ms Barons of the entry into the Ministerial Suite by Mr Lehrmann and Ms Higgins while they were intoxicated, that Mr Lehrmann had left the office around 2:30am and that a security guard had found Ms Higgins "naked and passed out"; she was also told that Ms Higgins was offered an ambulance and medical assistance, which she declined (although it would have been more accurate to say calling for such assistance was considered, but deemed unnecessary, after a check on Ms Higgins). She was also advised of the various remedial procedures to adopt. In particular, she was told that this was a "serious" security breach and Ms Barons outlined the relevant procedures, including workplace health and safety, Ministerial Staff Code of Conduct (**Staff Code**), and security protocols.

637 In the wake of this unwelcome news, Ms Brown had a further meeting with Mr Lehrmann and then several meetings with Ms Higgins, the details of which I have found are accurately recorded in Annexure B.

638 Given its importance, however, it is worth supplementing this by making specific findings as to what happened in the initial meeting between Ms Brown and Ms Higgins, which took place for about ten minutes commencing around 1:30pm on this day.

639 To Ms Brown's observation, Ms Higgins' demeanour at the start of the meeting was happy but changed somewhat when she saw some paperwork

on Ms Brown's desk, being the Employee Assistance Program (**EAP**) material and a copy of the Staff Code.

Ms Brown advised Ms Higgins that she had received advice that Ms Higgins and Mr Lehrmann accessed the Ministerial Wing and office after hours early on Saturday morning. After raising this point, Ms Brown asked her whether she "would you like someone to be here with you?", an invitation Ms Higgins declined. 640

Ms Brown then asked her "what time did you arrive at the office?", to which Ms Higgins responded with words like: "I don't remember accessing the office ... I'd been out and was drunk ... I remember coming through the security checkpoint in the Ministerial Wing basement ... I remember being woken up, but I don't know which time and that I was semi-naked". She also said: "I also remember waking up at about 8am on Saturday morning on the couch". 641

After Ms Brown asked her whether she was alright and pressed for more details, Ms Higgins then said she did not recall anything else and then said words to the effect: "I am responsible for what I drink and my actions". 642

Ms Brown recalls, and I accept, that she said she had been told that there was an ambulance requested or Ms Higgins had been asked whether she wanted an ambulance or a doctor. Ms Higgins did not recall this and, after again enquiring whether Ms Higgins was alright, Ms Brown provided Ms Higgins with a print-out from the M&PS site with details of the EAP and explained the independent support and service the EAP provides and apprised her of the fact that she could make a complaint about anything through M&PS at any time. 643

She then explained to Ms Higgins that entering the Ministerial Wing for non-work purposes, already inebriated, was a security breach along with a breach of the Staff Code and explained she would need to inform the PMO and the Government Staff Committee (**GSC**) of the incident. She had also been advised by M&PS that she should remind Ms Higgins of the Staff Code because she was an ongoing employee – unlike Mr Lehrmann who was winding up his deferral period. There was then some discussion of the Staff Code. 644

After a third enquiry as to how she was, Ms Brown suggested that she thought it best if Ms Higgins went home for the afternoon and take "a few days off or work from home", and "all you need to do is let me know". 645

Ms Higgins said "ok" and Ms Brown said: "you can also take a few days off to return to the Gold Coast to see your family". Ms Higgins then responded to a query as to whether there was anything else Ms Brown could do by then saying "no, I spoke to dad on the weekend, and he is coming down on the weekend to see me". Ms Brown noted: "I'm available any time should you wish to talk".

646 I have no doubt that Ms Brown was telling the truth about this meeting in her evidence-in-chief, which is consistent with the contemporaneous record and the logic of what was happening, including Ms Higgins' understandable shock at having to deal immediately with her becoming aware a senior person knew of the incident. What is plain is that at this point, Ms Higgins did not tell Ms Brown she had suffered any form of inappropriate conduct and Ms Brown's reaction to what she had been told was not only appropriate, but also solicitous of Ms Higgins' welfare and as to her need for any assistance.

647 At around the time of, and immediately following these events, several other things took place, including:

(1) Shaken by the meeting, Ms Higgins engages in several text message exchanges with Mr Dillaway, starting at 1:57pm (R99 (at 692–696)):

> *Ms Higgins* (1:57pm):
>
> So I think I may not continue to be employed with Linda.
>
> *Mr Dillaway* (1:59pm):
>
> What? Did something happen?
>
> *Ms Higgins* (2:05pm):
>
> Yeah it's pretty bad. I genuinely don't know how its going to play out/how I want it to play out
>
> *Mr Dillaway* (2:06pm):
>
> If you made a mistake/stuffed up. Just be honest to her and COS so it can be fixed. I've made some huge f**k ups but owned them, said sorry etc.
>
> *Mr Dillaway* (2:06pm):
>
> Can I call you? I realise you might be office [*sic*] so can't take call.

*Ms Higgins* (2:09pm):

So on Friday night how I ended up in the Ministerial Office it didn't play out how I made out. I don't remember getting there at all, vaguely remember Bruce being there and then I woke up in the morning half dressed by myself in the Ministers office on Saturday morning.

*Ms Higgins* (2:15pm):

Ive spoken with dad and he is flying down on Friday. Was pretty upset over the weekend so he's headed here to just hang out.

*Mr Dillaway* (2:16pm):

That's good hes coming down. Was it just you and Bruce who went back there or a group of people? Did you hook up in there or did someone take advantage of you?

*Ms Higgins* (2:23pm):

Yeah it was just Bruce and I from what I recall. I was barely lucid, I really don't feel like it was consensual at all.

*Ms Higgins* (2:27pm):

I just think if he though [*sic*] it was okay, why would he just leave me there like that.

*Mr Dillaway* (2:28pm):

So he f**ked you?

*Mr Dillaway* (2:29pm):

I hope you're ok. That's pretty serious horrible stuff. You probably need to report this.

*Ms Higgins* (2:31pm):

Fiona our CoS knows. She follow up [*sic*] on the security report about it. Bruce has been terminated early (he was leave post-budget for a department job apparently) she said I can come back in tomorrow but I'm considering just going home got the GC.

*Ms Higgins* (2:36pm):

That's so heavy. I am sorry to hear.

(2) Ms Brown forming the view, in the light of the further serious security incident, that there was "no workplace reason" why Mr Lehrmann needed to remain in the Ministerial office just to attend a farewell morning tea the next day, so he was told he could leave the office "immediately" (Brown (at [51])).

(3) Ms Brown attending a meeting the following day on Wednesday, 27 March, with the Minister and the Secretary of the DPS, where a report into the security incident was provided by the Secretary (Brown (Ex FB-7)); Ms Brown also contacted Dr John Kunkel, the Prime Minister's Chief of Staff and informed him of what Dr Kunkel described as being: "About a security incident the previous weekend ... which was essentially two staff members had ... come back into Parliament House and entered the ministerial office of Minister Reynolds and were drinking, um, late at night or early in the morning I think it was" (MC (at 32)).

(4) Ms Brown also communicated with the ASIO Director-General informing him about Mr Lehrmann's breach of document handling, unauthorised after-hours access and lying about why he came into the office, because they constituted breaches by a holder of an Australian Government Security Vetting Agency clearance, which was noted by ASIO (Brown (at [80]–[81])).

(5) As discussed in Section F.3 above, there was then the refusal by Ms Brown on Friday, 29 March (confirmed as being appropriate by Ms Barons of the Advice and Support Branch of M&PS) to follow instructions to report the incident (as it was then understood) to the police as she felt she could not accuse a young man of a criminal offence without the female telling her definitively that she had been raped and, moreover, because Ms Brown following such an instruction "would put Ms Higgins' welfare at risk as it would remove her power to make choices" (Brown (at [98(c)])).

(6) On 1 April, a number of events took place that received scant attention at the hearing; foremost among these was the meeting of the GSC, being a committee dealing with the number, classifications, salaries, recruitment and appointment processes for Ministerial staff; prior to the meeting, the Minister had formed the view that Mr Lehrmann's employment should be terminated based on his two prior security breaches; after hearing a presentation about the security breaches

and about lying to get into Parliament House after hours, the GSC "recommended Mr Lehrmann's employment be terminated on these grounds" (Brown (at [131], [136])).

(7) On 4 April, the evidence of Ms Brown at trial was that Assistant AFP Commissioner Leanne Close had told Senator Reynolds that a sexual assault had been reported to the AFP by Ms Higgins (T2145.12–15); in new material received following the reopening (MC (at 50–51)), more detail has now been provided of the meeting this day between Senator Reynolds, Ms Brown, Assistant Commissioner Close (wrongly referred to in MC as "Leanne Cross") and AFP liaison officer, Sergeant Paul Sherring. According to what appears to be a record of contemporaneous notes of Assistant Commissioner Close (which the parties have not suggested are anything but accurate), Senator Reynolds said "we became aware on Tuesday that this had happened on Saturday night – on my couch there!" (and that the incident had come to her attention "though a DPS report") (MC (at 39)). In context, I read this to mean that they had become aware on the Tuesday of the information as to the incident that had been reported to them by DPS on that day. Ms Brown further confirmed that Ms Higgins had initially said to her she did not want the matter reported and the "Minister wanted [Ms Brown] to go straight to the nearest police station" (MC (at 39)); and the following is then recorded in the notes (all misspellings are in the original):

> Minister - Bruce (alleged offended) has been stood down over other issues.
>
> Brown - end of contract on gardening leave. We had suspicious about him handling security material. Minister - There was a Home Affairs document in his possession that we kept asking for, it was classified and he shouldn't have had it. He only came to work in this office recently. He used to work for George and then Bridget McKenzie when George left Parl. Bruce made out he was getting a job at ASIO and was good friends with Duncan Lewis. It didn't add up and he looked shifty.
>
> Brown - I called Duncan Lewis who didn't know anything about this and not too good friends with Bruce.

Minister - wevee been trying to issue the end of contract papers to him but he wont come in.

I said first concerns about Brittany weneed to get her in contact with SACAT in ACTAP. Reg will ensure she is given specialist support + access to appropriate services. I want to understand what happened if there are any criminal charges that need to be investigated.

I also have concerns from info I heard that this may have happened before or could happen again. (I was referring to info that alleged victim may have been drugged).

Paul - we need to speak toa range of people. Security staff cleaners may have info

I said - we will need to speak to president of senate and other Presiding officer to give us access to CCTV + advise an investigation will require us to spend various people at **APH.**

Minister- she has already advised the special minister for state. Meeting concluded. Minister expressed gratitude that the AFP was taking charge of the matter.

Fiona Brown Paul Sherring + had a further brief conversation in the other room.

Brown went over details reviewing concerns about Bruce.

She then said that there was cleaning done in the office. She wasn't sure why the office had been cleaned although there is an email or something that seems to have been sent.

I said we will wait to understand how that occurred what security+ cleaners saw, heard+ did and why.

Paul+ I then left the minister's office.

(8) The same day, Ms Brown tried to contact Mr Lehrmann to arrange a meeting but was unsuccessful, she then received advice from the Advice and Support Branch of M&PS as to the appropriate procedure, including the provision of the show cause letter; which was sent on 4 April (Ex 23). Following receipt of a response, the Minister

> reached the conclusion that Mr Lehrmann had engaged in serious misconduct, had breached the Ministerial staff standards, and proceeded to terminate him.

I pause here to deal with some submissions made by Network Ten. In doing so, it is useful to bear in mind the incomplete and somewhat confused information about the alleged rape as at 4 April, which is well illustrated by the recently tendered evidence of the note made that day by Assistant Commissioner Close, as set out above (including its reference to the unsubstantiated rumours mentioned by Assistant Commissioner Close, to which I have already made reference). 648

Notwithstanding the lack of proof an assault had occurred and the then incomplete information as to the specifics of the allegation, it is said that it was "inexcusable" that in the show cause letter, no reference was made to Ms Higgins, the fact that she had been found naked and passed out, or to the allegation that Mr Lehrmann had sexually assaulted Ms Higgins. It is said to be "bizarre" that Mr Lehrmann was terminated for serious misconduct without "ever being confronted with or given the opportunity to respond to the allegation that he had sexually assaulted Ms Higgins in Senator Reynolds' office". It is further said, apparently seriously, that the "moving on": 649

> of an alleged rapist is reminiscent of the conduct of which a number of religious institutions stood rightly condemned in the Royal Commission into Institutional Child Sex Abuse, save that this time it occurred in the second decade of the 21st century in the heart of Australia's democracy on the eve of a federal election.

These overwrought and extravagant submissions ought never to have been made. If Ms Brown had wanted to move Mr Lehrmann on and try to sweep matters under the carpet, there would have been an obvious way of attempting to do so – he had left the office and was never to return and Ms Brown would not later have taken active steps to encourage Ms Higgins to report the incident to the AFP. But rather than letting things just slide, disciplinary steps were taken resulting in a termination for the security reasons put to, considered, and approved by, the GSC. Further, what the submission ignores or fails to appreciate, is that a show cause letter is a particular type of legal mechanism directed to providing procedural fairness. As those experienced in employment law would understand, it is critical 650 that if such a show cause letter is to be sent, that it specifies allegations that are cogent, objectively verifiable and are considered by an employer as able to be proven if any action is later taken to challenge any disciplinary decision adverse to the interests of an employee. It accords with prudence and is wholly unsurprising that the show cause letter would only focus on objective facts easily able to be established at the time the letter is sent and would avoid reference to contestable issues. To proceed otherwise ventured all sorts of legal complications. No doubt this is why Ms Brown received the advice from the Advice and Support Branch of M&PS in the form she did, and, as one would expect, the only evidence as to what occurred at the GSC is consistent with the reasons ultimately given for the dismissal (MC (at 34)).

651 Indeed, consistently with her personality, the great care Ms Brown took to deal properly with the employment aspect of what had occurred (and how it intersected with any ongoing criminal investigation) is the subject of some further information tendered following the recent reopening and made clearer by the record of Assistant Commissioner Close's notes (MC (at 54)). At 1:27pm on 5 April, the following is recorded by the Assistant Commissioner (errors in original):

> Called out be my EA to speak urgently to Fiona Brown COS to Minister Reynolds. She advised the employment of Bruce Lehrmann is to e discussed with him as he has finally responded to an email can she meet with him? I said, of course, but his employment matters are completely separate to the AFP investigation she should NOT raise the criminal allegations.
>
> Fiona said she doesn't want to become a witness. I said "you already are" as you may have been the first person Brittany spoke to about the allegation she was sexually assaulted.
>
> Fiona then sasid "how should we treat the issue of Bruce leaving a junior member of staff behind in that state?" I said I don't understand what you are referring to. She said - oh don't worry that's a separate issue. I assured her she could have a conversation with Bruce but not to discuss anything to do with the sex assault allegations AND advised her to take good notes of the conversation with him.

652 Ms Brown did what she did following taking careful and prudent employment and law enforcement advice. Network Ten's submission equating the

actions of Ms Brown in this regard as akin to protecting a paedophile is not only profoundly unfair but also legally misconceived.

Two further matters not already the subject of findings should be noted. Not because I consider that they are of particular significance to my consideration of any defence, nor relevant to Ms Higgins' credit, but because evidence was adduced about them, presumably because they were thought somehow relevant to Ms Brown's credit. 653

*First*, is cleaning. On Monday, 25 March, notably before Ms Brown or anyone other than Mr Lehrmann and Ms Higgins working for the Minister knew of the incident, the Ministerial private office was cleaned. As is evident from the contemporaneous records, this occurred by reason of actions commenced as early as 12:40pm on 23 March, involving the Chief of Staff of DPS (who had initially been called while Ms Higgins was still in the Ministerial Suite), as "someone may have vomited in there" (MC (at 13, 19, 22)). Ms Brown gave the cleaning no thought at the time, but when she later became aware that there had been unauthorised after-hours access to the Minister's office, she called "MinWing Support" to make enquires as to the details. Mr Stephen Frost, part of MinWing Support, saw Ms Brown and during this conversation, she discovered the Ministerial private office had also been cleaned on the previous Saturday, after Ms Higgins had left it. Ms Brown was initially concerned by hearing this, but Mr Frost advised her that it was "standard procedure for an office to be cleaned following after-hours access", and further explained there had been incidences over many years where offices had been left in a mess. There is no reason to doubt the evidence of what Mr Frost said to Ms Brown, which is supported by the contemporaneous record. 654

*Secondly*, not recorded in Ms Brown's notes, were meetings with Mr Payne which took place before Mr Lehrmann had left the office. I am satisfied these were inconsequential interactions whereby Ms Brown requested that Mr Payne initiate the necessary administrative action to finalise Mr Lehrmann's employment, but there evidently was also discussion of the incident in the context of Ms Brown enquiring of the Defence Liaison Officer whether the security incident, being the unauthorised access, would need to be reported to Defence (which Mr Payne responded in the negative) (T1421.24–31). It appears there may have been some discussion about *securing* CCTV footage of the security incident, which would 655 no doubt have been sensible given the serious security breach, but I am not satisfied the recollections of either participant is good enough, in the absence of any contemporaneous record, to ascertain specifics.

## I.3 The Role of the AFP and the 2019 Decision of Ms Higgins not to Proceed

656 Despite the representation made by Ms Higgins in the Commonwealth Deed that four days after the incident, on 27 March, members of the AFP Parliament House unit informed Ms Higgins that "they [the identity of the "they" is left undisclosed] had been told to investigate a sexual assault" (PL cl 3.13), this is not the case, and the involvement of the AFP came about differently.

657 On 27 March, Mr Dillaway came up from Melbourne to visit Ms Higgins and was giving her support – around this time Ms Higgins was saying her "main concern" was that she did not want anyone to know what had happened and she also "had concerns about becoming known as the girl who was raped in Parliament, and she was worried about how it could affect her job and her career" (T1223.33–35; T1224.16–26). Mr Dillaway explained to her that she had nothing to worry about because she was the victim and should have nothing to fear in terms of her job (T1224.42–45).

658 On 28 March, Ms Higgins had her discussion with Mr Payne (when she had made the contemporaneous representation it "would have been like f***ing a log" (T1422.39–43)). That afternoon, she also sent Mr Dillaway a text at 2:58pm referring to the fact that "Chris [Payne] just said apparently the AFP came into the suite during the night or morning sometime. And they just left me there" (Ex R99 (at 723)). Mr Payne's memory of this aspect of his conversation was unclear (T1423.23) but, of course, we know from the contemporaneous materials that this was an error, and it was security, not the AFP, that was involved in coming into the Ministerial Suite, as Ms Higgins explained in her evidence-in-chief (T659.27).

659 An assault had not been formally reported to the AFP by this time. This is not to say the evidence is clear about when a security incident had been communicated by DPS or others to the AFP. It is notable that a few months later Commissioner Andrew Colvin (Ex R94) complained about the AFP not being informed about the incident and asserted that "there

are significant discrepancies between the response to this incident and the existing agreements that our agencies share" and the "unacceptable" length of time it took DPS to share the Parliamentary Security Service incident report with the AFP.

In any event, what we do know is that on the following day, 660
the contemporaneous material (Annexure B) records Ms Brown called Ms Higgins on 29 March and offered to report the incident to police. This, of course, was at the time she was being pressured to report the incident, through Mr Reginald Chamberlain, because the Special Minister of State, Mr Hawke and Senator Reynolds wanted to protect their interests (T2126.14–32). Ms Higgins told Ms Brown "no", and said she wanted to see her father and, as I have already noted, Ms Brown appropriately respected her wishes.

Pausing here, Mr Chamberlain (Chief of Staff to Mr Hawke), gave evidence 661
he had first heard from the Department of Finance about the incident in "about late March or early April"; his knowledge was that two staffers had entered Parliament House late at night, which he thought odd (Chamberlain (at [6]–[7])). He obviously knew something happened before he was putting pressure on Ms Brown, so it must have been late March.

It was also on 1 April that Ms Higgins first went to the AFP 662
after the meeting between Ms Higgins, the Minister and Ms Brown as recorded in Annexure B. But despite this, the AFP must have become aware of the incident, other than through Ms Brown, prior to the meeting on 1 April. This is because when Federal Agents Katie Thelning and Rebecca Cleaves reported for duty on 1 April at 9:45am, they were notified by Sergeant Sherring "that there was a sensitive matter pertaining to a female who was attached to Minister Reynolds office" and Ms Cleaves was provided with a mobile contact number (T1386.23–25; T1402.36–38). How that information came to Sergeant Sherring is unclear on the evidence.

Ms Higgins now describes the meeting with the Minister, also attended 663
by Ms Brown, that preceded her meeting with the AFP on that day as "adversarial" (T783.33–34). When pressed, this was said to be because: (a) it was hosted in the same room as the incident had occurred; and (b) Senator Reynolds was saying "these are things that women go through", being evidence evidently meant to convey the impression, as Network Ten

submits, that the Minister "made her feel like she was trying to minimise what had occurred" (T783.38–46).

664 As to (a), I accept it makes sense, given what happened to her in the Ministerial private office; that she would have felt distress in the meeting being held around a small table, not far from the couch (however, I also accept the evidence of Ms Brown, however unfortunate, that she had not appreciated that Ms Higgins' statement "I remember him on top of me" was a reference to them being on the Minister's couch, and if she had been cognisant of this fact, she would have arranged the meeting to be held in another location). The meeting, of course, consisted mostly of Senator Reynolds talking to Ms Higgins (T664.4–11).

665 As to (b), contrary to the impression sought to be conveyed by Ms Higgins in selecting the words she used in the witness box, I have no doubt as to the correctness of Ms Brown's recollection (confirmed by the contemporaneous materials and the content of other representations made to and by Ms Higgins at around this time), that no minimisation of Ms Higgins' experience was attempted and, to the contrary, attempts were made to support and reassure Ms Higgins and, in particular, to encourage her to report her account to the AFP. More specifically, consistently with the contemporaneous record and Ms Brown's evidence, I find that during the meeting:

(1) the Minister explained the purpose of the meeting was to check on Ms Higgins' welfare; that she did not "know exactly what happened but something doesn't seem right" and "what you choose to do we will support"; and suggested counselling and talking to the EAP, which Ms Brown noted was an independent support process;

(2) the Minister suggested Ms Higgins speak to an AFP liaison officer to discuss what happened and explained the AFP could provide Ms Higgins advice the Minister was not in a position to do; in doing so, far from telling Ms Higgins that this an example of the "things that women go through", the Minister referred to times in her life where she had repressed things that had happened to her, and they popped back up again; she further said the AFP could quietly look into things and provide Ms Higgins with options and reiterated, first and foremost, that what was important was Ms Higgins' welfare and that she be in control, identify her options and then make decisions;

(3) Ms Higgins understandably said she was a bit overwhelmed, but being busy was a good thing; consistently with other contemporaneous representations made by her, I am satisfied she said Ms Brown had been "fantastic", and had gone "over and above to support" her; and that Ms Brown had been "caring" and "amazing"; Ms Higgins also said "I'm worried the impact this event could have on my career prospects";

(4) in response, the Minister said Ms Higgins' welfare was her primary concern and that Ms Higgins had her unconditional support and repeated that it was important that Ms Higgins take control today, talk to the AFP and know what her options were and that there would be no impact on Ms Higgins' career;

(5) by the conclusion of the meeting (and unsurprisingly given the level of encouragement she was receiving to speak to the AFP), Ms Higgins said she would like to talk to the AFP and the Minister asked Ms Brown to contact the AFP to arrange a meeting with Ms Higgins.

One of the most topsy-turvy aspects of this case is that putting what 666 occurred at this meeting and the events of the preceding days together, a clear picture emerges, but it is entirely at odds with the notion of an attempt being made to cover up an allegation of rape by discouraging it to be reported to the police.

Indeed, I am comfortably satisfied that the Minister considered it would 667 protect her personal interests that the *very opposite* occur. She wanted the incident to be reported to the police and was doing what she could to encourage Ms Higgins to see the AFP, having failed in her attempt to direct Ms Brown to report the incident the previous Friday. As I said during the hearing, it is the only alleged cover-up of which I am aware where those said to be responsible for the covering up were almost insisting the complainant to go to the police.

As noted above, the contemporaneous records make plain the AFP was 668 aware of the "sensitive matter pertaining to a female" prior to the 1 April meeting. It will also be recalled that Ms Brown gave evidence, which I accept, that she considered Mr Hawke and Senator Reynolds were being forceful in directing Ms Brown to report the allegation "because they were worried about covering themselves" (T2126.42). A rational conclusion is that someone said something to the AFP prior to Ms Higgins deciding she wanted to involve the AFP, which is perhaps unsurprising given the involvement of the DPS, the Chief of Staff of the Special Minister of State, the nature of the security breach, and the fact that Mr Chamberlain had the AFP's contact details. We know Mr Chamberlain had the contact details because after the meeting between the Minister and Ms Higgins, Ms Brown obtained the details for Sergeant Sherring and Agent Cleaves from Mr Chamberlain (who gave evidence that around the time he was dealing with Ms Brown, she asked him how to contact the AFP, and he sent her details of the AFP officers in Parliament House (Chamberlain (at [20]–[22])).

669 Ms Brown apparently spoke to Agent Cleaves about meeting Ms Higgins at 12pm (although this is not entirely clear). When the AFP officers came up to the office, Ms Brown observed they "looked like cops" and formed the view that it would be better for Ms Higgins' privacy to relocate the meeting to the AFP offices in the basement of Parliament House. Arrangements were made for Ms Higgins to go down to the basement (T1386.16–43).

670 Ms Brown offered to either attend the meeting, or wait and walk back with her, or return to pick her up, Ms Higgins declined these offers, but Ms Brown asked Ms Higgins to let her know "when she was back in the office, so I knew she was OK" (Brown (at [120])).

671 There is no need to recount in any great detail what was said at the initial meeting with the AFP by Ms Higgins as I am satisfied the officers recorded the information provided by Ms Higgins during that meeting in their official diaries (Ex R73 and Ex R77). It suffices to note they acted appropriately, professionally and asked "in-depth" questions (T1387.5). Ms Higgins told Agent Cleaves and Agent Thelning that she had been out drinking with colleagues, she ended up back at Parliament House and that "Mr Lehrmann was on top of her, participating in non-consensual sex" (T1387.24–45). The officers, recognising immediately that specialist assistance was required, then said they would refer the matter to SACAT (T667.1–7). Ms Higgins subsequently received a prompt referral to SACAT (T667.9; Ex R7).

672 Ms Higgins was no doubt still working through issues, was upset, and understandably appeared nervous (T1391.14–17). She was also apparently keen to downplay her drinking (falsely asserting she had drunk "four gin and

tonics") (T776.24–28) and although she explained that Mr Lehrmann had been quite "handsy" and (as recorded in Agent Thelning's diary) "[she] did not really mind" (Ex R77 (at 4); T1405.36), she underplayed the fact that they had been mutually intimate and that they passionately kissed at 88mph. She was also untruthful about saying she went to Phillip Medical Centre and had a test (Ex R77 (at 6); T780.17).

Ms Higgins gave evidence that she did not think it was true that she told the officers that she did not want at that point to progress with a "formal complaint" (T789.5). But she clearly did – it is evident from the notes (Ex R77 (at 5)) that she said: "I put what happened away so it wouldn't be a narrative to my life story. I am quite good at doing this"; and "I do not want to report this officially – just off the record". 673

At the end of the meeting, Ms Higgins said that she was aware that the matter would be referred to SACAT and knew that it was going forward in that sense (T788.33–789.10), despite what she told the officers about her lack of desire to proceed. 674

By 2 April, Agent Thelning spoke to an officer from SACAT; as we will see below, the available support services had been identified and the Canberra Rape Crisis Centre (**CRCC**) had been contacted (T1407.1–47). 675

After her contact with the AFP, it will be recalled that on 3 April, Ms Higgins was content for Mr Dillaway to "reach out to the PMO" (Ex R99 (at 814)) about expediting some counselling and about her desire to work close to home during the election (a matter to which I will return) and, after that occurred, Ms Higgins knew the matter would be discussed with Dr Kunkel. She then said to Mr Dillaway (Ex 99 (at 814)): 676

> Thank you for doing that. Honestly, I really appreciate it. The help is beyond welcome, I wouldn't say it had been handled poorly; just a difficult situation to manage. Seriously, Fiona is great. I just think there has been a lot of competing things going on.

As foreshadowed, Agent Cleaves contacted SACAT to arrange a "meet and greet" between Ms Higgins and members of that team (T1393.31–40) and informed Ms Brown of the fact Ms Higgins had been referred (T1393.42–1394.19). 677

It was not in dispute that in the ACT, a sexual offence investigation usually begins with what is called a "meet and greet" between the complainant 678 and officers from SACAT. Among other things, a complainant receives procedural information about the investigation and any future court proceeding. There may also be a referral to relevant support services.

679 After this comes a point of decision. If the complainant wants the investigation to proceed, the next stage involves a trained police officer obtaining evidence of the allegations by conducting a videotaped "Evidence-in-Chief interview". The interview is so-called because ACT law allows this interview recording to be adduced as the complainant's evidence-in-chief at an ensuing criminal trial (as the two interviews later given by Ms Higgins were adduced in the criminal trial of Mr Lehrmann with Ms Higgins in another room, supplemented by further evidence-in-chief adduced orally in Court).

680 As arranged, on 8 April (that is, just after a fortnight following the incident), Ms Higgins attended a meet and greet with SACAT officers. We know what happened in that meeting with clarity because of the contemporaneous records (Ex R72) produced by, and evidence given by, Detective Harman, an officer experienced in working with complainants, taking statements, and investigating matters by collecting evidence (T1288.16–39). Detective Harman had been allocated the matter on 4 April and had a conversation with Agent Cleaves (T1289.21–35; T1291.12–37). Consistently with Ms Higgins' express wishes conveyed to the AFP on 1 April, Detective Harman had been informed that Ms Higgins did not want to proceed with an investigation at that stage, but she did want further information about her options (T1289.17–19).

681 Detective Harman, and her colleague Detective Anderson, collected Ms Higgins from Parliament House and took her to the Winchester Police Centre where they met with Ms Kathryn Cripps from the CRCC (T1293.4–10), with whom she subsequently had many counselling sessions in person and by telephone (T1331.23–1334.16; Cripps (at [37]–[38])). Ms Higgins gave evidence as to the counselling but did not at trial repeat the claim made to Ms Maiden during an exchange two years later (Ex 50 (at 22)) that Ms Cripps, like, it appears, so many people Ms Higgins came across, acted in a "very weird" way. Ms Higgins asserted that she "ultimately stopped going [to counselling] because at one point [Ms Cripps] sort of made like a suggestion that I didn't seem like the type of vengeful person who would ever come forward, and I thought that that comment was really sort of like out of hand" (Ex 50 (at 22)). Although Ms Higgins made many vague claims about people acting weirdly or inappropriately, this one struck

me as particularly odd, having closely observed Ms Cripps giving evidence and being impressed by her experience, competence and acute sensitivity to persons alleging they are victims of sexual assault.

As I said during the hearing, I was conscious not to intrude upon what was said during the course of the counselling, except to the extent it was strictly relevant (T1332.30–32); understandably, there was no detailed exploration of the content of sessions, and in the absence of contemporaneous records, I do not consider it safe to make findings as to what was said during this counselling period based only upon snippets of material, subject to what follows. 682

Doing the best I can, and having taken the evidence of Ms Cripps into account, I consider it likely that Ms Higgins maintained her position, that she had articulated almost immediately to Mr Dillaway, that her main concern was that she did not want anyone to know what had happened and she had concerns about "becoming known as the girl who was raped in Parliament, and she was worried about how it could affect her job and her career" (T1223.33–35; T1224.16–26). This makes intuitive sense in circumstances where Ms Higgins told Ms Cripps she wanted to become a Member of Parliament (T1337.7–15). 683

Going back to the meeting on 8 April, consistently with the purpose of a "meet and greet", Detective Harman explained that her role was to explain available support services and to discuss what an investigation would involve, including conducting an Evidence-in-Chief interview, speaking to witnesses, and collecting evidence (T1293.16–44). 684

Detective Harman's evidence was that the day after the "meet and greet", she made some enquiries in relation to available medical services and tried to call Ms Higgins, including to see if she wanted to participate in an Evidence-in-Chief interview (T1298.35–45). Detective Harman tried to call Ms Higgins the next day, but there was no answer (T1299.28–32). 685

But Ms Higgins' intention not to pursue the complaint hardened given what had been conveyed to her. Again, here the contemporaneous records, not *ex post facto* reconstructions, are telling. She told Mr Dillaway on 9 April 2019, that the AFP "said pursuing it through the legal system usually takes around two years start to finish and is pretty involved" and that she "[h]onestly would rather just move on. Seems way too taxing" (Ex R99 (at 925)). Consistently with this, Major Irvine gave evidence of her 686 "distinct" recollection of a second and important conversation around 10 April (T1183.28–34) where Ms Higgins said she was no longer pursuing the AFP complaint because the police told her (T1183.44–46):

> it would take a really long time to get to court. It would be emotionally taxing on her and it would be difficult to reach, like, a conviction of – of Bruce from what happened.

687 I find this representation was made to Major Irvine, in whom she was confiding intimate matters at the critical time, notwithstanding she was not a close friend. I also find it reflected the candid belief of Ms Higgins at the time it was made.

688 The way Ms Higgins dealt with Detective Harman is reflective of her desire not to progress the complaint. For example, she did not take steps to provide the AFP with the name of the second venue (that is, 88mph), or where CCTV footage may have then been able to be obtained (despite what she later said was her intense desire to obtain access to CCTV footage from the Parliament). Although Ms Higgins did not have the name of the venue to hand, if she wanted to pursue the complaint, she could have discovered it. Further, Ms Higgins did not respond to messages and calls from Detective Harman (Ex R72; T1318.39–1319.17) and, although asked for photos from her phone and for the dress, they were not provided (T1317.21–45; T1324.29–41). This was all material central to the investigation and not providing it was consistent with her contemporaneous and candid representations as to her firm intention not to proceed.

689 The reality was that Ms Higgins was caught in the dilemma that countless women have faced in alleging they have been the victim of sexual assault. Her first and instinctive reaction (Ex R77 (at 5)) was to: "put what happened away so it wouldn't be a narrative to my life story. I am quite good at doing this"; but despite her thinking she could just compartmentalise what had occurred and move on, she naturally had the conflicting instinct to hold a perpetrator to account. I have little doubt Ms Higgins was experiencing a combination of antithetical elements; driven one way by self-protection – another way by a desire for justice – she was doing her best to think through whether it was best to change her mind from her instinctive reaction to move on.

690 In this regard she was hardly atypical. As is usefully summarised by Patrick Tidmarsh and Gemma Hamilton in the Australian Institute of Criminology

report, 'Misconceptions of Sexual Crimes against Adult Victims: Barriers to Justice' *Trends & Issues in Crime and Criminal Justice Report No 611* (November 2020) (at 3):

> Empirical evidence ... shows most victims who experience rape or sexual assault delay disclosing and reporting, or never disclose their experiences. Indeed, 83 percent of Australian women did not report their most recent incident of sexual assault to the police (Australian Bureau of Statistics (ABS) 2013; Cox 2016), and only six in 10 women who experienced sexual assault sought advice or help from others (ABS 2013).
>
> Members of the community, including legal professionals, may hold the misconception that reports of rape and sexual assault are easy to make and difficult to defend, and that most sex offenders are swiftly convicted and face severe punishment for their crimes (Eastwood, Kift & Grace 2006). However, both national and international research consistently demonstrate that incidents of rape and sexual assault are significantly under-reported, under-prosecuted and under-convicted.
>
> Common reasons for victims' non-reporting or delays in reporting or disclosure include:
>
> - confusion, guilt, or shock about the assault (Long 2006);
> - fear of the perpetrator (Cox 2016), and consequences of reporting (Cook, David & Grant 2001);
> - fear that they will not be believed (Cox 2016); and
> - rape myth acceptance, where victims do not recognise they have experienced sexual assault or blame themselves for what has occurred (Heath et al. 2013).
>
> Also, the criminal justice system is a difficult, stressful, expensive, and time-consuming process that requires exposing oneself to police and public scrutiny, and potential cross-examination. This may have serious legal and psychological consequences for both the complainant and others involved (Parsons & Bergin 2010; Wall & Tarczon 2013).

Ms Higgins is not an unintelligent woman. It is worth remembering that 691
much later, when we have some further candid indications of what Ms

Higgins thought, she was well aware of potential barriers to the difficulties she might encounter in assisting a criminal prosecution. Indeed, she was quite sophisticated in her understanding of the legal process. One only has to recall her telephone conversation with Ms Maiden when she "was really relieved" because given Mr Lehrmann's account, there would be no need "to have this very nuanced debate about consent and alcohol and all this kind of stuff" (T703.22–27), and in the first interview with the Project team, when she said she thought a finding of sexual assault had occurred may be able to obtained on the civil standard, but not to the criminal standard (T1015.19–24).

692 In any event, returning to the narrative, she did not change her mind in 2019 and her interactions with the SACAT officers simply fortified her initial view (as she then made clear to Mr Dillaway and Major Irvine). It followed she did not move down the path of an Evidence-in-Chief interview, because having confirmed her earlier indications, on Saturday, 13 April (the day she was later going to Perth) she wrote to Detective Harman that: "[a]fter careful consideration I have decided not to proceed any further" while remarking that she "really [did] appreciate your time, professionalism and assistance with this complaint" and that Detective Harman "helped more than you know" (Ex R9).

693 This far from unique and understandable response to what had been accurately explained to her by experienced AFP officers (engaging with her in the company of an experienced support person from a rape crisis centre) is the real reason why the complaint was not pursued in 2019.

694 But it does not end there. There is more in the contemporaneous record antithetical to the notion of any cover-up. Despite Ms Higgins making it plain she did not wish to proceed, the AFP then went to some lengths to ensure the complaint was concluded appropriately.

695 On 15 April, Agent Cleaves had left a message to arrange to view the CCTV footage and recorded a conversation she had with the SACAT that Ms Higgins did not want to proceed and had not called the CRCC (T1397.19–32). And again, even though there was no investigation on foot, on the following day (16 April), Agent Cleaves viewed the CCTV footage in the security room and made notes (T1396.31–36). She also followed up, obtained, and then reviewed an outstanding security report from the DPS (T1394.24; T1396.24–29).

Further, as Detective Harman explained (T1302.1–22) she "was still continuing ... to follow up the CCTV footage from Parliament House" and that: 696

> ... [Ms Higgins'] email didn't cause me concern because that was the ongoing theme throughout either my briefings or my interactions with her is that she didn't want to proceed at that time but may in the future. So that email that she sent to me wasn't out of the ordinary, or wasn't a shock to me that she had changed her mind vastly from a point. But Sergeant Rose did have – just wanted to make sure. So I did make some inquiries. And I know the victim liaison officer with ACT police was due to call her, so I did ask her as well that some time following when she did make contact, could she ensure that Ms Higgins did make that decision for herself. So I did get – you know, with my unanswered calls and text messages, I did get the impression that Ms Higgins perhaps didn't want to talk to me verbally at that point. So I was trying to get someone else to make that inquiry for me. I do know that Detective Sergeant Langlands did call her at some point ... I was made aware of a phone call that was made by him to ensure that it was her decision.

After his evidence was given, I asked whether Detective Harman recalled what was said about that telephone call with Detective Sergeant Langlands, to which she responded (T1302.27–32): 697

> I only read a case note entry on my job in relation to it, so I don't know what the – I wasn't present for the phone call. But it was a very brief case, and the entry I read from him saying that he called her and ensured that there was no pressure placed upon her by anyone to make the decision not to proceed with an investigation at that point.

By May 2019, what occurred is that Ms Higgins began to reflect on the unjustness of what had happened and was no doubt questioning whether she had done the right thing in not holding Mr Lehrmann to account. Her confusion and trauma understandably continued. From her perspective, Mr Lehrmann had moved on and she was distressed she had to cope as best she could. At this time, she was continuing to confide in Mr Dillaway and had been upset by a news story about a senior staffer in the office of the Hon Ken Wyatt MP allegedly engaging in bullying (T683.5–21; R99 (at 1420–1424)). 698

699 Ms Higgins heard Senator Reynolds say something like "[i]t's really awful that staffers would leak this about this woman", which Ms Higgins took as a comment supportive of someone behaving inappropriately (T683.8–16). Ms Higgins was obviously reflecting on her situation. She sent a text message to Mr Dillaway at 7:15pm on 6 May asking whether he had seen the story, and at 7:25pm (Ex R99 (at 1424)):

> It just sort of reminds me of my situation, I guess.
>
> How it can be turned into a story and everyone is basically just empathising with the perpetrator of the harassment.

700 Later, at 9:23pm, she texted that she was (Ex R99 (at 1428)):

> Kinda shitty.
>
> I'm not sure why, but I just feel super angry at the moment. It's probably misdirected and should be aimed at Bruce but I feel so pissed at the people in the party.

701 And at 9:44pm (Ex R99 (at 1429)):

> No, not really. It's just beyond shitty hearing Linda offering this obviously horrible Wyatt staffer all this support in the wake of the story and I'm, like ???
>
> I was literally assaulted in your office and I collectively maybe took 4 days off/was offered jack shit in terms of help.

702 Finally, at 10:05pm Ms Higgins texted (Ex R99 (at 1431))):

> If I want to maintain a job, I can't talk about it but I'm still getting follow up calls from the AFP to this dah [*sic*] and I'm just at the end of my rope with it.

703 I have little doubt that Ms Higgins considered, with justification, that it was wrong that as someone who had career (including political) aspirations, she had been placed in a situation where, to use the earlier words she had used to Mr Dillaway, she needed to have "concerns about becoming known as the girl who was raped in Parliament, and she was worried about how it could affect her job and her career".

704 For completeness, I should note that Ms Higgins, during the course of her evidence, gave a good deal of evidence about how she felt or what she perceived, usually expressed at a high level of generality. At the end of her evidence, in order to seek clarification of what she meant as to

obstructions or roadblocks, I requested Ms Higgins to identify with precision what were the express words or the actual actions of either (a) Ms Brown; (b) Senator Reynolds; (c) members of the AFP; or (d) anyone else she perceived to be in authority over her, which obstructed her, or threw up a roadblock, or forced her to choose between her career and pursuing her complaint up until she confirmed definitively she did not want to proceed in 2019. The exchange went as follows:

> HIS HONOUR: Now, so dealing first with Ms Brown. What I want you to do is to focus on the date when you raised the allegation of rape – and you've given evidence about that - - -?---Yes.
>
> - - - and the period up to 13 April 2019?---Yes.
>
> Now, you might recall on 13 April 2019, that's the date you emailed the Federal Police to say you really appreciated their time, professionalism and assistance with the complaint. "You've helped me more than you can know." And you thanked them for their sensitivity and care, but said after careful consideration, you decided not to proceed any further, okay?---Yes.
>
> So that's the period I'm asking you to focus on?---Yes.
>
> So dealing first with Fiona Brown. I just want to – I've heard what you said about your feelings and what you inferred, but I just want to understand what actually did she say to you or what actually did she do which you said put up a roadblock or obstructed you?---Of course. So the – the first major thing that really made me first doubt Fiona Brown was the difference of account between what Chris Payne knew and what she knew and what she was forthcoming and telling me, and that was the first time that I questioned Fiona Brown, because initially I really trusted what she was saying.
>
> So what is it that she said? That's what I want you to focus on: what she said - - -?---Yes.
>
> - - - or what she did, not what you took from things - - -?---Of course.
>
> - - - okay, because you've given a lot of evidence about what you felt?---Yes.

I want to know what she said or what she did which you said amounted to an obstruction so you had to choose between your career and making a complaint to the police?---Yes. So - - -

Specifically?---Yes. So she said that she didn't know about – she – she – okay. She – she said – she said that she didn't know certain things, or, like, she said that I had been found or was drunk or something, and then when I spoke to Chris Payne, I found out I had been found naked, and that was information she had that I didn't have. So she knew something and she was pretending like she had never heard or hadn't even considered a fact sexual assault could occur, and then, all of a sudden, these other people were coming to me telling me things that Fiona Brown obviously knew this, and yet - - -

So it was her fact of saying she didn't know something?---Yes.

Okay?---And that was the thing that first created doubt - - -

All right?--- - - - and first mistrust and broke down in the relationship.

All right. So what was the next thing that she did?---The next thing was the meeting in the office where the rape took place. It was the fact that they said if you go to the police, can you let us know, but it was done in a way where I felt threatened.

Don't worry about what you felt?---Of course.

I'm just asking you what they said or what they did?---Yes. And then - - -

So it said – they said if you go to the – so the next thing was, "If you go to the police, let us know"?---Yes.

Right?---And it was framed in the context – it made reference to the election.

What was said?---I can't specifically remember the wording.

Right?---But it was framed in the context that it – it was pertinent because of the election.

But you can't recall what was said about that?---Not – not the exact wording.

> Yes. Anything else?---The next thing was she asked about whether I could go to the Gold Coast, get paid out, and then I wouldn't return to work, and that was what I perceived to be - - -
>
> Don't worry about what you perceived?---Of course. That's the next thing?---She told me I could go to the Gold Coast and be paid out, but I wouldn't come back.
>
> Yes. Anything else?---Then she just disappeared. She left.
>
> Okay. Anything else – focusing now on Senator Reynolds, anything other than the matters that you referred to in the context of Ms Brown?---No. Senator Reynolds only spoke to me about the rape once, and it was on 1 April, and then later in October.
>
> All right. And what about members of the Federal Police between that period?---No, they were – they were good to me. The Federal Police at that point were really good. So is there anyone else you perceived in authority over you who said something or did something that you say obstructed you or threw up a roadblock in that period between the time when that person, as you understood it, knew about the rape, and 13 April 2019?---Not in overt vocalised ways.
>
> All right. Thank you. Anything arising out of that?
>
> DR COLLINS: Not from me, your Honour.
>
> HIS HONOUR: Anything arising out of that? That concludes your evidence. Thank you very much for your assistance - - -?---Thank you.

The bulk of these assertions are contrary to my findings based on the whole of the evidence, such as Ms Higgins' characterisation as to the evolution of the knowledge of Ms Brown, or as to the existence of some form of nefarious calculation being made as to the venue of the 1 April meeting, or any threatening of Ms Higgins if she went to the police, but it remains appropriate to address two final matters. 705

The *first* is Ms Higgins' assertion identified in her evidence above that those involved in failing to facilitate a move to the Gold Coast and guaranteeing her return were doing so in furtherance of an attempt to provide an obstacle to her pursuing her criminal complaint. The *second* is a matter which had been relied upon by Ms Higgins in out-of-court representations placed into evidence and gained some currency during the hearing 706 as consisting of a roadblock or obstruction – that of the CCTV footage at Parliament House.

707 Upon close examination, any suggestion that these matters are indicative of a cover-up forcing her not to pursue her complaint are devoid of merit.

## I.4 Why and When the PMO was told and Support Services

708 Despite speculation by some as to how and when various persons within the PMO came to know about the incident, like with so many things, contemporaneous material not provided to nor reviewed by Ms Maiden or the Project team before publication in 2021, if properly analysed, reveals the apparent answer.

709 As is evident from Ms Brown's records, following advice received from M&PS and telling Ms Higgins it was necessary to report the matter to the PMO because of the security breach at their initial meeting on 26 March, the following day, Ms Brown briefed Mr Wong, who worked in the PMO about the after-hours access. Not only was it known to Ms Higgins the PMO would be told about the security incident, she also consented to a later communication to the same office and knew it would be discussed with the Chief of Staff.

710 This necessitates some background and explanation.

711 As is evident from Ex R99 (being candid messages between Ms Higgins and her friend Mr Dillaway), Ms Higgins had messaged at 5:45pm on 31 March 2019 and said that she had "Hit a bit of a wall since dad left. Not too excited for the week ahead haha" (at 759). Mr Dillaway's response, four minutes later, was to say: "I'm excited for week ahead because of you" and separately a minute later: "I'll support and help you through next week" (at 759). This support continued, including at 9:13am on 1 April (which, as will be recalled, was the day of the meeting with the Minister and Ms Brown) with Mr Dillaway saying "[g]ood luck this morning. Let me know if you want to catch up afterwards, for a talk, coffee or just to give you a hug" (Ex R99 (at 764)). Mr Dillaway had obviously been unaware of the time of the meeting which, as Annexure B establishes, commenced at approximately 8:40am. Hence Ms Higgins responded: "All finished up. About to head down for a cup of coffee run if you are free" (Ex R99 (at 764)).

There are no messages then in evidence until 8:30am on 3 April, when Mr 712
Dillaway asks Ms Higgins whether she wanted him "to reach out to the PMO" (Ex R99 (at 813)).

Pausing there, Ms Higgins at some point had told Mr Dillaway that she 713
wanted to have the free counselling referred to in the EAP brochure that had been given to her but, upon enquiry, she had discovered there was no appointment available with a psychologist for two months (T644.45; T1260.40–45). I am also confident she was keen about the prospect of working with Mr Dillaway in Brisbane during the course of the election campaign. They certainly discussed her wish to move "closer to home" for the campaign at around this time (Ex R99 (at 814)).

According to a question asked of him in cross-examination, it appears Mr 714
Dillaway may have earlier told the AFP about the delay in fixing a psychological appointment at a get-together for the former staff of Mr Ciobo, who was giving a valedictory speech, but given that speech was on 4 April, it must have been earlier, and Mr Dillaway was characteristically hazy as to the details (T1260.36–7). In any event, it is apparent Mr Dillaway was concerned that Ms Higgins could not receive the sort of care he thought she needed, and I suspect he was also keen to see Ms Higgins work closer to home during the campaign.

What may not have been fully apparent to Mr Dillaway, 715
and did not receive particular attention at the trial, was the correct chronology and details of what occurred as to Ms Higgins seeking support (despite her complaints made about the initial delay in securing an EAP appointment):

(1) As noted above (at [643]), during her first meeting with Ms Brown on 26 March, the EAP contact details had been provided to Ms Higgins and Ms Brown had explained the independent support and service the EAP provides, and Ms Brown had checked up on her by phone twice later that day (Annexure B).

(2) During the third meeting with Ms Brown on 28 March, Ms Higgins had said "I am taking up the counselling" (which Ms Brown took to be a reference the EAP service) and to which Ms Brown responded: "good, I am pleased to see you are accessing it' (Annexure B) and it must have been around this time that Ms Higgins experienced a delay in getting an appointment (Brown (at [85] [86]).

(3) Later that day, Ms Higgins told Ms Brown she had made an appointment with a doctor for the following day (Annexure B) (Brown (at [91])) – she did not proceed with the appointment despite requesting and receiving the time off to attend because she was "terrified" (T782.35);

(4) As already noted, on 1 April, during the meeting with the Minister and Ms Brown, the Minister suggested counselling and talking to the EAP, which Ms Brown noted was an independent support process.

(5) After speaking to the AFP on 1 April, and Agent Thelning facilitating a "wraparound referral" which amounts to a "reach out to all different support services that a victim may require" and speaking to Ms Nikki Armstrong of the CRCC to discuss the matter and providing Ms Higgins with information as to the services available and contact details (T1407–8), Ms Higgins then spoke to Zara from the CRCC on 2 April, and had been promptly booked into an "intake appointment tomorrow 3rd April at 15:30 hours", which had been confirmed by the CRCC (Ex R90) – for reasons unclear on the evidence, she did not proceed with the appointment.

(6) On 3 April, Mr Dillaway spoke to his contact in the PMO, Mr Julian Leembruggen about "the need for councillor [*sic*] and desire to be closer to home during election" and in response to Mr Dillaway reporting that Mr Leembruggen had allegedly said "he was mortified to hear about it and how things has been handled", Ms Higgins reaction, as we have seen, was to correct that impression by saying "I wouldn't say it's been handled poorly, just a difficult situation to manage. Seriously, Fiona is great" (Ex R99 (at 814)).

(7) On 8 April, of course, as I have already explained, Ms Higgins attended a meet and greet with SACAT officers supported by the counsellor Ms Cripps from the CRCC (T1293.4–10), with whom she subsequently had many counselling sessions in person and by telephone.

(8) It appears in the background, efforts were being made to assist in also seeing a psychologist, because by 11:14am on 11 April, Mr Leembruggen checked in with Mr Dillaway "to see how [Ms Higgins was] doing and if you needed anything etc" (Ex R93), which was reported to Ms Higgins. I infer this prompted Ms Higgins to try to make a further psychologist's appointment at 1:53pm on that day,

which was fixed within 24 hours (12:01pm on 12 April) but the appointment was for 18 April. As she explained to Mr Dillaway later that day, however, without mentioning it seems the appointment (or, it is worth noting, anything about being pressured to leave): "Also I'm off to Perth on Sunday. My TA staying in a mid-range place will clock up around $4,500 over the course of the election" (Ex R93).

It is unclear on the evidence as to whether the psychologist with whom Ms Higgins made the appointment on 18 April was the same person Mr Sharaz referred to in the first meeting with the Project team, when he asserted, without any detail (Ex 36 (at 0:06:00)): 716

> I think it's worth mentioning, because I don't know if it's in this. The fact that you spoke to, the Liberal Party provided her a psychologist who encouraged her not to do anything about it.

Details were requested of a corroborating "email that you got from the psychologist" by Ms Wilkinson (Ex 36 (at 0:06:50)) which were never provided so far as I have been made aware (a topic to which I will return). 717

In any event, the above represents the true picture based on chorological records, not simply assertions, as to what happened about providing support services to Ms Higgins prior to her going to Western Australia approximately three weeks after the incident. It also explains the circumstances in which, with Ms Higgins' knowledge and then agreement, the PMO, at the level of Chief of Staff at least, was aware of the incident. 718

## I.5 The Move to Western Australia

What the contemporaneous materials and the evidence of Ms Brown reveal is that Ms Brown went to some lengths to arrange approval of a work base for Ms Higgins on the Gold Coast, where her family was located, in case she wanted to work from that location. Given the pendency of going into "caretaker mode" upon the calling of an election, Ms Brown was unsure whether an alternative work base could be approved during caretaker mode, or if it was best to obtain "in principle" approval to a proposed move. A discussion took place around 4 April with Ms Barons about appropriate steps and Ms Brown was informed a "prospective" approval could be given and exercised at any time that Ms Higgins wished (Brown (at [127])). Ms Brown was advised to email Dr Kunkel, copied to Mr Wong, who was in charge of the Government staffing process. Ms Brown then sent an email at 719

7:33pm to Dr Kunkel, copied to Mr Wong, seeking prospective approval of a non-standard base for Ms Higgins on the Gold Coast, noting that she was currently based in Canberra, however, for personal and family reasons she may wish to seek a non-standard work base with her family on the Gold Coast (Brown (at [128])).

720 Of course, part of the cover-up narrative was that Ms Higgins had to choose between her job and seeking justice. It is notable that at the time the contemporaneous records reveal (to the extent there is any doubt) that Ms Higgins well understood the reality of being in a deferral period and that her current employment was coming to an end. This can be seen from candid communications with an ex-boyfriend Mr Jacob Kay, on 28 March and 11 April, where she advises: "Honestly, I'm going to be unemployed pretty soon so won't be able to juggle both rents very shortly" and "Heads up election has been called which means have only 6 weeks left of employment (Ex R89 (at 1)).

721 By 7 April, Ms Brown was getting ready to relocate to Brisbane for the upcoming federal election and over the previous week, she had been discussing with Mr Dean Carlson (who would become Acting Chief of Staff) about providing options to all staff and giving clarity to them as to what their travel commitments and locations would be for the upcoming campaign (Brown (at [159]–[160])). It had been determined that two Canberra based staff were to be based out of Western Australia – Mr Carlson and a Ministerial advisor, Mr Burland, and no decision had been made as to the balance of the staff (Brown (at [160])). Ms Higgins had told Ms Brown her preference was to work at "Campaign Headquarters" in Brisbane (no doubt because she wanted to work with Mr Dillaway in the media team) (Brown (at [161])). Ms Brown explained to Ms Higgins that the Campaign Headquarters staff allocation had been settled many months prior to the election, and that Ms Brown was not involved in those decisions (Brown (at [161])).

722 Having already arranged approval for Ms Higgins to have a non-standard home base at the Gold Coast to be with her family during the deferral period, Ms Brown then gave Ms Higgins a choice of proceeding along those lines, or being based in Canberra, or working in Western Australia, or working from home (Brown (at [162])). It was up to her to make a choice.

723 At or about 12:14pm on 7 April 2019, Ms Brown sent the following text message to Ms Higgins, Mr Carlson and Mr Burland (Brown (at [163])):

> Hi Drew and Brittany, hope you're having a good weekend! Given the election announcement hasn't occurred, I think it best if travel to WA is determined after its called. Given I'm going to be in CHQ I'll hand over to Dean to advise you when to make plans. Any problems please let us know, thanks Fiona

Late Sunday, at 7:46pm on 7 April, Ms Brown then sent Ms Higgins a text message as follows (Brown (at [164])): 724

> Hi Brittany, hope you've had a good weekend! I thought I should clarify my message earlier which I sent to you, Drew and Dean. As we discussed the other day you can let me know if something doesn't work for you eg, a time to go to WA etc
>
> In my comms I didn't want to leave you off the CBR WA staff who were travelling.
>
> Dean may coordinate but if something doesn't work for you make sure you let me know. You'll also find Dean good to work with. I'm only a call away!
>
> Best, Fiona

Ms Higgins then responded: 725

> Hi Fiona,
>
> Absolutely, thank-you for the message. Yes, I figured as much and really appreciate it. I definitely will keep that in mind if there are any major issues. Enjoy CHQ!

Ms Brown replied with a "thumbs up" emoji (Brown (at [165])). 726

Ms Higgins chose to take up the offer to work on the election campaign in Perth and, on 13 April, travelled there for that purpose (Brown (at [169]); T993.43–4). Contrary to the representations in the "Timeline" document (Ex 42) (**Timeline**), she was not "[p]ausing the active case with the AFP following internal pressure to go to Perth for the 2019 Federal Election" as she had never had a firm intention to proceed and had expressed the considered view, before going to Perth, she would not pursue the matter. 727

I accept, however, that Ms Higgins would rather have not been in Perth. It is obvious her preference would have been to work with Mr Dillaway at Campaign HQ in Brisbane. I also accept she complained to her friend, Mr O'Connor, about how she felt "punted" over to Perth, in that she felt away 728 from the action in Canberra (T1922.16–31). Further, while Mr O'Connor could not remember specifics, when Ms Higgins was in Perth they discussed "mostly just the aftermath of the incident and her feelings about it", and she appears to have discussed the publicity that would be generated if she had pursued her complaint "and that it would define her" (T1923.2–12).

729 By this stage, based on Mr O'Connor's admittedly vague evidence, I also accept Ms Higgins had come to think "people were checking up on her" (T1922.28). The evidence for this checking up and what was said is opaque at best. Mr O'Connor gave evidence Ms Higgins mentioned the name Yaron, which Mr O'Connor understood to be a reference to Mr Yaron Finkelstein (T1922.16–37), the Prime Minister's Principal Private Secretary, who had been in contact around this time (evidence which makes sense given what occurred later).

730 But in the end, even though Ms Higgins was not particularly happy to be in Perth, far from presenting her with some sort of ultimatum, the truth is that Ms Higgins was treated no worse than any other staff member that needed to be dispersed during the election period (with the expectation that they would not be coming back following the expected defeat of the Coalition Government). Indeed, in her case, Ms Brown went to some effort to accommodate Ms Higgins, by giving her options. When the Government was unexpectedly returned, she was, of course, the recipient of three job offers from those within the Executive.

731 Finally, although it does not matter very much (save that it is relevant to a representation made in the Commonwealth Deed (PL cl 3.28)), the contemporaneous material does not support the notion Ms Higgins was somehow shunned by the Minister in Perth. Apart from this allegation finding no support in her contemporaneous text messages, there is Ex 40, being a photograph of Ms Higgins (wearing the white dress she had said on oath in the criminal trial was still under her bed), happily sitting next to Senator Reynolds at a dinner with staff, which Ms Higgins attempted to explain away as resulting from her "accidentally" sitting next to the Minister because she was among the last to be seated (T816.28–30). I do not accept this evidence. Apart from anything else, it is unlikely that the other members of staff were deliberately eschewing sitting next to the Minister leaving a vacant seat for the belated arrival of Ms Higgins. It is also not supported by the evidence of Mr Wotton who was present (T1094.8–11).

Of course, nothing about any of this detracts from the obvious proposition that those within the know in the Government would have been very sensitive about the adverse publicity that would flow if Ms Higgins changed her mind, and if her allegation of sexual assault was pursued. No doubt Ms Higgins and Mr O'Connor are right to think a senior person, such as the Prime Minister's Principal Private Secretary, would not be contacting someone in the position of Ms Higgins simply to assess whether she was coping well. Mr Finkelstein, no doubt, was anxious not to alienate her and would have been forming his own assessment as to whether Ms Higgins was likely to change her mind. Whatever Ms Higgins may or may not have "felt" while in Perth, there is no evidence that anyone was suggesting to her to not proceed to act in a way contrary to her own settled, informed and communicated judgment as to what was best for her (let alone pressuring or threatening her to do so). She was not being "forced" to do anything as that concept is properly understood. To the extent one can understand what "checking up" entailed, it is a not an intervention that could be relied upon as amounting to the serious wrongdoing of obstructing Ms Higgins pursuing a complaint of sexual assault. 732

## I.6 CCTV Footage

As I have noted above, Ms Higgins said to Ms Maiden (and, as I will later explain, in her initial Project interview) that Ms Brown had said that she had viewed the CCTV footage taken from Parliament House cameras that showed Ms Higgins to be inebriated and repeatedly rebuffed requests for Ms Higgins to see the footage. 733

But Ms Brown did not see the CCTV footage and Ms Higgins' representations in this regard are again false. In particular, Ms Brown was unaware in 2019 of there being any "issue" as to the AFP accessing the CCTV footage, prior to the allegations in media reports in 2021 and had never seen CCTV footage of Ms Higgins and Mr Lehrmann entering or leaving the Parliament or the Ministerial Suite; nor had she taken any steps to procure it for viewing (although she probably did sensibly raise *securing* the CCTV footage as a result of the security breach with Mr Payne) (Brown (at [156]–[157]); T2136.21–34; T2141.26–29). 734

Having said this, I accept that Ms Higgins wished to see this CCTV footage, and this was a point Ms Higgins repeatedly made to both Ms Maiden and the Project team. This was connected, however, to the distinct notion 735 that her failure to gain access to the footage, or the apparent "delay" in the AFP being able to view it (which amounted to no more than a fortnight since Ms Higgins made her initial complaint to the AFP) was somehow suspicious, or indicative of a cover-up, or demonstrated a "roadblock".

736 Three points should be made about this.

737 The *first* relates to the fact that Ms Higgins had yet to give an Evidence-in-Chief interview. The point of such an interview is for a trained person to procure a genuine account of a complainant's recollection for later forensic use at a criminal trial. It stands to reason that prior to obtaining a genuine account from the complainant, showing other material likely to be evidence, such as CCTV footage, may have the effect, either consciously or subconsciously, of influencing her genuine recollection and therefore risk what was recorded becoming partly a reconstruction based on the CCTV footage. It is hardly surprising that the AFP would not take steps to show her the CCTV footage unless and until she had indicated a willingness to proceed with the complaint and provided an account of her recollection in the Evidence-in-Chief interview. Indeed, as noted above, such was the thoroughness of Agent Cleaves that she viewed the CCTV footage in the security room and made notes (T1396.31–36), even though Ms Higgins had made it plain she did not want to proceed.

738 *Secondly*, even leaving aside the fact that some AFP officers could not obtain the CCTV footage as promptly as they would have liked, this is wholly unsurprising when one understands basic aspects of our Constitutional structure and the contemporaneous records. Despite the apparent incredulity of Ms Higgins, Mr Sharaz and the Project team in 2021 (each of whom variously referred to the AFP as having its "own weird little sovereign state" in Parliament or being the equivalent of the Vatican City) (Ex 36 (at 0:20:24–0:21:16)), there are important justifications for the legal separation of power between the Parliament and the Executive Government, which are unnecessary to canvass in these reasons. Parliament has asserted these rights as inheritors of a tradition going back to the 17th century. There are important Constitutional reasons why the Parliamentary precincts area is managed by the Presiding Officers, and the *Parliamentary Precincts Act 1988* (Cth) formalises the authority of the Presiding Officers to manage and control the Parliamentary precincts. Agent Cleaves explained that generally she was able to get CCTV quickly, but this request seemed to take longer, and she was required to make a

few phone calls to ensure the CCTV could be viewed and she felt frustrated (T1399.1–19; Ex 78). For over 450 years, agents of the Executive have had to confront the realities of Parliamentary privilege; a privilege which is of fundamental importance to our system of government. Agent Cleaves is one in a very long line.

*Thirdly*, the whole issue is a furphy in any event, as the reality is that the CCTV footage was, by reason of the prudent steps taken by the AFP, obtained for initial viewing and then preserved notwithstanding there was no extant complaint. It is, of course, to be expected that complainants *may* change their mind and hence the course of preserving the relevant CCTV footage was sensible and allowed it to be able to be played both at the criminal trial and in this proceeding. The implicit and sometimes express notion that there was something conspiratorial or improper about the way the CCTV footage was dealt with in 2019 does not bear scrutiny. I will return to this topic below when considering the conduct of Network Ten. 739

## I.7 Later Events

What is evident is that as time went on, the concerns of Ms Higgins grew and, when triggered, she felt significant trauma, most notably in around October 2019 when there was a media enquiry about an assault in Senator Reynolds' office by a journalist from the *Canberra Times*, which brought into focus the reality "there was already people, sort of, who knew or who peripherally somehow knew about the assaults in media circles in Canberra" and this was a "retraumatising event" (T687.18–25). 740

It is unnecessary for the purposes of these reasons to go into much detail of what then happened or the later dealings between Ms Higgins while she worked in the office of Senator Cash. It is, however, worth referring to two matters, which received some focus in the evidence. 741

### *1 The Canberra Times Enquiry*

What is evident is that by October 2019, neither Senator Cash nor her chief of staff, Mr Daniel Try, knew of the incident but, because of the *Canberra Times* enquiry, it was thought necessary to inform Mr Try, and through him Ms Higgins and then Senator Cash, of the possibility the incident could become public. 742

Mr Try had a meeting with Ms Higgins and explained he had received a call from Senator Reynolds' office about the media enquiry and that 743 someone from Senator Reynolds' office was going to come and speak to them. Mr Try told Ms Higgins: "God, I'm so sorry" (T694.28–30). The staffer, Ms Christie Pearson, told her the distressing news about the media enquiry and informed her "we're considering how to respond". Ms Higgins gave evidence that she told Ms Pearson and Mr Try about the sexual assault (T852.1–9) and that she was very upset and said (wrongly) that she had not told anyone, and she did not know how they (meaning the journalist) had found out (T695.36–42). Mr Try asked questions about how they could publish such a story without Ms Higgins' consent (T695.43–45). According to Ms Higgins, he talked about trying to "squash" the story (T849.25–29).

744 Obviously enough, at this time, there was a complete symmetry of interests between those within Senator Reynolds' office (and others within the Government) and Ms Higgins in the media story not being published. Ms Higgins was distraught at the prospect and those within the government wished to ensure the story was not published for political reasons.

745 At the conclusion of the meeting, after the unsettling prospect had been canvassed, Mr Try asked Ms Higgins if she would like to "tell the boss" (that is, the Minister, Senator Cash), or whether she preferred that he tell the Minister (T696.1–13). With Ms Higgins' consent, Mr Try immediately told the Minister. They were speaking privately for around 15 minutes and Ms Higgins was then invited into the Minister's office. Ms Higgins said that Senator Cash immediately embraced her in a hug. Ms Higgins was unable to recall what was said, but recalled the Minister said words to the effect that everything would be okay, and they would handle it (T696.15–31).

746 From this information, it was evident knowledge of the incident had spread, much to the distress of Ms Higgins. On 20 October 2019, Deputy Chief Police Officer Michael Chew directed Detective Harman to contact Ms Higgins about a media enquiry "concerning [the] incident and advise that the matter may be raised at senate estimates" (MC (at 61)). After initial attempts by Detective Harman that were unsuccessful because Ms Higgins was upset and "hung up abruptly", Agent Cleaves spoke to Ms Higgins over the weekend of 19–20 October about the media enquiry and informed her that the information could spark questions of the AFP and that a reference would be put in the AFP Commissioner's "Senate estimates pack" (T697.12–18; MC (at 61)). Ms Higgins said that she immediately

called Mr Try to let him know. She told him about the call and said that she was really upset and scared. Ms Higgins said that Mr Try thanked her for letting him know and said that he would handle it (T697.26–27).

Despite this solicitous attempt by the AFP to warn her about the possibility of unwanted publicity, Ms Higgins said this all made her change her view about the AFP, and then gave this evidence (T821–2): 747

> HIS HONOUR: Why did that make you change your view about the AFP? Weren't they, as a matter of courtesy, telling you about the – that there had been a media inquiry and there was a possibility, in response to a question asked, that they may have to answer truthfully about something, and they were giving you a heads up?---It made me scared about the relationship between the AFP and Parliament House, I guess. It wasn't the fact that she called me on the weekend. It was the fact that when the media inquiry came in and they said, "We will speak to Home Affairs. We will get them to squash the media inquiry." It – it spoke to the sort of relationship between the police and Parliament House that, in my view, sounded really close and it – it made me a bit intimidated and scared. So it did – it did change my opinion about what I perceived to be, I guess, the relationship between Parliament House and the police, it – it made me scared. It did, it intimidated me.
>
> Well, I understand you would be concerned and intimidated about the fact of disclosure. I'm just trying to understand a bit better than I do now, why you say that the fact that the AFP contacted you about something that might happen, changed your view about, I imagine – are you saying the integrity of the AFP?---No. I'm not questioning the integrity, but it was more so the – the level of information that was passed so readily between ministerial offices related to Home Affairs and the AFP itself. The – the way that media inquires worked, to the AFP, the fact that I knew media advisors get clearance on those responses, because that's just the way that it works, and – and that did make me feel scared.
>
> Scared of what, though?---Scared that if I re-enlived my complaint, that the Liberal Party would know pretty quickly, on the basis that minsters have oversight on responses on those sorts of matters, particularly sensitive ones.

748 This evidence, if accepted, reflects the extent to which Ms Higgins was starting at shadows. The original incident was, on any view of it, serious, and information as to the incident had now become known to a journalist and no doubt to others. There was a not insignificant possibility that the incident would become the subject of further publicity, either in the press or at a Senate estimates hearing. Indeed, five months later, anonymous, and inaccurate allegations related to the incident were spread by a letter sent to Senator Kitching, who then provided it to the Presiding Officers (MC (at 62)).

749 To quote H R Haldeman, "once the toothpaste is out of tube, it is awfully hard to get it back in". It was necessary to recognise that the information was out there in one form or another, and they may be some need, at some time, to deal with it.

750 Going back to October 2019, Ms Higgins, as the person most intimately involved, was being told of this publicity risk and it was consistent with the interests of everyone that information about a complaint of sexual assault (that an alleged victim, for her own good reasons, had decided not to pursue), not be the subject of unwanted publicity. Of course, if Ms Higgins changed her mind and enlivened her complaint, this information would spread and would likely become known as soon as any detailed investigation took place, including to members of the Liberal Party – but this had nothing to do with some sort of inappropriate conduct by the AFP. The apparent fear the AFP would not do its job if a complaint was pursued, even belatedly, is without rational foundation.

751 I have set out what the facts are about this incident in some detail. It is now particularly instructive to contrast this series of actual events as revealed in the evidence, with Ms Higgins' recounting of these events in her interview with Ms Maiden – which merit reproduction despite their length (Ex 50 (at 35–41)):

> *Ms Higgins*:
>
> ... Oh, so, Linda Reynolds then called my Chief of Staff in Minister Cash's office. He had obviously had no idea, so she briefed him.
>
> *Ms Maiden*:
>
> Linda did or Fiona?
>
> *Ms Higgins*:

Linda did. Linda called Daniel and briefed him on sort of the outline of what had happened.

*Ms Maiden*:

How do you feel about that?

*Ms Higgins*:

I don't know. I felt like I was always a passenger in the story. This thing happened to me, it was managed and it just. ... I was always just sort of the complication that was along for the ride. It was already happening, I was just sort of ...

Okay, but isn't that also some sort of breach or your privacy or ... ?

*Ms Higgins*:

Yeah, it was ... None of this was mine. Once again, it all just felt kind of normal ...

*Ms Maiden*:

It felt like it was something that was happening to you rather than you having a say in it.

*Ms Higgins*:

Yeah. Yeah.

*Ms Maiden*:

So how did you become aware that she'd had that conversation with Daniel?

*Ms Higgins*:

Because Daniel called me into the office. He let me know that Linda Reynolds had called. He said that he was so sorry and that he said -- 'cause he'd never heard it, so he was quite shocked.

*Ms Maiden*:

This is f***ing weird. I'm sorry but like I just don't think this is very appropriate.

*Ms Higgins*:

[LAUGHS] It's so weird. Like it's all weird.

*Ms Maiden*:

I don't understand why Linda things that she should tell Daniel that you were sexually assaulted. What's Daniel's last name, Daniel?

*Ms Higgins*:

Daniel Try.

*Ms Maiden*:

T-R-Y?

*Ms Higgins*:

Yeah. He like also works in PMO. It's a weird incestuous place.

*Ms Maiden*:

Okay. Are they Christians?

*Ms Higgins*:

[NO AUDIBLE RESPONSE]

*Ms Maiden*:

They're all Christians. Anyway, so he said to you ... Did he say to you, I understand that you were sexually assaulted?

*Ms Higgins*:

No, he said I had heard what happened to you in Linda Reynolds' office, I'm so sorry. He was quite ... Like you could tell that he was like freaking out.

*Ms Maiden*:

Upset.

*Ms Higgins*:

Yeah. And he said ...

*Ms Maiden*:

But.

*Ms Higgins*:

He said, yeah, pretty much. And he was like, they're sending someone up from Linda Reynolds' office, would you like me to be in the room with you? And I was like, yes, witness, you're coming with me.

*Ms Maiden*:

But why? I don't understand why are you being ... Oh, okay, keep telling the story, yep.

*Ms Higgins*:

So we went into the staff meeting room and it was this lady named Christy Pearson. She was working in Linda Reynolds' office during MinDef when she was Minister of Defence but has left since. And she pretty much ...

***

*Ms Higgins*:

Yeah, so she came and said, you know, an inquiry's come in, I know this is going to be really distressing for you but ... And it was pretty much, she told me what had happened and then the question kind of turned to, have you spoken to anyone. And it kind of felt really quickly ...

*Ms Maiden*:

Oh, like ...

*Ms Higgins*:

Yeah, like they thought that it was me.

*Ms Maiden*:

Yeah.

*Ms Higgins*:

But I was pretty distraught because it was like a long repressed trauma at that point.

*Ms Maiden*:

Did you cry in that meeting?

*Ms Higgins*:

Yeah, I was hysterical.

*Ms Maiden*:

Yeah, and what did you say?

*Ms Higgins*:

I obviously said that it wasn't me, that I was just ... I think I had a panic attack kind of. I think it was really ...

*Ms Maiden*:

How did that manifest itself? What were you?

*Ms Higgins*:

I don't know, it was just the prospect that I had not pursued it, that I had buried it, that I had pretty much internalised it and then that all of a sudden it was being leaked anyway, it was already going to come out and it was going to be like ...

*Ms Maiden*:

Become a thing once again that would embarrass the party.

*Ms Higgins*:

Yeah. Yeah, and I just ... I was ... Yeah, I knew like, you know, you're a media adviser, you learn to kind of sort of facilitate [49:56 UNCLEAR].

*Ms Maiden*:

And how was Daniel reacting to you being very distressed and ...?

*Ms Higgins*:

He was quite nice. Again, of everyone involved, he's quite nice. And, yeah, and so then the general tone is, well, they immediately thought it was the police. For some reason they became, both of them became dead set it was the police. And they were like, oh well, don't worry, we'll sort this, we'll call Dutton. And that was sort of the end of the conversation, where they just sort of [50:21 pulled me out]. And then the story never went anywhere, so it was just really weird.

*Ms Maiden*:

We'll call Dutton. How many people are they going to involve in this?

*Ms Higgins*:

I don't know how they solve problems. I don't know how

[50:30 UNCLEAR].

*Ms Maiden*:

But who said we'll call Dutton, Christy?

*Ms Higgins*:

Daniel.

*Ms Maiden*:

Daniel.

*Ms Higgins*:

Yeah.

*Ms Maiden*:

Okay. And then nothing happened.

*Ms Higgins*:

No, so Daniel was like, I'm going to tell the boss and he was like ...

*Ms Maiden*:

What the f***! Sorry.

*Ms Higgins*:

I don't know, staffing is weird. This is not ...

*Ms Maiden*:

Okay, so then he said, I'm going to tell Michaelia Cash.

*Ms Higgins*:

And he said, would you like to do a [50:55 UNCLEAR] ... feel like that's a your job, I don't want to tell my boss something very deeply personal to me; I'll let you do it. And so he did and then the boss called me in and she was very nice, she gave me a hug and, yeah, and then the rest was a sitting day at that point and I took the rest of the same day off, I went home.

*Ms Maiden*:

Phrrttt. And then you went into Senate estimates and nothing happened?

*Ms Higgins*:

Well one of the officers at SATAC called me and said that it was going to be in the Senate. I know, it's all weird. I don't know, it's all weird.

*Ms Maiden*:

So the cops must have had something to do with it.

*Ms Higgins*:

I don't know.

*Ms Maiden*:

Someone from SATAC called you?

*Ms Higgins*:

Called me and said it was going to be, 'cause it was the new AFP Commissioner in Canberra, the new guy ...

*Ms Maiden*:

Right, Kershaw or whatever is name is.

*Ms Higgins*:

Yeah. They said they were putting it in his Senate estimates pack. And I was ...

*Ms Maiden*:

Why?

*Ms Higgins*:

I don't know, 'cause it was AFP and it was logged as an incident and so technically ...

*Ms Maiden*:

This is very suspect.

*Ms Higgins*:

It's all weird. I don't understand it.

*Ms Maiden*:

There's something very suspect that has gone here. You get ... So the request from *The Canberra Times* was before the ...

*Ms Higgins*:

It was the week before.

*Ms Maiden*:

Sure, but then you also get ... The SATAC call was after *The Canberra Times* then?

*Ms Higgins*:

Yeah.

*Ms Maiden*:

And they tell you they're going to put it in the Senate estimates pack?

*Ms Higgins*:

Yeah, and they just wanted to give me like a heads up, like this is a courtesy because they knew it would probably impact me, like emotionally, if this conversation ...

*Ms Maiden*:

So they're putting it in the pack for him?

*Ms Higgins*:

Yes, just preparing in case he gets questions, they pre-prepare your talking points and your questions and your figures and your times and all that kind of stuff.

*Ms Maiden*:

And have you ever ... Did you ever get to say, thank you, I'd like to see that please?

*Ms Higgins*:

No. No, but you know, I was pretty much terrified so I thought I'd just call my boss again. I just was like, hey, heads up.

*Ms Maiden*:

You called Daniel?

*Ms Higgins*:

Yeah, and let him know.

*Ms Maiden*:

And what was his reaction to SATAC putting it in Kershaw's pack?

*Ms Higgins*:

He just told me to not worry about it. The issue was my boss reps Home Affairs in the Senate.

*Ms Maiden*:

Cash, yeah.

*Ms Higgins*:

> So they were worried that if Cash was sitting there with Kershaw at Senate estimates and they're in the pack and the query was almost just there, they were worried it was going to happen on that day.
>
> *Ms Maiden*:
>
> Okay, but as it turned out, no one asked anything about anything?
>
> *Ms Higgins*:
>
> No, not at all ...

752 Leaving aside the tone and nature of these interactions, including the journalist's notably leading and suggestive questions (and her apparent reference to the possible existence of some form of Christian cabal), these out-of-court representations of Ms Higgins, if scrutinised and investigated with any rigour, reveal the enigmatic nature of what Ms Higgins was saying; they also reveal the way benign actions revealed in the evidence were being characterised by her as (yet again) "weird" or suggestive of something sinister.

753 In truth, it was not complicated at all. It was plainly appropriate and prudent to warn an alleged victim (who was not, and did not at that time want to be, a complainant) that information had spread, that publicity may come out as a result, and to take prophylactic steps, including preparing answers to questions that might be directed to the AFP. At this time, everyone's interests were aligned. Only someone prone to speculation and avid for scandal could view the objective facts as forming a reasonable basis to suggest the perpetuation of an inappropriate, indeed criminal, cover-up.

### *II The Broadcast of the Four Corners Programmes*

754 The importance of the *Four Corners* ("Inside the Canberra Bubble") programme broadcast on 9 November 2020, as informing Ms Higgins' later conduct, is manifest. Ms Higgins had nothing to do with this programme and it is not to be confused with the 8 March 2021 *Four Corners* programme ("Bursting the Canberra Bubble"), which dealt with an historical rape allegation made against the then Commonwealth Attorney General after which Ms Higgins had sent Mr O'Connor a message, twelve days later, saying: "I feel okay. I worked with Four Corners behind the scenes to help piece it all together. I have been staying with Lisa W and Peter FitzSimons in Sydney for the past few days; they have been so wonderful" (T1936.39). It does not really matter in the overall scheme of things, but it is difficult to understand why this text was sent to Mr O'Connor, as it is

far from clear on the evidence that Ms Higgins did, in truth, assist in helping "piece it [that is, the *Four Corners* ("Bursting the Canberra Bubble") programme] all together" (Ex 66).

In any event, in her evidence-in-chief, Ms Higgins said (T687.8), in response to a question of what caused her to contact Network Ten, that "it was the Four Corners story. The Christian Porter Four Corners story is – is what triggered me, personally" (T687.7–8) but this appears to be a mistake, and the balance of her evidence, and other evidence, and the timing, establishes that the triggering event was the earlier, November 2020 story. 755

Moreover, it is important not to confuse these programmes with the 22 March 2021 *Four Corners* programme ("Don't ask, Don't tell"), which referred to Ms Higgins' "account of effectively being silenced for political reasons spark[ing] outrage and condemnation of the culture of Canberra" and was provocatively described as investigating "how and why Brittany Higgins' story was *kept* quiet for almost two years" (emphasis added). This is the programme which, when she became aware of it, had caused her to send messages to her friend (and that of Mr Sharaz), Ms Emma Webster, a "communications strategist", in which Ms Higgins had raised concerns about not being given a "right of reply" (T763.8) and after Ms Webster consoled her, she responded: "Thank you. After I had a bit of a breakdown to the Four Corners producer, he's going to give me a draft copy of her interview and give me an opportunity to reply" (T763.41). 756

But having sorted out her evidence as to the different *Four Corners* programmes, it was the airing of the 2020 programme that provided the moment when she said she felt she had a duty to speak (T859.38–41). Certainly, its catalytic importance in the formation of her antipathetic views towards the Prime Minister and his office can be seen from the following exchange with Ms Maiden (Ex 50 (at 1–2)): 757

*Ms Maiden*:

... Okay, so start from the beginning again. You were saying you watched the *Four Corners* and you felt that Morrison sidestepped it by saying it was in the past.

*Ms Higgins*:

Yeah, absolutely. I just ... It made me so angry on the basis of him dismissing this whole issue on the basis that it wasn't his government ... When I'd fundamentally lived that experience. It was handled by his team, [unclear] as Director of Operations, and he was saying that he was saying he was unaccountable. Kunkel was there, he had Daniel Wong, who's one of the other staff, they were intimately involved in this entire process as soon as it all kind of transpired. And it just made me so angry, in a way that I can't even ... 'Cause I was ashamed before or kind of like internalising it and I think it just. .. Yeah, it just ...

*Ms Maiden*:

So watching the programme was a trigger for you to start thinking about it all again.

*Ms Higgins*:

Yeah ...

758 As I have noted, obviously enough, both before, but especially after the 2020 *Four Corners* programme, Ms Higgins changing her mind and wanting to pursue her complaint would have been damaging politically to the Liberal Party, and various members of the Government would have very much wished Ms Higgins did not change tack.

759 Against this background, it appears a further telephone call was made by Mr Finkelstein to Ms Higgins on the day the 2020 *Four Corners* programme was broadcast, which was important in Ms Wilkinson's thinking (as we will see). The evidence is insufficient to form a view as to whether this call was to ascertain whether Ms Higgins' allegation was about to go public, or to ascertain whether another allegation was likely to be made in the future. Again, the evidence is far from pellucid, and it suffices to describe this communication as similar to the earlier contact referred to in the evidence of Mr O'Connor I have already discussed.

# J FACTUAL FINDINGS OF RELEVANCE TO THE SECTION 30 DEFENCE

## J.1 Introduction

It is important to recognise that this part of my reasons has, as its point of departure, the notion that the respondents cannot prove that Mr Lehrmann raped Ms Higgins and, consequently, the substantial truth defence is not made out. 760

Even if this was the case, the respondents say they have a defence. As I will explain in Section K, at the time of publication of the Project programme, s 30 of the Defamation Act provided a defence for the publication of defamatory matter if, among other things, the respondents prove their conduct in publishing the matter was "reasonable in the circumstances" (s 30(1)(c)). The first step in considering this defence is working out "the circumstances", that is, what happened as to the publication. 761

Before turning to the finding of facts, it is necessary to make a preliminary point. The submissions of the respondents are replete with reference to representations made in affidavits or in oral evidence being "unchallenged". This is understandable on one level because, as a general proposition, unchallenged evidence which is not inherently incredible, is generally accepted by the tribunal of fact. But there is a decided air of artificiality running through all the affidavit evidence to the extent it presents a picture of any real deliberation or any indecision as to whether the Project team would ever proceed with airing Ms Higgins' allegations. 762

This is an unusual case where there is a very comprehensive contemporaneous documentary record, including text and other messages and lengthy audio records. We know what people were saying (and can infer what people were thinking) by reference to real time records. I do not propose to accept representations, made at a high level of generality, about what was in a person's mind or what they said when the relevant state of mind 763 or action is contradicted by facts otherwise established by the contemporaneous material, or particular circumstances in that reliable material point to its rejection: *Precision Plastics Pty Limited v Demir* (1975) 132 CLR 362 (at 370–371 per Gibbs J, with whom Stephen J agreed, and Murphy J generally agreed); *Ashby v Slipper* (at 347 [77] per Mansfield and Gilmour JJ).

764 Although I do refer below to some aspects of the affidavit material, irrespective as to challenge by cross-examination, for affidavit evidence to be accepted, it must be *persuasive* in the sense that it does not jar with candid contemporaneous representations. In making this comment I am not saying anything different to what I said in *Lloyd v Belconnen Lakeview Pty Ltd* [2019] FCA 2177; (2019) 377 ALR 234 (at 269 [110]–[113]), where I also repeated the comment made by Lord Woolf MR contained in the *Access to Justice Report, Final Report* (London, HMSO), 1996 (at [55]) that:

> Witness statements have ceased to be the authentic account of the lay witness; instead they have become an elaborate, costly branch of legal drafting.

765 Or the reality known by any experienced litigator reflected in observations of Nettle and Gordon JJ (citing my observations in *Lloyd v Belconnen* with apparent approval) in *Queensland v Masson* [2020] HCA 28; (2020) 94 ALJR 785 (at 810 [112]):

> The oft unspoken reality that lay witness statements are liable to be workshopped, amended and settled by lawyers, the risk that lay and, therefore, understandably deferential witnesses do not quibble with many of the changes made by lawyers in the process – because the changes do not appear to many lay witnesses necessarily to alter the meaning of what they intended to convey ...

766 There was no denial of procedural fairness in this case: everyone knew what was in issue, and everyone had a chance to address those issues.

## J.2 The Genesis of the Story and the "Timeline" Document

767 The tone of the interactions between Mr Sharaz, on behalf of Ms Higgins, and the respondents was set by the first email of Mr Sharaz sent on Monday, 18 January 2021, at 10:13am. It was clear what the proposed story would be all about, and Mr Sharaz could hardly have chosen a more

glaring heading: "MeToo, Liberal Party, Project Pitch". Mr Sharaz got straight to the point (Ex R105):

> Hi Lisa,
>
> I hope you're well.
>
> I've got a sensitive story surrounding a sexual assault at Parliament House; a woman who was pressured by the Liberal Party and female cabinet minister not to pursue it. She's asked me to be the one to get the story told this year.

Mr Sharaz then continued: 768

> The girl has been through a lot, and I'm deeply protective of making sure this is done right, given going after the Liberal Party machine is no easy feat. (She'll only get one pull of the trigger before they try to discredit and shut the story down. My experience in politics and sky [*sic*] sadly gives me that insight.)
>
> I can say this, it's the first time something like that has happened under Prime Minister Scott Morrison's watch. He can no longer use the excuse: "This is a bubble" issue, or "this was before my time".

And then Mr Sharaz adopted the following valediction demonstrating his affection for (and apparently misconceived extent of familiarity with) Ms Wilkinson: 769

> Thanks so much.
>
> Much love,
>
> David Sharaz.

After some toing and froing, and reinforcing a conspiratorial and political theme, on 19 January Mr Sharaz sent the Timeline (Ex 42) under the cover of an email entitled, "Everything you need" in the following terms: 770

> Hi Lisa, thank you for your time over the phone today, and your sensitivity around what I truly feel is an injustice.
>
> I'm sending this on behalf of Britt, purely because, and this sounds paranoid, we just don't know who might be keeping a close eye on her.
>
> As discussed, we're happy for you to send this to your producer (and thank you for speaking to your EP for us).

771 Mr Sharaz then concludes:

> You can always chat to me over the phone if you need more, and I can put Britt on.
>
> Thanks again,
>
> David Sharaz

772 The Timeline was a curious document, as was the evidence given as to its creation.

773 Ms Higgins was emphatic in her evidence-in-chief it was prepared by her, the "intended audience" was initially her and the police, and it was an iterative document that evolved as she "thought of things". She also said: "I also provided it to, I believe, Samantha Maiden from news.com, and I provided it to, I believe, Angus Llewellyn from The Project" (T688.21–45). She believed the "final draft", which was provided to the Project team (which became Ex R11 and part of Ex 42) was "a final draft kind of one, but I'm not exactly sure" (T689.2–3).

774 In cross-examination (T819.27–41), Ms Higgins gave the following evidence:

> MR WHYBROW: ... who did you prepare [the Timeline] for? ---Originally, myself, ahead of going to the police, and then I ultimately circulated it to certain journalists on background.
>
> Okay. And was it prepared entirely by you?---Yes. I had – I sent it to my partner, so he also had a copy, and then also another friend of mine, and they may have circulated it on my behalf, but I was the one who wrote it.
>
> Okay. And do you remember when you prepared it?---Over that summer period. I couldn't say if it was the end of December 2020 or January 2021, but it was – it was over that Christmas period, I believe.
>
> Okay. And you, I think, have given evidence today that it was prepared in contemplation of reactivating a police complaint, was it?---Yes, yes. I was – I was preparing it for myself, ahead of doing what I knew I was going to do.

775 And later (T825–829) after accepting that it was not her, but Mr Sharaz, that had sent the Timeline, the following evidence was given:

MR WHYBROW: you just agreed with me that Mr Sharaz did in fact send this to Ms Wilkinson on your behalf?---He absolutely sent it on my behalf, but I wasn't over his shoulder as he typed the message.

No, but you knew that he had sent the timeline that you had prepared?---Yes, I asked him to.

***

You see Mr Sharaz indicates in the second-last line:

> *In addition to this, I've gone and looked up the ACT Policing crime stats for 2019, and there was one reported sexual assault during the time Britt's incident occurred*

Do you see that?---I see it.

And do you see on the second page of that document, I think, the attached printout or screen grab of some crime statistics, which include the area of Parliament House, it would appear?---Yes.

And were you aware that Mr Sharaz had done that search?---I remember him showing me the 2019 crime stats, and I remember I was discussing how unlikely – or what was the likelihood that there was another assault in Parliament House in that month. Yes.

***

And you see that that appears to be what Mr Sharaz was referencing when he said he looked up ACT police crime stats?---Potentially, yes.

Okay. And it appears to have highlighted 2019 April to June?---Yes.

And you first spoke to police - - -?---On - - -

- - - from 1 April 2019?---That's correct.

776 Although I have little doubt that Ms Higgins authored parts of the Timeline, her evidence that she was the only author is wrong. I am fortified in this view by reason of Mr Sharaz's initial representation he was asked to "be the one to get the story told this year" (Ex R105); his involvement in sending it (not only to the Project team but later to others); in doing searches; and the reference in the Timeline to Ms Higgins in the third person.

777 In any event, as distributed by Mr Sharaz, it purported to set out extensive details of Ms Higgins' allegations and a screenshot from the ACT Policing website. Ms Higgins gave evidence that she started preparing the Timeline at the end of 2020 because she had (T688.8–13):

> never really put it all together physically, so I wanted to start going through my texts to see, like, the timeline to figure out exactly what date because I had buried personally so far down.

778 I think there may be some truth in this, but as I have noted, the real catalyst for preparing it is the decision made in late 2020, after the *Four Corners* programme, for a document to be prepared to be provided to the media, initially to two journalists selected by Mr Sharaz, being Ms Maiden (a journalist described by Mr Sharaz and Ms Higgins as a "good friend" (MC (at 64)) and as "a friend of ours" (Ex 36 (at 0:06:24))) and also Ms Wilkinson, with whom Mr Sharaz felt affinity after doing some work experience on the *Today* programme.

779 Ms Wilkinson was in no doubt as to the significance of the "project" the subject of the "pitch". On the same day, she referred to the "explosive political story" as being "an extraordinary coverup involving Linda Reynolds, Michaelia Cash and the PMO" (Ex R117).

780 The following day, on 20 January, the Timeline document was sent by Ms Wilkinson to the rest of the Project Team. When the document was shared, the importance of the topic was recognised (Campbell (at [14]–[27]); Thornton (at [27]–[30]); Meakin (at [26]–[30])) and the Timeline document was thereafter used to guide lines of enquiry for the story (Ex R124; Wilkinson 28 July 2023 (at [34]); Llewellyn (at [71])).

781 One would have thought anyone reading it would have understood it not only contained some startling allegations that required close scrutiny, but that many people were apparently involved and aware of the cover-up. Relevantly, it alleged (page references are to Ex 42):

(1) Mr Payne and Ms Brown found out about the allegation "due to a security breach" (at 3);

(2) "[n]otification was sent to the Director of Public Prosecutions (DPP) from the Parliament House AFP Station" (at 4);

(3) after meeting with the AFP, "Brittany is flown to Perth" (at 5);

(4) in June "Brittany's original contract with Minister Cash from Star Chamber is rejected. (Note - Fiona Brown sits on Star Chamber)" (at 5);

(5) "[t]here was a noticeable presence of Daniel Wong/Kunkel in the office during the week following the incident" (at 7);

(6) "the AFP Unit in Parliament House had been informed [the week after] and would like to speak with me" (at 7);

(7) that she was given two options being: (a) "I could go home to the Gold Coast for the duration of the election campaign but that this would likely impact my ability to reapply for a job in the future"; or (b) "I could stay onboard and go to Perth, Western Australia for the campaign" (at 7–8);

(8) that she was "[p]ausing the active case with the AFP following internal pressure to go to Perth for the 2019 Federal Election" (at 11).

## J.3 The Investigation and Preparation

Ms Wilkinson also had a telephone conversation with Mr Sharaz on 20 January. One can gauge what was said about Ms Wilkinson's enthusiasm and the way in which she proposed to "hold britts hand through all this" by reference to a WhatsApp message sent after this call by Mr Sharaz to Ms Higgins (MC (at 64)): 782

> Lisa rang,
>
> Let's chat tonight, its good news.
>
> ...
>
> She wants to fly me and you down on Monday for a meeting with her and the EP at a non-disclosed location. She wants to potentially change the format of the show and do the 7.00-7.30 hour in this. Include Sam. Have Sam grabs thought [*sic*] the piece.
>
> She also said "we need to make sure we hold britts hand through all this. She can call me at any time."

At this time, Ms Wilkinson also resolved that Mr Llewellyn should be the producer of the story, given her assessment of his reputation and experience (Wilkinson 28 July 2023 (at [33])). 783

784 The decision was made to keep the details confidential, and a code name "ENVIRO" was adopted (Ex R431). Although Mr Llewellyn involved Network Ten's in-house solicitors from the beginning of the production process (Llewellyn (at [93]–[95])), the provision of legal advice does not go very far.

785 No assumptions ought to be made in this case, particularly when the only in-house legal advice revealed as to this matter was counterintuitive. I accept legal advice was obtained including (I assume) on the topic as to whether Mr Lehrmann ought to be named. Although no adverse inference as to the content of legal advice can be drawn from a party's decision to assert privilege, and the taking of advice itself could have some relevance, it does not assist in assessing reasonableness of conduct if it is said the *content* of advice relevantly informed that conduct, and yet the advice itself and the instructions given to procure the advice, are kept hidden. I cannot, and will not, act on speculation, but for all I know, the solicitors were given a request for advice along the lines of: "We are telling this explosive political story being an extraordinary coverup involving Linda Reynolds, Michaelia Cash and the PMO, we need to do everything to maintain exclusivity and publish at the same time as Maiden who also has the story, how do we best minimise litigation risk?".

786 In this regard, I should note Mr Lehrmann did not press for production of the advice relying upon an implied waiver of legal professional privilege.

787 In any event, as Network Ten properly accepts, the decision to broadcast ultimately turned upon Network Ten's confidence that Ms Higgins was telling the truth. This was quintessentially a decision for the production team, not solicitors, and as all contemporaneous records suggest, the truth of Ms Higgins' account was never in doubt in the minds of Ms Wilkinson and Mr Llewellyn.

788 Returning to the narrative, Ms Wilkinson came into direct contact with Ms Higgins from 21 January 2021, and Mr Llewellyn also engaged with Ms Higgins initially by phone on 26 January 2021.

### *I The First Interview, Weaponisation, Incomplete Data, and the Bruise Photograph*

789 Mr Llewellyn, Ms Wilkinson, Mr Sharaz and Ms Higgins met on 27 January 2021 at The Darling Hotel in Sydney over an almost five-hour period (Ex 36).

The respondents asserted the purpose of the first interview was for Mr Llewellyn and Ms Wilkinson to determine whether the story was worth pursuing and to assess Ms Higgins' reliability and credibility as a source. This does not ring at all true from listening to the audio recording (Ex 36). Ms Wilkinson was onboard with telling the explosive story before even meeting Ms Higgins. More realistically, the purpose was for Ms Higgins to tell her story so information obtained could be used by Mr Llewellyn to come up with themes to cover in the draft questions for the filmed interview, and to obtain information for conducting further investigations to support the narrative and to build rapport with Ms Higgins so that she felt comfortable. 790

In their affidavits Mr Llewellyn and Ms Wilkinson gave evidence they had formed the view that Ms Higgins was "traumatised", "raw", and "emotional" and felt she had been "let down by those she worked with": (Llewellyn (at [127]); Wilkinson 28 July 2023 (at [74])). They believed her when she said she did not pursue her complaint due to difficulties encountered by the AFP in obtaining CCTV footage from Parliament House; concerns she had about her job; and pressure she felt to go to Western Australia to help campaign for the Federal election. Mr Llewellyn said he thought Ms Higgins wanted to speak out about her experience to create change, to prevent it from happening to anyone else and did not consider she had a vendetta (Llewellyn (at [179])). 791

There may be some truth in this, but any suggestion Ms Wilkinson or Mr Llewellyn: (a) conscientiously considered the motives of Ms Higgins and Mr Sharaz; or (b) approached the story with disinterested professional scepticism, conflicts with the way they were prepared to assist in the plans of Mr Sharaz and Ms Higgins to use the allegations for immediate political advantage, and the lack of rigour with which Ms Higgins' account was examined and questioned during the meeting and thereafter. 792

It is notable how much in his evidence-in-chief Mr Llewellyn stressed the importance of this first meeting in terms of research and preparation of the programme, including that it allowed him to assess the demeanour of Ms Higgins and to determine whether the details provided would give more or less "confidence in her believability" and "whether to take the story further" (Llewellyn (at [98(d)]). I am sensible to the need to build rapport and for sensitivity in dealing with a person presenting as a victim of sexual assault, but assessing the credibility of someone making claims 793 of serious wrongdoing involves some degree of detachment and testing absent from the meeting and later interactions – all the more so when concerns (or at least matters requiring caution) ought to have become apparent to an independent mind.

794 The *first* of these matters was that Mr Sharaz's intentions in making and pursuing his "Project Pitch" were manifest: not only from his initial assertion that this was a story all about the Liberal Party and a female Minister in the context of the "MeToo" movement, but in the light of his expressed intention to liaise with an Opposition frontbencher to deploy the allegations against the Government during Question Time. Mr Llewellyn apparently thought this was of no moment and irrelevant to his stated purpose of assessing "believability", including the question of motive. When it was suggested in cross-examination that he knew that Mr Sharaz intended to assist the Opposition to pursue the issue in Parliament, his response was "maybe"; this qualified answer was said to be justified because "well he doesn't say that he's going to" (T1629.43). Mr Llewellyn then clarified his position to say that he did not know whether Mr Sharaz would go through with this plan, before saying "I didn't think [Sharaz] had a political agenda" (T1630.23).

795 It appears Mr Llewellyn was uninterested in reflecting upon Mr Sharaz's motives. In the light of what had been communicated by Mr Sharaz before and during this first interview, any journalist who did not think Mr Sharaz had a motivation to inflict immediate political damage would have to be wilfully blind. Of course, Mr Sharaz was perfectly entitled to work with the Opposition and to use any truthful allegations as to what happened to damage the Government. And the mere fact he had such a motive does not mean what is being said by his girlfriend was anything other than true. But it is important context, and a journalist acting reasonably would recognise this motivation and scrutinise what was being conveyed cognisant of it.

796 It does appear that prior to the meeting, Mr Llewellyn did conduct an internet search and knew Mr Sharaz had "married a political staffer" and sent it to Ms Wilkinson. Ms Wilkinson (who had seen the same details), in response, described Mr Sharaz, like Ms Higgins, as "two birds with broken wings who have seen the inside of Canberra and don't like what they see" – a zoomorphism with which Mr Llewellyn expressed his agreement (Ex R186; Ex R187). It does not appear anything changed, and they continued to believe this was an appropriate characterisation.

What we know is that insufficient recognition of motive did not only fail to cause increased care, but Mr Llewellyn and Ms Wilkinson expressed a willingness to assist in the political use of the serious charges they were supposedly interrogating and assessing with independent minds, as is evident from the following (Ex 36 (at 1:14:09–1:53:34)): 797

*Mr Sharaz*:

And for your reference, we'll get down to this later, but the reason we've chosen the timeline we've had is because it's a sitting week when we want the story to come out. A break and then –

*Ms Wilkinson*:

That's what we wanted to know. Why March?

*Mr Sharaz*:

And then the Senate goes to in March and that's when I'm going to talk to, I've got a friend in Labour, Katie Gallagher on the Labour side, who will probe and continue it going. So sitting week, story comes out, they have to answer questions at question time, it's a mess for them. March, Senate estimates. Hopefully we can try and get the footage, that sort of stuff, for Britt's clarity, and then he's going to call an election in whenever he calls it.

*Ms Higgins*:

Soon.

*Mr Sharaz*:

That's why Britt's picked that timeline.

*Mr Llewellyn*:

Ok.

*Ms Wilkinson*:

Because you're taking back ownership of your story and what happened to you to make sure that it can't happen to others. And it changes the culture as much as is possible. Because you're also riding on the back of the *Four Corners* story, as you know.

*Ms Higgins*:

Yep, yep.

*Mr Sharaz*:

Exactly.

***

*Mr Sharaz*:

And you can't prosecute the Liberal Party and the only, it's the court of public opinion that can get them. You can't get them in court.

*Ms Higgins*:

Yeah, I know. No. No, I'm not going to, I just, yeah.

***

*Mr Sharaz*:

The twenty-first of Feb you could do that story, that's ahead of that sitting week. And the March is when estimates is.

*Ms Wilkinson*:

Oh, right. So, we -

*Mr Sharaz*:

So, I don't know if that's too soon for you.

***

*Mr Llewellyn*:

So, twenty-first of Feb would be the ideal broadcast date.

*Ms Higgins*:

Yeah.

*Mr Llewellyn*:

When – so, there's questions in that next week, and then what does the, that first sitting week in March, is that Senate estimates?

*Ms Higgins*:

I think it's two weeks in, and I think it's mid-March is when Senate estimates is back.

*Mr Llewellyn*:

Okay. So, twenty-first or twenty-eighth, just as long as it's before Senate estimates?

*Ms Higgins*:

It'd be good to get a question time in, I think.

*Mr Llewellyn*:

Ah, right.

*Ms Higgins*:

Yeah.

*Mr Sharaz*:

So, you want to do it on the sitting week. So, that Sunday ahead of the sitting week.

*Ms Higgins*:

So, they're actually, they're all stuck in Parliament House with it.

*Mr Llewellyn*:

Got it. Okay. So, question time follows the twenty-first of Feb. Okay.

*Ms Higgins*:

Yep.

*Mr Llewellyn*:

Do you have friendly MPs you know that could fire questions in question time?

*Ms Higgins*:

We could find some.

*Ms Wilkinson*:

Oh, certainly, Albo.

*Mr Sharaz*:

Yeah. We just -

*Ms Wilkinson*:

Albo's a bit of a dead duck at the moment, but anyway.

*Mr Sharaz*:

Well, he's in a car crash, leave him alone, he got a lot coverage out of that.

*Ms Wilkinson*:

Tanya Plibersek, definitely.

*Mr Sharaz*:

Yeah.

*Ms Higgins*:

I'm nervous about the day after. You know how, I don't know if you guys do it, but you back in, you get friendlies to kind of back in your story. I'm kind of nervous that I'm going to be like a little -

*Mr Llewellyn*:

There'll be no friendlies?

*Ms Higgins*:

No.

*Mr Llewellyn*:

Yeah, if, I mean, Julia Banks, can we get her on ABC Breakfast or something? Like, you need people backing it in.

***

*Mr Sharaz*:

Because you want friendlies so that they don't saturate the airtime with Craig Kelly, oh, women just need to suck it up. You need, because they're going to –

*Mr Llewellyn*:

Yeah. Turnbull was the one, you know, when he was doing his book, came out and said it's like the nineteen eighties.

*Mr Sharaz*:

Yeah.

*Ms Higgins*:

He's already done *Four Corners*, though, and he'd want to make this his -

*Mr Sharaz*:

His thing.

*Mr Llewellyn*:

He does hate Morrison. Does he hate him that much?

*Ms Wilkinson*:

No, I don't, yeah, I think so. Malcolm, I know Malcolm well.

*Mr Llewellyn*:

Yeah.

*Ms Wilkinson*:

I've known him since I was in magazines.

*Mr Llewellyn*:

Yeah, I know.

***

*Ms Wilkinson*:

I reckon Malcolm will talk, Julie Bishop, I don't know. How close is she to Michaelia Cash and Linda Reynolds? They're all Perth girls.

***

*Ms Wilkinson*:

I'm a great believer in people's time will come. I'm incredibly salacious time -

*Mr Sharaz*:

Is it Linda's time, please, god, let it be Linda's time.

*Ms Wilkinson*:

Well, I think it might be.

***

*Ms Wilkinson*:

And if anybody wants to feel fired up about zeroing in on Linda Reynolds, I just found our private messages.

*Ms Higgins*:

Oh god.

*Ms Wilkinson*:

Did you see our private exchange?

*Ms Higgins*:

I did, I did, it was very scary.

*Ms Wilkinson*:

So, I said, we, she went for me, publicly, and then I tried to come back reasonably, and then I thought, I'm not going to do this publicly. I'm trying to work out who this f***ing woman is, I'd never heard of her. She's a nobody, I'd never heard of her.

***

*Ms Wilkinson*:

And it was literally about a week after I'd had the exchange with her. I just thought, this woman, this idiot is everywhere.

*Ms Higgins*:

Once again, she was sort of promoted really quickly, was never really sort of tried and put through her -

*Ms Wilkinson*:

Well, because they were plugging that hole.

***

*Ms Higgins*:

Broadly, I don't think they super care about my mental health. I don't think they are invested, personally, whether I'm smiling or -

*Ms Wilkinson*:

No, but the other three people at this table are.

*Ms Higgins*:

That's nice.

*Mr Sharaz*:

No, Linda cares.

*Ms Wilkinson*:

I've got, I've so got her in my sights now. Now that I've refreshed my memory on that.

*Mr Sharaz*:

Do you, because I said to Britt, ultimately, what do you want out of this. She goes, well, I want Bruce to forever have it difficult getting a job, like it's going to be difficult for me.

*Ms Wilkinson*:

Yeah.

*Mr Sharaz*:

And then you said, best case scenario, Linda Reynolds.

***

*Ms Higgins*:

Yeah, but obviously, you know who the biggest spender in Defence contracting is?

*Mr Sharaz*:

Linda Reynolds, yeah.

*Ms Higgins*:

Yeah. We're all shocked.

*Mr Llewellyn*:

The best bit is Linda Reynolds will see this story through my company, because we send her her media clips.

*Ms Higgins*:

We're doing a parliamentary showcase before all this starts. So, it's going to be great, we're having fun.

***

*Ms Wilkinson*:

The only problem with Julie [Bishop] is, do we let her know that we're doing this or do we just -

*Mr Llewellyn*:

No.

*Ms Wilkinson*:

- run great grabs of her, which, because she wanted to up her price on the corporate speaking circuit. So, in that period before Covid, she was making, like, forty grand a corporate speech to high level banks and all the big corporations. And the one topic they wanted her to talk about was how women need to be lifted up.

*Ms Wilkinson*:

So, I mean, she shat all over the Liberal Party at a *Woman's Weekly* Women of the Future Awards. I've seen her give the same speech about four times, and she always talks about the same stuff. So, if we worry that Julie will not play ball with us, then we just need to get those grabs. That's really what we need.

*Ms Wilkinson*:

Because that's when we got -

*Ms Higgins*:

Yeah.

*Ms Wilkinson*:

- the truthful Julie. Every other time she was asked to speak for the sisterhood, when it didn't work for her financially, she wouldn't do it. And I worry that she will get into someone's ear in the Liberal Party.

***

*Ms Higgins*:

Well, the best is the plausible deniability of Scott Morrison, post *Four Corners*, when he said that that was a Turnbull Government issue. And that's sort of what sparked my, I was like, f*** you.

*Ms Wilkinson*:

Yeah. Very much so. This one was under his watch.

*Ms Higgins*:

Yeah, it was his team.

*Ms Wilkinson*:

Yep.

798 *Secondly*, and relatedly, Mr Llewellyn knew it was Mr Sharaz who was "the one to get the story told", had pitched the project to journalists he personally selected, and was putting himself forward as a conduit for communication. At first glance, one would have thought this would have prompted efforts to ensure all important communications thereafter were with Ms Higgins directly. This does not mean Ms Higgins should have been patronised and it somehow assumed she was acting under the Svengali-like influence of Mr Sharaz, and it became evident she was very

much aware of what was going on, but it was unusual that he be used as the conduit for information. Although reasonable minds might differ, Mr Llewellyn genuinely thought it was appropriate to use Mr Sharaz as a conduit in order to communicate with Ms Higgins (T1536.28–29). In fairness to him, it also became apparent that Ms Higgins was quite content for Mr Sharaz to be the primary point of contact and she shared Mr Sharaz's views about the culpability and shortcomings of various politicians and they both very much wanted to hold them to account. But dealing with Ms Higgins in this way increased the need for care and caution.

*Thirdly*, was the remarkable assertion by Ms Higgins that her phone 799
might have been remotely wiped (Ex 36 (at 1:42:06)). Mr Llewellyn's evidence that he took that suggestion with a "massive grain of salt" and that he thought it sounded fanciful (T1514.13–1515.3) is significant and merits attention. One would have thought this was a warning light alerting to the necessity for care in assessing whether the maker of such a representation was open to speculation and conspiracies. Indeed, in written submissions, Network Ten accepted this amounted to a "conspiracy theory". Apart from the more general credit concern, it is decidedly odd that in these circumstances, Mr Llewellyn did not wonder why certain material was being provided but some was unavailable (T1516.9–33). In this regard, it is not obvious Ms Wilkinson, at least initially, thought this prospect of remote deletion was fanciful. I referred above to Mr Sharaz's accusation during the first interview (Ex 36 (at 0:06:00)) that "the Liberal Party provided [Ms Higgins] a psychologist who encouraged her not to do anything about it" (which was later not embraced by Ms Higgins). But the immediate response to the possibility an email existed corroborating this further claim was for Ms Wilkinson to say: "Given what happened to your phone, which we'll get to, I'd be retrieving that in the next 24 hours", that is, apparently entertaining the notion that such a document might also be deleted.

*Fourthly*, there was not only the incomplete data but also the nature of 800
the most important aspect of limited material said to be available, being corroborative photographs of a bruise. Importantly, Mr Sharaz had introduced the bruise photograph in establishing the credibility of Ms Higgins' rape allegation in the following exchange (Ex 36 (at 0:13:12–42)), in the context of discussing the difficulty of proving rape:

*Ms Higgins*:

... fundamentally, at the end of the day, it'll come down to my word against his. And if I don't have any corroborative evidence, whether it's the tapes, whether it's the logs, I don't, I think -

*Mr Sharaz*:

He can just say, oh, we just had consensual sex.

*Ms Wilkinson:*

Yeah.

*Mr Sharaz*:

You've got a, let me, **I'm sure you'll tell Lisa, you've got a photo of a bruise.** But there was no rape kit or anything. There's nothing that we can kind of -

*Ms Higgins*:

No.

801 As Mr Sharaz anticipated, towards the end of the meeting, Ms Higgins pointed out (Ex 36 (at 1:23:37)):

> **Yeah. Yeah. I've, on my phone, a photo of my leg.** I was, because he had pinned me down and I'm, I was in quite a lot of pain. I think that's kind of what woke me, sort of snapped me out of it, or woke me up. I was in a lot of pain, the way that my leg was sort of caught up against the couch. He was putting a lot of pressure on it. So, I had this big bruise on my thigh.

802 The following exchange then occurred (Ex 36 (at 1:24:21)):

*Ms Wilkinson*:

Have you got the photo there?

*Ms Higgins*:

Yeah, yeah, of course.

*Ms Wilkinson*:

So, you took that when you were in the office, just when it happened, or a couple of days later?

*Ms Higgins*:

Couple of days after.

*Mr Llewellyn*:

When the bruise appeared.

Pausing for a moment (as Ms Wilkinson and Mr Llewellyn ought to have done), here was an item of contemporaneous evidence said to elevate the accusation beyond a "she said, he said" contest. But both Ms Wilkinson and Mr Llewellyn moved on (by asking about seeing a doctor or contraception) at which time (and unresponsively to a question) Ms Higgins changed the subject to bring them back to something she and Mr Sharaz had evidently discussed and considered important to the credibility of her account (Ex 36 (at 1:24:58)): 803

*Mr Llewellyn*:

And were you on any contraception?

*Ms Higgins*:

No.

*Mr Llewellyn*:

Sorry, I know these are hideously private questions for me to ask.

*Ms Higgins*:

No, it's fine, it's fine. **I guess you can kind of see it in that photo, I've got a different one.** But it's, it was just, it was like this weird, largescale bruise, it was on my thigh.

*Mr Llewellyn*:

Yeah, so that's like -

*Ms Higgins*:

It was the whole leg, but it was, because it was really pressed -

*Mr Llewellyn*:

Because I can see the line there.

*Ms Higgins*:

Yeah. And it wasn't like a deep purple, but it was just this weird -

*Ms Wilkinson*:

Oh, right.

*Ms Higgins*:

- pressure bruise. I don't know. I don't know, it was weird.

*Mr Llewellyn*:

And -

*Ms Wilkinson*:

Oh, I see.

804 So now there were two photographs. Mr Llewellyn and Ms Wilkinson say they were concerned with assessing Ms Higgins' credibility. But Mr Llewellyn or Ms Wilkinson did not do all they could to obtain any information available as to these photographs (or at least the one photograph that was being shown to them), which were not only objectively important but were also regarded by the person they were interviewing as important (Ex 36 (at 0:13:12)).

805 What was done?

806 While the evidence was initially opaque, it became apparent the additional photograph referred to by Ms Higgins was never followed up on and instead was forgotten (T1512.30–31) and, as to the bruise photograph (Ex R222), it was "airdropped" by Ms Higgins to Mr Llewellyn's phone. That is, the photograph (not a screenshot) was airdropped to Mr Llewellyn's phone during the meeting (T1706.44–1708.38) but (for reasons not explained on the evidence) the airdropped photograph did not contain any metadata identifying when the original photograph was taken. Despite its importance, no attempt was made to obtain independent verification of when the original was taken.

807 Moreover, no attempt was made to ascertain how this corroborative document had survived in circumstances where Ms Higgins asserted that she had lost data from her phone.

808 In fairness, Ms Wilkinson was somewhat curious as to this general topic. A few days later, on 31 January, Ms Wilkinson and Mr Llewellyn exchanged the following messages on WhatsApp about the bruise photograph (Ex R203, 31 January 2021 (at 2:24:16pm)):

> I want to zero in a little on this whole phone thing. Have a look at my questions I've just added. I need to know what Vodafone are saying about her phone going to black. And if she says she took screenshots of crucial messages she now no longer has, how

> come she still has the bruise shot? I'm confused on this point. And why she is delaying - or at least appears to be delaying - getting answers on that. Without raising alarm bells with her do you think you can ask her today or first thing tomorrow? It's a crucial point when it comes to further blocking of her being able to gather evidence.

Her confusion was understandable. But rather than this prompting further action, Mr Llewellyn responded (Ex R203, 31 January 2021 (at 3:09:29pm)): 809

> No worries. Thanks. I'll talk to her. With no proof of my own though I suspect a stuff up more than anything else. My gut feeling is there's no covert monitoring or wiping of phones going on at all, it's just a stuff up. **And my gut feeling is to avoid the topic as it raises unanswerable questions and weakens rather than strengthens her very strong claims by adding in unnecessary doubt where there currently isn't any.**
>
> (Emphasis added)

This exchange is telling for several reasons: (a) Mr Llewellyn does not address Ms Wilkinson's question as to the evident difficulty with Ms Higgins' account as to the bruise photograph; (b) Mr Llewellyn ignores and does not question Ms Higgins' prevarication or apparent prevarication in providing an explanation as to why she selectively retained some data; (c) notwithstanding the issues now raised as to the bruise photograph, the second photograph of the bruise has been forgotten; (d) a statement that my "gut feeling is there's no covert monitoring or wiping of phones going on" is not the same as immediately dismissing what was being said as to covert monitoring and remote deletion as a conspiracy theory (which was the impression Mr Llewellyn gave in his evidence); (e) importantly, why was Mr Llewellyn intent on ignoring matters which raise "unanswerable questions" and weaken or sow doubt as to an aspect of Ms Higgins' claims? And (f), equally importantly, why was this regarded as a satisfactory response, clearing up the confusion, by a journalist as experienced as Ms Wilkinson? 810

The only other evidence of a related enquiry made was at 1:18pm on 8 February 2021, when Mr Llewellyn sent a message – not to Ms Higgins, but to Mr Sharaz saying (Ex R214): 811

> Hi mate
>
> A couple of non urgent questions for B. I don't want her having to wince when she sees a message from me so can I leave this up to you to find a good time to ask?
>
> Any idea what date the photo of the bruise was taken?

812 Ms Higgins responded to the message a couple of hours later, departing from her earlier account and indicating that the photograph was taken a "[c]ouple of days after" the rape (a representation Mr Llewellyn had apparently forgotten), by saying (Ex R292): "I'm not sure on the exact date but it was taken in Parliament House during budget week (1st - 5th of April)".

813 Even leaving aside this particular inconsistency, going back to the making of the enquiry through Mr Sharaz, one would think that instead of being concerned that Ms Higgins would "wince" upon contacting her, Mr Llewellyn would be pressing Ms Higgins to explain the anomaly as to the retention of (apparently two) bruise photographs and the selected data already provided, *a fortiori* when she had already embraced a theory as to the deletion of all data, possibly by reason of an event Mr Llewellyn said he dismissed as nonsense.

814 Although I accept that phone problems, including loss of data, are not extraordinary occurrences, the submission that it is to "Mr Llewellyn's credit that he discounted a conspiratorial explanation for the phone problems, and to Network Ten's credit that they were not ventilated" fails to grapple with the point that this was a potential problem with Ms Higgins' reliability.

815 Network Ten also submits that "Mr Llewellyn accepted that Ms Higgins' explanation about the death of her phone and the retention of the bruise photograph was inconsistent" but that this is why Network Ten "obtained a statutory declaration from Ms Higgins" (T1519.4–8). Reliance is placed on the following evidence (T1517.32–35):

> the only way we were going to use that – because of the lack of clarity, was whether we had a statutory declaration signed about that. Without that, we were unsure. Once the statutory declaration was there, we could use the photo. Otherwise, we wouldn't have used it.

816 But just before this answer, Mr Llewellyn had given the following evidence (T1517.11–21):

> MR RICHARDSON: - - - Mr Llewellyn, did it occur to you to wonder why it was that Ms Higgins was making certain material available to you and other material was not available?---The premise in your question, saying that Ms Higgins was not making stuff available to me, I don't know if there's anything that says that she was not making anything available to me.
>
> I want to suggest to you that the mere fact that she had supplied you with a handful messages and screenshots of emails attached to the timeline and the bruise photograph did not make her claims about the complete death of her phone any less strange?---Ms Higgins provided me with what she thought was relevant. That does not mean that I think things are relevant.

The submissions of Network Ten miss the point. 817

From the start, there was a failure to enquire into why Ms Higgins sought 818 to add verisimilitude to her account by reference to curated contemporaneous material. Even though, according to parts of Mr Llewellyn's evidence, he says he recognised an inconsistency and Ms Wilkinson had evidently been confused, rather than this inconsistency or confusion prompting enhanced scrutiny, the approach was to rely on further uncorroborated representations in a statutory declaration as to the bruise photograph, which, when referred to in the statutory declaration (R532 (at [7]–[8])), did not address the selective retention of data, let alone why this particular photograph had survived the "wipe" (T711–712).

It is well at this point to reject two of Network Ten's submissions related 819 to this point.

*First*, it was suggested that the absence of a contemporaneous transcript of 820 the first meeting explains why Mr Llewellyn forgot or overlooked inconsistencies as to: (1) when the bruise photograph was taken; (2) whether there was another photograph; or (3) why only some data had been provided by Ms Higgins. But according to Mr Llewellyn, he did recognise some inconsistency and, in any event, any journalist acting responsibly in a first meeting of such importance would have taken extensive notes or listened to the audio file.

*Secondly*, Network Ten made the point, more than once, that the bruise 821 photograph was adduced into evidence in Mr Lehrmann's criminal trial, even though there was no metadata available (Ex 67; T862.36–38) and the earliest version of the photograph was dated 19 January 2021 (Ex R883). In the light of this, it is said to be "perverse" if it were found that it was unreasonable for Network Ten to rely on the bruise photograph in its broadcast in circumstances where, "months later, and consistent with his obligations, the Director considered it reasonable and appropriate to put the photograph before the jury at Mr Lehrmann's criminal trial".

822 This submission does not withstand scrutiny, even if we assume the prosecution was conducted in a manner that could not legitimately involve criticism and there was a symmetry of information, in that the prosecutor appreciated all the inconsistences between retention of the one bruise photograph and the other information given to Mr Llewellyn and Ms Wilkinson during the initial meeting such as: entertaining a possibility there was a conspiracy to delete the data on her phone; the assertion of a complete wiping of her phone; and the existence of two bruise photographs.

823 Without objection, extensive extracts of the evidence of Ms Higgins at the criminal trial have been placed before me. Excerpts from the transcript (Ex 71 (at T128–9)) set out how the bruise photograph was adduced into evidence:

> MR DRUMGOLD: Now I am going to show you a photo. Now what are we looking at there?---My outside leg, my left leg. Your outside left leg?---Yes, I believe so.
>
> When did you take that photo?---It was the week of budget which was a week after the assault.
>
> If this night was Saturday, the 23rd - the early hours of Saturday, 23 March - - -?---Yes.
>
> - - - the next week started 25 March to 29 March. Is that the week you are talking about?---1 believe so, yes. I just remember it being the day before budget and I took a photo because it was still there and I - yes.
>
> Do you - what sort of - well let me ask it this way, are you in a position to estimate how many days after the 23rd of - well, including 23 March how many days after that?---It would be around five.
>
> Around five days.
>
> HER HONOUR: Mr Prosecutor, could you just clarify, it is not clear to me and it might not be clear to the jury, whether what is

shown is the inside of the thigh or the outside because the outside then the photograph, if it is the left leg, is in mirror.

MR DRUMGOLD: Yes.

HER HONOUR: If it is the inside, then it makes sense.

MR DRUMGOLD: Can we perhaps clarify, is that the outside or the inside of your leg?---If I was laying down it would have been - - -

MR WHYBROW: Object to that, your Honour. That is not the question.

MR DRUMGOLD: Perhaps it would - if I could ask the witness to stand and show on her leg where that bruise is, where that mark is.

HER HONOUR: Yes. Ms Higgins, you do not have to show your leg just on your clothing if you wouldn't mind, please?---Okay. Yes, of course. It looks like in that photo that it's taken on this leg but when I was assaulted I was pinned down on this leg so it looks like the bruise is more so on this side than this side.

Are you accepting that that photograph shows your right leg?---It does. It shows that leg, yes.

MR DRUMGOLD: Do you know when you sustained that bruise?---1 assume during the course of the assault.

Thank you. I will tender that photo, your Honour.

HER HONOUR: Exhibit F.

The following evidence was then given in cross-examination (Ex 71 (at T623–625)), demonstrating how the issue of the photograph became related to the issue of what Ms Higgins alleged she had told the AFP in 2019: 824

You have given evidence about a photograph of a bruise?---Yes.

You remember giving that evidence?---Yes.

Do you agree that you never mentioned that bruise or the photograph – two different things: the actual bruise, and the second thing is that you had taken a photograph of it. You didn't mention either of those things to the police officers on 1 or 8 April 2019? Sorry, I withdraw that; that's terrible. You took a photograph. I think from your statutory declaration you said that that photograph was taken on 3 April 2019?---Yes, that rings true.

In your evidence last week you said you took that photograph five days later. Do you accept that if you took it on 3 April, it would have been about 12 or 13 days after what you say happened on the night of the 22nd?---Yes. I just remember it being Budget week and the actual date itself I don't really recall specifically.

On - and I will break them down. When you spoke to Officers Thelning and Cleaves on 1 April, the first two ladies you spoke to - - -?---Yes.

- - - of 2019 - - -?---Yes.

- - - you didn't say anything about having a big bruise on your leg, did you?---Not that I recall to the police. Not at that point, no.

And on 8 April when you spoke to Detective Harman - you remember, from SACAT?---Yes.

Again, I suggest you didn't make any reference then to you having had a big bruise on your leg?---1 don't think that's true necessarily. They referenced keeping photos and the photos I think they were referring to were both the bruise and I took a stupid photo of a cocktail that I was drinking that night that I took a photo of that was like a Long Island Iced Tea joke because there was a teabag in a cocktail.

I suggest you didn't make any reference to having either had sustained a bruise on your leg to Detective Hannan on 8 April - - -?---No. I just answered that. I don't - - -

Did you make a reference to having sustained a bruise? Different to the photograph?---I believe so, yes.

And I want to suggest to you you made no reference to having taken a photograph of a bruise, and you have already given an answer to that?---I've already made reference - they asked me to give photos of those things, the drink and the bruise.

Is it your evidence that Detective Hannan specifically said, 'Please keep the photograph of the bruise'?---No, they said, 'Please keep any photos that are relevant', and I did.

I want to suggest that there is no reference - sorry, you didn't make any reference to anybody else before January '21 to having suffered a bruise on your leg?---1 don't believe that's true. I don't know who I would have particularly disclosed it to, but I think when I was relaying the events of the assault I think it would have come up.

I want to suggest to you the first reference that you make to having sustained a bruise is when you are speaking to Lisa Wilkinson and The Project in late January of 2020.

HER HONOUR: Just don't answer that question for a minute.

MR WHYBROW: Sorry. I might withdraw that question and put it in a different way.

HER HONOUR: Yes. I don't think you can put that.

MR WHYBROW: No, no, I will put it in a different way. I'll put a less broad proposition if I could?---Go for it.

You understand that on 25 May 2021 , the police, with your consent, done an extraction of things off your phone?---Yes. They took three of my phones and I had another three work phones I confirmed to them that existed, but they took stuff off all of them and they still have two of them.

And I want to suggest to you that on those extractions there is no reference to this bruise in messages or emails before January 2021? ---I don't think I sent it to anyone. I sent it Samantha Maiden at one point, I sent it to Lisa Wilkinson, but up until the point in which I was making a police complaint why would I send that around?

I suggest that the photograph of the bruise and your assertion that it was an injury that occurred during this assault is a fabrication?---Okay, sure. I reject you completely.

Thank you, and that - - -

MR DRUMGOLD: I'm sorry, your Honour, but the question is unfair, I think. I think the proposition advanced by this witness was she assumed. I think that was the word that was used. My friend is putting it definitively. I think she used the word 'assumed'. I can find the reference.

HER HONOUR: Well, there are two things. There's a different basis on which I can think the question might have been objected to but it wasn't and the answer has come, and if that's the submission that's going to be put, if there's a proper basis for putting it, then the question should be allowed. I think I'll leave it where it lies, Mr Prosecutor.

MR DRUMGOLD: Thank you, your Honour.

MR WHYBROW: Excuse me one second, if I may, your Honour.

HER HONOUR: My concern, Mr Whybrow, so I'm not being too Delphic, is the basis for putting as opposed to asking, if I could put it that way, given that you can't know the whole universe of information about that topic.

MR WHYBROW: No. That's why- - -

HER HONOUR: But if you're going to make the submission - - -

MR WHYBROW: That's why I confined it to something else and there's other - - -

HER HONOUR: But you are going to make the submission that it's a fabrication based on inference.

MR WHYBROW: Yes.

HER HONOUR: I think I have to allow it, Mr Prosecutor.

MR DRUMGOLD: Yes, your Honour.

825 We do not, of course, know what prior steps the prosecutor took to attempt to clarify matters with Ms Higgins in conference. He may have sought a detailed explanation and received some form of assurance or some of the evidence adduced in cross-examination may have come as a complete surprise to him (a hardly novel occurrence). As can be seen from the terms of the prosecutor's objection based on "unfairness", he was understandably trying to embrace the notion Ms Higgins had not been definitive as to what the bruise photograph depicted (although this might have been thought a forlorn endeavour forensically given the terms of her statutory declaration, a review of *all* the answers given in chief – rather than just the ultimate one – and the definitive answers given earlier in the cross-examination).

826 It is beyond argument that the prosecutor's obligation was to present all available, cogent and admissible evidence: *Nguyen v The Queen* [2020] HCA 23; (2020) 269 CLR 299 (at 314–315 [36] per Kiefel CJ, Bell, Gageler, Keane and Gordon JJ). Ms Higgins had made definitive

out-of-court representations, and the prosecutor was stuck with the reality of what had been said about the bruise photograph to the Project team. Given the defence also had these representations in the brief of evidence, the topic could hardly be ignored.

It is certainly easy to see why experienced defence counsel would seek to lock in what she had said about the bruise photograph on oath and then exploit accusations of recent invention of the bruise photograph and the existence of the bruise (allied to the broader topics of selective retention of data and inconsistences with what Ms Higgins had told the AFP in 2019) in an attempt to impeach the credibility of the complainant before the jury. 827

In these circumstances, from the perspective of the Crown, it might rationally be thought adducing evidence of the photograph in chief (which one ought to assume was a course open on the instructions received) would be the forensically preferable course to simply ignoring an important topic apt to be exploited in cross-examination. 828

The question of whether it was ethically open and prudent to adduce the evidence of the bruise photograph in chief at the criminal trial is separate to, and involves entirely different considerations from, the issues confronting the Project team when presented with the difficulties as to what Ms Higgins had first said to them about the bruise photograph and partial data retention. 829

It is tolerably plain what happened. The reason why insufficient scrutiny occurred as to these matters (which should have led to an informed assessment of Ms Higgins' general credibility) emerges from an objective review of the first meeting. From the get-go, all interactions are premised on the basis that what Ms Higgins was saying was true. It ought not be forgotten that prior to even meeting Ms Higgins, and only two days after receiving the first email from Mr Sharaz, Ms Wilkinson communicated to Mr Llewellyn that she had rung "Craig [Campbell, an Executive Producer] and Sarah [Thornton, the Network Executive Producer] and we're going huge with it" and that it would be a "March release" (Ex R117). 830

Although she was required to be dealt with sensitively, and even gently, and an empathetic and, at times, light-hearted approach was appropriate to build rapport, Ms Higgins' allegations were treated by Ms Wilkinson and Mr Llewellyn as a given. 831

## *II The Next Steps*

832 Two days later, on 29 January, a so-called "field debrief" was held. In attendance were Ms Wilkinson, Mr Llewellyn, Mr Meakin together with Mr Craig Campbell (who described himself as "the Creator and EP of *The Project*", and who had an entertainment background), Ms Laura Binnie (Head of Features), Ms Smithies and Mr Myles Farley (in-house solicitors).

833 Despite the suggestion in some parts of the evidence that the "commissioning" of the story was subject to further investigation, this does not ring true: at the risk of repetition, I am satisfied that Ms Wilkinson and Mr Llewellyn never departed from or questioned their immediate response that Ms Higgins was to be believed, despite the suggested need to conduct what Mr Campbell described as a "thorough investigation" (Campbell (at [26])).

834 The Project team also wanted to publish the story, and the primary reason why, as Mr Campbell explained, was not the sexual assault, but because "the involvement of the Federal Government and politicians" gave "this story a deep public interest" and the Project team had a "preoccupation with the involvement of the Federal Government and politicians in this story and the broader issue of safety inside Parliament House" (Campbell (at [38])). Ms Binnie had been told there "was an internal police force in Parliament House which the woman felt had not been able to properly investigate her claims, including by not being able to access key documents and CCTV footage from the night in question" and believed the story that the Project team "wanted to tell was about the treatment Ms Higgins said she had endured after complaining that she had been raped, rather than a story about the alleged rape itself" and that there was "an important difference between the two stories, and that, while both are in the public interest, the former is a story of greater public interest because Ms Higgins' then-employer was the federal government" (Binnie (at [24], [38]–[39])).

835 As Mr Campbell explained, in his view, "the villain in this case was the Government because of its lack of care for Ms Higgins" (Campbell (at [53])). Ms Binnie said that she was "always mindful of assessing what a person's motivations are for wanting to tell their story" and if "there are questionable or improper motives" she would not proceed (Binnie (at

[43])) but, as I have explained, despite this story being primarily about an alleged Government cover-up and coming from someone motivated to cause it damage, this sensible caution of Ms Binnie did not inform any heightened scrutiny by those assessing the account.

This is not to say no steps were taken. The rape allegation involved two people in a Minister's office and, apart from properly assessing Ms Higgins' credibility, the scope of available enquiries was relatively limited. Mr Llewellyn did: (a) seek confirmation as to whether the incident had been reported to others and investigated in 2019; (b) look up Mr Lehrmann online and on social media; (c) confirm the identity and positions of persons; (d) confirm with Ms Cripps that Ms Higgins had seen her for counselling; (e) spoke to Ms Higgins' then flatmate at the time of the rape (who confirmed that Ms Higgins' mood had changed following the incident); and (f) asked Ms Higgins (mainly through Mr Sharaz) to send him various documents. 836

But the story came as a coherent whole and Ms Higgins' credibility was critical. The steps he could have taken to investigate what he and others regarded as the most important part of the story (and which would perforce reflect upon the general credibility of Ms Higgins as to the rape allegation), were far from limited. 837

Mr Llewellyn gave evidence that at the first meeting (Llewellyn (at [127])): 838

> It was clear to me that Ms Higgins had called off the police investigation because the Australian Federal Police's (AFP) sexual assault unit had told her they had hit roadblocks with obtaining the CCTV footage from Parliament House.

Mr Llewellyn had conducted internet research and contacted a former Clerk of Senate and constitutional experts, including Professor George Williams, who provided information as to the workings of Parliament. Mr Llewellyn said (Llewellyn (at [189], [193])) he thought the fact "that two elected politicians were the ones who granted police access to Parliament House, sounded bizarre" and "anachronistic" and that he thought (oddly) he was in "Charles I territory". I say oddly, because the only sovereign to provoke a Civil War by Executive overreach (during the Eleven Years' Tyranny) was not exactly open to assertions of Parliamentary power. 839

840 The view of Ms Wilkinson that the system of policing within Parliament House was "archaic" led to the conclusion that the AFP police "operated at the directive of the parliamentarians themselves" and "no one was independently policing potentially criminal behaviour within Parliament House" (Wilkinson 28 July 2023 (at [83])) – needless to say (as I explained earlier (at [738])) this is a wrongheaded characterisation of the practical arrangements made for policing within the Parliamentary precincts in Canberra, and, for that matter, State Parliamentary precincts and, as far as I am aware, other Parliaments around the world that are inheritors of the Westminster tradition of an Executive responsible to a unicameral or bicameral Parliament. Even going further afield, there is a reason why the United States Capitol Police, very much in the news at around the time of the interview with Ms Higgins, unlike other federal law enforcement agencies, are appointed by the *legislative* branch of the federal government of the United States.

841 It is apparent Mr Llewellyn and Ms Wilkinson were operating on the basis that, in substance, there was a politically managed approach to policing within Parliament House such that it was open to members of the Executive to interfere with how the AFP went about their job in investigating crime. From this dangerous notion, it was a short step to embracing the idea that any delay in securing CCTV footage must be suspicious, rather than being the regular product of the need to obtain the permission of the Presiding Officers. The supposed institutional fetters on policing seem to have prompted the musings that Ms Higgins may have been spirited to Parliament House deliberately for the purposes of the assault because of roadblocks to recovery of evidence (apparently contributing to the notion that if one was to accept what Ms Higgins said, it was the safest place in the country to rape someone) (Ex 36 (at 0:25:09–0:28:33)).

842 Moreover, and even more importantly, insufficient work was done to ascertain or appreciate the fact that Ms Higgins had put a stop to the AFP investigation – not because of any delay – but only three weeks after the incident occurred (let alone ascertaining that the CCTV footage had been safely secured and was available).

### *III The Second Interview – 2 February 2021*

843 Even a failure to confirm an aspect of her story did not shake the conviction of Mr Llewellyn. For example, he noted that even though he was

"unable to confirm anything about the AFP investigation" this lack of information "did not mean that something was untrue or that the reliability of Ms Higgins' story was otherwise in doubt" (Llewellyn (at [184])). Put another way, if this important detail could not be confirmed, this did not mean there was any need for pause or mature reflection upon what other steps could be taken to procure information as to the *objective facts* surrounding Ms Higgins putting a stop to the AFP investigation shortly after the incident had been reported.

At one point in his evidence, Mr Llewellyn said he (Llewellyn (at [224])): 844

> ... thought that [Ms Higgins] was honestly expressing how she felt at the time as to the pressure not to report the allegations to police **based on the facts that were within her knowledge.**
>
> (Emphasis added)

But when it came to these facts, what were they? 845

He understood they were that "she said that she had received phone calls and the odd drop in from Yaron Finkelstein" which he "imagined that it would have been terrifying for her" (Llewellyn (at [224])). Nothing was done to investigate the existence of or timing of this or any other such "facts", which Mr Llewellyn assumed existed when it was said the cover-up caused her to choose between her career and pursuing the complaint. Moreover, Ms Higgins had made clear in the first meeting everyone's jobs were up, and employment in the Minister's office would cease shortly after the date of the election. Against this background, when Ms Higgins said at this meeting "[a]nd they intentionally made me feel as if I was going to lose my job so I wouldn't go to the police" (Ex R220 (at 2:07:56)), it seems not to have occurred to anyone on the Project team that given the pending election (which the Government was expected to lose) and the fact Ms Higgins would lose her job anyway (along with all the other staffers), that the whole premise of fear of losing her job merited investigation. 846

Returning briefly to further enquires relating to data, during cross-examination, Mr Llewellyn was taken to a portion of the second interview and gave the following evidence (T1522–3): 847

> MR RICHARDSON: Isn't it the case that after that meeting, you and Ms Wilkinson, in that exchange of messages, had reached a point where you both believed that there were serious problems

with her allegations on this topic?---No, no. We both – no. We both agreed that there was a lot of unanswerable things that we didn't have proof on. It was a – it was a very broad story about how an allegation was handled. It was not a story about a photo.

Mr Llewellyn, I want to suggest to you that when you say that it raised unanswerable questions, what you meant by that was that Ms Higgins couldn't answer those questions without appearing that she was either unreliable or a liar?---No, I reject that, because Ms Higgins didn't understand. She was going to Vodafone or Apple - - -

Well, she never did, did she?---At – I'm – I'm not aware one way or the other.

She never reported back to you that she had, in fact, visited Vodafone or Apple, did she?---She – we're talking about someone who is in an extremely – extremely – vulnerable state, who maybe for the second time has ever spoken to someone in detail about allegations of a serious rape. This photo was part of the story that she was – you know, a part – was something, but it – but it was, you know, something that – that was to be looked at over the next few weeks. Like, these – these questions are asked on 2 February. We – we weren't airing anything; it's a pre-recorded interview.

Mr Llewellyn, on 31 January, Ms Wilkinson had said to you:

> *Why is she delaying, or at least appears to be delaying getting answers on that? Without raising alarm bells with her, do you think you can ask her today or first thing tomorrow? It's a crucial point when it comes to further blocking of her being able to gather evidence.*

Ms Wilkinson thought it was a crucial point, didn't she?---I think the words just there, when it came to "gathering further evidence", so she was looking at, you know, if there were other things. It wasn't about specifically about the photo.

Mr Llewellyn, what Ms Wilkinson was saying is that there needs to be an explanation for why Ms Higgins is unable to produce all of this material. I suggest to you that's the plain meaning of what she was saying?---Ms Higgins – sorry, Ms Wilkinson is, like me, wanting to find out more.

> And despite the repeated promises Ms Higgins had made to have her phone checked, you - - -?---Sorry. There were repeated promises?
>
> Yes. She mentioned it twice in the meeting on 27 January and then Ms Wilkinson requested it again here. And, in fact, I think it's three times. I will pull up the references, but yes, she asked you at least – she told you at least twice that she was going to take her phone to be looked at, didn't she?---Look, from – from what I recall, I know that she – she definitely told us she was going to get her phone looked at, and - - -
>
> And she never did?---Well, like I said, I – I didn't expect Vodafone to be all that helpful.
>
> So did you even ask if she had had it checked?---I – I – I'm – I'm – I can't remember exactly when, but yes, I'm sure I would have.
>
> Well, it's not recorded, I suggest to you, in any document after 2 February?---That doesn't mean I didn't speak with her about it.

This evidence that he was "sure" Ms Higgins "checked" is uncorroborated 848 and, when given, was unpersuasive.

### *IV Further Steps Before Broadcast*

On 3 February, Ms Higgins signed an "Adult Appearance Release" (Ex 849 R350) in which she agreed to the following (cl 2):

> You warrant and represent to 7PM and 10 that any information contributed by you to the Program will be true and factually accurate, that you own or are entitled to all right, title and interest (including copyright) in any materials (i.e. documents, pictures or videos) provided by you to 7PM or 10 for the purpose of inclusion in the Program and that such materials do not contain confidential information or otherwise breach a duty of confidence owed by You to a third party.

The next day, on 4 February, Mr Llewellyn then began working on what 850 has been described as a "paper edit" of the proposed programme and highlighted the parts of the transcript that he thought were the most important (Llewellyn (at [243]–[244]); Ex R220). Mr Meakin worked with Mr Llewellyn and reviewed a Google Document that had been created and made changes to it (Meakin (at [56])). His involvement was not superficial, and in an email (Ex R385) he noted:

> I did notice a small point about Linda Reynolds' reaction.
>
> Brittany says her initial words were kind and supportive, but a moment later we're told she was uncomfortable with her; is there any explanation of the change of heart?

851 This prescient comment pointed to an apparent inconsistency, but Mr Llewellyn then responded by not engaging with the substance of the inconsistency but retorting that if one views the footage: "... I reckon once you see the way [Brittany] says all this stuff, you'll have a far better idea of the feel and the shifts in tone" (Ex R387).

852 Others such as Ms Binnie, Ms Smithies and Mr Farley were involved and the Project team spent several days, and possibly up to a week, on the paper edit (Meakin (at [58])), with Ms Wilkinson being provided with the paper edit on 10 February for review (Llewellyn (at [296]); Ex R493).

853 A good indication of Ms Wilkinson's mindset at around this time is provided by an email of 11 February sent to the other members of the Project team in which she expressed her view that it was important not to let Mr Finkelstein, the Prime Minister's Principal Private Secretary "off the hook", for having "checked in" with Ms Higgins at the time of the 2020 *Four Corners* programme being aired. Ms Wilkinson's view, which from her evidence at trial is one from which she has never departed, is that "it's not just the rape itself that is horrifying, it's the systemic coverup" (Ex R584).

854 The same day as Ms Wilkinson expressed this forceful view to the Project team, one of the recipients of the email, Mr Christopher Bendall, had become acting Executive Producer of *The Project*, having previously been a "co-EP" (with Mr Campbell as his superior). He was later appointed to the role in March (Bendall (at [22], [28]–[29])). As such, he was ultimately responsible for the production of everything that goes to air, including by providing the final "sign-off" and ensuring compliance with requirements relating to rights of reply, factchecking and legal processes (Bendall (at [30])). He was not involved in the preparation of the story but considered it "very sensitive" and was "concerned there was a risk of political interference or intervention if the story leaked prior to broadcast" (Bendall (at [47])).

855 How this risk of political interference or intervention would have manifested itself was not explained.

Mr Bendall made the formal decision to broadcast on 15 February. Mr Bendall said he viewed the script and "WIP video" on several occasions (Bendall (at [67])). He regarded Ms Higgins as credible and someone of high integrity because, among other things, he "found her recollection of what had happened to her consistent and compelling" and that he had been (Bendall (at [73])): 856

> … shown other evidence supporting Ms Higgins' allegations, including the photograph of a bruise that she said was taken just after the alleged assault. I do not recall who showed me this photograph. I felt this photograph added to the likelihood of her account as being true.

He would no doubt be right in this view if the bruise photograph could be relied upon. But it is unclear he was apprised of any inconsistences concerning the retention of data by Ms Higgins. It does not appear he was told there was no contemporaneous record of the existence of the bruise photograph at the time it was said to have been taken. Given the absence of evidence, it is more likely than not he was not told of any of these things. Indeed, he gave evidence of being unaware of "any inconsistencies in Ms Higgins' story" that caused him concern (Bendall (at [73])). 857

By the time of the interview there was no explanation as to what had happened to Ms Higgins' phone or why certain photos and text messages survived or why nothing was available in Ms Higgins' iCloud. Indeed, this general issue was not explored in any detail beyond Ms Wilkinson raising the topic of the mobile in relatively cursory fashion near the end of the interview (with Ms Higgins saying her WhatsApp had crashed and "even though I'd swapped previous handsets before, it lost all my previous sort of memory") and Ms Wilkinson commenting "Your phone, what, inexplicably died?" (a proposition with which Ms Higgins agreed) (Ex R220 (at 1:58:53)). 858

Moreover, with respect to the bruise photograph, Ms Wilkinson just assumed its veracity by asking (R220 (at 0:32:42)): "You have a photo that you took of a bruise that developed that night. What does that photograph show" and Ms Higgins replied the bruise was caused by Mr Lehrmann's leg pinning her down during the assault. 859

The lack of follow-up on these important topics reflected a general absence of detachment and investigative rigour. I should add, however, that I accept this suboptimal approach was at least partly well-intentioned. 860

861 From the time of the first interview, Mr Llewellyn concluded that Ms Higgins was traumatised and was acutely conscious of her mental health (Llewellyn (at [127])). Notwithstanding that he was the one supposed to be bearing the load of investigating, Mr Llewellyn considered "an important part of [his] job is duty of care for the talent" and providing Ms Higgins "with help and support through the process" (Llewellyn (at [219])). Indeed, as the EP of *The Project* was to observe, Mr Llewellyn was "very proactive about protecting Ms Higgins' wellbeing during this process" (Bendall (at [80])) and this appeared to be a predominant concern which led to dealing with her through Mr Sharaz and to be hesitant in pressing her. As Network Ten accepted, from "the outset, the production team was concerned about Ms Higgins' welfare ... [and] Mr Llewellyn and Ms Wilkinson immediately identified her as a very vulnerable and traumatised individual. It was for this reason, it was submitted, they used Mr Sharaz "as a buffer to minimise the stress caused by the production process to Ms Higgins" (see Ex R214). This might be all understandable from a human point of view, but in this case, it reflected the immediate assumption that Ms Higgins was telling the truth, and this was part of the reason why there was no proper examination and testing of her account.

### *V Seeking Comment*

862 Mr Bendall gave evidence of discussions with Mr Llewellyn, Mr Meakin and Mr Farley about seeking comment from people in relation to this story. He said that he thought it was important that the Project team went to affected, or potentially affected, persons for comment (Bendall (at [55])).

863 Mr Llewellyn gave evidence-in-chief that he "was aware that we were only airing one person's experience in the Higgins Segment" (Llewellyn (at [324])) and that it was "crucial to seek comment from any person affected by a feature story in the sense that they are the subject of any allegations (whether named or not) or otherwise mentioned in a material way in the story" (Llewellyn (at [321])). He also said he decided to seek Mr Lehrmann's comments on the allegations even though he was not named "because I thought it was the right thing to do" and a "basic tenet of good journalism that if you are airing an accusation about someone, you have to seek comment from them" (Llewellyn (at [323])).

864 This evidence is difficult to reconcile with the contemporaneous records and the objective facts as to seeking comment for this story.

As early as the first meeting, the participants had the following exchange (which is revealing as to the nature of the relationship) which touched upon several matters, including Mr Llewellyn's attitude to naming Mr Lehrmann and providing a right to respond (Ex 36 (at 0:45:22)): 865

*Mr Llewellyn*:

Yeah. Well, I mean, they're obviously, when it comes to naming Bruce.

*Ms Higgins*:

Yep, he, that's fine, I don't expect that ever to happen.

*Mr Llewellyn*:

Well -

*Ms Wilkinson*:

Depends on whether you want to press charges.

*Ms Higgins*:

If I can, after estimates, definitely.

*Mr Llewellyn*:

Yeah. And then, when it comes to defamation, he's reputation is clearly going to be lowered by being called a rapist. And whether people could identify him -

*Ms Higgins*:

I would love to -

*Mr Llewellyn*:

- by the story.

*Ms Higgins*:

- have the court case on civil. If he wants to go me after, like on a civil basis, I think, on the balance of probabilities, I think I could win. I think it's, if the onus of proof is beyond a reasonable doubt, I think that would be different. I don't think I could win that.

*Mr Llewellyn*:

Yeah. So, I mean, this is a discussion to have with -

*Ms Higgins*:

Lawyers.

*Mr Llewellyn*:

- the lawyers and stuff. But my feeling is that, if we didn't name him, and still, we may as well have named him. Because so many people would be able to identify him from the position and that kind of stuff. And various witnesses and stuff like that. So -

*Mr Sharaz*:

You toss up whether to just bother, just do it.

*Mr Llewellyn*:

Well, it's -

*Ms Higgins*:

He'll still come after us? Sorry, this is probably a conversation for a lawyer.

*Mr Llewellyn*:

Yeah, it's something that I'd need to sort of figure out with the lawyer and then come back to you and then decide. But if we, so, presuming that it's virtually impossible to, depending on how far, how many details you go through, it can either lead to identifying him or reducing that to quite a small number of people that it could possibly be. Which is still just as much as you could name him anyway. And so, therefore, we should be going, if we're making the accusation about him, as well as making the accusations against all the people who have been -

*Ms Wilkinson*:

The systems.

*Mr Llewellyn*:

The systems and covering up, then we, at the right time, so as to prevent there being injunctions and things like that.

*Ms Higgins*:

Yep.

*Mr Llewellyn*:

We would go to him and we would go to minister's office, if we're making accusations, we have to give everyone a reasonable chance to reply. **And reasonable can be pretty iffy, as long as it's not five minutes before broadcast. And if it's ten minutes, we should be okay.**

In cross-examination (T1643–4), Mr Llewellyn attempted to explain away this bolded comment by suggesting that he thought Ms Higgins and Mr Sharaz had been shocked by appreciating that Mr Lehrmann needed to be approached and that he had said this "to break the ice, I'm just sort of saying – using a bit of humour". 866

Given the way Ms Higgins had not been challenged and her account taken at face value, perhaps she and Mr Sharaz did believe that no attempt would be made to seek out those affected by the story before broadcast, however naïve that might seem. I accept that Mr Llewellyn was using humour, but it was humour revealing an underlying truth. 867

The approach taken was to ask "questions [which] are really to cover us off for defamation" (Ex R541), which Ms Wilkinson understood (T1862–1863). Despite the seriousness of the allegations to be made, there was no genuine desire to engage with anyone other than Ms Higgins in terms of content for the broadcast. This approach is unsurprising since those responsible for the programme had convinced themselves as to its veracity. Indeed, Mr Llewellyn went so far as to advise Ms Wilkinson that if any of the email recipients agreed to an interview, they were only going to be asked questions as to which Network Ten already knew the answer (Ex R541). 868

Reflecting this approach, Mr Llewellyn wanted the requests to go out as late as practicable and they went out late on Friday afternoon, 12 February, with a 10am Monday deadline. As Mr Meakin frankly acknowledged (T1958.34–37), it was unlikely that there would be time to re-interview Ms Higgins and, consistently with the process being a box-ticking exercise, the Project team did not contact her in relation to any of the information as it arrived. 869

Dealing with Mr Lehrmann, Network Ten sent detailed questions to Mr Lehrmann's Hotmail account at 2:46pm on 12 February (Ex R40) and a follow-up email on the morning of 15 February (Ex R756). No response was received. This was unsurprising for two reasons. 870

The *first* is that I am not satisfied Mr Lehrmann received either the 12 or 15 February request for comment via his Hotmail address (which together with an email address of a former employer had been sourced 871 from Mr Sharaz). The notion that such evidence was "incredible" is wholly overstated, he gave evidence as to the general frequency with which he reviewed his Hotmail account (Lehrmann (at [15(a)])) and, more significantly, there is no other contemporaneous record, such as texts, suggesting he was aware of what was about to hit him (until his first message with a friend after publication of the Maiden article at 10:29am on 15 February) (MC (at 69)).

872 The fact of receipt is not in itself important, but what is of significance is that Mr Llewellyn could not reasonably assume the Hotmail address would be regularly consulted. Nor was the use of a mobile number from a press release dated October 2018 (given it was known Mr Lehrmann had left government employment) likely to have been a useful contact. I accept the submission made by Mr Lehrmann that having regard to all the evidence, Mr Llewellyn's failure to make earlier and more detailed enquiries of how to contact Mr Lehrmann and his decision not to use Mr Lehrmann's known Facebook, Instagram or LinkedIn accounts suggest that he was doing the minimum he thought he needed to do in order to say he had made attempts to contact Mr Lehrmann. I reject the notion that for an investigative journalist genuinely trying to contact someone, adopting social media avenues, even for a very serious communication, was somehow akin to sending out "smoke signals" or "paper aeroplanes" (T1632.45–47). The suggestion that Mr Lehrmann somehow made an admission of receipt when he later presented to Royal North Shore Hospital on 16 February and said he had been "contacted by journalists in the morning [of 15 February] regarding an alleged incident occurring in early 2019" (Ex R95) is less than compelling.

873 The *second* reason was that before the Project programme went to air, Mr Lehrmann had obtained three separate pieces of advice not to respond to media enquiries and I am satisfied by reference to his evidence given in cross-examination that even if he had seen the communications, it was unlikely he would have contacted Network Ten (T434.1–34; T449.3–450.45; T451.37–452.5; T453.5–26).

874 Mr Llewellyn gave evidence about the reason for not sending out a request for comment to Mr Lehrmann sooner than the Friday before the Project programme aired on the Monday. He agreed with Mr Bendall's evidence (Bendall (at [88])) that the desire to protect the exclusivity of

the story was a reason for implementing strict confidentiality controls and processes around the story (T1620.11–26). But he then curiously denied that the desire to protect the exclusivity of the story was the reason why the request went out so late (T1620.28–1621.40). As counsel for Mr Lehrmann correctly submits, he was unable to offer any sensible explanation for why the request went out when it did, beyond that the requests went out when they were ready, and he considered it a "super reasonable" amount of time (T1620.33; T1621.11; T1621.36). It was only a "super reasonable" period if one was not interested in obtaining information from others and testing the veracity of that information with Ms Higgins.

## *VI The Treatment of the Government Response*

As I mentioned when making observations as to the credit of Ms Wilkinson (Section F.8), there was a substantive response received by the Project team. 875

The following exchanges took place between Mr Andrew Carswell, the media director for the PMO and Mr Llewellyn (Ex R716): 876

> *Mr Carswell (14 February 2021 at 4:20pm)*:
>
> Hi Angus. Andrew Carswell from the PM's office.
>
> Love to chat when you have a second.
>
> *Mr Llewellyn (14 February 2021, time unknown)*:
>
> Will give you a bell very soon Andrew.
>
> Cheers
>
> Angus
>
> *Andrew Carswell (14 February 2021 at 10:03pm)*:
>
> Here tis [*sic*]. Apologies for the delay.
>
> Please quote a government spokesperson.
>
> [first version of statement provided]
>
> Please let me know if you have further questions or need more on the record or on background.
>
> *Angus Llewellyn (14 February 2021, time unknown)*:
>
> Thanks Andrew.
>
> *Andrew Carswell (15 February 2021 at 11:16am)*:

Hi Angus, we have made some changes to the statement. I'll send in 10 mins.

***

The Government takes all matters of workplace safety very seriously. Everyone should feel safe in a workplace.

Reports today of an alleged sexual assault in 2019 in a Minister's office are deeply distressing. Throughout the entire process the overriding concern for Government was to support Ms Higgins' welfare in whatever way possible.

We understand this matter is under consideration by the police. This is an important step that the Government has consistently supported from the outset and we will await the outcome of this process.

At all times, guidance was sought from Ms Higgins as to how she wished to proceed, and to support and respect her decisions. This important best practice principle of empowering Ms Higgins is something that the Government has always sought to follow.

The Government has aimed to provide Ms Higgins with agency, provide support to make decisions in her interests, and to respect her privacy.

On Tuesday, March 26, 2019, senior staff in Minister Reynolds' office became aware the office was accessed after hours and that an incident had occurred. This incident involved two staff. It was initially treated as a breach of the Statement of Standards for Ministerial Staff.

After further consultation with Ms Higgins over the following days, it became clear to senior staff that there were previously unknown elements of the incident that may be of a more serious nature.

Ms Higgins was notified that should she choose to, she should pursue a complaint, including a complaint made to the police, and that to do so was within her rights. She was informed that she would be assisted and supported through that process.

Ms Higgins was told that if she did choose to pursue a complaint, she would have the full and ongoing support of the office and the Minister. This offer of support and assistance remains.

During this process, Minister Reynolds and a senior staff member met with Ms Higgins in the Minister's office. Given the seriousness of the incident, consideration should have been made to the location of the meeting with Ms Higgins, and in hindsight that oversight is regretted.

Minister Reynolds reiterated to Ms Higgins that whatever she chose to do, she would be supported. Minister Reynolds stated to Ms Higgins that her only concern was for her welfare and stated there would be no impact on her career.

Minister Reynolds encouraged Ms Higgins to speak with the police in order to assess the options available to her. At this meeting, Ms Higgins indicated she would like to speak to the Australian Federal Police, which Minister Reynolds supported and her office facilitated.

The Minister and her office continued to provide support to Ms Higgins through this period.

As part of this process, the Prime Minister's office provided support to Minister Reynolds and her office in assessing a breach of the Statement of Standards for Ministerial Staff by the other staff member involved in the incident.

It is important that Ms Higgins views are listened to and respected. The Government regrets in any way if Ms Higgins felt unsupported through this process.

Ms Higgins was told that if she did choose to pursue a complaint, she would have the full and ongoing support of the office and the Minister. This offer of support and assistance remains.

During this process, Minister Reynolds and a senior staff member met with Ms Higgins in the Minister's office. Given the seriousness of the incident, consideration should have been made to the location of the meeting with Ms Higgins, and in hindsight that oversight is regretted.

Minister Reynolds reiterated to Ms Higgins that whatever she chose to do, she would be supported. Minister Reynolds stated to Ms Higgins that her only concern was for her welfare and stated there would be no impact on her career.

Minister Reynolds encouraged Ms Higgins to speak with the police in order to assess the options available to her. At this meeting, Ms Higgins indicated she would like to speak to the Australian Federal Police, which Minister Reynolds supported and her office facilitated.

The Minister and her office continued to provide support to Ms Higgins through this period.

As part of this process, the Prime Minister's office provided support to Minister Reynolds and her office in assessing a breach of the Statement of Standards for Ministerial Staff by the other staff member involved in the incident.

It is important that Ms Higgins views are listened to and respected. The Government regrets in any way if Ms Higgins felt unsupported through this process.

Final statement, from a govt spokesperson

*Angus Llewellyn (15 February 2021, time unknown)*:

Thanks.

877 It will be recalled that when Ms Wilkinson read this response on Monday morning, she dismissed it (T1866.45) as a "very official response to a very difficult political situation that the government was in". She also gave the following evidence (T1868–70):

MR RICHARDSON: Well, did you believe it?---I believed that Ms Higgins' career would be impacted if she proceeded with the police investigation. I don't think she would have been a valued member - - -

I hear that?--- - - - of the Liberal Party workplace if she had proceeded with that police investigation.

Did you believe that Linda Reynolds said to Ms Higgins there would be no impact on her career?---Well, some nameless person from the Prime Minister's Office has said that there would be no impact.

The question was did you believe at this time, when you read this document, that Linda Reynolds had said to Ms Higgins there would be no impact on her career?---I don't know, I wasn't in the room.

So you had no state of mind one way or the other? You didn't know?---Well, this statement was put up on The Project website as the government's account of what they believed happened. So we very fairly put this up as the government response.

You recall yesterday you gave evidence – and this is at 1792, line 25. I said to you:

> *My note was this, that you didn't believe that Ms Higgins was alleging that Brown and Reynolds had actually discouraged her from going to the police.*

And your answer was:

> *Yes, I didn't believe that.*

Is that – you stand by that evidence?---Yes, I don't believe they discouraged her.

In that case, why wouldn't you have accepted the statement by the government that Minister Reynolds had said there would be no impact on her career?---Because I believe the way the political system works, that a young woman, who would very quickly become a scandal for the government were she to proceed down the path of a full police investigation, would have been a liability to the Liberal Party and it would have been very difficult for them to have her within their ranks.

Ms Wilkinson, I want to suggest to you that the statement that Ms Higgins had been encouraged and supported to make a police complaint did not corroborate what she had told you. Do you agree or disagree?---Would you mind asking that question again, please.

That the statement that Ms Higgins, by – in this statement from the government, that Ms Higgins had been encouraged and supported to make a police complaint, what I'm suggesting to you is that did not corroborate what she had been saying?---What she had been saying where? I had many conversations with Ms Higgins.

In any of her conversations. Do you agree or disagree? We went through them yesterday?---Sorry, I'm still struggling with your question, Mr Richardson.

When you received this document - - -?---Yes.

> - - - and you read those two paragraphs - - -?---Yes.
>
> - - - what I'm suggesting to you is that you knew they were not consistent with what Ms Higgins had been telling you?---Ms Higgins told me that Ms Reynolds was kind to her and that if she was to go ahead with the police investigation, that was okay.
>
> I also want to suggest to you that when you read the statement by the government suggesting that Ms Higgins had told there would be no impact on her career, that was also inconsistent with the allegation she had made to you?---Well, I believe and I still believe that if a full police investigation had got underway, given that her contract was going to finish in six or so weeks anyway, I believe beyond that it would have been very difficult for the Liberal Party – but we're dealing in unknowns here. I believe it would have been very difficult of the Liberal Party to continue to employ her when she would be seen as a liability. She would have been a liability.
>
> **I just asked you, Ms Wilkinson, whether you perceived any inconsistency between the government saying on the one hand no impact on her career, that that's what she was told, and the allegation she had been making to you. I suggest there was an inconsistency. Do you agree or disagree?---I wish I could comprehend your question better, Mr Richardson. I'm really struggling here.**

878 The response of Mr Llewellyn was similarly interesting. He gave the following evidence (T1670.17–42):

> You actually thought the information that Mr Carswell had provided you with was good for your program, did you?---It gave us – sorry. It gave us confirmation that an investigation had happened; it was very important.
>
> Was it because that he had admitted that the Reynolds' office was the wrong place for the meeting with Higgins to take place? Is that why you thought it was good for your program?---There was lots of good – it – confirmation; there was a lot of interesting stuff in it.
>
> Well, I'm just asking you why you thought it was good for the story?---It confirmed that there had been an investigation. It confirmed that meetings had happened. It confirmed where meetings had happened.

> Didn't it also suggest that a lot of what Ms Higgins was saying was wrong?---No, it confirmed a lot of what Ms Higgins right – was right; an enormous amount.
>
> Well, you recall – and I just took you to it – that The Project opens with the words:
>
> > *A young woman forced to choose between her career and the pursuit of justice.*
>
> **You remember that? And Mr Carswell had told you that Ms Higgins was told the incident wouldn't impact her job. Completely different, isn't it?---Yes, that's what Mr Carswell said.**
>
> Well, I'm asking you, as I said, why you thought what he said was good for the story?---Because it confirmed a lot of what Ms Higgins had said.

He also gave the revealing evidence that he thought the response contained an "element of victim-blaming" or a "suggestion that Ms Higgins had been at fault in some way", that is Ms Higgins *must* be believed and any information to the contrary is "victim blaming" (T1672.25–32). 879

By 2:17pm, Mr Llewellyn had also received, reviewed and forwarded to the Project team a further email reproducing two contemporaneous documents from Mr Carswell "[f]or background" which were said by Mr Carswell to confirm the support offered to Ms Higgins following the involvement of the M&PS division of the Department of Finance and Administration: being the lengthy and detailed summary of actions taken in relation to Ms Higgins up to and including six days after the incident sent to Ms Brown and the message sent by Ms Higgins to Ms Brown on 7 June 2019 noting Ms Higgins could not overstate how much she had valued Ms Brown's support and advice and praising her for being "absolutely incredible" (Ex R810). 880

On any view, those contemporaneous communications were important and gave substance to and corroborated the account given in the response earlier provided by Mr Carswell, being a response Mr Llewellyn had accepted was "completely different" to that recounted to the Project team by Ms Higgins about her job being at risk if she made a complaint to the AFP (T1670.37–39). 881

882 Notably, when Mr Meakin was taken to this material, which he did not recall (T1962.29) he gave the following evidence (T1962.31–42):

> I suggest it's a pretty significant email, isn't it, because it's contemporaneous and it records on 29 March what someone in an HR capacity was confirming had happened to Ms Brown?---Yes.
>
> **If you had read the email, you would agree with me, wouldn't you, that the first – that it would have been, obviously, important to go and check this account with Ms Higgins?---It certainly tells a different narrative, yes.**
>
> Now, Mr Meakin, could you - - -
>
> HIS HONOUR: Does that mean the answer to the question is yes, Mr Meakin?---I – **I think it would have been desirable, yes.**

883 Unlike Ms Wilkinson (who gave evidence she had difficulty understanding the question about inconsistency) and Mr Llewellyn (who understood the inconsistency but discounted it), the more experienced Mr Meakin recognised it and appreciated the desirability of going back to Ms Higgins in relation to contemporaneous documents that cut across what the Project team had been told. But the Project team had organised things in such a way as they needed to broadcast when they did and there was no time to make further enquires and reinterview Ms Higgins as any contradictory information or seek further material.

884 Mr Llewellyn's response to this material is telling. He focused on what he perceived to be the good parts of the response, while discounting and not pursuing the fact that the response clashed with the cover-up narrative. If Mr Llewellyn had been interested in uncovering the true position, it was incumbent upon him to put these documents to Ms Higgins and seek clarification. If he did so, perhaps it would have become evident, even to those who had been predisposed to being convinced of the cover-up narrative, that further work was necessary or even that the core allegation not based on facts (that is, what people said or did) and there was an insecure basis to make allegations that possibly amounted to criminal wrongdoing.

885 Mr Llewellyn also gave evidence (T1678–9) that he did not think it was "necessarily" important to alert Ms Wilkinson to the two contemporaneous documents. This evidence I accept. It was not important because Mr

Llewellyn knew Ms Wilkinson, like him, was committed to recounting what they thought was the most important part of Ms Higgins' account, irrespective of any comment they received.

### *VII Statutory Declaration*

Where a source has allegations that are or seem contentious, it is common for the Project team to obtain statutory declarations before the allegations are broadcast (Bendall (at [74]); Campbell (at [42])). Consistently with this practice, prior to 8 February, Mr Llewellyn had discussed with Ms Higgins and Mr Sharaz the fact that the Project team would require a statutory declaration from Ms Higgins. 886

The following day, Mr Llewellyn sent Ms Higgins a draft statutory declaration. Mr Llewellyn said he formed the view that a statutory declaration would give him an additional layer of comfort that she had been truthful during the second interview (Llewellyn (at [276])). I do not consider he believed there was a need for "comfort" but rather that it was a prudent step, like others that were being taken, to minimise defamation risk. As noted earlier (at [810]), on 10 February, Ms Higgins sent a signed copy of her statutory declaration to Mr Llewellyn by email (Ex R463). The statutory declaration (Ex R532) annexed the full transcript of the second interview and the bruise photograph and declared that everything she had said as transcribed was true and correct. 887

It was submitted by Network Ten that procuring the statutory declaration was not a "mere tick-a-box step". Although I accept the statutory declaration was detailed, as Network Ten accepted, the "statutory declaration did not, however, of course, replace the independent judgment formed by the production team as to Ms Higgins' credibility". And as I have explained, that ship had sailed long ago. 888

### *VIII The Broadcast*

The Project programme went to air at 7pm on 15 February 2021. 889

It did not bury the lede. 890

It commenced as follows: 891

> Welcome back to this special edition of The Project.
>
> Tonight claims of rape, roadblocks to a police investigation and a young woman forced to choose between her career and the

> pursuit of justice, and it all happened right in the heart of our democracy.
>
> Brittany Higgins says the government betrayed her …

892 The full broadcast is set out at Annexure A, but what that transcript does not convey is the unsettling, vaguely sinister "musical" soundtrack; the affirmation of Ms Higgins' account by the physical reactions of Ms Wilkinson including repeated nodding; the editorial decisions to show footage of Ms Higgins being emotionally upset; and the general tone of incredulity expressed at the various actions of security guards, senior advisors, and politicians leading up to Ms Wilkinson's statement: "If everything that you say is true, it sounds to me like the easiest place in this country to rape a woman, and get away with it, is Parliament House in Canberra" (line 164).

893 Only one change was made due to the materials provided by Mr Carswell (line 107) when a mention was made that the Government had stated that Senator Reynolds and Ms Brown had encouraged Ms Higgins to speak to the police, and Ms Higgins was guaranteed there would be no impact on her career. But as counsel for Mr Lehrmann submit, this was undercut by the succeeding segment regarding what Ms Higgins said happened to her. This was done advisedly. Mr Meakin suggested this structure to avoid the Government getting "the final word" (Ex R718), with the inclusion of the almost immediate reference to "the alleged assault left [Ms Higgins] feeling she had to choose between her career and seeking justice" and then further claims attacking what the Government spokesman had been reported as saying.

894 It is unnecessary to spend further time on what was broadcast, save to make three points.

895 *First*, at the conclusion of the broadcast, Ms Wilkinson said (line 167): "we of course approached all the people named in our story, and all our requests for interviews were declined". This was misleading in that: (a) Senator Cash was approached but was not asked if she was willing to be interviewed (Ex R625); and (b) Mr Meakin gave evidence (T1978.30) that this comment "was intended to refer to [Mr Lehrmann], even though he wasn't named in the story". Although literally correct because Mr Lehrmann was not named, in context, the clear impression to an ordinary viewer would have been as Mr Meakin explained, but, of course, he had not said that he declined to be interviewed.

*Secondly*, after the above comment, and referring to statements being available on the website, Ms Wilkinson said: 896

> But there is some good news for Brittany tonight, after almost two years, Parliament House authorities have finally told us the CCTV will be available to investigators.

This was misleading, and not in a minor way. As I have explained, the CCTV had been seen by the AFP as early as 16 April 2019; had been promptly secured; and had never been unavailable in the event it was required to be used for the purpose of a criminal prosecution. The only rationale for this form of words was to: (a) reinforce the notion that Ms Higgins had been improperly denied access to CCTV footage by Ms Brown, an allegation expressly made earlier in the programme; and (b) implicitly suggest that some "roadblock" had finally been removed, presumably because of the pending publicity, thus reinforcing the validity of the cover-up allegation. 897

*Thirdly*, although disputing relevance, Ms Wilkinson in submissions surprisingly doubled down on the notion that there was a proper basis for suggesting in the programme that "roadblocks" were put in place to obstruct the investigation. She called in aid a miscellany of matters such as no ambulance being called; the fact that Parliament House had no independent Human Resources department; the location of the meeting with the Minister; the "delay" in obtaining the CCTV; and that "the internal police in APH answer to politicians and different rules apply". Some of these matters are misconceived, but even to the extent they are true, or partly true, they are beside the point. The submission relying on the existence of these facts (to the extent they existed) is devoid of merit. These were not "roadblocks" to obstruct an investigation requiring someone to choose between her career and pursuing justice. An extraordinarily serious allegation was being made, pregnant with the notion of conscious wrongdoing to secure a perceived advantage. Leaving aside any comfort that could be derived from what Ms Higgins said she felt, there was no real factual basis, let alone a reasonable factual basis, for the allegation. 898

## J.4 The Position of Ms Wilkinson

As I explained in the cross-claims judgment (at [32]–[35]), the s 30 defence requires a focus on the conduct of each of the respondents: that is, the conduct of Network Ten and Ms Wilkinson separately, and 899 it follows that there is a need for the trier of fact to make findings in respect of *each* publisher as to what, in fact, occurred, before turning to the statutory mandate to have regard to all the relevant circumstances in considering whether the conduct of each publisher was reasonable. I also noted that as the trial went on, the more it became evident as to how Ms Wilkinson seeks to distinguish her role from the role of others within Network Ten as to the investigation and publication of the Project programme.

900 In Section J.3 above, I have already made several findings as to the relevant conduct of Ms Wilkinson. I will focus on the distinguishing factual matters called in aid by Ms Wilkinson as to her conduct in Section K.5 below, when evaluating the availability of the s 30 defence.

# K THE SECTION 30 DEFENCE

## K.1 Introduction

As at the time of publication of the Project programme, and prior to the coming into force of the *Defamation Amendment Act 2020* (NSW) on 1 July 2021, s 30 of the Defamation Act provided as follows: 901

> (1) There is a defence of qualified privilege for the publication of defamatory matter to a person (the "**recipient**") if the defendant proves that:
>
> > (a) the recipient has an interest or apparent interest in having information on some subject, and
> >
> > (b) the matter is published to the recipient in the course of giving to the recipient information on that subject, and
> >
> > (c) the conduct of the defendant in publishing that matter is reasonable in the circumstances.
> >
> > ...
>
> (3) In determining for the purposes of subsection (1) whether the conduct of the defendant in publishing matter about a person is reasonable in the circumstances, a court may take into account:
>
> > (a) the extent to which the matter published is of public interest, and
> >
> > (b) the extent to which the matter published relates to the performance of the public functions or activities of the person, and
> >
> > (c) the seriousness of any defamatory imputation carried by the matter published, and

(d) the extent to which the matter published distinguishes between suspicions, allegations and proven facts, and

(e) whether it was in the public interest in the circumstances for the matter published to be published expeditiously, and

(f) the nature of the business environment in which the defendant operates, and

(g) the sources of the information in the matter published and the integrity of those sources, and

(h) whether the matter published contained the substance of the person's side of the story and, if not, whether a reasonable attempt was made by the defendant to obtain and publish a response from the person, and

(i) any other steps taken to verify the information in the matter published, and

(j) any other circumstances that the court considers relevant.

902 Given it is not in dispute that the recipient has an "interest or apparent interest in having information on some subject" (s 30(1)(a)) and the matter is published to the recipient in the course of giving to the recipient information on that subject (s 30(1)(b)), it is the question as to whether the conduct of the respondents in publishing the matter is "reasonable in the circumstances" (s 30(1)(c)) that is determinative in evaluating the defence in this case.

903 I recently had cause in *Russell (No 3)* (at [272]–[307]), in considering the new defence of "public interest" in s 29A of the Defamation Act, to survey at length the genealogy of the qualified privilege defence and the concept of "reasonableness" at statute and common law. I will not repeat that analysis here, and it suffices to make some initial general observations and then deal only with a legal issue that separated the parties, being the proper construction of s 30.

904 It seems to me there is a danger in overcomplicating the relevant task.

It was long established under s 22 of the *Defamation Act 1974* (NSW) that a publisher was required to demonstrate its conduct in publishing each imputation that was conveyed was reasonable in the circumstances. It followed that the more serious the meaning conveyed, the more onerous was the obligation cast upon the publisher to ensure that its conduct in relation to conveying the meaning was reasonable. If the publisher intended to convey the meaning found to have been conveyed, the publisher was required to establish that it had an actual or attributed belief in the truth of the imputation (save those exceptions where belief in the truth of what was published was not required at common law – such as where a publisher was under a duty to pass on, without endorsement, a defamatory report made by some other person or analogous circumstances: see *Echo Publications Pty Limited v Tucker (No 3)* [2007] NSWCA 320 (at [20] per Hodgson JA, with whom Mason P and McColl JA agreed)). 905

Finally, the publisher was required to establish that before publication it exercised sufficient care to ensure that proper enquiries were made; checks were made on the accuracy of sources; the conclusions drawn followed logically; fairly and reasonably from the information obtained; the manner and extent of publication did not exceed what was reasonable; and that each imputation conveyed was relevant to the subject matter about which information was being conveyed. Obviously enough, the steps required to be taken to establish that the publisher had acted reasonably was a contextual enquiry depending upon the nature of what was conveyed. 906

The relevant evaluative assessment occurred in circumstances where the defence fell to be considered if other defences (such as substantial truth or comment) had not been established in relation to the imputations conveyed and there would be cases where, despite all appropriate reasonable steps being taken by the publisher, the journalist got the facts wrong: see *Austin v Mirror Newspapers Ltd* (1985) 3 NSWLR 354 (at 364–365 per Lord Griffiths on behalf of the Privy Council). 907

With respect, Wigney J in *Chau v Fairfax Media Publications Pty Ltd* [2019] FCA 185 (at [109]–[115]) drew together the relevant principles conveniently as follows: 908

> [109] First, in most cases, the more serious the imputation that is conveyed, the greater the obligation upon the respondent to

ensure that its conduct in relation to the publication was reasonable: ***Morgan*** *v John Fairfax & Sons Ltd (No 2)* (1991) 23 NSWLR 374 at 387C (per Hunt A-JA, with whom Samuels JA agreed); see s 30(3)(c) of the Defamation Act.

[110] Second, a respondent who intended to convey an imputation that was in fact conveyed must generally establish that they believed in the truth of that imputation and that the imputation conveyed was relevant to the subject: *Morgan* at 387F and 388C.

[111] Third, the fact that the respondent may not have intended to convey the imputation that was in fact conveyed does not necessarily mean that their conduct in publishing was unreasonable: *Austin* at 362; ***Roberts v Bass*** (2002) 212 CLR 1 at [81]-[82]. In such a case, the respondent must generally establish that they believed in the truth of the imputation that they intended to convey, and that their conduct was nevertheless reasonable in relation to the imputation which they did not intend to convey, but which was in fact conveyed. In that regard, it may be relevant to consider whether it was reasonably foreseeable that the publication might convey the unintended imputation and, if so, whether the respondent considered that possibility and took appropriate steps to prevent that imputation being conveyed: *Morgan* at 387G-388A; *Obeid v John Fairfax Publications Pty Ltd* (2006) 68 NSWLR 150 at [70]-[75]; *Evatt v Nationwide News Pty Ltd* [1999] NSWCA 99 at [40]-[43].

[112] Fourth, the respondent must generally establish that reasonable steps were taken before publishing to ensure that the facts and conclusions stated in the publication were accurate. That would generally involve making proper or reasonable inquiries, checking the accuracy and reliability of sources of information and ensuring that the conclusions followed logically, fairly and reasonably from the information that had been obtained; *Morgan* at 388B; see generally ss 30(3)(g) and (i) of the Defamation Act. In that context, the respondent must ordinarily disclose both the nature

and source of the information which was possessed: *Sims v Wran* [1984] 1 NSWLR 317 at 327F.

[113] Fifth, in relation to sources, the respondent's belief or perception of the position, standing, character and opportunities of knowledge of the source must be such as to make the respondent's belief in the truth and accuracy of the information reasonable in the circumstances: *Morgan* at 388D; s 30(3)(g) of the Defamation Act.

[114] Sixth, a respondent must show that the manner and extent of the publication did not exceed what was reasonably required in the circumstances: *Morgan* at 388C.

[115] Seventh, the respondent must also establish that the respondent gave the person defamed an opportunity to make a reasonable response to the defamatory imputation: *Stephens v West Australian Newspapers Ltd* (1994) 182 CLR 211 at 252; referred to by the High Court in ***Lange** v Australian Broadcasting Corporation* (1997) 189 CLR 520 at 574.

## K.2 The Proper Construction of Section 30

### *I The Respondents' Submissions*

Both the respondents submitted on the proper construction of s 30, the 909
enquiry as to the reasonableness of a respondent's conduct turns on its conduct with respect to the "defamatory matter", that is, the aspects of the publication that the applicant has selected for complaint as embodied in the imputations and not "the matter" as defined in s 4 of the Defamation Act, which provides:

**"matter"** includes –

(a) an article, report, advertisement or other thing communicated by means of a newspaper, magazine or other periodical, and

(b) a program, report, advertisement or other thing communicated by means of television, radio, the Internet or any other form of electronic communication, and

(c) a letter, note or other writing, and

(d) a picture, gesture or oral utterance, and

(e) any other thing by means of which something may be communicated to a person.

910 This means the defence does not invite some form of "roving commission of inquiry into every aspect of the broader publication, untethered from the applicant's complaint".

911 The starting point is that positive defences at common law in defamation are pleas in confession and avoidance, and a plea that defamatory matter was published on an occasion of qualified privilege is predicated upon the existence of a defamatory imputation, that is, it assumes that the applicant's case is established (that is, it confesses the defamatory meaning). Hence it makes sense that the subject matter of the defamation, in relation to statutory defences other than justification and contextual truth is expressed as the *defamatory matter* not the *defamatory imputations*.

912 Put another way, the *defamatory matter* described throughout the Defamation Act is the matter the subject of the action in defamation, that is, the matter that is defamatory of the person bringing the action. The defences only come to be considered in relation to a pleaded matter if, and only if, the Court finds that the matter was defamatory of the applicant.

913 It is said any textual argument relying on the non-exclusive definition of "matter" is of no moment. The section needs to be read as a whole and words defined in legislation apply "except in so far as the context or subject-matter otherwise indicates or requires" (see s 6 of the *Interpretation Act 1987* (NSW) and cognate provisions).

914 Although the term "defamatory matter" is not defined, it is contended its meaning is clear from its deployment, including its deployment in contradistinction to the term "the matter" elsewhere in the Defamation Act, such as:

(1) *s 28* which provides that it is a "defence to the publication of defamatory matter if the defendant proves that the matter was contained in ... a public document or a fair copy of a public document, or ... a fair summary of, or a fair extract from, a public document"; if the terms "defamatory matter" and "the matter" in s 28 were references to the publication as a whole, then the words "was contained in" would have no work to do;

(2) *s 29* which provides that it is a "defence to the publication of defamatory matter if the defendant proves that the matter was, or was contained in, a fair report of any proceedings of public concern"; again, if the terms "defamatory matter" and "the matter" were references to the publication as a whole, then the words "or was contained in" would be otiose; and

(3) *s 31* which provides for a defence of honest opinion that applies, relevantly, "to the publication of defamatory matter if the defendant proves that ... the matter was an expression of opinion of the defendant rather than a statement of fact..."; the words "defamatory matter" and "the matter" cannot be a reference to the publication as a whole; otherwise there would never be a defence of honest opinion available in relation to a matter that admixed fact and opinion, which, as the respondents correctly point out, is the reality in almost every honest opinion case; hence the provision only makes sense if the words "defamatory matter" and "the matter" are understood as referring to the aspects of the publication selected for complaint by the applicant: see *Massoud v Nationwide News Pty Ltd; Massoud v Fox Sports Australia Pty Ltd* [2022] NSWCA 150; (2022) 109 NSWLR 468, where Leeming JA (with whom Mitchelmore JA and Simpson AJA agreed) explained (at 521 [195]) that the issue is not whether the matter published was an expression of opinion rather than a statement of fact, but whether the matter published insofar as it conveys the defamatory imputation is an expression of opinion.

There are also three aspects of s 30 which are said to point to the use of the 915
same distinctions, being:

(1) that the defence begins in the same way as the defences in ss 28, 29 and 31 by describing the defence as a defence for the publication of "defamatory matter" and that term "is apt to describe and should be understood as a reference to the field of battle in the action as defined" by the imputations;

(2) s 30(1) distinguishes between "defamatory matter" (chapeau); "the matter" (s 30(1)(b)); and "that matter" (s 30(1)(c)), and if the legislature had intended a broader enquiry, then the words "the matter", not "that matter", would have been used in s 30(1)(c); it follows the words "that matter" in s 30(1)(c) "can only rationally be understood

as a reference to the words 'defamatory matter' in the chapeau" and are to be distinguished from that in s 29A, which I recently considered in *Russell (No 3)* (at [309]–[316]);

(3) s 30(3) defines the relevant enquiry as being "whether the conduct of the defendant in publishing matter *about a person* is reasonable in the circumstances" and hence focuses upon the allegations concerning the applicant; that is, the defamatory matter, not the entirety of the publication.

916 It is further submitted this approach is confirmed by other objects of the Defamation Act including "effective and fair remedies for persons whose reputations are harmed by the publication of defamatory matter": s 3(c); that is, the focus is not upon "the regulation of journalistic standards in respect of parts of publications not selected for complaint".

917 It was said to be "absurd" if the Court were to conclude that Network Ten's conduct in respect of the publication of the rape allegation selected for complaint by Mr Lehrmann was reasonable, and yet go on to award damages to Mr Lehrmann because Network Ten's conduct was unreasonable in relation to the cover-up allegations. Such an outcome would, it is submitted, be inconsistent with "the objects of the Act, the policy of the cause of action and would defy common sense to the point of bringing the law into disrepute".

918 This approach accords with the fact that the predecessor to the s 30 defence, namely s 22 of the predecessor Act, was clearly intended to widen the scope of qualified privilege: see *Austin v Mirror Newspapers* (at 359 per Lord Griffiths on behalf of the Privy Council). The Privy Council (at 354C, 363G), consistent with a defence of confession and avoidance, identified that the starting point of the assessment of reasonableness under s 22(1)(c) is the facts on which the attack (that is, the defamatory meaning or allegation as opposed to the matter) was based, which the jury has found were not true.

### *II Conclusion on Construction Issue*

919 Although I am grateful for the well-considered and scholarly submissions on this point, I think they overcomplicate the issue.

920 As support for the construction advocated, both respondents called in aid the judgment of Hodgson JA (with whom Basten JA and McClellan CJ

at CL agreed) in *Griffith v Australian Broadcasting Corporation* [2010] NSWCA 257. In that judgment, his Honour observed as follows (at [117]–[121]) in relation to s 22 of the predecessor Act:

> [117] ...What has to be shown to be reasonable under s 22(1)(c) of the Act **is the conduct of the publisher in publishing that matter, in its character as making the imputation complained of; not, in my opinion, the matter in all of its aspects.**
>
> [118] This view is supported by the following passage from *Morgan* at 383:
>
>> Those opposing arguments require further discussion of the nature of the requirement imposed by s 22, that the conduct of the defendant in publishing the "matter" was reasonable in the circumstances.
>>
>> The extent of this requirement was first considered by this Court in *Wright v Australian Broadcasting Commission* [1977] 1 NSWLR 697. Moffitt P (with whom Glass JA agreed) said (at 705):
>>
>>> "... s 22(1)(c) requires that particular attention is paid as to [the] reasonableness of the conduct in relation to [the] publication of this particular matter, ie that which carries the defamatory imputation."
>>
>> He then gave an example which underlines the issue as being whether the defendant acted reasonably in publishing the particular imputation concerning the plaintiff. The defendant, his Honour made it clear, must establish that the particular imputation against the plaintiff was reasonable. Reynolds JA (with whom Glass JA also agreed) said (at 712):
>>
>>> "... Section 22(1)(c) calls for the consideration of a wide range of matters. Some are to be found in the published material itself and the manner and extent of its publication, and others from the whole of the surrounding circumstances. The connection between the subject and defamatory imputation remains

> relevant. It may be tenuous, or it may be real and substantial. If what was said includes comment, it is relevant to consider whether it was fair and whether it followed logically from facts known or stated. Questions of the exercise of care before the defamatory utterance are also relevant, and questions as to whether the maker of the statement knew whether he was likely to convey a misleading impression."

[119] **This passage indicates that the relevant conduct is the conduct of a defendant in publishing the particular imputation, not its conduct in publishing the whole matter; so that different results might eventuate in relation to different imputations:** *Vilo v John Fairfax & Sons Ltd* [2000] NSWSC 937 at [51] per Simpson J. See also *Makeig v Derwent* [2000] NSWCA 136 at [43] per Spigelman CJ (Mason P and Heydon JA agreeing).

[120] Accordingly, in my opinion, unreasonableness of the respondents' conduct in publishing matter in its character of making imputations against Mr Macartney-Snape does not constitute relevant unreasonableness so as to defeat a defence under s 22 to the appellant's claim. **It may conceivably have some factual relevance to the question whether the respondents have proved they have acted reasonably in publishing the matter in its character as making the imputation against the appellant**, but not otherwise. In my opinion, the appellant has not identified any respect in which the primary judge should have taken unreasonableness as against Mr Macartney-Snape into account in this way, but did not do so.

[121] I have said that, as part of establishing reasonableness, the onus is on the respondents to exclude malice; that is, in my opinion, relevantly an onus to show that their purpose in publishing the matter, **in its character of conveying the defamatory imputation**, was to give the audience information which the audience had an interest (or apparent interest) in having, and that the respondents did not have

> any other reason for this publication which was the dominant reason: cf *Roberts v Bass* [2002] HCA 57; (2002) 212 CLR 1 at [104].
>
> (Emphasis added)

It seems to me there is force in the proposition that the approach explained in *Griffith* remains the principled way to approach this defence of confession and avoidance. What needs to be the subject of focus is the matter, but in *its character of conveying the defamatory imputation*. 921

## K.3 Introduction and the General Approach of the Respondents

As touched on above, my analysis of the reasonableness of the conduct of the publishers starts from the premise that the rape allegation has not been proven to be true. This is because if the defamatory imputation is true, it is unnecessary to consider this separate defence which recognises that a publisher can publish untrue material but still act reasonably. In this regard there is a need to guard against judging a publisher by unrealistic standards, adopting a counsel of perfection, or adopting hindsight bias. 922

At the outset, it is worth dealing with, and then rejecting, two related submissions made primarily by Network Ten. 923

*First*, no doubt recognising the difficulties the respondents had in defending the reasonableness of the cover-up allegation, the approach urged on me was less a principled focus on the matter *in its character of conveying the defamatory imputation*, but rather putting those parts of the programme that dealt specifically with the rape in a hermetically sealed box, entirely separate and insulated from any context that surrounded it. The evaluation of reasonableness must focus on the defamatory imputations, but the conduct which led to the publication must be considered by reference to all the circumstances, including how the Project team approached the task of publication. 924

*Secondly*, and relatedly, the assertion that the whole of the attack upon the respondents' conduct in relation to the conception, research and presentation of the programme concerned matters "wholly unrelated" to the imputations (other than the bruise photograph, and the adequacy of the opportunity afforded to Mr Lehrmann to respond to the allegations against him) is superficial because the focus must be on *all the relevant* 925 *circumstances*, including what steps were taken before publishing the defamatory matter to ensure that the facts and conclusions stated were accurate and, in this regard, making proper or reasonable inquiries, checking the reliability of sources of information and, most importantly, the credibility of sources.

926 Part of this context is that from the period when Mr Sharaz first contacted Ms Wilkinson until the time of broadcast, a relatively short period elapsed. Network Ten knew that Mr Sharaz had chosen Ms Wilkinson and Ms Maiden advisedly. He and Ms Higgins wished to ensure co-ordinated publicity be given to their allegation of rape and a political cover-up preventing Ms Higgins from obtaining justice. As I have explained, the first time Network Ten sought and obtained any other information (which was contradictory to the narrative developed by Ms Higgins), there was no time for reflection or further enquiry prior to the co-ordinated publication, and for some time, Mr Sharaz had been pressing for publication.

927 During submissions, any suggestion that there should have been some scrutiny given to Ms Higgins' credit as being relevant to her allegations as a whole (including the allegation of rape), particularly given the vagueness of what was perceived to be the most important component of her allegations, was dismissed as being a counsel of perfection demonstrating naïveté as to the way that politics and journalism works. The "worldly" approach of Network Ten was to support someone perceived from the start to be a victim of two wrongs and, in the absence of verifiable facts, to "read between the lines".

928 Despite any suggestion to the contrary, to deprecate the general approach adopted by Network Ten and Ms Wilkinson in this case is not a counsel of perfection, nor does it somehow lack sophistication.

929 The Media, Entertainment and Arts Alliance (**MEAA**) (the industrial association successor of, among other things, the Australian Journalists Association), binds its members to the MEAA *Journalist Code of Ethics* (**Code**). The Code has a very long history and, as Callinan J observed in *Australian Broadcasting Corporation v Lenah Game Meats Pty Ltd* [2001] HCA 63; (2001) 208 CLR 199 (at 305–306 [268]) "[f]rom time to time, the [Code] finds its way into evidence in defamation cases". Although the Code is not in evidence in this case, and under MEAA's rules (registered with the Fair Work Commission), it only applies to MEAA journalist

members (which does not include the Project team), I raised with the respondents whether the Code is a useful guide to the responsible and reasonable conduct of journalists.

I did so because as can be seen from Section K.1 above, the question as to whether the relevant conduct is "reasonable in the circumstances" is determinative of this defence; and after making findings as to the circumstances, when one comes to the process of evaluation, the court may take into account the specified s 30(3)(a)–(i) factors, but also "any other circumstances that the court considers relevant" (s 30(3)(j)). 930

Deconstruction and particularism abound in submissions made by defamation practitioners when considering reasonableness. But in this, like in other areas of the law, one must be astute not to "seek a false certainty" by seeking out some defining element given that it is "human behaviour that is to be evaluated and characterized": for a discussion of this topic, see the Hon J L B Allsop, 'The Judicialisation of Values', Speech to the Law Council of Australia and Federal Court of Australia FCA Joint Competition Law Conference Dinner, 30 August 2018. 931

Without detracting to the guidance as to norms of behaviour and considerations provided by the text of s 30(3), as I said in the cross-claims judgment (at [33]), the governing notion of reasonableness is open-textured and value-laden; and when Courts are required to apply such a standard, as Professor Julius Stone observed: "judgment cannot turn on logical formulations and deductions, but must include a decision as to what justice requires in the context of the instant case ... [Such standards] are predicated on fact-value complexes, not on mere facts": see Legal System and Lawyers' Reasonings (Stanford University Press, 1964) (at 263–264). 932

The assessment of reasonableness has, implicit within it, the identification of values against which conduct is measured. Some assistance is derived from the non-exclusive s 30(3) factors, but one cannot ignore other norms or values one would expect to inform the conduct of responsible and reasonable journalism. Despite the resistance of the respondents to the notion, the usefulness of the Code is that it provides, among other things, a pointer as to what might be expected of a journalist. 933

The respondents are correct to stress the lack of any direct relevance of the Code in this case, but that is not to say (nor in fairness do I think 934 the respondents are saying) that I would be wrong in having regard to whether the publisher was: (a) reporting and interpreting honestly, striving for accuracy, fairness, and disclosure of all essential facts; and/or (b) not allowing any belief or commitment to undermine fairness or independence.

935 As I will explain, taking all relevant considerations into account, including the desirability of not allowing any belief to undermine fairness or independence, the conduct of Network Ten and Ms Wilkinson in publishing the matter in its character of conveying the defamatory imputations of rape fell short of the standard of reasonableness.

## K.4 Why the Network Ten Conduct was not Reasonable

936 Returning to specifics, and relying on the findings identified in Section J above, to the extent they are relevant, there are several pointers in the evidence demonstrating why the conduct of Network Ten fell short of being reasonable in publishing that matter, in its character as making the imputation of rape:

(1) The rape allegations were intertwined with the cover-up and the Project team had strong indications of the unreliability of their main source, particularly as to how she lost material on her phone and selected material survived; her explanations were implausible and rather than this being a flashing warning light, Mr Llewellyn's instinct was to avoid "unnecessary doubt" (Ex R295) and was not even followed up. The lack of curiosity about investigating the bruise photograph is especially unreasonable given its subjective and objective importance and given it was said to viewers to be physical evidence corroborating Ms Higgins' rape allegation (Annexure A (lines 35–37)).

(2) Further relevant to credibility as to the allegation of rape was the fact that her account was, as Mr Lehrmann submitted, "replete with inconsistencies and implausibilities"; a fair review of the first meeting reveals, to an objective observer, how vague Ms Higgins was as to any concrete detail, repeatedly asserting that people or things were "weird" or saying what she felt and, to the extent there was any detail, those details shifted, moving from Senator Reynolds and Ms Brown

representing "we wouldn't stop you", to accepting she was offered support, to saying she was not offered support and was made to feel that going to the police was not an option, to Ms Brown making it plain that if she went to the police she would not have a job. Sensibly, Ms Thorton had stressed (Ex R190) that she wanted "clarity on what was said by who means to who [*sic*] in terms of Brittany not pressing charges. And whether there's a paper trail or [*sic*] notes or witnesses or anything to corroborate that part of it". Despite this caution, and without this detail, the serious allegation of a cover-up was immediately accepted as being inherently credible, resulting in a want of reasonable scrutiny as to her general credibility, which was directly relevant to assessing the cogency of the allegation of rape. Rather the approach of Ms Wilkinson and Mr Llewellyn was to encourage the cogent articulation of an obstruction narrative, with this exchange occurring in the first meeting (Ex 36 (at 1:08:39–1:10:55)):

> *Ms Wilkinson*:
>
> The answer you really need to think about is -
>
> *Ms Higgins*:
>
> Yeah.
>
> *Ms Wilkinson*:
>
> - why didn't you press charges?
>
> *Ms Higgins*:
>
> Yeah.
>
> *Ms Wilkinson*:
>
> I'm, I have every confidence that you will answer that very eloquently, but it's one you just need to really think about.
>
> *Ms Higgins*:
>
> Yep, I'll -
>
> *Ms Wilkinson*:
>
> And you need to -
>
> *Ms Higgins*:
>
> - whittle it down to a bite.

***Ms Wilkinson*:**

**Yeah, but speak about the culture that, I don't want to put words in your mouth, but if you can enunciate the fact that this place is all about suppression of people's natural sense of justice. Because you see around you the way that this place works.**

***Ms Higgins*:**

**Yeah.**

***Ms Wilkinson*:**

**That will help. And that people who work there feel like they've reached the top of the mountain, and you don't want to leave the top of the mountain. Because this is where -**

***Ms Higgins*:**

**This was the pinnacle.**

***Ms Wilkinson*:**

**- this is government. This is everything you've ever wanted, and it's either, you play by their rules or you're out of there.**

***

*Mr Llewellyn*:

Okay. Because I think the story will clearly have an explosive element of there is just no moral compass. That everyone is treated as a political weapon, rather than as a human.

*Ms Wilkinson*:

And it exists within its own set of rules. I mean -

*Mr Llewellyn*:

Own set of rules, yeah.

*Ms Wilkinson*:

- the whole situation with the police. The fact that you can't get access to CCTV footage that a whole bunch of other people have seen.

*Ms Higgins*:

Have seen. Yeah.

*Ms Wilkinson*:

And that you asked for it, repeatedly, you were never given access to it, the police outside of the parliamentary set of police, asked for it and were stonewalled.

(3) The motivations of Mr Sharaz in selecting the journalists to tell and use the story were manifest and rather than this motive being a cause of some degree of circumspection, but Mr Llewellyn and Ms Wilkinson indicated their willingness to assist in the political use of the allegations as Ms Higgins and Mr Sharaz intended.

(4) As noted above in Section J.2, the Timeline document, according to Network Ten, confirmed the view that the story was potentially an issue of great public interest and should be pursued. Despite this, there was no proper investigation of representations made in the document, including as to why: (a) it was said notification was sent to the DPP from the "Parliament House AFP Station" (an allegation never explained); (b) the tension between the notion there was something sinister about the ominous comment about a "contract with Minister Cash from Star Chamber [being] rejected. (Note - Fiona Brown sits on Star Chamber)" with the fact that Ms Higgins was in truth offered three jobs after the 2019 election; (c) the wrongful implication that Mr Lehrmann was fired because of the assault; or (d) Ms Higgins' assertion that she met with the Parliament House AFP on 26 March (which was not only wrong factually, but necessarily confused the fact that Ms Brown organised the initial visit after the meeting on 1 April).

(5) The ahistorical and misconceived notion embraced by Mr Llewellyn and Ms Wilkinson that there was an Executive Government-controlled approach to AFP policing within Parliament House, which obstructed investigation and caused delays, contributing to the withdrawal of Ms Higgins' complaint and suggesting, together with the other things Ms Higgins was alleging, that according to Ms Wilkinson, Parliament House was the safest place in Australia to rape someone (see [841] above).

(6) The approach to seeking comment from Mr Lehrmann including the steps taken to contact Mr Lehrmann (from which approach there was no dissent by Ms Wilkinson) when the contacts provided by Mr Sharaz were obviously inadequate (and the Project team were warned not to research Mr Lehrmann via LinkedIn in case Mr Lehrmann was notified of that research – "Worth noting that if you click on the alleged perpetrator's LinkedIn profile he could get a notification – something we clearly wish to avoid" (Ex R180; see also R126)).

(7) If Network Ten wanted to get in contact with Mr Lehrmann, there were ways of ensuring that contact could be achieved. He was not living the life of a hermit – he was working for a public company in Sydney. The approach lacked reasonableness in the circumstances of the publication of an allegation of such seriousness. Network Ten were not to know that Mr Lehrmann was unlikely to take up any invitation.

(8) Finally, was the dismissal of contradictory information received from Mr Carswell and failing to follow it up with Ms Higgins; but this is a mere instance of the broader problem that Mr Llewellyn, like Ms Wilkinson, started from the premise that what Ms Higgins said about her allegations was true. They resolved from the start to publish the exclusive story and were content to do the minimum required to reduce unacceptable litigation risk.

937 In the end, standing back and evaluating the conduct of Network Ten in publishing the matter (in its character of conveying the serious defamatory imputation of rape about Mr Lehrmann), and notwithstanding the broadcast was on a topic of high public interest, Network Ten falls short of discharging its burden.

## K.5 Ms Wilkinson: Distinguishing Matters and an Evaluation

938 Having identified and evaluated Network Ten's conduct, I now turn to Ms Wilkinson. In the light of my findings above, however, extensive overlap is apparent, not only because it is accepted by Network Ten that Ms Wilkinson's conduct can be attributed to the corporation (and I have taken it into account in considering the position of Network Ten); but also because much of the other conduct to be attributed to Network Ten,

by reason of the actions of others, occurred while Ms Wilkinson was present or was conduct of which she was aware.

The most significant point made is the heavy reliance placed upon Ms Wilkinson's actual role in the publication, to which I have already referred. Although Mr Sharaz approached Ms Wilkinson, as she points out, the ultimate decision to proceed with the story was made by others and the final approved script was not distributed until 5:22pm on the day of broadcast (Ex R842). More generally, Ms Wilkinson submitted she was not a "decision maker in relation to any aspect of the final production, broadcast and publication of the matters" and her "role" was limited. 939

The distancing of this experienced and high-profile journalist from the circumstances of publication might somehow be linked to the falling out between Network Ten and Ms Wilkinson revealed in the evidence adduced on the cross-claims, but it is unnecessary to form any view about the reason behind the unusual circumstance of there being differences between the defences of the media company and a journalist employed by it. Ms Wilkinson is correct to submit the defence is focused on conduct, and all the attributed conduct of Network Ten is not her conduct. 940

This tension between the picture of a limited role as to publication painted in Ms Wilkinson's final submissions and the Logies speech has already been pointed out, but it also conflicts with other evidence. As Mr Richardson SC colourfully, but accurately, put it in final submissions (T2439.12–34): 941

> MR RICHARDSON: ... And now we see her instructing her counsel to say, "Well, I didn't really have that much to do with the programme, particularly near the end". Truly. It's peculiar, your Honour, to say, "Well, the mistakes lie at Ten's door, not mine". The real point is Ms Wilkinson was there at the point of the assessment of Higgins' credibility, the timeline, the five hour meeting on 27 January, the two hour interview on 2 February. She had heard all of the inconsistencies and problems with what Higgins said about the phones, the photograph, Brown, Reynolds and so on. She was gleefully anticipating her hit on Linda Reynolds and the then Coalition government.
>
> Now, we heard yesterday that some kind of actuarial analysis has been undertaken to show that she wasn't copied on something

like 80 or 90 per cent of the emails during the editing process, and also that she had no decision making powers. That is well and good, your Honour. What the evidence was, was that she was kept informed of the responses as they arrived, that's paragraph 125 of her affidavit, she was kept informed of the timing of when the requests for comment would go out and also contributed to those requests. That's at paragraphs 112 and 113. And when Mr Llewellyn observed to her that those requests were to cover us off for defamation, she said "cool, understood". That was the conduct she did, and now we hear the submission about her having some kind of lesser responsibility.

If your Honour squints into the horizon and looks far, far away down the end of the river, your Honour will see Mr Llewellyn on a barge destined for the next market town, fate unknown.

942 It is apparent that Ms Wilkinson was eager to assist Ms Higgins in telling her story and that Ms Wilkinson was doing so for reasons personal to her. This was the case from soup to nuts. In this regard, there is a revealing exchange at the first meeting:

*Mr Sharaz*:

Yeah. I guess, what's your, obviously, we're not stupid, we know that this sort of stuff's transactional. What are you getting out of it, what do you want out of it?

*Ms Wilkinson*:

Champion for women who are being suppressed.

*Mr Sharaz*:

And I assumed that, because I tried to show.

*Ms Wilkinson*:

No, I'm always about exactly the same thing. The inequality that exists out there, whether it's white privilege, whether it's male domination, whether it's criminal activity that is suppressed. I'm a girl from the western suburbs of Sydney, I'll always be motivated by exactly the same thing. People who deserve to be heard, not being heard.

***

> *Ms Wilkinson*:
>
> David just asked me an important question that you probably, well, you should know the answer to. David said, what's in it for me, as a journalist. And my background is, I was a kid from Campbelltown, who knew no-one, went to public school, and just got into media and love what I do. So, I come from a place of, I know what it is to be nobody. And to see good people repressed, suppressed, and their stories not heard. And certainly, particularly, writing my book at the moment and looking back on the treatment of women. And we've come a long way, if you look at the history of the world, we've come a long way in a very short space of time. But we can't stop. And this is, like, if you were a bloke, you wouldn't be getting this treatment.
>
> *Ms Higgins*:
>
> No, not at all.
>
> *Mr Sharaz*:
>
> No, it's much easier.
>
> *Ms Wilkinson*:
>
> Yeah. And it's not necessarily, it's certainly not just a gender story, it's a Canberra bubble story. But women in particular, it's, I mean, so often you hear, Canberra is not a safe place for women.

From the moment she received information from Mr Sharaz (and before even seeing Ms Higgins), and without any further detail or checking, she wanted to tell the "explosive political story" of "an extraordinary coverup" as revealed in the fact she immediately had consulted with the powers that be and had expressed her resolve that "we're going huge with it" in a March release (Ex R117, 19 January 2021 (at 7:19pm)). 943

Although I accept that various communications did not go to her (see, for example, Ex R673 on 14 February, and Ex R782 and Ex R793 on 15 February); Ms Wilkinson did not write the script (T1898.30); and it was not possible for Ms Wilkinson to be involved in any late additions (T1873.33–41), the focus, to use the statutory words, must be on whether Ms Wilkinson can establish that her "conduct ... in publishing [the] matter is reasonable in the circumstances". This inquiry into conduct goes well beyond what happened immediately prior to broadcast. 944

The attempt to seal her off from the final content and publication of the programme is unpersuasive.

945 Within the Project team, it is evident they did not think Ms Wilkinson's conduct was somehow peripheral to what was going on by the time of publication. Mr Bendall's contemporaneous praise sent by text at 6:17pm, immediately before the broadcast, reflects the perception within Network Ten. It was that Ms Wilkinson had "done an outstanding job developing, conducting and delivering this story. Everything is perfectly in order and on track" (Ex R845). And despite the attempted minimisation of her role, as Ms Wilkinson candidly accepted in cross-examination, she thought her role was to develop, conduct and deliver the story (T1726.1–11).

946 Having said this, as I have already noted, I accept Ms Wilkinson did rely in performing her work upon trusted and experienced producers and reposed confidence in the expertise of each of Mr Campbell, Mr Meakin, Ms Binnie, and Mr Bendall in doing their jobs in supervising and approving the work undertaken.

947 I do not accept, however, that she "relied on the production team to fact-check Ms Higgins' allegations as she continued with her daily commitments as a host" to the extent this suggests that she had a reasonable basis to conclude sufficient work was being undertaken. As I have explained, she was there when the issues regarding credibility arose as to the floating of a conspiracy theory, the bruise photographs, and selective production of data. She gave the following candid evidence about what Ms Higgins was telling her about data (T1736.38–43):

> MR RICHARDSON: And what I want to suggest to you is that when you heard her say that you understood her to be saying that she had lost all of her photos and all of her screenshots?---I actually can't follow what she is saying there, Mr Richardson.
>
> All right. Did it concern you at this point that what she was saying seemed to be barely comprehensible?---Yes.

948 Despite the initial flirtation, to which I have referred, with the notion an email from a Liberal Party-selected psychologist might be deleted if not recovered within 24 hours, Ms Wilkinson had the chops to spot the confusion about data and that it was a potential problem going to the general credit of Ms Higgins. But she allowed her well-tuned and correct journalistic instincts to be fobbed off by a self-evidently inadequate response.

Moreover, although Ms Wilkinson again submits she understood that Mr Llewellyn was "engaging in extensive fact checking" supervised and supported by others, she must have known that this fact-checking was not starting from a point of independence and professional detachment but from Mr Llewellyn's acceptance of the veracity of Ms Higgins' account. 949

I also accept she understood the Project programme was the subject of "legalling" by Network Ten's experienced in-house solicitors (Wilkinson 28 July 2023 (at [12])). She also understood that Mr Llewellyn spoke to Network Ten's in-house solicitors. Indeed, the extent she generally relied on legal advice emerged fairly clearly in the evidence adduced on the cross-claims. Without objection, I now have before me the fact that those acting for Ms Wilkinson initially pleaded a draft defence based upon the provision of legal advice but then Network Ten directed Ms Wilkinson to delete this from the draft defence, given those parts of the pleading were said to constitute a waiver of a jointly held privilege (Ex X1 (at 1120–1121)). But, as I have explained, I remain in the dark about the precise content of interactions with solicitors prior to broadcast. 950

Having said this, on the basis of all the evidence now adduced, I am satisfied that Ms Wilkinson was informed that the content of the Project programme would be checked by Network Ten solicitors prior to broadcast to reduce litigation risk. Although I think it is likely Ms Wilkinson would have complied with any advice or requests made by the solicitors, I do not know what precisely the solicitors were told, or what their detailed advice was, and to whom it was given. 951

It is contended that Ms Wilkinson also relied on her own background knowledge and experience and her own background research on the "workplace culture" that existed at Parliament House: she "believed the allegations that Ms Higgins made" and "was not provided with any information that led her to doubt the allegations made by Ms Higgins that were ultimately published". I do not doubt her sincerity, but I have already explained why this subjective view, which informed her conduct in not further testing Ms Higgins, does not withstand objective analysis. 952

A point made with some force in the submissions of Ms Wilkinson is the necessity to separate the state of mind of Ms Wilkinson from her conduct when it comes to considering the applicability of the defence. This is correct, in that whether Ms Wilkinson had an unreasonable *state of mind* is 953 not the issue in determining the s 30 defence, and her state of mind is only relevant insofar as it assists in fact-finding as to what happened, or as it can be seen reflected in the reasonableness of her *conduct*.

954 I am not being in the least critical of Ms Wilkinson holding the views she expressed to Mr Sharaz and Ms Higgins (and holding them strongly). Many would find the sentiments reflected in them worthy, particularly insofar as they relate to advocating for those who are victims of sexual assault, which the empirical evidence suggests is an underreported crime. But no doubt the strength of her views presented challenges to prevent any belief undermine fairness or independence when reporting upon an allegation of sexual assault and a political cover-up of such an event.

955 Naturally enough, her state of mind informed her conduct, and it is the reason why she so associated herself with Ms Higgins; was willing to assist in the politicalisation of her account; helped craft Ms Higgins' responses; and was dismissive about anything which might be seen to constitute information contrary to what Ms Higgins said right up to the time of publication.

956 The fact she did allow this commitment to undermine her independence emerges clearly from the evidence.

957 Apart from the nature of her interactions with Ms Higgins I have already described, it is well illustrated by a contemporaneous message on the day of broadcast. Ms Wilkinson watched live the Prime Minister's comments about Ms Higgins' allegations and saw other Parliamentarians, including Senators Gallagher, Wong and Reynolds, comment on the allegations in the Senate. At 2:46pm, she sent a message to Mr Llewellyn: "Okay. Have you been watching Question Time? Lots of focus on the story. Penny Wong magnificent. Reynolds lying through her teeth" (Ex R203). Of course, at this moment, as Ms Wilkinson accepted (T1895.33), the only information she had about Senator Reynolds' interactions with Ms Higgins, was derived from either: (a) Ms Higgins' account; or (b) what Mr Carswell had said in the response she had received that morning, being a response which: (i) referred to contemporaneous material; (ii) was contradictory to what Ms Wilkinson considered to be the core aspect of Ms Higgins' account; and (iii) had not been raised with Ms Higgins.

958 She instinctively believed Ms Higgins *must* be telling the truth and Senator Reynolds *must* be lying. Of course, she was perfectly entitled to

her view, but it is not redolent of the conduct of a highly experienced journalist dealing with facts, not instincts, and ensuring any belief or commitment did not undermine fairness or independence. Mr Meakin's assessment that it "would have been desirable" (T1962.41–2) to go back to Ms Higgins to try to check this contrary account, based on apparently contemporaneous materials, is clearly correct.

It is also illustrated, after the event, by her evidence, to which I have already referred above (at [318]), that "every new piece of information received up to broadcast" corroborated the version of events given to her by Ms Higgins. Although I accept Ms Wilkinson believed that Mr Llewellyn was responsible for seeking responses on the advice of the Network Ten solicitors and understood that the production team was amending the script (as evidenced by her saying: "I'm utterly fascinated by [the Carswell] response!! Have we had to cut much?" (Ex R203, 14 February 2021 (at 11:00:23pm)), her view was to dismiss the Carswell material peremptorily, which was treated by her as not even being contradictory and in a way reminiscent of the riposte of Mandy Rice-Davies in the trial of Stephen Ward arising from the Profumo affair (when Ms Rice-Davies was asked by counsel whether she knew that Lord Astor had denied having sex with her, she responded: "well he would, wouldn't he?"). 959

The same commitment to ensuring Ms Higgins' story was told, but in manner and with an emphasis that accorded with what Ms Wilkinson believed ought to be conveyed, can be seen by her saying: "I don't want to put words in your mouth" but then immediately putting words into Ms Higgins' mouth by advising her as to the desirability of "enunciat[ing] the fact that this place is all about suppression of people's natural sense of justice. Because you see around you the way that this place works" (Ex 36 (at 1:08:56–1:09:18)). 960

Ms Wilkinson asserts that one cannot "ignore the fact that outside the curial environment and before the effects of publicity, Ms Higgins, as recorded on 27 January and 2 February 2021, was a genuine, compelling and highly credible young woman" and Ms Wilkinson's motivation was to report on issues that were plainly of the highest public interest. 961

For reasons I have explained, this puts the point far too highly. I do not think it is a counsel of perfection to conclude that to an objective observer, there were warning signs ignored and obvious steps not taken, particularly 962 in telling a story of such importance and conveying such serious allegations of wrongdoing.

963 For largely the same reasons as Network Ten, although looked at from a different perspective and recognising the evidence as to her role, I do not accept she has established that her conduct in publishing the matter, in its character of conveying the defamatory imputations as to Mr Lehrmann, was reasonable in the circumstances.

# L OTHER DEFENCES

## L.1 General Observations

I do not propose to add to an already too lengthy judgment by dealing with the miscellany of subsidiary defences except briefly. 964

## L.2 Common Law Justification

This defence was not pleaded by Ms Wilkinson, and Network Ten accepted that on the present state of the authorities, there is no relevant distinction between the test at common law and the test under s 25 of the Defamation Act, and that if the statutory defence was made out, justification must also succeed at common law; with the converse being true. 965

It is only pressed because Network Ten submits the common law presumption of falsity in defamation law imposes an intolerable burden on freedom of expression and contends formally, at this stage of the judicial hierarchy, that the common law should develop such that falsity is an element of the cause of action in defamation (cf *Roberts v Camden* (1807) 103 ER 508 (at 509 per Lord Ellenborough); *Motel Holdings Ltd v Bulletin Newspaper Co Pty Ltd* [1963] 63 SR (NSW) 208 (at 212 per Sugerman J, with whom Wallace J agreed)). 966

## L.3 *Lange* Qualified Privilege

Again, this defence (derived from the High Court's decision in *Lange v Australian Broadcasting Corporation* (1997) 189 CLR 520) is not pleaded by Ms Wilkinson but is pleaded by Network Ten. It appears it is pleaded only if (contrary to the conclusions I have expressed above) the s 30 defence invites some form of "broad inquiry beyond the parts of the program[me] selected for complaint by Mr Lehrmann". It is a little unclear why it is pleaded, as Network Ten concedes that the outcome of the s 30 and *Lange* defences is necessarily the same if the s 30 analysis 967 is performed correctly. It does not really matter, but the point would go nowhere in any event, because if the relevant inquiry as to reasonableness was untethered from the defamatory meanings pleaded, the position as to the want of reasonableness in publishing the matter generally would be even worse for Network Ten.

## L.4 Common Law Qualified Privilege

968 I will deal with the common law qualified privilege defence pleaded by Ms Wilkinson very briefly.

969 It was pressed because it was contended that the defamatory matter about Mr Lehrmann was only published to a limited and select number of persons who already possessed special knowledge about him and was not defamatory when published to persons without that special knowledge. It is then said to follow that each of the people that could have reasonably identified Mr Lehrmann had such specialised knowledge about him (or proximate relationship to him), such that Ms Wilkinson, having conducted a recorded interview with a person accusing him of rape, had an interest in communicating that interview to those persons through the Project programme, and those persons had an interest in receiving the Project programme such that each publication to those persons was a privileged occasion.

970 This novel argument founders on the reality that: (a) Ms Wilkinson had no special or particular interest in relation to the allegations above their general newsworthiness; and (b) the Project programme was published to the general television public (even though there was an indeterminate number of people who had the specialised knowledge that allowed them to identify Mr Lehrmann). But merely because some of the persons viewing had a particular interest in receiving the Project programme, this did not mean that publication to the others was incidental and there was no relevant and necessary community of interest between Ms Wilkinson and the recipients: see *Daily Examiner Pty Ltd v Mundine* [2012] NSWCA 195 (at [77]).

# M DAMAGES AND OTHER RELIEF

## M.1 Introduction

In *Roberts-Smith*, Besanko J (at [2615]) identified some complex issues relating to damages in that case and then observed (at [2618]) that his Honour had: 971

> assumed for a time in preparing these reasons that I would assess damages on the hypothetical basis that I was wrong and I had considered a number of matters associated with damages. I had proceeded on that assumption because it is generally desirable for the Court hearing the proceedings to resolve as many issues as is possible. However, on working through the issues, it has become apparent to me that largely because of the significant number of possible alternative outcomes if I am wrong and to a much lesser extent (but relevant nevertheless) the extreme difference between the decision I have reached and the assumptions I would need to make, that that would not be an appropriate or useful exercise. Neither of these matters are decisive in themselves as judges not infrequently consider matters on alternative bases, including that they might be wrong. However, the force of the matters together in this case has led me to conclude that I will not embark on an assessment of damages on a hypothetical basis.

I am in a somewhat different position. As I will explain, the issues as to damages in this case do not give rise to the extent of complications confronting Besanko J, and I respectfully agree it is generally desirable for a trial judge to resolve as many issues as possible against the prospect the judge has fallen into error. 972

If I was wrong to have found Mr Lehrmann raped Ms Higgins, it would be necessary to deal with questions of relief, which, as finally pressed, is a claim for ordinary and aggravated compensatory damages. 973

974 Counterfactual reasoning is when a reasoner is asked to assume for one purpose that a fact the reasoner previously thought was true, is now false, and to draw a conclusion on that basis. Obviously enough, it can present logical difficulties. What can be obscured is that the reasoner is required to make what amounts to a choice in selecting the fact or facts to change to entertain the counterfactual. As a general proposition, it is best to approach the task from the perspective of doing as little violence to the known facts as is possible (consistently with *Lewis v Australian Capital Territory* [2020] HCA 26; (2020) 271 CLR 192).

975 But the theoretical complications that can arise are absent here, as the choice of counterfactual for the purposes of assessing damages is relatively straightforward: I will only deal with the most realistic choice, given my findings and the legal consequences that flow from those findings. That is, I will not address a fantasy world where Mr Lehrmann is to be believed on his French submarine fiction, but the far more realistic scenario where sex took place, but I ought not to have found that the non-consent and/or the knowledge elements were established by the respondents so as to make out the substantial truth defence.

## M.2 General Observations

976 The award of damages is governed by the provisions of Pt 4, Div 3 of the Defamation Act. The requirement is that by s 34 of the Defamation Act, the Court is "to ensure that there is an appropriate and rational relationship" between the harm sustained and the amount of damages awarded.

977 Further, by reason of the operation of s 35(1) of the Defamation Act, and by declaration of the Minister pursuant to s 35(3), the maximum amount of damages for non-economic loss that may be awarded is limited – the so-called "cap". The cap was increased from 1 July 2023 in accordance with s 35(3) to the sum of $459,000, with the applicable cap being that in force at the time of judgment (New South Wales Government Gazette No 250 (9 June 2023) (at 15)). Two further matters should be noted about the cap: *first*, the cap is not to be treated as establishing an award for a worst-case scenario and then mandating the scaling of damages downward from that range; and *secondly*, if the Court determines that an award of aggravated damages is warranted, the cap is not applicable.

Unsurprisingly, as to the general principles applied when calculating damages, including when aggravated damages may be awarded, there was common ground. The three purposes of an award are: *first*, consolation for the personal distress and hurt caused by the publication; *secondly*, reparation for the harm done to the person's reputation; and *thirdly*, vindication of reputation. The assessment is an intuitive, evaluative process conducted "at large", but subject to the provisions of Pt 4, Div 3 of the Defamation Act. 978

I discussed the relationship between the three purposes of damages and the relationship between damage to reputation and vindication in *Palmer v McGowan (No 5)* [2022] FCA 893; (2022) 404 ALR 621 (at 726–727 [497]–[498]), where I noted that: 979

> [497] ... the relationship between the three purposes of damage, particularly damage to reputation and vindication, ought not to be forgotten. As Windeyer J explained in *Uren v John Fairfax & Sons Pty Ltd* (1966) 117 CLR 118 (at 150):
>
> > It seems to me that, properly speaking, a man defamed does not get compensation for his damaged reputation. He gets damages because he was injured in his reputation, that is simply because he was publicly defamed. For this reason, compensation by damages operates in two ways — as a vindication of the plaintiff to the public and as consolation to him for a wrong done. Compensation is here a solatium rather than a monetary recompense for harm measurable in money.
>
> [498] Chief Justice Mason and Justices Deane, Dawson and Gaudron echoed this feature of damages in *Carson v John Fairfax & Sons Ltd* (1993) 178 CLR 44 (at 60), when their Honours said that the purposes of an award of damages "overlap considerably in reality and ensure that 'the amount of a verdict is the product of a mixture of inextricable considerations'" ...

## M.3 Three Particular Issues as to Ordinary Compensatory Damages

But having identified these uncontroversial principles, and leaving aside aggravated damages (which I will deal with separately below in Section 980

M.6), there are three somewhat connected aspects of this damages assessment that emerged in submissions meriting separate consideration: *first*, whether it is legally possible to award no damages instead of nominal or derisory damages; *secondly*, the relevance of an English line of authority relied upon by the respondents as to an alleged abuse of process on the part of Mr Lehrmann; and *thirdly*, the principled approach to dealing with evidence of misconduct on the part of Mr Lehrmann in the counterfactual (that is, following the rejection of the defence of substantial truth for the reasons assumed).

### *I No Damages or Nominal Damages*

981 At common law, once an applicant has proved the publication of a libel, and in the absence of a successful defence, an entitlement arises to an award of damages, even if they are nominal. The presumption of damage reflects the emphasis that the common law of defamation gives to protecting reputation.

982 In *Palmer v McGowan (No 5)* (at 727 [502]), I turned to the question of the proper approach when having considered the three purposes of an award of compensatory damages, the conclusion is reached that no substantial damages should be awarded and I said (at 727–728 [503]–[506]):

> [503] … The best statement as to the meaning and incidence of nominal damages is given by Lord Halsbury LC in *The Mediana* [1900] AC 113 (at 116):
>
> > "Nominal damages" is a technical phrase which means that you have negatived anything like real damage, but that you are affirming by your nominal damages that there is an infraction of a legal right which, though it gives you no right to any real damages at all, yet gives you a right to the verdict or judgment because your legal right has been infringed.
>
> [504] "Nominal damages", remarked Maule J in *Beaumont v Greathead* (1846) 135 ER 1039 (at 1041), "means a sum of money that may be spoken of, but that has no existence in point of quantity". The authorities reveal that after an early period in which the amount could be miniscule, such as a farthing in *Mostyn v Coles* (1862) 7 H & N 872; (1862) 158

All ER 723, in England, the amount eventually crystallised at the figure of £2, although £1 was sometimes awarded. In the last half the twentieth century, the amount buffered between £2 and £5, but the new century has seen a reversion to £2, which amount has said to be "the traditional sum": *Village Investigations Ltd v Gardner* [2005] EWHC 3300 (QB) (at [77] per Seymour J). Although, again, £1 has sometimes been awarded.

[505] A distinction has sometimes been drawn between "nominal damages" and "contemptuous damages" or "derisory damages", connoting damages in the amount of the lowest coin of the realm. Two key points of distinction between nominal damages and contemptuous damages appear to be: *first*, that contemptuous damages may be awarded in respect of any tort, whether actionable *per se* or not, and *secondly*, contemptuous damages are tantamount to an expression of disapproval of, or contempt for, the plaintiff: see *Habib v Nationwide News Pty Ltd (No 2)* [2010] NSWCA 291 (at [45] per Hodgson, Tobias and McColl JJA).

[506] In Australia, some awards of nominal damages have been somewhat higher than the equivalent of £2. For example, in *Bahonko v Sterjov* [2007] FCA 1244; (2007) 167 IR 43 (at 104 [186]), Jessup J awarded nominal damages of $50 in an action for defamation in which no harm was found. In a number of cases in non-Superior courts, damages purportedly labelled "nominal" have reached $1,000. Given the way nominal damages have been awarded in some cases in recent times, the precise line between what is nominal award and what is a modest award can be blurred. It seems to me, with respect, that awards of thousands of dollars are inconsistent with the fundamental nature of a *nominal* award.

In 2014, Gibson DCJ, a judge highly experienced in defamation law, 983
remarked on the distinction between "nominal" damages and "contemptuous" damages in *Allen v Lloyd-Jones (No 6)* [2014] NSWDC 40, noting (at [140]) that "awards of nominal damages are rare, and contemptuous damages non-existent". Incidentally, her Honour referred (at [139]) to

a submission made by Mr Evatt calling in aid the one farthing damage awards in *Kelly v Sherlock* (1866) LR 1 QB 686 and *Dering v Uris* [1964] 2 QB 669. I digress to note that the latter case, of course, was brought by a former prisoner-doctor at Auschwitz who accused the noted author Leon Uris and his publisher of a libel in a passage from the 1958 novel *Exodus*, and the ensuing courtroom drama led to an award of the (then) lowest coin in the realm (a halfpenny), and then to the author writing a bestselling fictionalised account of the case, being *QB VII*.

984 However, as noted in the introduction to this section of my reasons, an award of damages is now regulated by statute. Justice McCallum (as her Honour then was) in *Dank v Nationwide News Pty Ltd* [2016] NSWSC 295, in the course of awarding a plaintiff $0 for the publication of the false claim Mr Dank had injected a blood-thinning agent into football players (when in truth he injected a horse feed supplement), explained (at [75]) that:

> The need to nominate a nominal sum in this jurisdiction may be doubted. The *Defamation Act 2005* [s 22(3)] expressly contemplates the possibility that, even where no defence to a defamatory publication has been established, the judicial officer may determine that no amount of damages should be awarded. So much is explicit in the requirement to determine "the amount of damages (if any) that should be awarded to the plaintiff".

985 *Dank* has been referred to in two cases in this Court, without analysis, being *Palmer v McGowan (No 5)* (at 728 [507]) and *Greiss v Seven Network (Operations) Limited (No 2)* [2024] FCA 98 (at [368], [371] per Katzmann J) and in the Supreme Court of Victoria (*Tawhidi v Awad* [2022] VSC 669 (at [367] per Keogh J)) and *Charan v Nationwide News Pty Ltd* [2018] VSC 3 (at [765] per Forrest J), including when referring to Neil LJ's observations in *Pamplin v Express Newspapers* [1988] WLR 116, when his Lordship (at 120B–D) said a defendant is entitled to rely in "mitigation" of damages on any other evidence which is properly before a Court so a defendant "may be able to rely upon such facts as he has proved to reduce the damages, perhaps to vanishing point" (a matter to which I will return).

986 The section relied upon by McCallum J, s 22 of the Defamation Act, is headed "Roles of judicial officers and juries in defamation proceedings"

and, by subsection (1), applies to defamation proceedings that are tried by a jury. It is not applicable to this proceeding because I am the trier of fact and, even if, as I initially contemplated, I ordered a jury to deal with aspects of this case (see *Lehrmann v Network Ten Pty Limited (Tribunal of Fact)* [2023] FCA 612) it would not have present applicability as there is a direct inconsistency between s 40 of the *Federal Court of Australia Act 1976* (Cth) and s 22 of the Defamation Act (and hence s 22 is not picked up as "surrogate" federal law in determining this justiciable controversy by reason of s 79 of the *Judiciary Act 1903* (Cth)). I hasten to add such a result is *not* a conclusion that a section of the Defamation Act is invalid under s 109 of the *Constitution*, as has been recently suggested: see *Scott v Bodley (No 3)* [2023] NSWDC 47 (at [44]).

But the issue, properly analysed, is not whether s 22 is picked up. The real 987 questions are whether the presumption of damage, long regarded as deeply rooted, reflects the current state of the common law of Australia (which Network Ten disputes) and, if not, whether the Defamation Act, including Pt 4, Div 3 which deals with "Remedies", evinces a legislative intention to do away with the presumption of damage existing at common law.

Without deciding the point, I incline to the view that the express statu- 988 tory requirement to ensure "that there is an appropriate and rational relationship between the harm sustained by the plaintiff and the amount of damages awarded" (s 34) sits uncomfortably with an award of any damages – even nominal or derisory – when the tribunal of fact finds no harm whatsoever has been suffered. But in any event, as will become evident, there is no need to decide the point.

### *II The English Cases on Abuse of Process by a Claimant*

Anticipating my findings that Mr Lehrmann had sexual intercourse with 989 Ms Higgins but guarding against the possibility neither defence was made out, the respondents submit that this would necessarily mean that Mr Lehrmann: *first*, cheated on his girlfriend despite using his apparently monogamous relationship with her as a reason to deny Ms Higgins' allegations; *secondly*, perverted the course of justice in lying to the police; and *thirdly*, instructed his counsel to cross-examine Ms Higgins on a false basis twice and presented her as a fantasist. Following the reopened case, the respondents also *fourthly* allege Mr Lehrmann breached his *Hearne v Street* obligation and then wilfully mislead this Court, by way of submissions and evidence, in his denial of engaging in such conduct (collectively, the **Relevant Misconduct**).

990 The Relevant Misconduct is said to be so serious that no damages ought to be awarded.

991 More particularly, relying on a line of English authority, they submit this is the kind of "very exceptional case of abuse of process" where it would be open to the Court to reduce to a vanishing point any damages on account of Mr Lehrmann's conduct: *Wright v McCormack* [2023] EWCA Civ 892 (at [76] per Warby LJ). In that case, Warby LJ (with whom Singh and Andrews LJJ agreed) considered *Joseph v Spiller* [2012] EWHC 2958 (QB) and *FlyMeNow Ltd v Quick Air Jet Charter GmbH* [2016] EWHC 3197 (QB), two decisions in which nominal damages were awarded in circumstances where the plaintiff had advanced a false case and supported it with false evidence in an attempt to deceive the court: *Wright* (at [62]–[63]); see also C Gatley, R Parkes R and G Busuttil, *Gatley on Libel and Slander* (Thomson Reuters, 13th ed, 2022) (at 10-005).

992 In *Joseph v Spiller*, Mr Justice Tugendhat held (at [166], [177]) the relevant conduct was "a sophisticated deception" which involved relying on a false document to mislead the court (at [55]), and that the plaintiff "abused the process of the court by deliberately pursuing a false claim for special damages" (at [177]). That deception, "massive as it was", did not affect the whole claim, because adequate vindication of reputation was given in the reasons for judgment and an award of nominal damages was considered appropriate (at [178]).

993 By parity of reasoning, it is said in the present case that Mr Lehrmann has asserted "he has been destroyed by a manipulative fantasist" and that "he is true victim of a vendetta". It is submitted that this is more than a case involving dishonesty about some aspect of a claim – it is "dishonesty at the very core of the claim" and Mr Lehrmann has offered no honest account of the incident and Mr Lehrmann's denial of sex with Ms Higgins should be characterised as "a hideous lie that undermines the very foundation of bringing this action". In this way, it is said his "wicked conduct" rises to the level of a very exceptional case of abuse of process and it would bring the administration of justice into disrepute to award Mr Lehrmann any damages.

994 I confess to finding the reasoning in this line of English cases somewhat problematical, as it does not distinguish between abuse of the process with

the distinct notion of the appropriate remedial response where a claimant is entitled to some relief, but has engaged in disreputable conduct (and, more particularly, on how relief by way of damages is to be assessed in the light of that conduct).

As the High Court explained in *Batistatos v Roads and Traffic Authority of New South Wales* [2006] HCA 27; (2006) 226 CLR 256 (at 262–265 [2]–[8] per Gleeson CJ, Gummow, Hayne and Crennan JJ), the term "abuse of process" is used in a number of contexts and what amounts to an abuse of process is insusceptible of a formulation comprising closed categories. It is fundamental to the proper functioning of a principled legal system that a judiciary can safeguard its own processes. A core mechanism used by courts to guard against judicial proceedings being converted into instruments of injustice or unfairness is the inherent or implied power to stay (or dismiss) proceedings where there is an abuse of process (see Emerson Hynard and Aiden Lerch, 'The Tort of Collateral Abuse of Process' (2021) 44(2) *UNSW Law Journal* 714, a paper which contains a useful summary of the tort of collateral abuse of process). 995

But here, we are not talking about a disentitlement to continue using the Court's processes as an instrument of oppression, which must be ended by granting a stay or dismissal, but the different concept of a Court granting appropriate relief, after its processes have been used by the party seeking that relief, in part, inappropriately. 996

I adhere to the view I recently expressed in *Russell (No 3)* (at [471]), that it would be erroneous to "reduce" any component of ordinary compensatory damages otherwise appropriate to be properly awarded on the evidence because of general misgivings as to a claimant's conduct on the basis it is said to be some form of abuse of process. 997

### *III How to Use Evidence of Misconduct*

What then is to be done with evidence of misconduct on the part of Mr Lehrmann when the misconduct is relevant to his true reputation, but a defence of justification or substantial truth has not been made out? 998

I provided an answer to that question in *Kumova v Davison (No 2)* (at [97]–[102]), when I explained that such evidence may be considered on the question of damages, to the extent that it is directly relevant to the subject of the defamatory matters in the relevant "sector" of the applicant's 999 reputation. The following is taken from the above referenced paragraphs of that judgment.

1000 The use of this type of evidence on damages has customarily been referred to as being in "mitigation" of damages. Although this jargon is very well-entrenched (and adopted in the Defamation Act), it seems to me to obscure what is going on. Some common factors in "mitigation" of damages are identified in s 38 of the Defamation Act (for example, an apology or other compensation). But this is not an exclusive list of factors (see s 38(2)).

1001 Usually, of course, in other areas of the law, the term "mitigation" is used in the phrase "a plaintiff's duty to mitigate" (albeit mistakenly, as there is no so-called duty, because claimants are completely free to act as they perceive to be in their best interests, but defendants are not liable for all loss suffered by claimants in consequence of so acting): *Sotiros Shipping Inc and Aeco Maritime SA v Sameiet Solholt, The Solholt* [1983] 1 Lloyd's Rep 605 (at 608 per Donaldson MR); *Borealis AB v Geogas Trading SA* [2010] EWHC 2789 (Comm) (at [42]–[50] per Gross LJ). Such a factor might be best described as not being in "mitigation" of damage, but as being simply a factor, among others, informing the Court's assessment. The concept can be viewed through the prism of causation of loss as the use of such evidence is relevant to, and impacts upon, the actual, causally-related harm suffered.

1002 But leaving aside terminology, the correct approach was usefully explained by Wigney J in *Rush v Nationwide News Pty Ltd (No 2)* [2018] FCA 550; (2018) 359 ALR 564 (at 573 [32]–[33]):

> [32] In *Warren v Random House Group Ltd* [2009] QB 600; [2009] 2 All ER 245; [2008] EWCA Civ 834, the Court of Appeal of England and Wales explained the *Burstein* principle in the following terms (at [78]):
>
> The decision of this court in *Burstein v Times Newspapers Ltd* [2001] 1 WLR 579; [2000] All ER (D) 2384; [2000] EWCA Civ 338, cited above, established two important interlocking propositions. (a) In relation to the court's assessment of damages for libel it is open to a defendant to seek to rely upon such facts as fall within the "directly relevant background context" to the defamatory publication.

See in particular the judgment of May LJ, at para 42. (b) It is illogical and undesirable that a defendant can seek to rely upon such facts in relation to such assessment only if he has presented them as part of a substantive defence to liability, in particular within a plea of justification of the publication. He can rely upon them as freestanding matters pleaded as relevant only to the assessment of damages: see in particular the judgment of May LJ, at para 47.

[33] That rather simple statement of the propositions flowing from Burstein somewhat belies the uncertainty that has arisen concerning the application of those propositions. That uncertainty mainly revolves around the vague and unhelpful expression "directly relevant background context". Judges are often rightly sceptical when the tender of evidence is sought to be justified on the basis that it provides "background" or "context". Those words often conceal or obscure, rather than explain, whether or why the evidence is relevant. Careful attention to what was actually decided in Burstein, however, tends to remove some of the uncertainty.

The facts pleaded and proved in the light of *Burstein v Times Newspapers* 1003
*Ltd* [2001] 1 WLR 579 must, in Wigney J's terms (at 577 [45]):

> **concern specific conduct that is directly relevant to either the subject matter of the alleged defamatory statement, or the claimant's reputation in the part of his or her life the subject of the defamatory publication** ... courts, including this Court, must proceed with caution in applying Burstein, should guard against "extending too creatively" the concept of "directly relevant background", and should subject the proposal to adduce facts under the Burstein principle to careful scrutiny. Mere resort to the label "directly relevant background context" will not suffice.
>
> (Emphasis added)

The underlying rationale is to prevent trials such as this one from 1004
becoming "roving inquiries" into an applicant's reputation, character or disposition: *Burstein* (at 596 per May LJ); *Speidel v Plato Films Ltd* [1961] AC 1090 (at 1143–1144 per Lord Denning).

1005 Two further points should be made.

1006 *First,* there is no contest in this case that the Relevant Misconduct is directly relevant to Mr Lehrmann's reputation in the part of his life the subject of the defamatory publication.

1007 *Secondly,* the Relevant Misconduct relied upon occurred well after the publication of the Project programme. Despite Sugerman ACJ considering that defamation law is concerned with a person's "actual" or "current" reputation as at the date of defamatory publication (see *Rochfort v John Fairfax & Sons Limited* [1972] 1 NSWLR 16 (at 22–23)), as was explained by McColl JA in *Channel Seven Sydney Pty Ltd v Mahommed* [2010] NSWCA 335; (2010) 278 ALR 232, like the continuing nature of damage to reputation that may occur after the defamation, any evidence of post-publication material going directly to reputation and that is otherwise admissible should be considered to ensure that the damages awarded in accordance with s 34 of the Defamation Act accurately reflect the applicant's reputation at the time the damages are awarded (although, as noted above, any so-called *Burstein* use must be approached with caution and must be carefully confined (at 283–284 [246] per McColl JA, with whom Spigelman CJ, Beazley JA, McClellan CJ at CL and Bergin CJ in Eq agreed)).

1008 All in all, this is a more complex way of saying that an assessment reflecting an appropriate and rational relationship between the harm sustained and the quantum of damages does not occur "in blinkers".

## M.3 Mr Lehrmann's Submissions on Ordinary Damages

1009 Unsurprisingly, Mr Lehrmann asserts that the starting point for the assessment of damages should be the fact that the central allegation, that Mr Lehrmann raped Ms Higgins, is extremely serious; indeed, it is one of the most damning allegations which could be made. It is also said that the severity of the "base allegation is aggravated by the features delineated in the separate imputations pleaded by Mr Lehrmann", which I have already described.

1010 Damages should also be assessed on the basis that, even though he was not named in the Project programme, actionable publication occurred to a "wide circle" of people and the publication should not be treated as limited to a small number of people personally acquainted with Mr Lehrmann.

The evidence relevant to the impact of the Project programme on Mr 1011
Lehrmann's reputation and the hurt feelings he experienced because of it are, it is submitted, devastating.

It is said that even if the Court formed an adverse view about Mr 1012
Lehrmann's credit on other issues, it would accept his evidence of hurt feelings and the reaction he described in his evidence is plausible. It is submitted that it is natural that a young man accused of such a crime on national television would be extremely upset, frightened, and angry, as he described.

Mr Lehrmann points to the fact that neither of the respondents pleads 1013
that Mr Lehrmann had a bad reputation in general prior to the publication and that he was an ordinary young man just starting out in his career, not much known to anyone outside the circle of his direct acquaintances. But the Project programme had the effect of bringing Mr Lehrmann to the attention of a wide range of people who had never had much reason to know or care who he was (including some who did not know him at all), immediately ruining his reputation within that wider circle of people.

It follows that the need for vindication in this case is very high, and not 1014
just because of the serious nature of the allegation but because of the national controversy that has aroused very strong feelings. An award of damages "sufficient to convince a bystander of the baselessness of the charge" in this context must be very substantial: *Broome v Cassell & Co Ltd* [1972] AC 1027 (at 1071 per Lord Hailsham of St Marylebone LC).

Mr Lehrmann accepts some damage was caused to him by the antecedent 1015
publication of the Maiden article, the supervening criminal proceeding and the media attention following the charges being preferred on 7 August 2021 (T555.11–21). But the significance of the Maiden article to the causation of loss should not be overstated. The Project programme went to air that same night, so the article only had a head start of a couple of hours and both publications were co-ordinated with the respondents seeing the article as a means to "build the hype for us having the only interview with the woman at the centre of it all", with Mr Campbell previously commenting that it "solves our promo issue" (Ex R419; T1954.12). Moreover, the Project programme had greater impact because the broadcast was based

around the interview with Ms Higgins, and it was the interview that "seared Ms Higgins' allegations into the national consciousness" with the "spectacle and pathos of seeing her tell her story on prime time television" making the case notorious. The Maiden article, it is said, had none of this colour and movement, and this substantially lessened its impact.

1016 Mr Lehrmann also accepts in broad terms that it is open to the Court to take into account the matters relied on by the respondents in "mitigation" and, more particularly, accepts "that it is open to the Court to make adverse findings about some of his conduct" and those findings, if they are made, "are to his discredit and are relevant to assessing the real damage caused to his reputation by the defamation".

1017 But in considering what relevance any adverse findings have to the assessment of a proportionate award, those findings must be considered in context of the very serious nature of the defamation and the resultant high need for vindication. Once that is recognised, it is submitted the reduction on account of such findings should be "relatively small".

1018 Presciently, Mr Lehrmann's submissions deal expressly with what is described as the:

> maximal findings which could in theory be made, short of upholding the justification defence – that intercourse probably happened in Senator Reynolds' suite, and that Ms Higgins was not capable of consenting to it because of her state of intoxication, but that Mr Lehrmann did not have knowledge of her inability to consent.

1019 As I have explained, I am proceeding to assess damages on this basis, and Mr Lehrmann's contention is that should still lead to an award of damages which is substantial given that the distinction between findings of this kind "and a finding that rape occurred (particularly in the manner described in the [Project programme]) is real and significant" and where the allegation is so serious, the distinction "should not be elided by a low award of damages which signals that what was published was 'close enough'".

1020 More specifically, it is further accepted that if it was found: (a) Mr Lehrmann did have intercourse with Ms Higgins; (b) he did it despite being in a relationship; and (c) that he told a lie about it to the AFP, these matters would be relevant to the assessment of damages, as would the termination of his employment for a security breach. However, apart from the telling of a lie to the AFP, it is submitted that these matters would have no significant effect on the assessment of damages.

It is said that "infidelity in a monogamous relationship is a question of personal morality" and that "many people would regard it with indifference when it did not concern a person to whom they were close". Similarly, if Mr Lehrmann left Ms Higgins drunk and naked on the couch it is accepted (with considerable understatement) that this "was certainly ungentlemanly, but not much more could be said about it than that" and it could not make any meaningful difference to the huge reputational damage caused by the publication of the untrue allegation of rape. 1021

Finally, it is contended that the "mitigatory effect" of the News Life and ABC settlements would only be small, because the payments were characterised publicly as contributions to costs only and there was no apology, admission of liability, or entry of judgment, those settlements did not and could not do anything to vindicate the damage to Mr Lehrmann's reputation. The need for a substantial award of damages to satisfy the purpose of vindicating his reputation remains despite the settlements. 1022

## M.4 Matters Relevant to Aggravated Damages

### *I The Bases Pressed*

In considering aggravated damages, the Court is entitled to look at the whole of the conduct of a respondent from publication to the time of judgment and the applicant must establish that the respondent's conduct was improper, unjustifiable, or lacking in bona fides: *Triggell v Pheeny* (1951) 82 CLR 497 (at 513–514 per Dixon, Williams, Webb and Kitto JJ). 1023

The relevant grounds relied upon by Mr Lehrmann shifted somewhat. Five bases were eventually particularised at the conclusion of the evidence (which can be usefully summarised into three) being: 1024

(1) the respondents were recklessly indifferent to the truth or falsity of the imputations in publishing the assertions and allegations giving rise to the imputations without giving Mr Lehrmann a reasonable opportunity to respond;

(2) the failure by the respondents to make reasonable efforts to contact Mr Lehrmann for comment and Mr Llewellyn cynically refraining from giving Mr Lehrmann a reasonable time to respond;

(3) the making of the Logies speech, "on behalf of, and/or with the approval and/or authority" of Network Ten, and Network Ten's "continuing public adherence to advice given by Ms Tasha Smithies, being Ten's Senior Litigation Counsel, to Ms Wilkinson in June 2022 to the effect that the speech should have been given" the "original provision of that advice and Ten's refusal to apologise for or retract that advice is unjustifiable" noting that "even if such advice had never been given, the conduct by all persons involved remains unjustifiable".

1025 I will make findings as to each of these bases in turn (and will separately deal with the consequences of these findings at Section M.6 below).

### *II Reckless Indifference to Truth of the Imputations*

1026 Despite not articulating detailed submissions in support of this ground, Mr Lehrmann pleaded that Network Ten was recklessly indifferent to the truth or falsity of the imputations in publishing the assertions and allegations giving rise to the imputations without giving Mr Lehrmann a reasonable opportunity to respond (SOC [9(a)]).

1027 Importantly, the focus of this particularised conduct is a reckless indifference to the truth of the *imputations*, not the matter generally and as pleaded. It relates to the failure to give Mr Lehrmann an opportunity to respond, which I will deal with separately.

1028 The shortcomings of Network Ten and Ms Wilkinson canvassed while dealing with the statutory qualified privilege defence, while preventing a finding their conduct was reasonable in publishing the matter in its character of conveying the defamatory imputation, were not of such a character, nor so improper and unjustifiable as to amount to reckless indifference as to the truth or falsity of the pleaded defamatory imputations. Put another way, even though Network Ten or Ms Wilkinson acted unreasonably in relation to the publication of the imputations, and irrespective as to whether they behaved improperly in relation to other matters, this aspect of their conduct cannot be stigmatised as improper or lacking in good faith.

### *III Failure to Seek Comment Adequately*

1029 In considering the s 30 defence, I have already dealt with the unreasonable approach to seeking comment reflected in Mr Llewellyn's statement to Ms Wilkinson on 11 February 2021, that the "questions are really to cover us off for defamation" (Ex R541), and his comments to Ms Higgins and Mr Sharaz during the first meeting.

Although Mr Llewellyn's box-ticking exercise (and Ms Wilkinson's acquiescence in it) was unreasonable in the circumstances, I do not consider it reaches the level of improper and unjustifiable conduct demonstrating a lack of *bona fides*. Moreover, I have difficulty accepting the evidence of Mr Lehrmann that he feels increased hurt by reason of this aspect of this conduct when I am satisfied he never had any intention of providing a comment. 1030

It is not conduct justifying an award of aggravated damages. 1031

### *IV The Logies Speech and Ms Smithies' Advice*

Ms Smithies gave evidence she considered it was her role, not that of Mr Drumgold, to give advice about the proposed Logies speech to Ms Wilkinson. This was an understandable view, but it was not strictly accurate. As Kaye AJ explained in *Drumgold v Board of Inquiry (No. 3)* [2024] ACTSC 58 (at [471]), it is a fundamental principle that a prosecutor, as a minister of justice, has "an obligation to ensure that a trial is conducted in accordance with the dictates of fairness to an accused person, and to ensure that the integrity of a trial is appropriately preserved". Ms Smithies was correct in appreciating, however, as the solicitor who accompanied Ms Wilkinson, that she owed an independent duty to give Ms Wilkinson "appropriate legal advice": *Drumgold v Board of Inquiry (No. 3)* (at [472]). 1032

Ms Smithies was well qualified to give this advice. She is a highly experienced solicitor of the Supreme Court of New South Wales of about 27 years' standing and has been the Chief Litigation Counsel of Network Ten for ten years. Since 1999, her duties have included "providing pre-publication and broadcast advice to media companies, initially in [her] role at Gilbert + Tobin and then at Nine Entertainment Co, Australian Associated Press and, currently, at Network Ten". She reports to Mr Stewart Thomas, who holds the curious title (to Australian ears) of "Vice-President, Legal and Corporate Affairs for Network Ten" and works with the "primary lawyer" being the Senior Legal Counsel of Network Ten, Mr Farley (introduced earlier), who "also provides pre-publication advice" (Smithies (at [13]–[15])). 1033

At the conclusion of the evidence of Ms Smithies, I sought to clarify and summarise Ms Smithies' evidence about the Logies speech and her related advice given to Ms Wilkinson. Ms Smithies gave the important evidence, bolded below, as to the state of her mind, but out of fairness, it is 1034 appropriate to extract the entire exchange to give context to this evidence, despite its length. It was as follows (T2614.17–617.6):

> HIS HONOUR: Ms Smithies, I just wanted to clarify something about the evidence yesterday about your state of mind at various stages. I just want to remind you of some evidence you gave. At transcript page 2546, these questions and answers, line 40:
>
> > *And you advised that the speech was okay?---Yes, yes.*
> >
> > *You understood that she was relying on you to advise her if that was not the case?---Yes.*
> >
> > *You understood that she was relying on you to warn her if there were any risks associated with the speech?---Yes.*
> >
> > *And you didn't?---No, I didn't.*
> >
> > *No. And you accept you should have, don't you?*
>
> And you said:
>
> > *I do not accept that.*
>
> Then you were asked:
>
> > *No. I see. You appreciated that once the court in the Australian Capital Territory who granted the stay that Ms Wilkinson became the subject of intense public and media criticism?---Yes.*
> >
> > *Criticism that was harmful of her professional reputation and future?---Yes.*
> >
> > *You appreciate at the time that on – that is, on 22 June and following that the advice that you gave that the speech was okay had exposed Ms Wilkinson to that public criticism, correct?---I don't accept that.*
>
> And you gave the following evidence at transcript 2569, line 5:
>
> > *It would be a matter of very substantial and obvious personal embarrassment for you, correct? That is, for the information that Ms Wilkinson had acted on her advice – had become public.*
>
> And your answer was:

*I do not accept that. I am not professionally or personally embarrassed by the advice that I provided to Ms Wilkinson.*

*Is that right?---Yes.*

Now, I just want, as I say, to clarify your state of mind. That was your view – that is, that the advice that you gave – so I understood your answers – you were satisfied that at the time Ms Wilkinson gave the legal advice, your advice was correct?---Yes.

And – now, by 22 June, three days later, Ms McGarvey was writing to the Associate to the Chief Justice of the Australian Capital Territory. You recall that?---Yes.

And you were involved in the preparation of that letter?---Yes.

And were satisfied that it was true and correct, given it was being sent to the Associate to the Chief Justice?---Yes.

In that letter, it was said that there was no objective intention to interfere with the administration of justice. You recall that?---Yes.

But it expressed profound regret and also an apology. Do you recall that?---Yes.

And by [representing] to the Chief Justice that you had profound regret and apology – that is, Network Ten – I presume you were seeking to convey a recognition that there was something that Channel Ten had done that was worthy of regret or a profound apology. Would that be fair?---I think the regret and profound apology, in my view, was in relation to the fact that the trial had been vacated and that, in my view, your Honour, it was that that we were addressing in the letter, not, in my view, anything in relation to the advice that had been given, because her Honour also wrapped up consideration of the advice with the warning that had been given or not given. And so in my view, that's what we were trying to address.

So your view at the time that the Chief Justice was contacted was that advice to that speech was completely appropriate advice?---Yes.

All right. And so you – would it be fair to say that you still hold that view?---I do.

And [I] take it then, that you disagree that the combination of the speech and the posts amount to Ms Wilkinson endorsing the credibility of the complainant, who in terms celebrated Ms Wilkinson's endorsement of the complainant's credibility?---No, your Honour. I accept that the speech did that. However, in my view, with the circumstances available, that was a preferred course because it was entirely consistent with the position Ms Wilkinson had taken in the preceding 18 months. And I had genuine concern that to deviate from that position would actually, in effect, create a greater problem because she would – she would be a witness, then, who could be perceived as wavering in her support of Ms Higgins, which is a stance that she had taken for the preceding 18 months. And if I can just elaborate slightly, your Honour.

Sure. I want you to be able to say everything you wish to say - - -?---Yes.

- - - concerning this?---Yes. It was my view that from the time after the broadcast of the story, Ms Wilkinson was inextricably intertwined with Ms Higgins. And the words I would use is Ms Wilkinson became part of the story. That continued through the Justice March in 2021. It continued throughout 2021. And that continuing support continued through the anniversary of the story. There were comments by Ms Wilkinson in press about that. There were also comments about how Ms Higgins' courage had inspired her to tell her own story in her book. There was – it was linked in – with the friendship and support between Higgins and Grace Tane. And this was clear and unequivocal, in my mind, for the 18 months preceding the Logies speech. So to deviate from that position in the speech, in my mind, was more prejudicial because it would be seen that she was wavering in her support of Ms Higgins.

But when you say prejudicial, do you mean prejudicial to – it might create doubt in the fact that she may not be believing Ms Higgins' account? Is that what you mean?---When I say prejudicial, I mean prejudicial in terms of affecting the trial. So - - -

**Well, her Honour in paragraph 29 said, after saying the Crown accepted that the Logies awards acceptance speech was unfortunate for that reason, her Honour went on to say the Crown also accepted this proposition – that Ms Wilkinson's status as a respected journalist is such to lend credence to the representation of the complainant and a woman of courage whose story must be believed?---Yes, I – I've read that.**

**And you understood when the speech was being made that what Ms Wilkinson was doing was lending credence to the representation of the complainant as a woman whose courage – whose story must be believed. Would that be fair?---I would accept that. Yes, your Honour.**

**And you as a solicitor thought that that was appropriate to occur by a Crown witness eight days before a criminal trial of a man who is facing a serious criminal charge?---I think, given all the circumstances available, that that was the preferred course to her not giving a speech.**

Right. Thank you. Anything arising out of that?

MR ELLIOTT: No, your Honour.

I conclude from this and her other evidence that Ms Smithies not only turned her mind to the issue as to whether Ms Wilkinson should give the speech in the terms it was given, but it is also apparent she: (1) actively considered how the content of representations made by Ms Wilkinson may or may not be "prejudicial" to the assessment of the credit of Ms Higgins in the pending criminal trial; and (2) gave the advice in order to ensure Ms Higgins' credibility was not undermined by speculation Ms Wilkinson was wavering in her belief as to the truth of the accusation of rape. 1035

At the very least, she must have known the speech, when broadcast in the ACT, would involve a prominent figure (just endorsed and acclaimed by her professional peers), making comments relevant to the guilt of an accused when he was facing an imminent jury trial for a serious offence exposing him to the prospect of a significant gaol sentence, being a trial in which the prominent figure was proposed to be called in the Crown case. She also knew that the speech amounted to "endorsing the credibility of the complainant" and was "lending credence to the representation of the complainant as a woman... whose story must be believed" (T2616.41–44). 1036

1037 For reasons which defy commonsense, Ms Smithies thought Ms Wilkinson faced a binary choice: to continue to endorse the credibility of the complainant in a pending sexual assault trial; or to act in a way that would be perceived as "wavering" in supporting her credibility. It appears it did not occur to her that there was another obvious and far more responsible option: merely saying thank you, or making an anodyne speech which did not say things such as "the truth is, that this honour belongs to Brittany" and having a Network star and witness endorse the complainant's "unwavering courage" in accusing Mr Lehrmann of rape.

1038 As an experienced media lawyer, Ms Smithies should have been alive to the concept of *sub judice* contempt of court and that it can occur when a publication, as a matter of practical reality, tends to interfere with the course of justice in a particular case: *John Fairfax & Sons Pty Ltd and Reynolds v McRae* (1955) 93 CLR 351. The tendency to prejudice proceedings is assessed objectively having regard to the nature of the material and all the circumstances. The tendency must be clear, and there should be a substantial risk of serious interference: *Hinch v Attorney General (Vic)* (1987) 164 CLR 15; *Attorney General v John Fairfax & Sons Ltd* [1980] 1 NSWLR 362 (at 368–369 per Street CJ, Hope and Reynolds JJA); *Director of Public Prosecutions v Wran* (1987) 7 NSWLR 616 (at 626 per Street CJ, Hope, Glass, Samuels and Priestley JJA).

1039 When the balloon went up following the speech, leading to the Chief Justice in *R v Lehrmann (No 3)* making findings as to the significant prejudice occasioned by representations going to the credibility of the complainant being "so widely reported so close to the date of empanelment of the jury", it is little wonder that Ms Smithies and Network Ten became very concerned about contempt. It is also unsurprising that thought was given to limiting the perceived damage, including by consideration being given to not appearing in Court to proffer an apology and advice being taken from experienced senior counsel (who had publicly remarked the speech was ill-advised) as to how to best mollify the evident concern of the Chief Justice.

1040 The approach taken by Network Ten was then carefully considered and resulted in a letter being sent to her Honour's Associate, which although using words such as "profound regret" and "apology", when closely parsed, is directed at regret for the *consequences* that ensued, and not for the fact the speech was given. According to Ms Smithies, it amounted to an apology for things for which Network Ten bore no responsibility. It was not disclosed to the Chief Justice that Ms Wilkinson gave the speech based on considered advice, nor that it was given for the specific purpose now explained by Ms Smithies and that Network Ten's Chief Litigation Counsel continued to stand by the appropriateness of the giving and content of the speech.

The conduct of Network Ten through its employees in procuring Ms Wilkinson to give the speech in the form it was given, for the reason it was given, was grossly improper and unjustifiable. It was conduct apt to cause disruption to the criminal justice system and, without the Chief Justice making the orders she did, could have imperilled Mr Lehrmann's right to a fair trial. 1041

During his cross-examination, the following evidence was given by Mr Lehrmann (T514.13–34): 1042

> You heard the Prime Minister refer to Ms Higgins as having the "courage to stand". Do you remember that?---In his stupid Parliament speech, yes.
>
> ...And "the terrible things that took place"; he apologised to her for that?---Yes.
>
> And the leader of the opposition also:
>
> > *...pay tribute to the courage of Brittany Higgins, who is with us today.*
>
> ?---Yes, and a number of party leaders and other Labor party front benchers, yes.
>
> And the next day was the Press Club speech over which you sued the ABC in early this year. Did you hear that speech?---Yes.
>
> And is it correct that you heard that, during that speech, Ms Higgins broadcast – sorry, Ms Higgins recounted her allegations against you?---Yes.
>
> And that was a few months before your trial was set to be heard?---Yes.

Senior counsel for Ms Wilkinson, relying on these events, said in closing submissions that I ought not assume people watch the Logies, and that there was no evidence that anyone in Canberra who would have been in 1043 the jury pool did watch them (T2283.23–26) and then, presumably more seriously, submitted (T2284.25):

> We say, your Honour, in light of the history of the matter, and the fact that my client had said such things about Ms Higgins in the past, it is – it was a drop in the ocean, having regard to everything else that was online about Mr Lehrmann, the Press Club speech, the Prime Minister's speech in Parliament, Mr Albanese - - -

1044 I accept that senior politicians used the protection of absolute privilege to make representations which had the effect of endorsing the credibility of a complainant and prejudging that a "terrible" thing had taken place, despite an upcoming jury trial of an Australian citizen entitled to the presumption of innocence. To similar effect, senior counsel for Ms Wilkinson also cross-examined on a report of the Australian Human Rights Commission, *Set the Standard: Report on the Independent Review into Commonwealth Parliamentary Workplaces* (Ex R54), of 30 November 2021, which notwithstanding Mr Lehrmann had been charged three and half months earlier and was scheduled to stand trial in 2022, stated in the Commissioner's Foreword:

> The global #MeToo movement and associated momentum for reform has seen numerous brave women publicly sharing their experiences of workplace violence and harassment. **In February 2021, Brittany Higgins courageously shared her experience.**
>
> (Emphasis added)

1045 It is beyond the scope of these reasons to characterise these public comments while a criminal trial in relation to the complainant's allegations was pending, but however one describes them, they did not later give members of the media, including Network Ten, open slather to pay no regard to an accused's fundamental common law rights to a fair trial. The fact that others in positions of power made (much earlier) pre-trial comments endorsing Ms Higgins' courage and thus necessarily endorsing her credibility in making the rape allegation may, however, be relevant to the *extent* of aggravation caused by the Logies speech, in that Ms Wilkinson says she merely repeated what had been said by others in public positions and so any incremental aggravation to Mr Lehrmann was minor, a matter to which I will return.

1046 Ms Wilkinson then makes the following submissions:

(1) "the judgment [of the Chief Justice] was irregular by reason of the Chief Justice accepting (what was incorrect evidence) from the DPP and by denying Ms Wilkinson natural justice" and that to rely upon factual findings of McCallum CJ, contrary to s 91(2) EA, "based on the evidence before her not currently before this Court ... would lead this Court into error";

(2) a "support or belief from a public figure in the guilt of an accused more than one week before trial" would not have the necessary tendency to affect the juror pool who would be "given strict directions in light of existing extreme publicity and notoriety and the numerous articles still online";

(3) Ms Wilkinson's "unchallenged evidence" is that she was asked by Network Ten through Ms Thornton to give the speech in early June and she "was placed in an invidious position of balancing her concerns (raised first in her email on 3 June 2022) with her obligations to comply as an employee with directions from her employer" and she relied "on the advice given to her by her employer's lawyers and the judgment of those to whom she reported".

I do not regard these submissions as helpful. 1047

The notion the Chief Justice denied Ms Wilkinson natural justice is 1048
wholly misconceived. Although her Honour made adjectival factual findings based on the evidence before her (and I am required to make any findings on the basis of the evidence adduced in this proceeding), as is evident from even a cursory reading, the determinative reasoning of her Honour in vacating the hearing date was that (pinpoint references below are to *Lehrmann (No 3)*):

(1) "the combination of the speech and the posts amounted to Ms Wilkinson endorsing the credibility of the complainant who, in turn, celebrated Ms Wilkinson's endorsement of the complainant's credibility" (at 280 [25]);

(2) "the distinction between an untested allegation and the fact of guilt has been lost" and "Ms Wilkinson's status as a respected journalist is such as to lend credence to the representation of the complainant as a woman of courage whose story must be believed" (at 280 [29]);

(3) "the prejudice of such representations so widely reported so close to the date of empanelment of the jury cannot be overstated. The trial of the allegation against the accused has occurred, not in the constitutionally established forum in which it must, as a matter of law, but in the media" (at 280 [30]); and

(4) the "public at large has been given to believe that guilt is established" (at 280 [30]).

1049 This reasoning meant the order to be made and the result was not dependent upon what advice had been received as to the making of the speech and from whom (although the inaccurate impression given to her Honour the speech had been made in the teeth of advice from the DPP, no doubt made the action in giving the speech more inexplicable). Ms Wilkinson was not a party and had no right to appear, but if Ms Wilkinson was aggrieved by a *finding* of the Court, it was open for her to approach the Court to seek leave to appear as a person affected by a finding to correct the record and seek the specific finding as to her ignoring advice be withdrawn. For her own reasons, she did not do so after having been talked out of it by Network Ten. On no view of it, does this amount to a denial of natural justice, or, more specifically, a denial of procedural fairness.

1050 The submission that support or belief from a public figure in the guilt of an accused more than one week before trial televised nationally would not tend to affect the juror pool is unsustainable and reflects a worrying continued insistence by Ms Wilkinson to understate the seriousness of what occurred notwithstanding the vacation of the hearing date which was, for the reasons explained by her Honour, inevitable in the circumstances.

1051 I do not accept the implicit premise in the submission now advanced by Ms Wilkinson (on the basis of "unchallenged" evidence) that she was somehow vexed and reticent in making the speech upon receiving the award at the Logies and she "was placed in an invidious position of balancing her concerns ... with her obligations to comply" with lawful directions by her employer. The notion of reluctant Ms Wilkinson being forced by her employer to make the speech does not ring true at all.

1052 Although I regard Ms Wilkinson's conduct in giving the speech to be improper and unjustifiable, she has less culpability than those encouraging her to make the speech. Ms Wilkinson at least had the insight to seek advice and might not be expected to have the objectivity of others within

Network Ten given the fact that she had, as Ms Smithies noted, become part of the story.

Although these findings are sufficient for the purposes of identifying the 1053
actual and attributed conduct of both respondents as an aggravating circumstance, I cannot responsibly leave this topic without remarking that the most disturbing aspect of this part of the case is the insouciance of Ms Smithies as to the real criticisms made by the Chief Justice and the repeated fastening upon Mr Drumgold's separate failure as some form of excuse.

There has been ample time for mature reflection and yet there is no recogni- 1054
tion, even now, that the speech could have undermined the administration of justice and caused it to be disrupted. It is one thing to make a mistake, even a serious mistake – after all, to err is to be human. But I regret to say that the continuing lack of insight by Ms Smithies as to the inappropriateness of her conduct related to the speech reflects, in my view, a lack of proper appreciation of her professional obligations as a solicitor and her paramount duty to the Court and the administration of justice: see r 3.1, *Legal Profession Uniform Law Australian Solicitors' Conduct Rules 2015* (NSW).

## M.5 Conclusions on Ordinary Compensatory Damages

Without losing sight of the fact that an assessment of damages is an 1055
intuitive, evaluative process conducted at large, but within the parameters of Pt 4, Div 3, I will now proceed to deal with various matters of particular relevance to the assessment of damages being: (1) the severity of the defamatory sting; (2) the purposes of an award of damages in defamation, being consolation for hurt to feelings, recompense for damage to reputation and vindication; and (3) the extent of publication. In doing so, I will deal with Mr Lehrmann's submissions summarised at Section M.3 above.

### *I Severity*

The nature of the imputations speak for themselves and there is no need to 1056
elaborate on them, save to note that the defamatory publications convey an allegation of grave criminal misconduct.

### *II Hurt to Feelings*

Although Mr Lehrmann contends that any young man accused of rape on 1057
national television would be upset, frightened, and angry, after having the opportunity of observing him closely in the witness box, it seemed to me

that where his *real* hurt emerged was when he gave evidence as to how the conduct of others had prejudiced his ability to have a fair trial. Certainly, this included the improper conduct of the respondents relating to the Logies speech, but extended to those who made statements which were implicitly but necessarily premised on his guilt, and the headlong rush to judgment by those who unthinkingly obliterated "the distinction between an untested allegation and the fact of guilt" (to use the words of McCallum CJ).

1058 He also was visibly angered and upset about aspects of the conduct of the Director of Public Prosecutions during his criminal trial and, after trial, when Mr Drumgold implied, while making a public declaration praising Ms Higgins, that he personally believed her complaint was true and therefore Mr Lehrmann was guilty, even though the law continued to presume his innocence. Wholly unjustifiably, he also seemed to harbour resentment at the way in which the Chief Justice summed up the case to the jury.

1059 To a disinterested observer conscious of the importance of the rule of law, his white-hot anger as to his right to a fair trial and the presumption of innocence being undermined by persons presuming his criminal guilt and then expressing their conjecture publicly before the allegation was tested (and later when it was to be no longer tested in the criminal justice system), is perfectly understandable. But from my observation, this reaction seemed to be qualitatively different to the evidence he gave as to his subjective reaction to the publication of the imputations as to the underlying allegation of rape. This is likely to do with the fact that on the premise I am calculating damages, he well knew he had sex with Ms Higgins, which gave rise to at least some questions as to consent (remembering that we are presently dealing with a counterfactual).

1060 Mr Lehrmann was curiously phlegmatic when giving evidence as to the publication of the rape allegation itself, although I recognise it is important not to make too much of such demeanour assessments. As I have noted elsewhere (*Kumova v Davison (No 2)* (at [296])), ordinary human experience reveals there are people who express themselves in an understated way, and others who emote freely and are otherwise less restrained. This does not mean that the subjective hurt of the former person is any less than that of the latter. What matters is the genuineness of the evidence as to hurt to feelings, which is best assessed by the evidence-in-chief on this topic being given *viva voce* and in person. What was notable here, from close observation of the oral evidence, was the difference in demeanour between Mr Lehrmann's evidence as to his reaction to the publication of the imputations, and his manifest distress when speaking of the actions of those who acted without regard for his right to a fair trial.

My task is to decide all disputed questions of fact, including the extent 1061
to hurt to feelings, according to the evidence adduced, not according to some speculation about what other evidence might possibly have been led: *Australian Securities and Investments Commission v Hellicar* [2012] HCA 17; (2012) 247 CLR 345 (per French CJ, Gummow, Hayne, Crennan, Kiefel and Bell JJ (at 412 [165]–[166]). It would be wrong to draw any adverse inference from the absence of any witness on this topic, but ultimately this is a matter where Mr Lehrmann was required to prove the extent to hurt to feelings to my reasonable satisfaction, and his evidence was less than compelling and, unusually, there was no evidence from family members, friends or others about his contemporaneous or ongoing hurt to feelings or as to aggravation (cf *Russell (No 3)* (at [484]–[488])).

A solatium for injured feelings should form a component of the damages, 1062
but it should not be significant, given the lack of connexion between the respondents' wrong and what I have found to be the real cause of most of Mr Lehrmann's distress and hurt. In making this finding, I am not ignoring the Logies' speech, which will be dealt with below.

### *III Damage to Reputation*

The real issue in the present case is the overriding need to ensure an appro- 1063
priate and rational relationship between the actual harm sustained and the damages awarded.

It is in this context that one comes to two issues that assumed importance 1064
in this case: (1) how one isolates any damage to reputation caused by the publication of the Project programme from the Maiden article and subsequent events by which Mr Lehrmann received a tsunami of adverse publicity damaging his reputation (which might be termed an issue of causation); and (2) the conduct of Mr Lehrmann directly relevant to his reputation in the part of his life the subject of the defamatory publications.

#### *Causation*

A complication in this case is that before broadcast on 15 February 2021, 1065
the accusation had been conveyed to those who, without Mr Lehrmann being named, could identify him. As Mr Sharaz had planned, Opposition

members of Parliament had referred to Ms Higgins and were pressing members of the Government on her serious allegations just after lunch – at around the same time Mr Sharaz's efforts in disclosing Mr Lehrmann's name to members of the media were bearing fruit, with Ms Lewis from *The Australian* contacting Mr Lehrmann's employer and precipitating his suspension from his position.

1066 A further complication is that the reputational damage caused by the publication of the Maiden article, or the Project programme, came to be swamped by the avalanche of reputational damage after Mr Lehrmann was charged and named publicly. I accept the submission of the respondents that this was when the real damage to Mr Lehrmann's reputation was caused.

1067 It follows from these complications, that the task of identifying causally related reputational damage caused by the Project programme is not straightforward.

1068 That said, as Mr Lehrmann correctly notes, the Project programme drove the allegations home on 15 February and contained the emotional account of Ms Higgins. There is some compensable damage caused by the broadcast (in the sense the broadcast materially contributed to the first wave of reputational damage) and for which the respondents are responsible, including some shunning of Mr Lehrmann manifested in his exclusion from chat groups (including Ex 11).

*Conduct of Mr Lehrmann*

1069 But before we leave reputational damage, as explained above, it is necessary to have regard to the evidence of the Relevant Misconduct of Mr Lehrmann, being conduct directly relevant to reputational damage. This conduct does rationally bear upon Mr Lehrmann's true reputation in the relevant sector and thus is of some significance in fixing upon a rational assessment of damages.

1070 At this point it is worth referring to the "concession" of senior counsel for Mr Lehrmann (T2444.37–38), relied upon by the respondents, that if the Court were satisfied sexual activity occurred, then Mr Lehrmann's conduct of this proceeding would amount to an abuse of process. In isolation, this exchange may indicate that a "*Joseph v Spiller*" type approach was conceded to be open depending on my findings of fact, but when

Mr Lehrmann's submissions are considered as a whole, it reflects an agreement that the principled way of dealing with the Relevant Misconduct is the approach explained by Wigney J in *Rush (No 2)* (at 573 [32]–[33]).

Mr Lehrmann behaved disgracefully. He defended the criminal charge on 1071
a false basis, lied to police, and then allowed that lie to go uncorrected before the jury. He instructed his unwitting and hence blameless senior counsel to cross-examine a complainant of sexual assault, in two legal proceedings, on a knowingly false premise.

Any other instances of conduct relevant to his true reputation relied 1072
upon by the respondents (such as behaving like a blackguard to his girlfriend and leaving Ms Higgins as he did) are also unworthy, but pale by comparison.

As to the final aspect of the Relevant Misconduct, being the provision 1073
of information protected by the *Hearne v Street* undertaking to a third party, it is necessary to deal with an aspect of the submissions of Network Ten that is said to bring that aspect of the conduct into a different, and serious category. Dr Collins submits a raft of information was provided to the *Spotlight* programme for publication with the intention of intimidating proposed witnesses in this proceeding. Although Mr Lehrmann's provision of some information to the *Spotlight* programme was seriously wrong, I am far from convinced it was done for the *purpose* of intimidating witnesses. Ms Higgins had been held up by numerous public figures as a woman of courage; she had been hailed widely for her criticism of what she asserted was an unjust legal system; and, with the assistance of her supporters, had shaped the public relations narrative. It is likely that Mr Lehrmann's motivation to "light some fires" (Ex R43) was to tell his (factually wrong even on the counterfactual) side of the story and try to expose what he thought had gone wrong in the criminal justice system. It was his attempt to counter a narrative hostile to him and that was already extant. Part of his conduct in pursuit of this end reflects very poorly upon him, but the respondents' characterisation is inaccurate.

The consequence of all this is that the actual damage proven to be occa- 1074
sioned to Mr Lehrmann's reputation by the broadcast could only be slight in respect of the defamatory publications unsuccessfully defended, because he is only entitled to be compensated for the reputation he deserves.

### *IV Extent of Publication*

1075 This is also a matter of some significance in this assessment.

1076 As would be evident as to my findings as to identification (see Section D.4 above), this is a case where the rumours causing relevant persons to identify Mr Lehrmann had commenced when the Maiden article was published, and the Project programme would likely have involved a further, albeit more graphic, publication to the relatively limited class of persons able to identify Mr Lehrmann reasonably.

## M.6 Conclusions on Aggravated Damages

1077 I have found one aspect of the respondents' conduct to be improper and unjustifiable. Insofar as Network Ten is concerned, its conduct in relation to the Logies speech given by Ms Wilkinson was egregious.

1078 But it does not follow axiomatically that this conclusion leads to an augmentation of the damages to be paid to Mr Lehrmann.

1079 Justice Brennan in *XL Petroleum (NSW) Pty Ltd v Caltex Oil (Australia) Pty Ltd* (1985) 155 CLR 448 (at 471) explained that an award of exemplary damages "is intended to punish the defendant for conduct showing a conscious and contumelious disregard for the plaintiff's rights and to deter him from committing like conduct again". I am, however, prevented from making an award of exemplary damages by dint of s 37 of the Defamation Act. Punishment for the wrongful conduct of Network Ten and notions of specific deterrence are inconsistent with a compensatory award and, as Hunt J explained in *Bickel v John Fairfax & Sons Ltd* (1981) 2 NSWLR 474 (at 496):

> The distinction between compensatory damages and punitive damages cannot be overemphasized. Compensatory damages are given to compensate the plaintiff for the harm done to him by the publication of the matter complained of; aggravated compensatory damages (which are also known as merely "aggravated damages") are given to compensate him when that harm has been aggravated by the defendant's conduct. Punitive damages, on the other hand, are given to punish the defendant and relate only to the defendant's conduct; they do not depend upon any effect of that conduct on the harm of the plaintiff.

Mr Lehrmann is not automatically entitled to an award of aggravated damages even though a necessary condition for the making of such an award has been satisfied. He must still prove that his harm has been exacerbated by the respondents' improper and unjustified conduct. 1080

There has been some debate as to the precise justification for aggravated damages at common law. The Law Commission of England and Wales in its report, *Aggravated, Exemplary and Restitutionary Damages*, Law Com No 247 (1997) (at [1.9]) suggested the label "damages for mental distress" should be used instead of the misleading phrase "aggravated damages" and remarked that once it is appreciated that aggravated damages are concerned with circumstances in which the victim of a civil wrong may obtain compensation for mental distress, a more coherent perception, and so development of, the law on damages for mental distress should be possible. 1081

But despite these debates as to the underlying justification of aggravated damages, insofar as the common law of Australia is concerned, the basis of aggravated damages was explained by Hodgson JA in *State of NSW v Riley* [2003] NSWCA 208; (2003) 57 NSWLR 496 (later approved by Tobias AJA, with whom Meagher JA, Bergin CJ in Eq agreed in *MacDougal v Mitchell* [2015] NSWCA 389). 1082

In *Riley*, Hodgson JA noted that having assessed the appropriate level of damages, the compensatory nature of aggravated damages leaves room for the award of further compensation without incurring the risk of double counting and noted (at [131]) that the principled explanation for this is that: 1083

> [it] is extremely difficult to quantify damages for hurt feelings. In cases of hurt feelings caused by ordinary wrong-doing, of a kind consistent with ordinary human fallibility, the court must assess damages for hurt damages neutrally, and aim towards the centre of the wide range of damages that might conceivably be justified. However, in cases of hurt to feelings caused by wrong-doing that goes beyond ordinary human fallibility, serious misconduct by the defendant has given rise to a situation where it is difficult to quantify appropriate damages and thus where the court should be astute to avoid the risk of under-compensating the plaintiff, so the court is justified in aiming towards the upper limit of the wide range of damages which might conceivably be justified.

1084 His Honour added (at [133]) that there must be a justification for this approach, which he acknowledged was one of degree so that "the worse the defendant's conduct, the further from the centre of the range and towards the upper limit of the range the court may be justified in going".

1085 In the end, however, the fundamental point is that aggravated damages are compensatory damages.

1086 As with other aspects of Mr Lehrmann's case on compensatory damages, a complication arises: although he was initially extremely distressed and hurt by the conduct of the respondents in undermining his right to a fair trial, this only lasted for a short period and has had no ongoing effect. Mr Lehrmann gave evidence that it became evident soon after the speech that Ms Wilkinson, ironically, did him a favour by making the Logies speech.

1087 Although denying that the Logies speech saved him from conviction (T526.38–42), Mr Lehrmann said in the *Spotlight* programme that the adjournment occasioned by the Logies speech fortuitously allowed his legal team sufficient opportunity to "dig deeper ... go down the rabbit holes ... find the golden nuggets" with the potential result that "if they had not done what they did [it] would have been catastrophic" (T526.16–36). It follows that in his opinion, the improper conduct quickly redounded to his considerable forensic advantage.

1088 Although I am satisfied that Mr Lehrmann was justifiably angry and hurt at the giving of the Logies speech (as would any accused when the conduct of others may adversely influence the disposition of likely jurors), and the giving of the speech did serve to increase his subjective hurt, the evolution of his state of mind to the recognition that the Logies speech significantly reduced his chances of conviction, diminishes the practical and ongoing effect of the aggravating conduct.

## M.7 Quantum

1089 Despite both being compensatory in nature, where applicable, in relation to post-1 July 2021 publications, s 35(2B) of the Defamation Act requires an award of aggravated damages to be made separately from ordinary compensatory damages. That provision does not, however, apply in this proceeding and I will proceed to make a single award as has been the traditional common law approach.

Mr Lehrmann would have been entitled to more than a nominal award 1090
but as the above analysis demonstrates, his award of ordinary compensatory damages would be very modest. Hence any augmentation of damages occasioned by the aggravating conduct, comes from a very low base. If it had been necessary to assess damages in favour of Mr Lehrmann, the appropriate and rational relationship between the actual harm sustained and the damages awarded would lead to total damages of $20,000.

## N CONCLUSION AND ORDERS

1091 Having escaped the lions' den, Mr Lehrmann made the mistake of going back for his hat.

1092 As I stressed at the commencement of these reasons, there is a substantive difference between the criminal and civil standards of proof. To make the grave finding Mr Lehrmann raped Ms Higgins, it is unnecessary for me to reach a level of certainty indispensable to criminal liability. The respondents have not won because I can exclude all other possibilities as to what happened, but because they have proven that such possibilities that are open on the evidence, both individually and collectively, are unlikely; and further because I am satisfied that the evidence provides an appropriate basis upon which to reach a conclusion. Put another way, they have proven that the whole of the evidence, properly analysed, establishes a reasonable satisfaction on the preponderance of probabilities of facts sufficient to make out the substantial truth defence.

1093 As a result of the inconclusive criminal trial, Mr Lehrmann remains a man who has not been convicted of any offence, but he has now been found, by the civil standard of proof, to have engaged in a great wrong. It follows Ms Higgins has been proven to be a victim of sexual assault.

1094 At first glance this might be thought to be an odd outcome. But if one leaves aside superficial reactions and appreciates the high value the common law has always placed upon the importance of securing against the conviction of the innocent, it is not at all peculiar. Ensuring an accused is deprived of their liberty *only* if the prosecution can exclude all reasonable hypotheses consistent with innocence, has been as elemental to our criminal justice system as the presumption of innocence and the related "golden thread" running through the criminal law that the prosecution bears the burden of proof: *Woolmington v DPP* [1935] AC 462 (at 481–482 per Viscount Sankey).

Mr Lehrmann is not entitled to the vindication of his reputation. The respondents, however, are entitled to vindication by the entry of judgment on the statement of claim. 1095

But even though the respondents have legally justified their imputation of rape, this does not mean their conduct was justified in any broader or colloquial sense. The contemporaneous documents and the broadcast itself demonstrate the allegation of rape was the minor theme, and the allegation of cover-up was the major motif. 1096

The publication of accusations of corrupt conduct in putting up roadblocks and forcing a rape victim to choose between her career and justice won the Project team, like Ms Maiden, a glittering prize; but when the accusation is examined properly, it was supposition without reasonable foundation in verifiable fact; its dissemination caused a brume of confusion, and did much collateral damage – including to the fair and orderly progress of the underlying allegation of sexual assault through the criminal justice system. To the extent there were perceived systemic issues as to avenues of complaint and support services in Parliament, this may have merited a form of fact-based critique, not the publication of insufficiently scrutinised and factually misconceived conjecture. 1097

I will direct that an outline of submissions on costs be filed and then will list the matter to hear and determine all outstanding issues, including the residuum of the issues arising on the cross-claims. 1098

I certify that the preceding one-thousand and ninety-eight (1098) numbered paragraphs are a true copy of the Reasons for Judgment of the Honourable Justice Lee.

Associate:

Dated: 15 April 2024